INDIVIDUAL DIFFERENCES
AND THE
COMMON CURRICULUM

INDIVIDUAL DIFFERENCES
AND THE
COMMON CURRICULUM

Eighty-second Yearbook of the
National Society for the Study of Education

PART I

By

THE YEARBOOK COMMITTEE
and
ASSOCIATED CONTRIBUTORS

Edited by

GARY D FENSTERMACHER AND JOHN I. GOODLAD

Editor for the Society

KENNETH J. REHAGE

Distributed by THE UNIVERSITY OF CHICAGO PRESS ● CHICAGO, ILLINOIS

The National Society for the Study of Education

Founded in 1901 as successor to the National Herbart Society, the National Society for the Study of Education has provided a means by which the results of serious study of educational issues could become a basis for informed discussion of those issues. The Society's two-volume yearbooks, now in their eighty-second year of publication, reflect the thoughtful attention given to a wide range of educational problems during those years. A recently inaugurated series on Contemporary Educational Issues includes substantial publications in paperback that supplement the yearbooks. Each year, the Society's publications contain contributions to the literature of education from more than a hundred scholars and practitioners who are doing significant work in their respective fields.

An elected Board of Directors selects the subjects with which volumes in the yearbook series are to deal, appropriates funds to meet necessary expenses in the preparation of a given volume, and appoints a committee to oversee the preparation of manuscripts for that volume. A special committee created by the Board performs similar functions for the Society's paperback series.

The Society's publications are distributed each year without charge to more than 3,000 members in the United States, Canada, and elsewhere throughout the world. The Society welcomes as members all individuals who desire to receive its publications. For information about membership and current dues, see the back pages of this volume or write to the Secretary-Treasurer, 5835 Kimbark Avenue, Chicago, Illinois 60637.

The Eighty-second Yearbook includes the following two volumes:

Part I: *Individual Differences and the Common Curriculum*
Part II: *Staff Development*

A complete listing of the Society's previous publications, together with information as to how earlier publications still in print may be obtained, is found in the back pages of this volume.

Library of Congress Catalog Number: 82-62381
ISSN: 0077-5762

Published 1983 by
THE NATIONAL SOCIETY FOR THE STUDY OF EDUCATION

5835 Kimbark Avenue, Chicago, Illinois 60637
© 1983 by the National Society for the Study of Education

No part of this Yearbook may be reproduced in any form without written permission from the Secretary of the Society

First Printing, 6,500 Copies

Printed in the United States of America

Officers of the Society
1982-83

(Term of office expires March 1 of the year indicated)

HARRY S. BROUDY

(1985)
University of Illinois, Champaign, Illinois

LUVERN L. CUNNINGHAM

(1984)
Ohio State University, Columbus, Ohio

ELLIOT W. EISNER

(1983)
Stanford University, Stanford, California

JOHN I. GOODLAD

(1983)
University of California, Los Angeles, California

A. HARRY PASSOW

(1985)
Teachers College, Columbia University, New York, New York

RALPH W. TYLER

(1984)
*Director Emeritus, Center for Advanced Study in the Behavioral Sciences
Stanford, California*

KENNETH J. REHAGE

(Ex-officio)
University of Chicago, Chicago, Illinois

Secretary-Treasurer

KENNETH J. REHAGE

5835 Kimbark Avenue, Chicago, Illinois 60637

v

The Society's Committee on
Individual Differences and the Common Curriculum

GARY D FENSTERMACHER

(Cochairman)
College of Education
Virginia Polytechnic Institute and State University
Blacksburg, Virginia

JOHN I. GOODLAD

(Cochairman)
Graduate School of Education
University of California, Los Angeles
Los Angeles, California

ARTHUR BERCHIN

Graduate School of Education
University of California, Los Angeles
Los Angeles, California

LEE S. SHULMAN

School of Education
Stanford University
Stanford, California

Associated Contributors

HARRY S. BROUDY

College of Education
University of Illinois
Champaign, Illinois

CHARLOTTE CRABTREE

Graduate School of Education
University of California, Los Angeles
Los Angeles, California

vii

MARGARET EARLY

School of Education
Syracuse University
Syracuse, New York

LOUIS FISCHER

University of Massachusetts
Amherst, Massachusetts

THOMAS L. GOOD

Center for Research in Social Behavior
University of Missouri
Columbia, Missouri

MICHAEL W. KIRST

School of Education
Stanford University
Stanford, California

HUGH MUNBY

Faculty of Education, Queen's University
Kingston, Ontario, Canada

THOMAS S. POPKEWITZ

School of Education
University of Wisconsin
Madison, Wisconsin

THOMAS A. ROMBERG

School of Education
University of Wisconsin
Madison, Wisconsin

ROBERT ROSEN

Department of Physiology and Biophysics
Faculty of Medicine, Dalhousie University
Halifax, Nova Scotia, Canada

THOMAS L. RUSSELL

Faculty of Education, Queen's University
Kingston, Ontario, Canada

GAIL P. SORENSON

School of Education
State University of New York at Albany
Albany, New York

DEBORAH J. STIPEK

Graduate School of Education
University of California, Los Angeles
Los Angeles, California

Chapter Reviewers

COURTNEY CAZDEN

Harvard University
Cambridge, Massachusetts

ROBERT DREEBEN

University of Chicago
Chicago, Illinois

JOHN JAROLIMEK

University of Washington
Seattle, Washington

JEREMY KILPATRICK

University of Georgia
Athens, Georgia

STANLEY MADEJA

CEMREL
St. Louis, Missouri

ARTHUR E. WISE

Rand Corporation
Washington, D.C.

Acknowledgment

The problem of reconciling the concept of individual differences with the concept of a common curriculum is by no means new to educators. In one way or another, that problem has been a central focus of discussions in educational circles for a very long time, as can be amply demonstrated by a review of the titles of previous volumes in the series of yearbooks published by the National Society for the Study of Education. We believe it is particularly appropriate for the Society to make available at this time yet another effort to illuminate the problem and to search for new insights that can assist educators in dealing with it.

Professors Gary D Fenstermacher and John I. Goodlad, coeditors of this volume, have secured the assistance of a distinguished group of authors whose treatments of their respective topics merit the attention of thoughtful professionals at all levels of education. The Society is extremely grateful to the editors, their committee, and to each of the authors for their contributions. We also wish to acknowledge the assistance of several reviewers, each of whom offered helpful comments on a particular chapter.

The Society is pleased to present this volume as Part I of its Eighty-second Yearbook.

KENNETH J. REHAGE
Editor for the Society

Table of Contents

xi

CHAPTER I

Introduction

GARY D FENSTERMACHER

People differ. Almost no one disputes this point. What provokes disagreement is how people differ and what, if anything, should be done about their differences. In the field of education it is generally believed some differences among learners are so important that they justify differences in what is taught and how. Precisely what these important individual differences are is not always clear, nor is it in most cases obvious what specific curricular or instructional variations ought to follow from important individual differences.

Much of the scholarship and research on individual differences over the last fifty years has been devoted to increasing our understanding of the ways people differ and to determining educational treatments most appropriate for differences believed crucial to learning. By comparison, little attention has been given to the consequences of our belief that individualization enhances teaching and learning. Not much is heard about the confusion individualization may bring to teachers' conceptions of their work, the costs borne by those who pay for schooling, the complexity of programs and systems developed in response to demands for individualized instruction, and the feelings of students who are grouped and tracked in hopes of realizing gains in their achievement.

That our commitment to individual differences in education may have untoward consequences for teachers and learners justifies a closer look at the concept and its practical permutations. Of special concern are the ways curricular and instructional practices are varied in order to accommodate relevant differences among learners. The question to be raised here takes the form: Does difference D justify treatment T?

1

Difference D may represent a personality variable like sociability or self-concept, a motivational variable such as need to achieve, or a learning variable like aptitude or cognitive style. Treatment T may represent an instructional variation, such as pacing, sequencing, or grouping; or a curricular variation, such as alternative texts, materials, courses, programs, or tracks (where the actual content studied differs from text to text, course to course, and so forth).

Grouping and tracking are among the most profound responses to notions about individual differences. Grouping within and across classes is a treatment variation frequently linked to individual differences in aptitude, ability, or interest. Tracking is a procedure for streaming secondary school students into programs of study formulated according to the students' career aspirations. The most common tracks are academic (college preparatory) and vocational; some schools offer a general track intended for semiprofessional careers or for those students unable to decide between the academic or vocational tracks. Grouping, as it is typically practiced in the elementary school, is considered more an organizational and instructional than a curricular response to individual differences. That is, it is assumed that younger learners are grouped in order to permit variation in instructional practices without great variations in content studied. However, if the concepts, knowledge, skills, and ideas taught to one group are different from those taught to another, then grouping constitutes a curricular variation as well as an instructional variation. While grouping is thought of primarily as an organizational and instructional variation, tracking is clearly understood as a curricular and organizational variation, though instructional variation may occur within different tracks.

Do differences in ability, aptitude, or interest justify the kinds of curricular variations apparent in grouping and tracking? Behind this question lies the editors' conviction that curricular variation is far more prevalent than instructional variation as a treatment response to individual differences—despite the fact that the putative reason for so zealously pursuing the study of individual differences is to enhance the teacher's capacity to provide the most appropriate instructional treatment. It is, in other words, the editors' belief that educators have accommodated to individual differences primarily through curricular and organizational rather than instructional variations. Grouping and tracking practices are the most visible and far-reaching manifestations of this accommodation.

The consequences of accommodating individual differences by curricular variation are enormous. Using individual differences in aptitude, ability, or interest as the basis for curricular variation denies students equal access to the knowledge and understanding available to humankind. Students grouped as slow learners and later tracked into vocational programs often are effectively barred from the literature, history, fine arts, and science—and the training in intellectual skills accompanying these disciplines—believed most likely to free their minds from convention, dogma, and cliché. Students grouped as fast, highly motivated learners and later tracked into college preparatory programs usually are prevented from developing the practical skills and traits of character typically associated with good work at a trade or craft. No theory of education known to us permits such selective access to knowledge and ideas based upon individual differences in aptitude, ability, or interest. Of course, it is possible that some students may not benefit equally from unrestricted access to knowledge, but this fact does not entitle us to control access in ways that effectively prohibit all students from encountering what Dewey called "the funded capital of civilization."

The knowledge and understanding, the skills and traits that mark a person as well educated, should be open to all who can profit from what schools are able to provide. The curriculum that encompasses this knowledge and understanding, these skills and traits, is a common curriculum. It is common in the sense that what it contains is common to all who would lead enlightened lives in a state of civilization, and in the sense that all who would lead enlightened lives must possess this knowledge and understanding, these skills and traits, in common. Assuming that such a curriculum were available and generally accepted, the point of our inquiries into individual differences would be considerably altered. Instead of studying individual differences to learn how we may most effectively and efficiently teach whatever outcomes we have in mind for different learners, we would seek the means to teach the common curriculum successfully to all students. We would, in short, strive for those instructional variations that permit us to avoid making the kinds of curricular and organizational variations which selectively limit access to common studies.

In the context of the beliefs and convictions mentioned above, the editors addressed the following question to the authors whose work appears in this volume: "Do we know enough about differences between or among individuals to entertain, in a practical way, the possibility of providing most learners with a common curriculum, adapted to account for individual differences but without compromising their chances for a rational, moral, and authentic life?" We chose to examine this question from the perspective of several disciplines germane to the study of individual differences: psychology, sociology, law, and biology.

In chapter 2, Good and Stipek review the psychological basis for individual differences. They conclude that there are some variations in instructional treatment that show promise for accommodating to individual differences. However, they find no single form of instructional treatment powerful enough to accommodate all the ways individuals may differ, nor do they find any one kind of individual difference that positively requires a specific instructional treatment. Their analysis of the literature leaves open the question of whether too little is yet known about the psychology of individual differences to generate the kinds of instructional variations a common curriculum may require.

In chapter 3, Popkewitz sets forth the social and political elements that influence conceptions of the individual, and hence our understanding of how individuals differ. His analysis is an antidote for the temptation to fix and reify the concept of individual differences. Popkewitz concludes by expressing doubt that pedagogical practices geared to individualization can serve as a means to realizing a common curriculum. He, too, leaves the reader with an open question: Are the social and political ideologies which shape our understanding of individual differences in opposition to the philosophical ideals of a common curriculum?

Fischer and Sorenson (chapter 4) explore the legal basis for individual differences. They ask how much of our current attention to individual differences is the result of legal intervention in the schools, and in what ways the law requires educators to attend to various individual differences. To those who would assert that the law compels consideration of individual differences, Fischer and Sorenson offer reasons to believe otherwise. The major impact of the law has been to prevent educators from using certain differences as a basis for variation in curriculum and instruction, on the grounds that consideration of these differences violates the rights and privileges of individuals. The contentions advanced in this chapter imply that there are no legal barriers to the development and implementation of a common curriculum.

The final chapter on individual differences examines the biological basis for variation. This chapter demonstrates the extraordinary sophistication biologists have developed for classifying the similarities and dissimilarities among organisms, and accounting for their variability. By comparison, our efforts as social scientists and practicing educators seem paltry. Yet Rosen's discussion of the difference between discriminability and variability may profit our inquiries into molar differences among individuals. His analysis of genetic and epigenetic variability suggests new ways of thinking about the influence of nature and nurture on individual differences. This chapter leaves no doubt that human beings vary biologically, and that environment—including education—impacts on biological variation. The precise nature of this impact and its implications for education are not detailed here. Is this detail missing because the state of knowledge in biology is such that it cannot be provided now, or because the implications of biological variation for education are yet to be established? Rosen does not say, but we may reasonably guess that it is a measure of both.

Relative to the question posed to the authors, what conclusion may be drawn from these four chapters? I believe one may validly conclude that we do not yet know enough about individual differences to decide whether sufficiently powerful instructional treatments can be devised to offset the effects of human variation on an individual's chances for success in a common curriculum. Another way to state this point is that what is currently known about individual differences does not constitute a major resource for aiding teachers and schools in the implementation of a common curriculum. This conclusion does not bear on whether we should or should not provide a common curriculum, for the chapters raise a number of questions about the logic and conceptual integrity of the very notion of individual differences. What seems clear enough is that the editors' original convictions are neither confirmed nor repudiated by the chapters on individual differences. We began in the belief that schools are responding to individual differences primarily through curricular variations, which in turn prohibit students from equal access to human knowledge, and from experiencing a common curriculum. We reasoned that it is unjust to deny equal access to human knowledge, and that it is morally necessary to provide a common curriculum. Therefore, individual differences should be accommodated through instructional, not curricular variations in treatment. It now seems clear that sufficiently powerful instructional variations are either unavailable or perhaps not required to the extent we originally thought. We remain in some doubt whether matters of individual difference are a red herring or a red flag when considering the feasibility of a common curriculum. Nevertheless, in the hope of enhancing learning, it appears both reasonable and appropriate to assure learners in a common curriculum access to the full array of instructional alternatives known to educators.

Regardless of the status of individual differences in education, the moral argument for a common curriculum remains undisturbed. As such, we sought for a number of specialists in subject fields, asking them to identify what all learners can and should learn about their respective subjects. We asked these authors what a reasonably well-educated youth ought to know about the author's subject area upon completion of its study (typically by the time of graduation from high school). Authors were requested to take account of a broad range of individual differences among learners, such that their proposals would not apply solely to academically talented students. In an effort to add further perspective to this charge, the authors of the common curriculum chapters were asked to write as if they were answering a parent who wished to know what it is reasonable to expect his or her child to gain from studying that subject for the number of years it is offered in school. It was and is our hope that these chapters would be accessible to interested parents, students, school administrators, and board members, as well as those engaged in the formal study of education.

The charge given these authors is virtually impossible to fulfill in thirty-five manuscript pages. Yet the authors met it with zeal, each saying they looked forward to analyzing their subject areas in this way. We are grateful to them for accepting the challenge, and thankful for the extraordinary efforts they expended. Despite the complexity of the task, we believed it must be done if the educational community is to take seriously the idea and ideals of a common curriculum.

Any attempt to summarize these chapters and tease out related threads is bound to founder, for the chapters are delightfully diverse in approach, process, and outcome. The one conclusion that can be drawn is that a common curriculum is within the reach of educators who wish to incorporate it. On reading these chapters, it is apparent that nearly all students can be granted equal access to "the funded capital of civilization," and achieve success undiminished by their individual differences. In part, this success is achieved by modest curricular as well as instructional variation. But the curricular variation proposed by the authors is not fundamental variation, in the sense of providing different themes, ideas, and understanding to individually different learners. Rather it is variation in approach, in materials, and in experiences, though always in pursuit of the same fundamental understandings, skills, and traits.

The final section of this volume contains two chapters. The first deals with the policy implications of individual differences and the common curriculum; the second, with implications for practice. In chapter 11, Kirst calls attention to what is required to translate reform proposals into functional educational policy. In the belief that local districts should play a more vital role in the formation of curricular policy, he proposes a series of questions for local personnel to use in deciding such policy. These questions illuminate the nature of deliberations on curricular matters, and constitute a useful guide for debating the adoption of a common curriculum. In the second chapter of this section, Goodlad advances the practical implications of the theme and content of this yearbook. Using the results of his "Study of Schooling," he offers evidence in support of the convictions that impelled our work on this volume. He concludes with specific recommendations for changing school practices.

Several of the chapters in this volume were reviewed by editorial consultants who prepared extensive critiques of the chapters assigned to them. The editors and the authors are grateful for the excellent assistance provided by these consultants.

Essays by individual authors on an assigned theme can easily become a disparate and confusing collection when bound together. We are deeply indebted to our authors for their careful attention to our charge and their willingness to take into account the criticisms offered by the editors and the reviewers of chapters. We hope the reader benefits as much from the product as we did from the process.

Part One
INDIVIDUAL DIFFERENCES

CHAPTER II

Individual Differences in the Classroom: A Psychological Perspective

THOMAS L. GOOD AND DEBORAH J. STIPEK

"This roof is like a sieve!" said Toucan. Rain drops splashed on her bill. "More like a colander" said Sloth. "There are lots of dry spots." Like these characters in Diane Redfield Massie's children's book, *Sloth's Birthday Party*, children in a classroom perceive and interpret the "same" event differently. This is because children vary in competence, self-confidence, emotional maturity, need for nurturance, and in countless other ways. Moreover, children's perceptions, and consequently their behavior, vary considerably across different situations. A frown from the teacher on one occasion may engender embarrassment and silence; on another, it may provoke defiance.

Mischel aptly describes the variability of human behavior and the interacting influences of person and situation: "One of the most impressive—and obvious—lessons from the history of personality measurement is the recognition that complex human behavior tends to be influenced by many determinants and reflects the almost inseparable and continuous interaction of a host of variables both in the person and in the situation."[1] While this diversity is basic to our existence and, within limits, should be accepted and encouraged, the variability and

Lee S. Shulman served as the editorial consultant for this chapter. The authors also acknowledge the excellent editorial suggestions provided by Gail Hinkel, as well as the typing assistance of Janice Meiburger and Pat Shanks at the Center for Research in Social Behavior, University of Missouri—Columbia, and Diane DeRosa at the Graduate School of Education, University of California, Los Angeles.

unpredictability of human behavior pose enormous problems to teachers.

Teachers are expected to produce optimal learning in all students, despite significant differences on so many dimensions. Historically, educators and researchers have proposed many "solutions" to the problems of student diversity, a few of which have gained considerable attention, at least for brief periods. Some of these solutions are reviewed in this chapter.

Although we believe that it is important for teachers to be responsive to the unique cognitive and affective needs of their students, we take the position that there are no simple, generalizable methods to achieve optimal learning in a diverse group of children. We know of no dimension of individual differences that has unambiguous implications for instructional method. Accordingly, we will argue that teachers need to have extensive knowledge about how children learn and develop and about the diverse ways students perceive and understand instruction. Teachers need to apply this knowledge selectively to particular students (and combinations of students), taking the instructional content and myriad other situational variables into consideration.

Because problems posed by student diversity have been discussed in the educational literature for many decades, we begin with a brief and selective review of the history of educators' efforts to deal with those problems. We turn later to more recent research on two dimensions of individual differences—ability and cognitive style—chosen to illustrate among other things, the impossibility of finding one best solution to student variability, even within a specific dimension.

Adapting Education to Individual Needs

A BRIEF HISTORY

For many years, the National Society for the Study of Education has encouraged the study of individual differences. Its twenty-first yearbook presented considerable evidence indicating that a pronounced range of differences (in capacity and achievement) exists among students within grade levels.[2] In the twenty-fourth yearbook, noted scholars addressed the issue of adapting the curriculum to individual differences and articulated specific plans for doing so (most notably the Dalton and the Winnetka plans).[3] However, even during this period of initial concern for adapting education to individual differences, there was considerable debate about both the philosophical and practical issues related to individualized instruction. Kilpatrick dramatically describes the history of this controversy:

Up to about a century ago, the children of our schools had only individual instruction, and in this absence of group effort and cooperative activity much was lost. The coming of class teaching was counted a great advance. For some purposes it was a great advance. It remains, we may confidently assert, a permanent contribution to educational procedure. But as we developed class procedure to its completer form and contrived textbooks and groupings and promotions to fit it, we began to find that not all was good. No one procedure would fit equally well all the children put into any one class. It was the old problem of institution and individual all over again. And, as always, the easiest solution was to hold to the institution and let the individual suffer. So we did. . . . We now know, where heretofore we guessed about, the inadequacy of our treatment. The situation is now shown in its ugly nakedness and is intolerable.[4]

The sixty-first yearbook of the Society was also devoted to individualizing instruction. Although new evidence pertaining to the variability of student performance and novel and useful concepts for organizing instruction were presented, the book reminds us that between 1925 and 1962 no consensus was reached about successful strategies for responding to individual differences.[5]

Ability grouping within classrooms has been perhaps the most common measure taken to accommodate to individual differences in rate of learning.[6] This method illustrates the kind of problems produced by most "solutions" to individual differences. Indeed, ability grouping apparently causes as many problems as it solves. The most common criticism of homogeneous ability grouping is that it stigmatizes children in lower groups, and there are many potentially negative consequences (for example, a negative self-concept) associated with this stigma.[7] Teachers tend to be less motivated to teach low-ability groups,[8] and their expectations, behavior toward children, and perceptions of children's performance and instructional needs may be largely determined by children's group placement. Evidence that group placement is highly stable over time suggests that ability grouping is less flexible than would be expected if children were all learning at an optimal rate.[9]

Ability grouping may also have failed to solve problems caused by individual differences in rate of learning because homogeneous groupings do not improve the teachability of groups. As Tyler argued, homogeneous grouping on a *single* ability measure does not reduce variance in other abilities that students bring to the learning situation.[10] One danger of homogeneous ability grouping is that some teachers believe that because students have been grouped, they will benefit from the same treatment. Ironically, teachers who instruct larger, more diverse classes may feel a stronger need to ascertain whether they have been understood by all students.

Most early attempts to accommodate individual differences in learning style had similarly disappointing results. In a review of the major individualization techniques used in reading instruction during the 1900s (the scientific movement, the activity movement, grouping for instruction, self-selection reading, language-experience reading, individually prescribed instruction, computer-assisted instruction, skills-management systems, and so on), Artley notes that despite many desirable features, the effectiveness of each of these techniques is seriously limited.[11] Specifically, Artley claims that any program helps the reading problems of some students, but creates (or at least fails to respond to) difficulties for other students.

Over the last half century, many educational adaptations to individual differences have been tried. Cronbach notes that "adapting education to the individual has meant many things in educational discussions."[12] He delineated four basic responses to individual differences in school settings (and countless variations on these basic themes). First, it is possible to have *adaptation to a predetermined program* (that is, a fixed curriculum where students are "weeded out" at particular times or forced to stay at a level until they master the curriculum).

A second response is *adaptation by matching educational goals to the individual* (goals are modified so that some students are assigned to general mathematics and others to algebra, or students are allowed to select courses, activities, and so forth). A third possible way to respond to individual differences, particularly in rate of learning, is *adaptation by remediation* (same goals for all students and the basic program is added on to rather than modified; students who need extra time are given remedial work). Cronbach claims all three of these responses are basically administrative. A fourth response involves altering instructional behavior—*adaptation by altering instructional methods* (teach different pupils with different methods).

Despite the disappointing results of early attempts to accommodate instruction to individual differences in rate and style of learning, instructional adaptation to individual needs remains one of the most important issues in educational research. To be sure, educators continue to experiment with all four of the basic adaptations described by Cronbach. Ability grouping, for example, has been used in classrooms for decades. More typically, an approach becomes fashionable for a few years and when it does not live up to its promise, alternative methods are sought. Tracking, Cronbach's second response, was socially approved for a while, but has been controversial since the common school movement flourished in the 1950s. Compensatory programs, a variation of Cronbach's third category, were extremely popular during the 1960s, but in the last decade, enthusiasm for compensatory education has waned considerably.

Cronbach's fourth category, matching particular instructional methods to students' learning styles, has recently gained attention, particularly among educational researchers. Recent research on distinctive educational treatments for students who differ on one dimension or another falls under the rubric of "aptitude by treatment interaction" (ATI). Like earlier research on student diversity in the classroom, few clear implications for classroom instruction have resulted from recent ATI research, despite systematic attempts to derive theoretical and practical principles. Because of its current popularity, we summarize below some of the most common problems in ATI research.

APTITUDE BY TREATMENT INTERACTION MODES

There are many reasons why research on aptitude by treatment interaction has failed to provide solutions to the problems of student diversity. First, the preoccupation of earlier researchers with status variables was, in some respects, counterproductive. Status variables, including sex, race or ethnicity, and socioeconomic status, while important, do not provide a systematic basis for planning instruction.

Consider sex as an example. There is a wealth of information describing sex differences in terms of physical, psychological, and cognitive development,[13] and there is much observational research describing classroom behavior of male and female students.[14] Perhaps the most important finding from research on sex differences is that the distribution of males and females overlaps markedly on almost every variable studied to date (for example, there are high-anxious males and there are high-anxious females). Even though there are many variables on which group differences emerge, the relevance of these differences to educational planning is questionable. The educator who concludes that all girls or boys need more of a particular kind of instruction because, on the average, they are somewhat less proficient, will probably be incorrect at least 60 percent of the time. For example, if 20 percent of males appear to be deficient in a reading skill, emphasizing that skill in instructional programs for all boys will result in needless instruction for many and may neglect other areas where they need instruction. Likewise, the belief that girls generally are good at a particular skill may lead teachers to de-emphasize that skill when instructing the 10 percent of girls who are deficient in it. We are not arguing that information about status variables is entirely irrelevant to educational planning, or that some general tendencies should be ignored. However, overemphasizing status variables is counterproductive.

A second explanation for the disappointing results of many educational programs based on the ATI model is that educators overestimate the speed with which they can design and implement programs.[15] Often, too little conceptualization and time go into the design of curricular materials for particular types of students. Furthermore, the duration of a treatment is often short (a few days or a few weeks). Cronbach and Snow note that aptitude by treatment programs producing relatively promising results generally expose students to the treatment for a relatively long period of time.[16] Hence, there is reason to suspect that the quality of the treatment (Is it really suited to the student type?) and the length of the treatment are both important factors. More promising results may yet emerge from this tradition if more adequate and longer treatment programs are utilized.

Disappointing results may also occur because treatments are not fully implemented as they had been conceptualized. Classroom observation sometimes is a part of research on aptitude by treatment interaction and, in some studies there is evidence that students in treatment "A" received different forms of instruction than students in treatment "B"; however, the observational data are typically not extensive enough to assure that the treatment was performed adequately. Finally, in the few studies with rigorous conceptualization and adequate observational measures, the teacher sample is small, making generalization risky.[17] Also, teachers often administer both treatments. While this procedure excludes extraneous teacher variables such as personality, energy, and the like, as sources of influence, it makes it difficult for teachers to become specialists, or at least accomplished in one treatment area.

A fourth problem with ATI research is that it often ignores quality of teaching as a factor affecting the success of instructional techniques. Teachers who communicate actively, thoughtfully, and clearly may be able to teach a common curriculum to students with a wide range of abilities with only minor adjustment (for example, individual projects or curricula for a few students in the class). Teachers with poorer skills may be unable to teach successfully either a common or a specialized curriculum. Quality of instruction cannot be ignored in planning and evaluating the extent to which a "program" fits the needs of particular students. Unfortunately, in much of the ATI research that has been conducted, instructional quality has been ignored.

Specific educational treatments may also have been applied to the wrong students. To be sure, teachers need considerable information and skill to be able to match treatments to students. As Cronbach notes: "The poorer the differential information, the less the teacher should depart from the treatment that works best on the average. . . . Modifying treatment too much produces a worse result than treating everyone alike."[18] Too often in the 1960s and 1970s, teachers taught in programs in which students were exposed to unique but haphazard curriculums.

Perhaps the most fundamental, even insurmountable, reason for educators' inability to derive principles from most ATI research is that even when aptitudes and skills are precisely specified and the instructional program is taught by a good teacher, there is simply no single effective educational treatment. Cronbach claims that ATI research is characterized by inconsistent results and higher-order interactions.[19] Apparently, techniques that work in one setting with one group of students do not necessarily work in another setting with another group of students, even for the same teacher.

Consider, for example, how societal change may alter the effectiveness of particular instructional procedures. A teacher who teaches reading in 1980 the same way (with equal thoughtfulness and energy) as he or she did in 1960 may obtain different results from students because of the effects of television on readiness skills, shifts of school boundaries, changes in the characteristics of the neighborhood surrounding the school, the presence of mainstreamed children, and countless other factors.

Our knowledge of schools, and particularly of classroom interactions, has improved notably in the past twenty years. However, group and individual needs can only be resolved as a result of judicious planning, monitoring, and revising of instruction and curricula by school staffs as they consider their goals and the needs of the specific children they serve in the specific context in which they teach. Accordingly, this chapter will not provide any definitive recommendations for dealing with student diversity. Rather, we hope to emphasize the complexity of the concept of individualization and the difficulties associated with implementing individualized programs, and to encourage educators to think about effective techniques within the contexts and constraints of their own particular educational settings.

Students vary on many dimensions that influence how and under what conditions they learn. They vary in the rate at which they learn, their learning style, and on many personality dimensions. In this chapter, we focus on only two of the many educationally important individual difference variables. First, the dimension of ability was selected to illustrate attempts to adjust the organization of instruction to the variable rates at which children master curricula. Most educational accommodations to differences in rate of learning have *not* involved different instructional methods. Rather, classroom organizational features (for example, large- versus small-group instruction; homogeneous versus heterogeneous grouping) and reward structure (for example, competitive versus noncompetitive; individual versus group) have been studied. The goal of most of this research is to identify the classroom structure that optimizes children's learning at all ability levels. Second, cognitive style was selected as an example of an individual difference variable that has inspired researchers to match particular instructional methods to children's particular learning styles. Consequently, research on cognitive styles illustrates one form of the currently popular aptitude by treatment interaction model.

We stress that choice of any two dimensions on which students vary is bound to be somewhat arbitrary because there are so many individual difference variables that influence learning. However, general ability is the first variable that educators consider when designing instructional programs. Cognitive style is a variable that, although ignored by many teachers when planning instruction, has received considerable attention from educators and researchers. We include these two dimensions also because they illustrate many of the problems associated with individualizing instruction.

We will emphasize one classroom structure variable related to general ability (reward structure) and one particular cognitive style (psychological differentiation). By restricting our scope, we can summarize what is known about each variable, including research evidence linking instructional practice and student achievement, and discuss both the utility and limitations of research for classroom practice.

Ability Differences

Ability is perhaps the most important and certainly the most controversial individual difference variable related to education. Notwithstanding the ideological ideal—that all persons are created equal—the indisputable fact is that most teachers begin each year with a class of students who vary widely in their skill levels and the facility with which they learn new skills. These individual differences are present at kindergarten and continue throughout the school years.

We use the term "ability" in the way that aptitude is defined by Snow, as readiness to profit from a learning experience.[20] We recognize that individual differences in ability or facility for learning result from a variety of factors, including the quality of previous instruction, social-emotional development, motivation, and so on. Ability is, therefore, considered as both an input variable and an outcome of instruction. The term "input" emphasizes that children bring to each new class an "initial state of competence" and a facility for acquiring new knowledge.[21] Their performance in each class is the consequence of an interaction between these input factors, which we call ability, and characteristics of the learning environment.

This conceptualization is admittedly problematic because we can only infer children's "initial states of competence" from their performance and behavior. Indeed, most extant studies on the classroom variables discussed below use "ability" and "performance" almost interchangeably. Yet there are many reasons why a child may perform poorly, and the stable, immutable trait that the term "ability" usually implies may be one of the least important factors. For example, one third grader having difficulty learning to read may have older brothers who devalue academic excellence and ridicule the child for practicing. Another child's difficulty may be explained by poor eyesight, or fatigue, or any one of myriad factors. While all of these problems can produce the same outcome—poor academic performance—each may require a different educational environment for correction and for optimal learning. It is, therefore, important to keep in mind that the appearance of poor ability has multifarious causes and these underlying causes, which are often difficult to identify, have important implications for planning appropriate learning environments. Note also that performance levels for a child may vary from subject to subject. It is therefore often inappropriate to categorize children as high, average, or low achievers. Classroom interventions make assumptions about the source and the extent of a "student problem." When those assumptions are correct, and when a program is adequately implemented, positive changes are likely to occur. However, when the assumptions are wrong, the intervention is likely to have little positive effect.

Ability or performance differences among children in a class, whatever their causes, are particularly important because motivational and other individual differences result from an interaction between the classroom environment and children's ability levels. For example, a competitive reward structure may enhance the motivation of children who begin the competition with high levels of skill, but inhibit the motivation of children who begin at a disadvantage and consequently have no hope of winning. Since motivation is undeniably a factor in ultimate performance, the differential effects of competition and other classroom practices on motivation may only widen the variance in skill level.

In this section, we discuss educational research related to the problem of optimal learning by both high- and low-ability students. Many classroom organizational features have been studied in an attempt to optimize learning for groups of students who vary in the rate at which they learn. The size of the instructional group has been varied, as has the constitution of small groups (for example, groups that are homogeneous or heterogeneous in ability). Classroom reward structure, in which reward is based on individual or group performance using normative standards (comparative or mastery), is currently an area of active research. It is widely believed that low-ability students perform below their optimal capacity because of motivational problems, not necessarily because of inappropriate instruction, and that reward structure is a critical variable affecting motivation.[22]

Modifications in reward structure often require modifications in instructional format (for example, group reward contingencies are usually associated with small-group, cooperative instructional units). It is, therefore, difficult to evaluate separately the effectiveness of the various types of reward structures and instructional formats that have been tried. We will discuss these two aspects of classroom organization independently when this is possible. Note also that the organizational accommodations discussed in this section do not represent an ATI approach to meeting students' individual needs. Rather, the research reviewed next represents a search for a uniform treatment that benefits all children equally.

We shall take the perspective of the teacher who, on the first day of class, is presented with twenty to thirty students grouped by age. Some pupils have achieved a high level of mastery and others are far below grade level. Some can learn new material quickly; others require a great deal of repetition. The teacher wants to organize the classroom in a way that will optimize learning for *all* of the children. The dilemma is that most classroom organizational and reward structures differentially affect the learning of low- and high-ability students.

We should emphasize that the effect of various classroom structures on children's achievement is currently so complex that it would tax the mind of even the most formal operational thinker. We provide here only a few samples of research illustrating the importance of asking a more complex question than we are accustomed to asking. The issue is not which reward structure or instructional format is best, or even which structure is best for which students and under what conditions. Variations in teacher abilities and skills, as well as those of students, and the content being taught will necessarily dictate different strategies for optimal learning.

REWARD STRUCTURE AND INSTRUCTIONAL FORMAT

Evaluation is omnipresent in educational settings.[23] Nevertheless, important variations exist in the performance criteria used to evaluate students and to allocate rewards.[24] The traditional practice of evaluating individual students on the basis of their relative performance necessarily involves competition, which is believed to affect low-ability students negatively. Some critics of individual normative evaluation have urged group reward structures in which the same grade or reward is given to all children in a group.[25] Group reward can be based on either a competitive model in which groups compete for rewards or on a mastery model in which groups are rewarded for achieving a predetermined standard. Alternatively, individualized reward contingencies, which base grades and other rewards on how much material each student masters rather than on a normative basis, have been touted because they provide all children with the hope (and presumably the motivating power) of success.[26]

Individual competitive model. In the individual competitive model that characterizes most classrooms, rewards are allocated among individuals according to their relative performance. Slavin points out that a competition between individuals of equal ability should be particularly effective in optimizing effort because success is largely a function of effort.[27] However, in more typical classrooms composed of competing individuals of unequal abilities, the outcome is determined only in part by ability; increments in effort by any competitor do not necessarily increase his or her probability of success. Accordingly, an individualistic competitive situation could inhibit high effort in high-ability students because they can succeed without great effort when they are competing against students of lower ability. Individual competition may also inhibit effort in low-ability students because no amount of effort will lead to success against faster students. Perhaps average-ability children exert the most effort in individual competitive reward structures, since effort may be a particularly important determinant of their relative success or failure.

Low-ability students are probably the most disadvantaged by an individual competitive structure. High-ability students can compete with each other and, consequently, be motivated to exert high effort. The low-ability students may learn that no amount of effort will bring them success. When performance gains are made, they are seldom reinforced (for example, by high grades) because despite significant gains, their performance remains relatively poor as compared to other students in the class. The typical "D" student who achieves a "C+" with a great effort usually receives less recognition for this accomplishment than an "A" student who receives yet another "A". Hence, low-ability students may infer that effort is not related to performance, or at least to evaluation of performance.

The effect of noncontingency of reward on low-ability students' efforts in an individual competitive evaluation environment has been discussed at length in the literature on learned helplessness.[28] Children who begin competition at a disadvantage and who fare poorly no matter how hard they try eventually cease trying. Many educational writers have documented the lack of attention and persistence and other behaviors exhibited by children who repeatedly fail in competitive educational environments.[29] Competition has also been shown to accentuate the negative affect associated with failure.[30]

For these and other reasons that have been discussed by critics of individualized competition in the classroom, teachers and educational researchers have sought alternative reward structures. Their task is, in part, to design a reward structure that minimizes maladaptive behavior in low-ability students (behaviors that result from continued failure and hopelessness) without impeding the motivation and learning of higher-ability children.

Group reward model. A group reward structure may relieve motivational problems some low-ability students have in individual competitive situations, perhaps without inhibiting the performance of high-ability children. Evidence suggests, for example, that simply being a member of a successful group, regardless of a child's own performance, allows the child some of the advantages of success, such as high self-perceptions of ability, satisfaction, and peer esteem.[31] Unfortunately, in one study, each child in a cooperative group that failed was derogated, even if he or she had performed well.[32] It seems that group competition may not enable an individual to avoid the effects of failure. However, group settings may diffuse failure, so that every child in the class experiences equal proportions of success and failure. Moreover, if groups are matched on ability level, all groups have an equal chance of winning. This may help students recognize that failure is a normal and expected part of the learning process. According to Ames and Felker, individual group members share equally the advantages of success and the disadvantages of failure; all members, therefore, should be motivated to contribute to the likelihood of success of their group by working as hard as possible.[33] (However, as we shall see later, when psychological differentiation is discussed, some individuals work better in groups than others.)

Cooperative groups do not necessarily have to compete with each other. If a mastery model is applied, groups are rewarded when they meet a specified standard. Consequently, all groups have the opportunity to succeed. However, the advantages of a mastery model over a competitive model in cooperative reward structures are questionable. Unlike the individualized competitive situation, in which some children know that they have no chance of winning regardless of their efforts, group competition presumably pits groups of equal ability against each other. As a consequence, the competitive-cooperative model may increase motivation, since effort should be the major determinant of relative success. If competition enhances the performance of groups roughly equal in ability, as it is assumed to do for individuals,[34] then a mastery-based cooperative structure may be less motivating for both high- and low-ability students than a competitive-cooperative structure.

Mastery learning model. The mastery learning model is perhaps the most radical departure from usual classroom structures because it modifies both the reward contingency and the instructional format. It is designed specifically to achieve optimal learning in a class of students varying in ability. Instructional pace is fully individualized and performance is evaluated according to each child's own personal standard. Note that like the classroom reward structures described above, mastery learning is not an aptitude by treatment interaction model. An ATI approach involves different kinds of instruction for different kinds of children. In mastery learning programs all children receive essentially the same kind of instruction; only the rate at which they pass through the instructional sequence varies.

The mastery model is believed to have important implications for motivation. Because an individualized standard is used for evaluation, students at all ability levels can expect success to result from their efforts.[35] Low-ability students, in particular, should benefit from a mastery-based reward contingency. Indeed, many researchers have reported impressive gains in the performance of low-ability children when a mastery-based model was introduced into their classrooms.[36] Regrettably, we know of no data bearing on the mediating role of students' perceptions of success, that is, that they are positively affected by mastery programs. Consequently, we do not know if the improved performance of low-ability children is due to their higher expectations for success and increased effort or to more appropriate selection of curriculum content or more systematic teaching.

Does the gain for low-ability children necessitate a loss for high-ability children? Is there any reason to believe that mastery models inhibit performance of high-ability children? Block reports that students who are accustomed to success in a competitive situation are often less motivated in a noncompetitive situation.[37] The possibility of outperforming other students may add to the incentive value of success for students who have some expectation of winning, and the removal of the competition may decrease their motivation. The positive effect of a competitive situation on "winners" is demonstrated in a study by Ames and Felker.[38] When stories about hypothetical winners and losers were read to them, children judged the winners in the competitive situation as more deserving of reward than winners in the individual mastery-based system.

Mastery learning models may be a disadvantage to high-ability students in another way. The idea that children vary in the amount of time they need to master skills, not in the level of mastery they can achieve, is basic to mastery learning theory.[39] That is, if all children are provided the time they need for mastery, all (or at least most) will master the entire school curriculum. Since the amount of time children need to master material varies greatly, a program that allows the slowest child to achieve mastery risks holding back faster learners.

In a review of mastery learning research, Block and Burns note that some mastery learning programs require more study time than non-mastery-based models of learning.[40] The additional study time is reduced in the long term, but the evidence nevertheless suggests that a mastery learning program requires more time to cover the same curriculum than other methods. Consequently, while average- or low-ability children reach a high level of mastery in the mastery learning program, high-ability students may be required to wait for the slower students before they can go on to the next curriculum unit. Cohen and Spady have both suggested that this negative outcome of mastery-based learning can be avoided if the curriculum is open-ended, that is, if the fast learners are always provided new material to master.[41]

On a practical level, it is noteworthy that children can undermine the purpose of the mastery model. For example, some children introduce normative evaluation into mastery-based programs by informally creating a "race to the end of the curriculum." While the teacher reinforces each child for his or her gains, children sometimes focus their attention on their relative positions in the steps toward finishing the entire curriculum.[42] In this situation, low-ability students regain their positions as losers and suffer the same motivational consequences that are found in an individual competitive program, but without the benefits that occur in many nonmastery classrooms (frequent teacher modeling of positive problem-solving approaches and other forms of teacher instruction which are sometimes omitted in more individualized mastery-oriented programs).

Ames and Ames suggest that the deleterious effects of competitive or normative standards are only likely to be present in mastery learning programs in which children are given external criteria by which to judge their performance.[43] For example, in an experimental study, they found that children who had only their own past performance to use as a standard were more likely to attribute their failure to lack of effort than were children in a competitive situation in which their performance could be compared to another child's performance. In some studies using individualized performance standards, external performance criteria were available and the desirable attributional relationship between effort and outcome was not found.[44]

It may be impossible to create a learning environment with no external standards of performance. Although social comparison in mastery learning programs may be minimized to some degree by reducing public evidence of each child's mastery level,[45] children often appear to be highly motivated to seek normative information, even when such behavior is discouraged by the teacher.[46] Indeed, Levine argues that the act of reducing public evidence related to ability may enhance the need, at least in some students, to gain such information. Furthermore, teachers may inadvertently reinforce the notion of normative ability in mastery classrooms by referring to the speed at which a student is working, or by otherwise providing normative information.

In summary, there is some evidence that a mastery learning evaluation structure can positively affect the achievement of low-ability students. The effects of mastery learning on high-ability students depend on several factors, such as whether the students have been previously socialized in a competitive reward structure and whether fast learners are required to wait for slow learners. For slower learners, the advantage of a mastery learning program over a competitive reward structure probably depends to a significant degree on the presence or absence of external normative criteria by which children can evaluate their own and each other's performances.

MEDIATING VARIABLES

Overall, research comparing these various reward structures and instructional formats has produced inconsistent results.[47] Some researchers attribute the inconsistency in findings on group reward models to mediating variables such as the nature of the task,[48] the academic subject,[49] the composition of the group,[50] or the degree to which individuals have resources to share in the cooperative situations.[51] Most likely, all of these factors influence the effectiveness of cooperative learning. Moreover, their effects on learning surely also interact with characteristics of learners, such as their ability levels or learning styles. For example, some studies comparing high and low achievers suggest that low achievers benefit most from a group reward structure.[52] However, the evidence on this interaction is inconsistent, probably because other variables influence the relative effectiveness of group reward structures for low and high achievers.[53]

With regard to the effects of group composition, Laughlin found that high-ability students performed better in a group comprised of other high-ability students than if they worked alone or with lower-ability students.[54] Low-ability students did not benefit from working with other low-ability students, but did benefit from working with high-ability students.

In a program of related research, Webb reported that middle achievers did less well in groups where both high and low achievers were present than in uniform ability groups.[55] The advantage of the uniform-ability grouping for middle achievers was probably related to an additional finding that average-ability students in uniform-ability groups received more explanations than average-ability students in mixed-ability groups. Receiving explanations was associated with higher achievement. Apparently both *composition* factors (which students are placed in a group) and *process* factors (the form of academic and social exchange in the group) affect group learning.

The specific nature of the reward contingency appears to be another important factor influencing group learning outcomes. Litow and Pumroy delineate different kinds of reward contingencies in cooperative learning structures.[56] For example, the reward can be contingent on the performance of a subset of the group's members, or it can be contingent upon the entire group's performance, either by summing or averaging the performance of the individual members.

The enhanced performance of cooperative groups in which reward is contingent on average performance could be due to the high-ability members giving the answers to the medium- and low-ability students. However, the finding in one study that even the achievement of high-ability students was enhanced in one cooperative learning situation suggests that group performance was not enhanced because the high-ability students gave answers to other students.[57] Nonetheless, since the reward was contingent on the group's performance, the high-ability students may have been largely responsible for the overall gain.

Indeed, in the long term, rewards contingent upon an average or total group score might even negatively affect the learning of low-ability children. The total or average score could represent the performance of some children who had mastered a skill and others who had not. If the group advanced despite the lack of mastery of some members, these slower learners could move through the curriculum on the coattails of the faster learners without ever mastering the material. Such a negative effect of cooperative learning is a risk any time a total or average group score is the criterion for reward, either in a mastery model where a predetermined level of performance must be achieved, or in a competitive-cooperative model.

Hamblin, Hathaway, and Wodarski suggest that the achievement of high- and low-ability students is optimized in cooperative situations by making the reward contingent on the performance of the low-ability students.[58] They found that peer tutoring and increments in achievement occurred most often when reward for each child was contingent on the average of the four lowest performers in the group. Presumably, tutoring enhanced the learning of the high-ability tutors and their students. In a later study, peer tutoring was again enhanced by making reward contingent upon the performance of the bottom four students in the group.[59] Moreover, the performance of both the bottom four students and the top four students was enhanced somewhat by this reward contingency.

Perhaps the most important variable mediating the effect of reward structure or instructional format on low- and high-ability children's learning is the teacher. Teachers largely determine the effectiveness of any instructional format. Indeed, the quality of teaching may overwhelm any effect of classroom organization on student motivation or learning.

For example, there is evidence that teachers often expect too little from students perceived as low in ability and they do not make serious attempts to teach them. Some teachers have been found to offer inadequate response opportunities and academic stimulation for students perceived to be low in ability. Moreover, these differences have been found in classrooms with individualized and whole-class organizational structures and by investigators using quantitative and qualitative observation strategies.[60]

Teachers who group students for instruction or who create individualized learning programs, but who spend more time with high achievers, have not solved the "motivational problem." Clearly, the small-group or individual learning settings typically associated with noncompetitive reward structures do not guarantee optimal conditions for learning.

Comparisons of small-group teaching also illustrate the potential irrelevance of the format when other teacher qualities are considered. In a large naturalistic study, Good and Grouws found that elementary school teachers (teaching comparable students) who were getting the highest gains from students in mathematics used a whole-class teaching technique.[61] Furthermore, high gains were not necessarily obtained at the expense of one type of student. However, teachers who obtained the lowest gains also used whole-class techniques. Most teachers who tended to be "middle gainers" used individualized formats or taught mathematics in small groups.

Subsequent work indicated that the group format was less critical than other aspects of instruction. Systematic differences in instructional techniques were found between relatively effective and relatively ineffective teachers using whole-class teaching techniques. Moreover, the instructional techniques used by successful whole-class teachers could be effectively taught to other teachers.[62] Note, however, that the training was very effective for certain types of teachers and students, but had only marginally positive effects upon other teacher-learner combinations.[63] The importance of considering student characteristics is also clear from research by Peterson and Janicki.[64] They found that some children learned better in large-group settings and others in small groups. Low-ability students, for example, actually had a more positive attitude toward large-group than small-group approaches.

All classroom organizational formats, apparently, have potential problems as well as potential advantages. The advantages of a particular format depend upon the teacher's skills, the needs of particular students, the content taught, and specific instructional goals.[65] When implemented well and when suited to student characteristics, small-group, individual, and large-group instruction, and individualized and group reward structures can have a positive impact on student learning at all ability levels.

The educational implication that we draw from research on classroom organizational and reward structure is that no particular structure maximizes learning in children of all ability levels. Thus, this research supports our initial claim that a search for the single best solution is likely to fail. There are many variables that must be considered in designing a classroom organization that meets the individual needs of students. Teachers need to be wary of packaged programs or pat solutions and they need to be well trained to assess the particular needs of their own students.

Ability is only one of many individual difference variables complicating instructional decision making. Other factors such as student preferences and learning styles must also be considered in educational planning. We now turn to a discussion of cognitive style, another variable that teachers may want to consider when planning instructional activities.

Cognitive Style

We examine cognitive style for several reasons. Students vary widely on this dimension and we suspect that few teachers consider this variable when planning instruction. This is despite increasing evidence that variation in students' learning styles have important educational implications.

Cognitive style has received considerable attention from researchers in recent years. Most of this research follows the currently popular aptitude by treatment interaction model; different kinds of instruction are recommended for children with different kinds of cognitive style. However, like research on other dimensions of individual differences that have become fashionable to study, research on cognitive style has had limited utility for educators. Indeed, even though cognitive style is one of the individual difference variables we know most about, few unambiguous pedagogical principles can be derived from research. This is, in part, because attempting to develop "packaged" programs (with predetermined and presumably generalizable solutions) is an inappropriate response to individual differences in cognitive style (despite the claims of some enthusiastic program developers).[66] This field of research provides a good example of the potential hazards of overemphasizing a single dimension in instructional decision making.

We object to packaged curriculum programs and to standardized forms of instruction for students who have particular learning styles because these solutions neglect other variables affecting student learning. We do think that cognitive style should be considered in planning educational programs that accommodate to individual differences. In this section we briefly explain the concept of cognitive style and we explore the implications for educational research and practice of one type of cognitive style, psychological differentiation. Specific ways in which this individual difference variable may be used in instructional planning are suggested.

Cognitive style variables concern *how* a person learns rather than *what* is learned or the competence with which an individual performs a task. An important distinction between "ability" and "style" is that ability is viewed as unipolar. More of an ability is better than less of it. In contrast, cognitive styles are conceptualized as bipolar and independent of context or of task. Being at one end of the continuum is neither good (adaptive) nor bad. Extreme behavior in a cognitive style (for example, risk taking) may have advantages in some tasks (for example, certain card games); being at the other extreme may have advantages for other tasks (for example, investing in the stock market). Hence, a particular style should not necessarily be taught in the classroom.

It should be emphasized that the distinction between style and ability is relative because all "style" measures reflect some degree of ability. Cognitive style measures often include individual students' cognitive *preferences* (what they like to learn and under what conditions) as well as dimensions of *motivation* and general *personality*. Various measures of cognitive style focus upon different cognitive operations. For example, Kagan, Moss, and Sigel have developed a cognitive style measure that emphasizes preferences.[67] Other measures of cognitive style have a stronger ability component, although they include aspects of preference and motivation. For example, the distinction that Bruner, Goodnow, and Austin make between focusers and scanners and the distinction that Witkin and his colleagues make between field independence (analytic) and field dependence (global) include both ability and motivational variables.[68]

Many cognitive style variables have been studied by educational researchers: extensiveness versus intensiveness of scanning, leveling versus sharpening, risk taking versus cautiousness, cognitive complexity versus simplicity, impulsivity versus reflectiveness. Several cognitive style variables have had sufficient theoretical attention to merit examination for potential educational application. Among these are conceptual level (abstract-concrete), conceptual tempo (fast-slow responders), and psychological differentiation (field-dependence versus field-independence). We focus here on the concept of psychological differentiation.

FIELD INDEPENDENCE/FIELD DEPENDENCE

Witkin and Goodenough conceptualize psychological differentiation in terms of a greater or lesser degree of self-segregation, which is represented in individuals' tendency to rely upon the external field (for example, other people) or themselves. Psychological differentiation refers to individual differences in autonomy from external referents. At one extreme are field-independent persons (autonomous) who have an impersonal orientation, and at the other end of the continuum are field-dependent persons who have an interpersonal orientation.

At the outset, several conceptual and methodological caveats deserve mention. First, some researchers have contended that a distinction between ability and cognitive style cannot be defended logically or empirically.[69] While ability surely affects psychological differentiation, recent conceptualizations[70] and empirical work[71] provide some support for the independent construct of psychological differentiation.

A second caveat to keep in mind is that psychological differentiation is a continuous dimension with most people falling between the two extremes. Moreover, there is considerable within-person variation (for example, an individual may rely on others in some contexts—an unfamiliar social setting—but rely primarily on self in other settings— the office). Within-person variation is, of course, true of ability or any other individual difference variable. Nevertheless, there appears to be enough consistency in individuals' style across situations to merit consideration from educators.

Because extreme field-independent persons tend to be autonomous, it is not surprising that they are typically described as more concerned with ideas than with people, analytical, cold, rude, and aloof. On the other hand, extreme field-dependent people, with their tendency to seek and use information from others, are often described as warm, interested in people, liking to be with others, and socially adept.

An individual who falls at either extreme of this cognitive style variable (field dependence/field independence) has qualities that are more or less adaptive in particular circumstances. In an interesting cross-cultural comparison, Witkin and Berry have shown that environmental demands influence style preferences.[72] For example, more field independence was found in a hunting society than in an agricultural society. It seems reasonable that personal autonomy and analytical skills would have more value in a hunting society, and that a social orientation would have more adaptive value in an agricultural society where interdependence and close physical proximity prevail. However, in a multifaceted society such as ours, it is difficult to designate one style as more adaptive than the other. There are times to cooperate and to achieve consensus and there are times to evaluate ideas and plans analytically.

There is no consensus on the cause of individuals' tendency toward a field-independent or field-dependent orientation. Witkin and Goodenough tend to stress socialization (for example, parent-child interaction, opportunities for independent functioning, decision making, and so forth); however, others have argued that cerebral lateralization is a more compelling explanation.[73]

We will not discuss research on socialization or cerebral lateralization. However, the issue of causation deserves mention because the timing and nature of educational intervention may depend upon our understanding of the antecedent factors related to cognitive styles as well as our knowledge of the environmental factors that reinforce different cognitive styles. There is evidence to suggest that field dependence and field independence can be altered to some degree.[74] However, the value of such intervention depends in part upon the philosophical assumptions that educators, parents, and policymakers hold.[75]

CLASSROOM IMPLICATIONS OF PSYCHOLOGICAL DIFFERENTIATION

Psychological differentiation is related to a variety of variables relevant to education.[76] Field-dependent students usually prefer to work in groups and to interact frequently with the teacher; field-independent students may respond better to more independent and more individualized approaches. Field-dependent students tend to work to please the teacher and are more motivated by praise and encouragement from the teacher than are field-independent students, who tend to pursue their own goals. Field-independent students tend to prefer to structure their own learning tasks to a degree, and they are typically better at doing so. Field-dependent students may, therefore, need more explicit instruction in problem-solving strategies or more exact definitions of performance outcomes.

Field-independent students prefer mathematics and science and generally perform well in these subjects. Field-dependent people generally prefer and do better in the humanities and social studies. Field-independent people are oriented toward occupations requiring a theoretical and analytic orientation: mathematician, physicist, chemist, biologist, architect, engineer, physician, dentist, production manager, carpenter, forest service, farmer, mechanic, artist. Field-dependent students are oriented toward occupations that require social skills: social worker, minister, counselor, probation officer, teacher, seller, advertiser, administrator, politician.[78]

Psychological differentiation is an important variable for teachers as well as for students. From what has been said so far, it is not surprising that many teachers of mathematics, science, and industrial arts, compared to teachers of social studies, humanities, and teachers in the elementary school, organize their classrooms in ways consistent with a field-independent rather than a field-dependent orientation. In addition, teachers' psychological differentiation affects to some extent the ways that they teach.

Relatively field-independent teachers prefer impersonal teaching situations oriented toward more cognitive or theoretical matters, whereas field-dependent teachers prefer frequent interaction with students and tend to stress class discussion.[79] Field-independent teachers have been found to use questions primarily as instructional tools. Field-dependent teachers use questions primarily to assess student learning following instruction.[80] Field-independent teachers tend to emphasize their own standards and to formulate principles themselves when explaining material to students. In contrast, field-dependent teachers generally involve students more in organizing the content and sequences of the teaching-learning process and encourage them to formulate principles independently.[81] Field-independent teachers are more likely to believe that students should be informed when they are incorrect and be told why they are incorrect; they express displeasure with students who are performing below capacity. Field-dependent teachers are less likely to provide negative feedback.

Several studies indicate that field-dependent teachers are interested primarily in creating and maintaining positive attitudes and good group dynamics, and only secondarily in subject content; field-independent teachers have been found to have the opposite set of priorities.[82] Finally, students perceive field-independent teachers as focusing on general principles and field-dependent teachers as stressing facts.

This cognitive style dimension also appears to be associated with learning outcomes. For example, field independence has been found to be positively associated with mathematics and spatial abilities, even when general intelligence is controlled.[83] More generally, as noted above, students tend to achieve more in subject matter areas that are compatible with their cognitive styles. There is additional evidence suggesting that students perform better when matched in cognitive style with their teachers.[84]

Grieve and Davis, for example, report that a discovery treatment (with more teacher-learner exchange and a friendlier social context) was best for boys who were low in field independence and that an expository teaching model was associated with more learning gains in boys who were high in field independence.[85] Significant interactions were *not* found for girls in this study.

Even so, it is not clear that students, teachers, and educational environments should necessarily be matched on this dimension, especially for students who are at the extremes of this psychological differentiation dimension. Extreme field independents often have social adjustment problems, and extreme field dependents are highly conforming. These individuals might benefit from environments that require them to function in their nonpreferred orientations. Indeed, there is some empirical evidence to suggest that mismatches may, under certain conditions, be beneficial for students.[86]

Although the issue of teacher-student styles merits additional research attention, it is important for teachers to learn to recognize and respect both orientations, to build on existing student strengths, and to avoid letting stylistic differences lead to discriminatory practices or personality clashes. Field-independent teachers can help meet the needs of field-dependent students by structuring learning experiences sufficiently for students to be able to cope effectively. Teachers can also provide encouragement and praise for success but remain objective and supportive when criticizing mistakes, and they can develop a generally positive personal relationship with field-dependent students. Field-dependent instructors accustomed to indirect, subtle communication may need to deal more directly with field-independent students. Also, since extreme field-independent students are not likely to respond strongly or even positively to warmth or praise from the teacher, the teacher should not feel rejected when this occurs. Finally, it is important that field-dependent teachers respect field-independent students' needs for privacy and distance, and avoid penalizing the students' low social participation.

The value of teacher sensitivity to students' cognitive styles was shown in a recent study by Doebler and Eicke.[87] Fifth-grade teachers in the experimental group were given information about their students' field dependence/field independence and suggestions about teaching strategies likely to be successful with each type. Compared to students in control classes whose teachers were not given this information, experimental students showed better self-concepts and attitudes toward school on measures taken in December and adjusted for prescores taken during the sixth week of school. Most teachers will not have access to such data on their students, of course, but they should be able to identify students' cognitive styles by observing and interacting with them.

We conclude with Cronbach and Snow that the research evidence for adapting instruction for students solely on the basis of students' cognitive styles is not compelling.[88] Extant research does suggest that in some instances students who are high in field independence react differently to the same instructional treatment from those who are low in field independence. However, there is only weak support for the claim that instructional treatment should always be consistent with students' learning styles.

It is important to note that we believe we would have reached the same conclusion (that is, no immediate, specific implications for practice) with an analysis of *any single variable*. Some field-independent students are intelligent, but low in persistence. Other students high in field dependence may be less intelligent, but very persistent. They try hard because they are intrinsically motivated. The examination of students' cognitive styles in terms of psychological differentiation clearly provides some important information about their learning needs. However, this construct, like any other, fails to provide other important information about students that is relevant to the design of instruction. Consequently, overemphasizing this one individual difference variable in instructional planning could have harmful effects.

Nevertheless, teachers' awareness that some students may perceive a stimulus situation quite differently than the teachers do may cause them to include more variety in their instruction than they would otherwise (for example, teachers might realize that not all bright students benefit from a fast-paced questioning style or they may understand that some students prefer to work alone, and so forth). For this reason, we suggest that teachers be sensitized to the educational implications of psychological differentiation and familiar with the literature on cognitive style. Existing research and theory do not offer instructional prescriptions, as advocated by some researchers. However, tentative guidelines for instructional planning can be derived and a reading of current research can enhance practitioners' sensitivity to the issue of adapting instruction to students' learning styles.

Diversity in the Classroom

To be sure, there are no single solutions for meeting diverse student needs. Instructional formats or reward structures designed to maximize children's learning at all ability levels typically benefit some students while harming others. Programs or recommendations designed for particular types of student learning styles generally have disappointing results. We have discussed many reasons why a search for a single cure for the problems posed by individual differences is likely to fail and why many instructional and classroom organizational accommodations have not been as effective as they might have been. In this final analysis of research related to student diversity in the classroom we consider some further implications for researchers and teachers.

To researchers we suggest that treatment effects may be more powerful when teachers select a treatment group because they have confidence in a particular treatment, possess skills compatible with the treatment, or are willing to spend extra time to implement the treatment well. Some time ago, Jackson made an eloquent plea for more attention to the individual needs and preferences of teachers.[89] Yet, researchers have paid little attention to teacher preferences or other teacher characteristics. Although, as noted above, it may not be profitable to match teachers and students on cognitive style (for example, field-independent teachers teach only field-independent students) or some other particular variable, some accommodations or recognition of teachers' preferred styles might be made.

In our pursuit of adapting instruction to the personal needs of students, we must keep in mind teachers' unique skills and personalities. Perhaps rather than ask teachers to do all things well for all types of students we should help them become more adept at a few skills and instructional styles. If teachers utilize instructional skills suited to their personalities and educational goals, they are more likely to use their skills effectively. Research attempting to adjust school to teachers is far too rare.[90]

Researchers' failure to find "one best solution" for meeting the needs of individual students has further implications for teachers. Every classroom presents its own unique combination of characteristics. Moreover, classroom dynamics change continuously throughout the year. Consequently, an instructional program that worked effectively with one group of students may not work at all with another; methods that were effective at the beginning of the year may not be effective in the middle.

In any instructional program teachers will necessarily have to adjust instruction to fit students' skills and other characteristics, as well as the teacher's own life circumstances. Teachers should begin with an instructional program that they can implement competently and effectively. However, they must also be trained as problem solvers, quick to adjust to individual children and circumstances.

As we have seen in the discussion of field-dependent and field-independent students, only the few students at the extremes of this cognitive style would appear to need specialized treatment. Most students will adapt successfully if clear and meaningful instruction is provided, and if the teacher is sensitive to students and is flexible in classroom style (some lecture, some discussion, some group work). We suspect the same is true for other student individual difference variables as well.

We believe that research on aptitude by treatment interaction is important and that continued research in this tradition is warranted. Indeed, there is some evidence that certain aptitude-treatment results can be replicated.[91] However, the research suggests that teachers in regular classrooms who attempt to design special programs for the "visually alert" and other programs for the "affectively aware" students are fighting an uphill, and ultimately losing, battle. There are too many individual difference variables within classrooms, and a special program in one area often offsets gains in other areas. Hence, there is always the question of which individual difference does one wish to accommodate.

What teachers need (in addition to a coherent sense of their instructional values and skills suited to those philosophic goals) are a better understanding of student development variables (at the grade levels they teach) and an improved set of observational skills for learning from students.[92] Amarel provides an example of how teachers and researchers can combine awareness of students' developmental levels with close classroom observation in order to become more sensitive to students' "learning styles" and to derive sensible instructional hypotheses and strategies for building in meaningful variations in classroom instruction.[93]

Educational policymakers need to be aware that students and teachers vary in many ways and they must also *continuously* monitor and respond to school programs to allow flexibility of expression for students and teachers alike. However, educators should simultaneously strive to offer all students meaningful experiences, and in many (but certainly not all) instances, *common* experiences. Educators or researchers who advocate more individualized programs often assume that students receive the *same* content but need *different* programs. As was noted earlier, it appears that in some settings students receive distinct treatment (for example, unequal access to teacher) when a more similar treatment would be better. In future research on individualization it will be important to place more emphasis upon the *quality* of the instruction afforded to particular types of students rather than to the *form* of instruction.

FOOTNOTES

1. Walter Mischel, "On the Future of Personality Measurement," *American Psychologist* 32 (April 1977): 246.

2. Guy M. Whipple, ed., *Intelligence Tests and Their Use*, Twenty-first Yearbook of the National Society for the Study of Education, Parts I and II (Bloomington, Ill.: Public School Publishing Co., 1922).

3. Guy M. Whipple, ed., *Adapting the Schools to Individual Differences*, Twenty-fourth Yearbook of the National Society for the Study of Education, Part II (Bloomington, Ill.: Public School Publishing Co., 1925).

4. William H. Kilpatrick, "An Effort at Appraisal," in *Adapting the Schools to Individual Differences*, ed. Whipple, p. 273.

5. Nelson B. Henry, ed., *Individualizing Instruction*, Sixty-first Yearbook of the National Society for the Study of Education, Part I (Chicago: University of Chicago Press, 1962).

6. Warren G. Findley and M. W. Bryan, *Ability Grouping, 1970: Status, Impact, and Alternatives* (Athens, Ga.: Center for Educational Improvement, University of Georgia, 1971).

7. Joan C. Barker Lunn, *Streaming in the Primary School* (London: National Foundation for Educational Research in England and Wales, 1970); Walter R. Borg, *Ability Grouping in the Public Schools*, 2d ed. (Madison, Wis.: Dembar Educational Research Services, 1966).

8. Nell Keddie, "Classroom Knowledge," in *Knowledge and Control: New Directions for the Sociology of Education*, ed. Michael F. Young (London: Collier-Macmillan, 1971).

9. Ray C. Rist, "Student Social Class and Teacher Expectations: The Self-fulfilling Prophecy in Ghetto Education," *Harvard Educational Review* 40 (August 1970): 411-51; Rhona S. Weinstein, "Reading Group Membership in First Grade: Teacher Behaviors and Pupil Experience over Time," *Journal of Educational Psychology* 68 (February 1976): 103-116.

10. Fred T. Tyler, "Intraindividual Variability," in *Individualizing Instruction*, ed. Henry.

11. A. Sterl Artley, "Individual Differences and Reading Instruction," *Elementary School Journal* 82 (November 1981): 143-51.

12. Lee J. Cronbach, "How Can Instruction Be Adapted to Individual Differences?" in *Learning and Individual Differences*, ed. Robert Gagné (Columbus, Ohio: C. E. Merrill, 1967), p. 23.

13. Eleanor Maccoby and Carol Nagy Jacklin, *The Psychology of Sex Differences* (Stanford, Calif.: Stanford University Press, 1974).

14. Jere Brophy and Thomas L. Good, *Teacher-Student Relationships: Causes and Consequences* (New York: Holt, Rinehart and Winston, 1974); Barbara J. Bank, Bruce J. Biddle, and Thomas L. Good, "Sex Roles, Classroom Instruction, and Reading Achievement," *Journal of Educational Psychology* 72 (April 1980): 119-32.

15. American College Testing Program, *Promoting Student Learning in College by Adapting to Individual Differences in Educational Cognitive Style*, Final Evaluation Report (Iowa City, Iowa: American College Testing Program, 1977). ED 158 699.

16. Lee J. Cronbach and Richard E. Snow, *Aptitudes and Instructional Methods: A Handbook for Research on Interactions* (New York: Irvington Publishers, 1977).

17. Terence C. Janicki and Penelope L. Peterson, "Aptitude-Treatment Interaction Effects of Variations in Direct Instruction," *American Educational Research Journal* 18 (Spring 1981): 63-82.

18. Cronbach, "How Can Instruction Be Adapted to Individual Differences?" p. 30.

19. Lee J. Cronbach, "Beyond the Two Disciplines of Scientific Psychology," *American Psychologist* 30 (February 1975): 116-27.

20. Richard E. Snow, "Requirements for a Theory of Aptitude" (Invited address at the annual meeting of the American Educational Research Association, Los Angeles, 1981).

21. Robert Glaser, *Adaptive Education: Individual Diversity and Learning* (New York: Holt, Rinehart and Winston, 1977).

22. Martin Covington and Richard G. Beery, *Self-Worth and School Learning* (New York: Holt, Rinehart and Winston, 1976); John G. Nicholls, "Quality and Equality in Intellectual Development: The Role of Motivation in Education," *American Psychologist* 34 (November 1979): 1071-83.

23. Philip W. Jackson, *Life in Classrooms* (New York: Holt, Rinehart and Winston, 1968).

24. Steven T. Bossert, *Task and Social Relationships in Classrooms: A Study of Instructional Organization and Its Consequences*, Arnold and Caroline Rose Monograph Series of the American Sociological Association (Cambridge, Eng.: Cambridge University Press, 1979).

25. David W. Johnson and Roger Johnson, "Instructional Goal Structure: Cooperative, Competitive, or Individualistic," *Review of Educational Research* 44 (Spring 1974): 213-40; Robert E. Slavin, "Classroom Reward Structure: An Analytical and Practical Review," *Review of Educational Research* 47 (Fall 1977): 633-50; Robert E. Slavin, "Cooperative Learning," *Review of Educational Research* 50 (Summer 1980): 315-42.

26. James Block and Robert B. Burns, "Mastery Learning," in *Review of Research in Education*, ed. Lee S. Shulman (Itasca, Ill.: F. E. Peacock and the American Educational Research Association, 1976); Covington and Beery, *Self-Worth and School Learning*; Nicholls, "Quality and Equality in Intellectual Development."

27. Slavin, "Classroom Reward Structure."

28. For a review, see Carol S. Dweck and Therese E. Goetz, "Attributions and Learned Helplessness," in *New Directions in Attribution Research*, vol. 2, ed. John H. Harvey, William J. Ickes, and Robert F. Kidd (Hillsdale, N.J.: Lawrence Erlbaum Associates, 1978).

29. See, for example, Covington and Beery, *Self-Worth and School Learning*.

30. Carole Ames and Donald W. Felker, "An Examination of Children's Attributions and Achievement-related Evaluations in Competitive, Cooperative, and Individualistic Reward Structures," *Journal of Educational Psychology* 71 (August 1979): 413-20; Susan B. Crockenberg, Brenda K. Bryant, and Lee S. Wilce, "The Effects of Cooperatively and Competitively Structured Learning Environments on Inter- and Intrapersonal Behavior," *Child Development* 47 (June 1976): 386-96.

31. Carole Ames, "Competitive versus Cooperative Reward Structure: The Influence of Individual and Group Performance Factors on Achievement Attributions and Affect," *American Educational Research Journal* 18 (Fall 1981): 273-88; Ames and Felker, "An Examination of Children's Attributions and Achievement-related Evaluations in Competitive, Cooperative, and Individualistic Reward Structures."

32. Ames and Felker, "An Examination of Children's Attributions and Achievement-related Evaluations in Competitive, Cooperative, and Individualistic Reward Structures."

33. Ibid.

34. Slavin, "Classroom Reward Structure."

35. Benjamin S. Bloom, *Human Characteristics and School Learning* (New York: McGraw-Hill, 1976).

36. See, for example, Alan S. Cohen, "Dilemmas in the Use of Learner-responsive Delivery Systems" (Paper presented at the annual meeting of the American Educational Research Association, Los Angeles, 1981); William G. Spady, "Outcome-based Instructional Management: A Sociological Perspective" (Unpublished manuscript, American Association of School Administrators, Arlington, Va., 1981).

37. James Block, "Motivation, Evaluation, and Mastery Learning," *UCLA Educator* 19 (Winter 1977): 31-36.

38. Ames and Felker, "An Examination of Children's Attributions and Achievement-related Evaluations in Competitive, Cooperative, and Individualistic Reward Structures."

39. Benjamin S. Bloom, "Learning for Mastery," *Evaluation Comment* 1 (May 1968): 2; Bloom, *Human Characteristics and School Learning*; John Carroll, "A Model of School Learning," *Teachers College Record* 64 (May 1963): 723-33.

40. Block and Burns, "Mastery Learning."

41. Cohen, "Dilemmas in the Use of Learner-responsive Delivery Systems"; Spady, "Outcome-based Instructional Management."

42. Crockenberg and Bryant, "Socialization: The Implicit Curriculum of Learning Environments"; J. M. Levine, "Social Comparison and Education," in *Teacher and Student Perceptions: Implications for Learning*, ed. J. M. Levine and M. C. Wang (Hillsdale, N.J.: Erlbaum Associates, in press).

43. Carole Ames and Russell Ames, "Competitive versus Individualistic Goal Structures: The Salience of Past Performance Information for Causal Attributions and Affect," *Journal of Educational Psychology* 73 (June 1981): 411-18.

44. See, for example, Ames and Felker, "An Examination of Children's Attributions and Achievement-related Evaluations in Competitive, Cooperative, and Individualistic Reward Structures"; John G. Nicholls, "Causal Attributions and Other Achievement-related Cognitions: Effects of Task Outcome, Attainment Value, and Sex," *Journal of Personality and Social Psychology* 31 (March 1975): 379-98.

45. Susan J. Rosenholtz and Bruce Wilson, "The Effect of Classroom Structure on Shared Perceptions of Ability," *American Educational Research Journal* 17 (Spring 1980): 75-82.

46. Levine, "Social Comparison and Education."

47. Johnson and Johnson, "Instructional Goal Structure"; James W. Michaels, "Classroom Reward Structures and Academic Performance," *Review of Educational Research* 47 (Winter 1977): 87-98; Shlomo Sharan, "Cooperative Learning in Small Groups: Recent Methods and Effects on Achievement, Attitudes, and Ethnic Relations," *Review of Educational Research* 50 (Summer 1980): 241-71; Slavin, "Classroom Reward Structure"; Slavin, "Cooperative Learning."

48. David W. Johnson, Roger Johnson, and Linda Skon, "Student Achievement on Different Types of Tasks under Cooperative, Competitive, and Individualistic Conditions," *Contemporary Educational Psychology* 4 (April 1979): 99-106.

49. David L. DeVries and Robert E. Slavin, "Teams-Games-Tournaments (TGT): Review of Ten Classroom Experiments," *Journal of Research and Development in Education* 12 (Fall 1978): 28-38.

50. Patrick R. Laughlin, "Ability and Group Problem Solving," *Journal of Research and Development in Education* 12 (Fall 1978): 114-20.

51. Slavin, "Classroom Reward Structure."

52. Keith J. Edwards, David DeVries, and John P. Snyder, "Games and Teams: A Winning Combination," *Simulation and Games* 3 (September 1972): 247-69.

53. Noreen M. Webb, "A Process-Outcome Analysis of Learning in Group and Individual Settings," *Educational Psychologist* 15 (Summer 1980): 69-83.

54. Laughlin, "Ability and Group Problem Solving."

55. Noreen M. Webb, "Peer Interaction and Learning in Cooperative Small Groups" (Unpublished manuscript, Los Angeles, Calif., 1981).

56. Leon Litow and Donald K. Pumroy, "A Brief Review of Classroom Group-oriented Contingencies," *Journal of Applied Behavior Analysis* 8 (Fall 1975): 341-47.

57. Johnson, Skon, and Johnson, "Effects of Cooperative, Competitive, and Individualistic Conditions on Children's Problem-solving Performance."

58. Robert L. Hamblin, Craig Hathaway, and John S. Wodarski, "Group Contingencies, Peer Tutoring, and Accelerating Academic Achievement," in *A New Direction for Education: Behavior Analyses*, ed. Eugene A. Ramp and Bill L. Hopkins (Lawrence Kans.: University of Kansas Press, 1971).

59. John S. Wodarski, Robert L. Hamblin, David R. Buckholdt, and Daniel E. Ferritor, "Individual Consequences versus Different Shared Consequences Contingent on the Performance of Low-achieving Group Members," *Journal of Applied Social Psychology* 3 (July-September 1973): 276-90.

60. See, for example, Kathryn Anderson-Levitt, "Memory and Talk in Teachers' Interpretations of Student Behavior" (Paper presented at the annual meeting of the American Educational Research Association, Los Angeles, April 1981); Brophy and Good, *Teacher-Student Relationships*; Harold Levine and M. Katherine Mann, "The Negotiation of Classroom Lessons and its Relevance for Teachers' Decision Making" (Paper presented at the annual meeting of the American Educational Research Association, Los Angeles, April 1981).

61. Thomas L. Good and Douglas A. Grouws, "Teaching Effects: A Process-product Study in Fourth-grade Mathematics Classrooms," *Journal of Teacher Education* 28 (May-June 1977): 49-54.

62. Thomas L. Good and Douglas A. Grouws, "The Missouri Mathematics Effectiveness Project: An Experimental Study of Fourth-grade Classrooms," *Journal of Educational Psychology* 71 (June 1979): 355-62.

63. Howard Ebmeier and Thomas L. Good, "The Effects of Instructing Teachers about Good Teaching on the Mathematics Achievement of Fourth Grade Students," *American Educational Research Journal* 16 (Winter 1979): 1-16.

64. Penelope L. Peterson and Terence C. Janicki, "Individual Characteristics and Children's Learning in Large-group and Small-group Approaches," *Journal of Educational Psychology* 71 (October 1979): 677-87.

65. Thomas L. Good and Jere Brophy, *Looking in Classrooms*, 2d ed. (New York: Harper and Row, 1978).

66. For an especially good example of an evaluation of an instructional program based directly on students' cognitive style, see American College Testing Program, *Promoting Student Learning in College by Adapting to Individual Differences in Educational Cognitive Style*.

67. Jerome Kagan, Howard A. Moss, and Irving E. Sigel, "Psychological Significance of Styles of Conceptualization," in *Basic Cognitive Processes in Children*, ed. John C. Wright and Jerome Kagan, *Monographs of the Society for Research in Child Development* (Serial no. 86) 28, no. 2 (1963): 73-112.

68. Jerome Bruner, Jacqueline Goodnow, and George Austin, *A Study of Thinking* (New York: Wiley, 1956); H. A. Witkin, C. A. Moore, D. R. Goodenough, and P. W. Cox, "Field-Dependent and Field-Independent Cognitive Styles and Their Educational Implications," *Review of Educational Research* 47 (Winter 1977): 1-64. The reader interested in an extended discussion of basic distinctions in cognitive style measures should consult Richard H. Coop and Irving E. Sigel, "Cognitive Style: Implications for Learning and Instruction," *Psychology in the Schools* 8, no. 2 (1971): 152-61, or Kenneth M. Goldstein and Sheldon Blackman, *Cognitive Style: Five Approaches and Relevant Research* (New York: John Wiley, 1978).

69. Cronbach and Snow, *Aptitudes and Instructional Methods*.

70. Herman A. Witkin and Donald R. Goodenough, "Field Dependence and Interpersonal Behavior," *Psychological Bulletin* 84 (July 1977): 661-89.

71. Marcia Linn and Patrick Kyllonen, "The Field Dependence-Independence Construct: Some, One, or None," *Journal of Educational Psychology* 73 (April 1981): 261-73.

72. Herman A. Witkin and J. W. Berry, "Psychological Differentiation in Cross-Cultural Perspective." *Journal of Cross-Cultural Psychology* 6 (March 1975): 4-87.

73. Witkin and Goodenough, "Field Dependence and Interpersonal Behavior"; Wendell E. Jeffrey, "The Developing Brain and Child Development," in *The Brain and Psychology*, ed. M. C. Wittrock (New York: Academic Press, 1980).

74. Witkin and Goodenough, "Field Dependence and Interpersonal Behavior."

75. This section of the paper has been adapted from Thomas L. Good and Jere Brophy, *Educational Psychology: A Realistic Approach*, 2d ed. (New York: Holt, Rinehart and Winston, 1980).

76. Witkin et al., "Field-Dependent and Field-Independent Cognitive Styles and Their Educational Implications."

77. Ibid.

78. Ibid.

79. Ibid.

80. Carol Ann Moore, "Styles of Teacher Behavior under Simulated Teaching Conditions" (Doct. diss., Stanford University, 1973).

81. Marshall Gordon and Robert J. Gross, "An Exploration of the Interconnecting Perspective of Teaching Style and Teacher Education," *Journal of Curriculum Studies* 10 (April-June 1978): 151-57; Witkin et al., "Field-Dependent and Field-Independent Cognitive Styles and Their Educational Implications."

82. These studies are reviewed in Witkin et al., "Field-Dependent and Field-Independent Cognitive Styles and Their Educational Implications."

83. David J. Satterly, "Cognitive Styles, Spatial Ability, and School Achievement," *Journal of Educational Psychology* 68 (February 1976): 36-42.

84. Witkin et al., "Field-Dependent and Field-Independent Cognitive Styles and Their Educational Implications"; Janis Packer and John D. Bain, "Cognitive Style and Teacher-Student Compatibility," *Journal of Educational Psychology* 70 (October 1978): 864-71.

85. Torrance D. Grieve and J. Kent Davis, "The Relationship of Cognitive Style and Method of Instruction to Performance in Ninth-grade Geography," *Journal of Educational Research* 65 (November 1971): 137-41.

86. Bernard M. Frank and J. Kent Davis, "Effect of Field-Independence Match or Mismatch on a Communication Task," *Journal of Educational Psychology* 74 (February 1982): 23-31.

87. L. K. Doebler and F. J. Eicke, "Effects of Teacher Awareness of the Educational Implications of Field-dependent/Field-independent Cognitive Style on Selected Classroom Variables," *Journal of Educational Psychology* 71 (April 1979): 226-32.

88. Cronbach and Snow, *Aptitudes and Instructional Methods*.

89. Philip W. Jackson, "The Teacher and Individual Differences," in *Individualizing Instruction*, ed. Henry.

90. For an exception, see Herbert A. Thelen, "Grouping for Teachability," *Theory into Practice* 2 (April 1963): 80-89.

91. See, for example, Janicki and Peterson, "Aptitude-Treatment Interaction Effects of Variations in Direct Instruction," and Ebmeier and Good, "The Effects of Instructing Teachers about Good Teaching on the Mathematics Achievement of Fourth Grade Students."

92. Good and Brophy, *Looking in Classrooms*.

93. Marianne Amarel, "Literacy: The Personal Dimension" (Paper presented at the annual meeting of the American Educational Research Association, Los Angeles, April 1981).

CHAPTER III

The Sociological Bases for Individual Differences: The Relation of Solitude to the Crowd

THOMAS S. POPKEWITZ

Introduction

The words *individual* and *individual differences* can be viewed as important symbols for our most cherished feelings and beliefs. In everyday life we look for the realization of the individual; we glorify personal happiness as a worthy human goal; we believe the individual is responsible for his or her own destiny. The myths of our institutions affirm our belief in the sanctity of the individual and often downplay the importance of social context, cultural circumstances, or social class. Our government is to provide for freedom, justice, and pursuit of happiness, each defined as a birthright of the individual; in schooling, the language of education includes phrases such as "individualized instruction" and "individual differences" and statements such as "education is to enable the individual to realize his or her own potential."

The importance of "individual differences" lies in its creation of a symbolic canopy for school practices. To use the slogan is to legitimate school programs as responding to a variety of deeply held social and cultural beliefs. At the same time, however, the social complexities and issues that emerge as people respond to some notion of individuality must be considered. While the language of individual differences may make the individual seem alone, the ability to be an individual is formed within worlds of crowds that have culture and

---

Robert Dreeben served as the editorial consultant for this chapter.

history. The relation of individual to social worlds provides one of the more profound and most intensely debated issues in Western history, underlying the political arguments of Locke, Rousseau, Jefferson, and Marx. Nor does our educational thought about enlightenment and autonomy avoid the moral and political issues. Linked to our theories of individuality are assumptions, world views, and ideological systems that tie an individual to a structure of society.

Just as central to our deliberations are the pressures of the social context upon the meaning and values of "individual differences." Teaching responds to fundamental transformations of social relations, politics, and economics that occur in the society as a whole. This relation of pedagogy and society is apparent in the history of schooling. The emergence of the French secondary school, the early twentieth century progressive educational reforms, and contemporary school reforms—each in their own time—define individual differences in ways that give moral as well as intellectual values to the organization of classrooms. These moral and intellectual responses to individualization, however, are not one-dimensional. There are divergent and conflicting currents running through any one society to influence pedagogical practice. To understand the assumptions and implications of individual differences requires that we consider how our conceptions of the individual vary over time and social circumstances.

The social and political elements that come into play through the idea of individual differences is the theme of this essay. The first section focuses upon issues of social control, authority, and legitimacy that underlie any conception of individuality. The following discussion considers the ways in which cultural circumstances and social environment modify and alter pedagogical schemes. It is the thesis of these sections that educational ideas and consequently the appropriate means of responding to individual differences change as social conditions and values are transformed. In the present, as in the past, schools mediate social values through conceptions of individuality that underlie classroom organizations.

The problem of individual differences in schooling is not in any final sense logically resolvable, as it entails tension between the individual and the crowd that has roots in social conditions and visions of how people live and interact in a society. It is these complexities that made the writing of an essay on individual differences an intellectual struggle. The piecing together of what seem very disparate parts— philosophy, pedagogy, sociology, and history—is only partially resolved in this discussion.[1]

Social Visions and Values: The Individual in a Crowd

When we talk about individual differences or individualized instruction in schools, we cannot just talk about the individual. A child is a *child in a class*, a context of social expectations and demands that gives definition to individuality.[2] The patterns of school conduct, for example, establish what forms of relationship are to exist between a teacher, children, and the materials (books, chalkboards, libraries) of classroom life. These patterns of activities establish certain rules for personal competence and identity. For example, learning about the world is to come from textbooks rather than from personal interactions, examinations are to evaluate personal worth and esteem within the school context, and specialized people (teachers, principals, or counselors) are to establish definitions about whether a person is to be defined as educated or not. Psychologies of instruction are linked to these institutionally defined patterns. To talk about learning, motivation, individual attributes or traits presupposes a concept of schooling in which a student interacts with a given organization of knowledge, establishes relationships with teachers, and achieves according to institutionally established criteria.

To say that individual differences exist within a social context, however, does not go far enough in clarifying the relationship. To live in a world is to participate in social relations that establish ways in which the individual is to encounter the world and to challenge the possibilities of existence. To view a person as developing in a specific community is not only to consider individuality but, at the same moment, the basis of authority, legitimacy, and order.[3] In feudal times, for example, individual differences were tied to positions in a hierarchy of social order: the serf's life was to be reconciled to position in the order of lord, king, and God. The conventions of social interactions, law, work, and the church reinforced the givenness of that order. Personality and individuality meant sublimating the "self" to prearranged destinies.

With transformations accompanying industrialization came new sets of social conditions and new views of the "self" as a participant in the creation of history, culture, and destinies. One could begin to talk about society as a contract among people, of inalienable rights, of people making history, and of psychologies of individuals that express personal intent, will, and autonomy. These changes in larger social-individual relationships became embedded in the concept of education and in the construction and organization of schooling.

The complexities of individuality are compounded when we realize that the contemporary world has many different and competing visions of itself and of its individuals. For some, the individual is an autonomous actor for whom society is organized to provide the conditions of growth. For others, the individual is not autonomous but is a cultural and historical being, with human growth intricately tied to the relationship permitted in one's community.

These two views provide major strands in debates about the relation of cognition and community and can be considered by focusing upon two philosophers—the seventeenth century English liberal political theorist, John Locke, and the eighteenth century German philosopher, Immanuel Kant. While we may want to consider the philosophical arguments of Kant and Locke as just that—philosophical arguments that are fine for the philosopher but have little relationship to our everyday work—we must recognize that the assumptions about the world and individual underlying the works of these men, though modified by time, are embedded in the practices of our everyday world. Behavioral sciences and behaviorism in psychology, behavior modification, learning psychologies, and instructional management systems to individualize education have their origins in Lockean philosophy. Much of the curriculum work of John Dewey and the "reformist" strand of progressive education bears a relation to Kant's attempt to consider the relation between individual and community.

While Locke is known primarily as a political philosopher, many of his assumptions about human nature and cognition have come to dominate Western thought and underlie much contemporary social science and pedagogical practice.[4] For Locke, the individual is an essentially receptive, reflective organism whose qualities are shaped over time by the environment. That is, there exists a world of objects that the individual senses through the body. The individual thinks and reasons about these objects in forming consciousness. But the objects and people's ideas about those objects are separate and distinct from one another.

While the intellectual and social world in which Locke lived was radical in rejecting the metaphysics of religion and establishing a basis for the development of a scientific outlook, the distinction between people and objects maintains certain fundamental religious assumptions. A separation between the soul and the material world is maintained. The assumption that ideas and the material world are distinct has been refined and often relabeled, persisting in learning theories of American schooling in which the individual is viewed as a receptive, reflective organism and cognition is the assimilation of knowledge about the material world. Criterion-referenced measures, for example, fix the world as discrete objects that the child is to assimilate and replicate.

Kant offers a different view of cognition and individuality. He was interested in the way in which community and the human psyche are integrally related and mutually reinforcing. In Kant's theory of cognition, the individual plays an active and creative role in the constitution of experience. A dynamic unity exists between individual and society. Both the community and individual are viewed as developing and mutually changing as they interact. The relationship between object and individual is not the monologue of a solitary thinker, but a dialogue.

As with Locke, Kant's views became immersed in a larger debate about how people exist in a social world and develop consciousness and personality. The recent educational interest in social psychology, "information processing," the pragmatism of John Dewey, the view of the school as a "community," as well as the emergence of qualitative studies of classroom interaction are believed to be appropriate because of assumptions that can be traced to Kant's belief about the interplay of individual and culture.[5] Classroom knowledge is thought to result from a dynamic process involving joint creation.

To pursue the notion of individuality, it is essential to recognize that theories of cognition never stand alone as psychologies of individuals. Psychologies posit views of society in which the individual is to participate. Embedded in Locke's view of the separation of objects and ideas is the separation of people from society. The individual is the proprietor of his own person or capabilities. "The individual [is seen] neither as a moral whole nor as a part of a larger social whole, but as an owner of himself." The individual, it was thought, is free inasmuch as he is proprietor of his person and capacities.[6]

The proprietary nature of the individual becomes critically important in determining the nature of society. Society is composed of free, equal individuals "who are related to each other as proprietors of their own capacities and of what they have acquired by their exercise. Society consists of relations of exchange between proprietors. Political society becomes a calculated device for the protection of this property and for the maintenance of an orderly relation of exchange."[7] The basis of society is the social contract, in which the interests of individuals are harmonized by natural, market forces.

The individualistic principle of Locke is transformed into a moral norm, a model for individual liberty, a basis of community, and the theoretical underpinning for socializing the youth in the society. Education assumes a particular meaning—it is to enable each individual to develop his or her particular attributes and abilities and to become a free, rational adult. Education is to train the specific and discrete aspects of individual mental reasoning. As society assumes a neutral role in facilitating individual capacities, schooling is to be a mechanism of calculated devices to provide the most efficient means for promoting the exchanges of individuals and the development of their capacities. This technical view of society and community permeates the "systems" approaches to curriculum design, differentiated psychology, and the view of educational science as a problem of management.

A contrasting view is that humanity develops as individuals assimilate the residues of culture and history and, at the same time, are active participants in their world. For Kant, individuals develop consciousness and compassion through an evolutionary process. This evolution occurs within a community that has patterns of social conduct, world views, and language to underlie everyday practice, giving coherence and purpose to the individual. The private and public—subjective and objective—are not separate entities but exist in relation to each other. Purposeful action is tied to the larger social and moral whole and is important for establishing and maintaining a human society.

These cognitive assumptions have implications for pedagogy. Education becomes a mediating experience between the world and our knowledge of the world. This idea emerges in the "open classroom," the British Infant School, or the John Dewey School. The intent is to develop conditions in which both individual and community grow, in which reciprocal relationships of authority exist among students and between students and teachers, and where a child shares in the work of his or her community.

The linkage of a model of community to a theory of cognition creates values for pedagogical programs. To treat the world atomistically and to separate it objectively from the individual, as did Locke, is to deny the individual as an actor in the creation of history and culture. It is also to obscure the interrelation of social, economic, and political institutions in fashioning and shaping the world in which we live. Social life becomes unyielding and resists intervention. The interrelation of individual and community, from a Kantian view, establishes a dynamic in which individuals can, to some extent, play active roles in determining the possibilities of human conditions. But the nature of that activity, the sources of domination, and the challenges of involvement are still at issue.

While the two views do not exhaust the possibilities of relationship, they help to illuminate a continuing tension between the individual and society. Individual psychologies, pedagogical practices, and social and political theories interrelate to provide conceptions of cognition and individuality. To accept a psychology of individual differences, is also to accept a view of individual relations with the social world, of the possibilities and strategies for coming to be educated in that world.

Individuality and Cultural Transmission

The political and social issues associated with individual differences have concrete implications within particular institutions and institutional processes. Schooling is both a process of cultural transmission and learning. It organizes knowledge and provides cognitive styles or habits of thinking for individuals to act upon that knowledge. The everyday patterns of classrooms establish webs of meaning that allow an individual to navigate through ordinary events and encounters with others. To do a reading assignment, manipulate objects for an art lesson, or answer questions on a social studies test is to be involved in learning ways in which an individual is to express individuality and establish social identity. The formal content merges with the social processes of classroom life to posit dispositions that guide individuals as they act in the world.

These choices of cultural transmission are not without substantive meaning for defining individuality. The everyday patterns of classrooms provide one cultural mechanism for negotiating the constantly evolving views of individuality that lie in society. We can identify, for example, two orientations for responding to individual differences that have their roots in larger social aspirations and expectations. One orientation is to develop rational and efficient methods for increasing individual achievement. A standard curriculum is identified and instruction is made flexible to allow differentiation of pacing for mastery learning. Systems of instructional management and "engaged" time in content learning become central to classroom organization. A second approach considers knowledge as personal, emerging from group interactions and face-to-face negotiation. Instruction provides a flexible curriculum and classroom organization to enable children to develop communication and problem-solving skills. Viewed in isolation from the institutional processes of schooling, the two approaches seem to be strategies or procedures of schooling that have no deeper meaning.

Placed in a context of schooling as cultural transmission, these two strategies provide for different moral and intellectual qualities of character development. Bernstein points to these two pedagogies as situated within a context where different interests in society exert indirect and direct pressures upon schools to transmit certain types of knowledge and the appropriate definitions of individuals capable of carrying that knowledge.[8] These pedagogies, "visible" and "invisible," maintain different organizations of knowledge and cognitive styles that are linked to social transformations in the middle class of contemporary Western industrial societies.

The visible pedagogy involves a clear and orderly process of learning and teaching. There is believed to be an explicit hierarchy of knowledge and roles to be transmitted in schooling. The sequences and rules for acquiring content are fixed and criteria for evaluating children's mastery of the subject matter are objective. For example,

Bloom's taxonomy, which identifies items for mastery learning, provides an aspect of the visible pedagogy.[9] Logical systems by which the knowledge and skills of learning can be ordered and made available to children are sought. Instruction becomes the technologies of managing children as they proceed through the different objectives and levels of mastery. We can recognize in this pedagogy some of the assumptions about individuals and society articulated by Locke—the individual is essentially a receptive organism; knowledge is composed of discrete parts; social institutions are calculated devices to maintain orderly development; and education trains specific and discrete aspects of mental reasoning.

A second social form in classrooms is the "invisible pedagogy." The "invisible" pedagogy, as illustrated in Summerhill, the British Infant School, Open Education, or progressive educational practices, is less concerned with a clear hierarchy of learning and mastery of specific skills. Emphasis is placed upon the teacher's creating a context in which children are expected to rearrange and explore, and upon children's attitudes and dispositions toward learning. The child is to have some power over selection, over structuring of time, and apparently over social relationships. In these schools, the transmission and acquisition of specific skills are subsidiary. As with Kant, the invisible pedagogy defines humanity and knowledge as interrelated in an evolutionary process in which the person is tied to the growth and development of community.

The visible and invisible pedagogies contain contrasting definitions of individuality. The focus of the visible pedagogies is on the "individual." It presupposes explicit and unambiguous values and roles which the pupil is to internalize. The emphasis is upon atomized individual relations and a belief that each individual will be able to develop personal abilities and attributes. The invisible pedagogy emphasizes the "person." This pedagogy encourages children to display more ambiguous role definitions through decreased specialization in the school subject matter. Children are to learn how to use language and to gain interpersonal control through involvement in group interaction and discourse.

Bernstein argues that the emergent social forms of these pedagogies contain principles of legitimacy and authority. Implicit in the ideas of person and individual are fundamental social assumptions about the work, knowledge, and role of people in institutional life. The visible pedagogy contains a view of knowledge that is fixed and unyielding, defined by experts. The role of the individual is to internalize and to reflect about those external conditions. Social institutions are made to seem static and unchanging. Control is explicit, according to seemingly clear criteria of success or failure. The invisible pedagogy, in contrast, places control in the patterns of communication. Consensus and legitimacy are built by interpersonal negotiation and skills. Knowledge is presumed to be flexible and negotiable. While teachers arrange contexts for children to explore, they also monitor and evaluate children through informal methods of control that include attitude formation.

The conflict between invisible and visible pedagogies, Bernstein continues, cannot be understood solely as a pedagogical problem. The differing conceptions of education and individual are rooted in deeper social strains and transformations within the middle class. The visible pedagogy responded to the interests of the older middle class of merchants. Less dependent upon the creation of knowledge and more upon the accumulation of capital, the merchant middle class used the school to train the individual in the specific cultural habits and traits that were necessary to compete with the aristocracy. The closed nature of school knowledge served that purpose of training the individual. In contrast, the invisible pedagogy responds to the cultural requirements of a new stratum within the middle class, the professional occupations such as lawyers, psychologists, or educators. This new middle-class stratum of society is dependent upon generating and controlling social knowledge and it requires a different approach for the socialization of the young to the sensibilities and awareness necessary for the professional occupations.

It is perhaps easy to overlook the relationship of pedagogy to larger social and philosophical issues because many of our attempts to theorize about schooling define educational practice as separate and distinct from the social world in which we live. Yet pedagogical practices are social forms and as such contain lines of thinking, reasoning, and acting that emerge from our more general relationships and issues. Bernstein's argument enables us to understand how the central social issues of individuality become immersed in institutional practices and how the resolutions of these issues are located in time and cultural place. Which knowledge is transmitted and its assumptions and implications for individuality cannot be taken for granted.

Individual Differences in Times of Social Transformation

We have begun to formulate the response to individual differences as one that is related to the social predicament of schools.[10] At any one time, there are various social demands that are made upon schools to establish particular forms of consciousness and individuality. The social and cultural demands, however, are not presented in the form of carefully worked out arguments or as forcefully documented concerns. Rather, cultural and social expectations provide background assumptions as to the social organization of classrooms and are constantly negotiated in educational theories and classroom interactions.

These background assumptions about individual differences become more apparent in times of social change and transformation. In periods of social change, this relationship between self and community is made problematic. The dominant webs of meaning and cherished values are challenged by other conceptions of society and individuality. The social tensions and struggles become part of the school's definition of pedagogy and individuality, for schools are central institutions in the socialization of the young. Pedagogy is a mediating link between the subjective consciousness of the individual and community lifestyles and cognitive styles.

The relation of social transformations and pedagogical practices to individualization can be illustrated by focusing upon two educational reform movements. One is the Jesuit response to the Reformation during the sixteenth century. A second consists of the progressive educational reforms in American schools. Each response contained formulations of individual differences that are situated in the institutional contexts in which the reforms are realized.

INDIVIDUALIZATION AND THE COUNTER-REFORMATION

Perhaps the most comprehensive discussion of the relation of individual differences to social conditions is Durkheim's study of the events, ideas, and conditions that led to the emergence of the French secondary school. An important element in the evolution of that school was the development of individualized pedagogies in the sixteenth-century Jesuit schools.[11] Instruction involved teachers continually monitoring student work through recitations, written assignments, and group competition. The individualization of instruction was in sharp contrast to previous periods where teaching occurred in large, impersonal settings.

The emergence of the new individual pedagogy occurred under pressures of significant changes in the social, cultural, and economic world within French and European societies. Education in antiquity was to decorate the mind with certain ideas and habits. There was no idea of personality or individuality as we now think of it. With the development of Christianity, the purpose of education shifted to a concern with the soul, and a concomitant awareness that underlying the particular conditions of our intelligence and sensibilities were more profound dispositions that determine and give unity to our overt habits and ideas. For Christianity, education was to create within people a general disposition of the mind and will and to make them see things in a particular light.

Underlying the education of the Christian was the notion of conversion. Education was a profound movement in which the soul changed its world outlook. To accomplish conversion, the child was to be subjected to influences that are not dispersed in different directions, as in antiquity, but vigorously concentrated toward one and the same goal. A child was to live in a completely enveloping moral environment, the influence of which was inescapable. In its conception, the aim of Christian education was to educate the whole child, a conception of education that is still with us.

The Christian idea of the soul and conversion took on concrete meaning in the development of an individualized pedagogy during the Counter-Reformation and under the guidance of the Jesuits. Under Loyola, the Jesuits formed to combat heresy through a new kind of religious militia. The Jesuits strove to move closer to people so as to be able to influence them. Loyola saw the education of the young as an important instrument in the struggle for mastery of the human soul and developed an educational program that would appeal to youth, yet be conservative to preserve the faith.

There were two central issues that the Jesuits had to deal with in forming educational practice. One was the humanism of the sixteenth century, which maintained pagan values. A second was the emergence of the idea of individualism. The roots of heresy were seen in the sixteenth-century intellectual interest in humanism, the study of the literature of antiquity. This content of secondary education emerged as greater wealth in the society and a newly formed bourgeois created demand for an education appropriate for a polite society. Education was to provide the tasks, delicate pleasures, and manners that were before reserved only for the aristocracy. The response of teaching was to develop the art of intellectual analysis and moral temperament through the reading of the great literature of Greece and Rome. This literature, however, contained its own crisis for the Church. The moral environment of humanistic literature was related to a pagan world and therefore seen as antagonistic to Christianity.

To teach the Christian ethos effectively, the subject matter was organized for individualized instruction. This pedagogical strategy reflected the changing social awarenesses of a person's personality. The sixteenth century saw the emergence of particular personalities standing out from the homogeneous moral and intellectual mass that had been the rule in preceding centuries. It was no longer adequate to have the teacher addressing large and impersonal audiences. The individual was conceived as no longer merely an undifferentiated fraction of the whole. The individual had self-consciousness and a personal manner of thinking and feeling.

As people's consciousness became individualized, education itself had to become individualized if it was to effect the Jesuits' goals. An educational system developed to bring teachers close to individuals and accommodate their intellectual and temperamental diversities. Education became extraordinarily intensive. The use of written assignments, for example, appeared as an important part of instruction to keep the pupil busy. During every recitation period, students who were not involved in recitation were to remain active by doing assignments. A teacher would have a whispered dialogue with a pupil while others engaged in practice. Diversity of exercises was introduced to prevent monotony.

The form of the individualization of the program was related to the purpose of the Jesuits. The plethora of written assignments forced the pupils to stretch their active resources incessantly, to produce work prematurely and without genuine thoughtfulness. The written assignments were important because the Jesuits wanted pupils to learn to speak and write Greek and Latin but not to consider in depth the meaning of those civilizations.

The social structure of the individualized classroom reflected the single goal of conversion. The Jesuits believed that there was no good education without contact which was at once continuous and personal. The principle served a double purpose. It ensured that the pupil was never left alone; molding the child required that the pupil be subjected to unrelenting pressures. It also enabled the Jesuits to study the character and habits of the pupils to discover the most suitable methods of directing each individual child. Education thus became more personal and better suited to the personality of each pupil. It was not enough, however, to surround pupils and envelop them at close quarters with solicitude and vigilance, for the work was lacking in substance. Competition was included as an important aspect of instruction to develop motivation.

We can identify three important characteristics for understanding the Jesuit reforms to individualize. First, schooling is a social organization that involves moral, intellectual, and political imperatives. The organization of pedagogy contains social values, principles of legitimacy and authority. Second, these imperatives involve larger issues of social life. Individualization was to create a character and personality suitable to the Jesuits' vision of Christianity. Third, implementation was neither unidimensional nor straightforward. The Jesuits were in competition with the University and other interests in society. From the interaction of the various groups emerged a secondary school in which practices reflected that competition, altering the original proposals in ways not envisioned by the planners.

INDIVIDUALITY IN SCHOOLING AND INDUSTRIALIZATION

By the eighteenth century, the social organization of pedagogy shifted from a class of individuals in directed sets of studies to the classroom in which group-based pedagogies began to dominate the more individualized forms of teaching and learning. The shift to classrooms, however, did not alter the conception of schooling that evolved from Christianity. The moral quality of schooling to provide a way of thinking and feeling remained in a secular form of having people acquire a human manner of feeling and thinking. While the abstract outline did not change, the means employed to respond to the evolving social conditions did change.

Nowhere is this concern of education for the creation of a moral environment to form individual character more evident than in the creation of the classroom in the late eighteenth century.[12] New pedagogies emerged in England and Scotland that followed the transition from individual to mass production (the early factory system) and were intertwined with changing social networks and intellectual ferment in the general society. Borrowing and modeling Adam Smith's ideas about the moral economy, the pedagogies sought to find a resolution between the requirements of simultaneous instruction and a market orientation in which the association in classes would provide a meritocratic system for individual advancement. The response to individual differences was to provide differentiation of instruction that would motivate the individual toward self-improvement through emulation of the successful.

Similar social concerns for character formation in classrooms emerged in the early twentieth-century development of American schools. The intellectual, moral, and social purposes of schooling were retained in the progressive educational reforms, but with new sets of social conditions and pressures to influence policy and practice. Progressive education was a response to industrialization and the influx of Mediterranean and Eastern European immigrants after 1880. By this time, the organization of schools into classrooms was taken for granted and the challenge was to find new pedagogical solutions to the tensions created by the relations between individual and society. The children of the working classes and immigrants had to learn how to adapt to a complex, massive, and concentrated industrial economy. The notion of the rugged individual no longer fit; a new idea of individual was needed that combined individual initiative with a corporate economy and its diverse occupations. Children had to learn cooperation; but individual potential would have to be realized within the confines of an elaborate industrial order built by science.

The belief in science that underlies industrialization also became a guiding force in the redefining of schooling. Two conflicting interpretations of science, however, were formulated by the progressives for organizing classrooms. One approach was that schools should contribute to a more efficient selection process for social occupations. A second response was for schools to provide a social atmosphere that would serve to teach children how to use science as a method for renewing as well as sustaining social conditions. These contrasting approaches to school reform had concomitant views of individual differences. The two approaches also reflected the different social location and the publics of the major advocates of the progressive reforms.

During the first decades of the century, David Snedden was a noted proponent of the social efficiency movement.[13] A professor at Stanford and at Teacher's College and a Massachusetts Commissioner of Education, he argued that education must provide the moral, social, and occupational skills that fit a child into society. Instruction was to meet individual needs, not on the basis of methods of teaching, but according to aims which are different for different groups. For Snedden,

"educational equalitarianism" was a "gross superstition," likely to deprive a large number of children and youth of the educational opportunities they deserved. He felt that educators under the spell of this belief provided mere sameness of educational opportunity in the confused belief they were providing equality of opportunity. Instead, [Snedden] argued, the student should be fitted to achieve optimum success in the environment in which he found himself so far as his natural endowment would permit. He recognized differences in endowment and opportunity as "immutable facts," and his program was intended to develop the individual to live within his predetermined limits. In this way the needs of a "team society," based upon the "coordinate complementary contributions" of all its members, would be satisfied.[14]

The emphasis upon fitting the individual to the environment and to the possibilities of employment produced recommendations for instruction and the organization of content. Snedden believed that not all children should go to high school and receive a general academic education. Instead, training should be for specific functions. Particular "case" groups were to be organized in school based upon native ability, environmental background, and "future prospects as imposed by the socioeconomic group from which the student came."[15] Many traditional subjects such as Latin, literature, or physics had to be eliminated or restructured to respond to the future vocation of the student. Three different courses of study were recommended for physics, for example; one was to include easy electives to provide a general cultural appreciation of physics, another incorporated courses of general utility that covered the application of the knowledge of physical sciences to everyday activities, and the third was made up of prevocational physics courses for students studying engineering or gardening or "for homemakers who expected incomes of less than two thousand dollars a year."[16]

Courses tailored to future vocations were to evolve from the development of a science of instructional management. Snedden sought to incorporate newly developed sociological theories of social control into school organization. Sociology had emerged as a profession which some believed could provide the expertise for maintaining social harmony and stability. Snedden viewed himself as such a sociologist. Relying upon statistical formulas, random sampling techniques, and other procedures that gave science an aura of precision, Snedden believed that science could provide a mechanism for organizing and molding individuals in schools toward the demands of society. The educational science included a concern with precisely stated and measurable objectives. Educators were to define what selective habits, what items of knowledge, and what ideals must be engendered in pupils of various groups to achieve the correct moral and vocational training.

In contrast to the view of individual differences embedded in the social efficiency movement was a belief in the school as an agency of social service and reform. John Dewey, one of the most articulate proponents of this view, saw the need for schools to respond to social and economic demands: to businessmen who saw the school functioning as an apprenticeship, and to civic reformers who wanted schools to assume functions of socialization no longer performed by other institutions, such as teaching hygiene, domestic science, manual arts, and child care. But, in contrast to Snedden, Dewey did not want schools to make merely acquiescent citizens or workers. Dewey sought to reconcile the conflict of individuals and groups and to recognize the importance of individual autonomy and initiative. Further, by making school life more worthy, appealing, and harmonious, schools were to be model communities that could serve as levers to improve the larger society.

Dewey attacked the separation of thought and action, of individuality and association, of method and subject matter. Dewey's vision of science was a fusion of hand and head, of craft and intellect. The curriculum was to focus upon stimulating a child's impulses to converse, to inquire, to construct, and to express as well as to provide the technical information and discipline of traditional education. Science and industrial studies were to increase pupils' awareness of the world around them. Vocational studies were not merely utilitarian but intellectual ventures into the life and meaning of industrial society. In the Laboratory School of the University of Chicago, for example, the youngest students studied the home to see connections of the home to the productive and commercial activities of the wider community and interdependence in society.

A theory of growth and a belief in a democratic society that encouraged free interaction and mutual adjustment among different groups influenced Dewey's conception of individuality in school programs.[17] His pedagogic strategies sought to replace external authority with voluntary interests and disposition, to promote both individual initiative and adaptability, and to encourage individual reconstruction and reorganization of experience.

[Dewey] wanted education constantly to expand the range of social situations in which individuals perceived issues and made and acted upon choices. He wanted schools to inculcate habits that would enable individuals to control their surroundings rather than merely adapt to them. And he wanted each generation to go beyond its predecessors in the quality of behavior it sought to nurture in its children.[18]

Dewey's conception of science and curriculum existed within a specific context of American society that gave plausibility to its mandates. It was a time in which professionalization and skilled groups were growing as people moved from the older middle-class stratum of commercial and business careers to this new stratum of society.[19] The "invisible" quality of Dewey's pedagogy responded to the pressures of the changing situation as it offered a means for the class ascent and professionalism by focusing upon the knowledge, skills, and interpersonal competencies required for entrance to the new social stratum.

Each of the pedagogical innovations discussed in this section was accomplished within a context of particular political, economic, and philosophical debate and change. The pedagogical innovations of the Jesuits, of Snedden, and of Dewey were not merely the result of philanthropic or benevolent people but were situated in complex political and social and material worlds to which they responded. These worlds contained varying and conflicting visions of individuality and society, which filtered into and gave meaning to schooling.

Differentiated Schooling: Variations in Themes

In one sense, the interplay of school and society is obvious and noncontroversial: citizenship education, back-to-basics, and the discipline-centered curriculum reforms reflect efforts of larger social interests to achieve influence upon the values and knowledge taught in the schools. What is not as obvious is the different notions of consciousness and individuality carried in the day-to-day activities of schooling. While Locke's and Kant's theories about society point us to different visions about solitude and the crowd, an examination of reforms indicate that different conceptions of individuality are transmitted in different times and places. What becomes transmitted is modified and altered as the reforms confront the everyday practices and values in schools.[20]

As we look at the styles of working and communicating in schools, we must realize that what occurs in the everyday life of schools is not unidimensional.[21] There are different types of schooling that emphasize different linguistic, intellectual, and social competencies. DeLone argues, for example, that schools are organized differentially for children of different social, economic, and racial backgrounds.[22] Teachers of students from low-income families minimize cognitive interactions with children while emphasizing rote learning. When these children ask questions that are marginal or tangential to points under discussion, their answers are rebuked or ignored. Schools for middle-class children, on the other hand, stress cognitive growth and student satisfaction; in the dialogue of the classroom, children's questions are taken seriously; classroom practices provide greater opportunities for students to work in communities, and there are more tasks leading students to classroom discussion. The different treatment in school, DeLone argues, performs a function of occupational screening and selection, and awards status on the basis of inheritance, while obscuring the different expectations by means of the popular belief that those who succeed have been meritorious in the competitive, neutral system.

The implications of differentiated schooling for individual differences can be considered by focusing upon a reform program to individualize instruction, Individually Guided Education (IGE).[23] An elementary school reform project, IGE is a management plan for pacing children through a standardized, objective-based curriculum. The program includes a comprehensive set of procedures for grouping children so instruction can be responsive to individual abilities and skills. This includes team teaching, objective-based curriculum management systems, testing, and record keeping to monitor children's movement through the hierarchy of objectives.

Because of the uniform character of the reform technologies, one would expect that all the schools that adopted Individually Guided Education would be similar and that differences would give reference only to the pacing of children through the standardized curriculum. In the six schools identified as models of the IGE program, there was a formal appearance of sameness as each school used its public language and technologies. The program's technologies to individualize, however, were used in different ways within the schools and established different definitions of individuality. Particular configurations of school work, views about cognition, and teacher ideologies emerged to give concrete definitions to individuality and individual differences. The organization of life in these classrooms provided unique definitions of what it meant to learn, to interact, and to assert individuality. To capture the meaning of these differences in the organization of social experience and thinking, the schools were called "technical," "constructive," and "illusory" schools. These differences, however, are only partially explained by analysis of classroom interaction. The views of individual differences were made plausible by the social predicaments of the individual schools.

TECHNICAL SCHOOLING

In three schools called technical schools, the implementation of the management procedures of the reform became an end in itself. The curriculum was organized into systems of hierarchically ordered objectives, and record-keeping procedures were developed to control children's progress. Emphasis was upon measurable outcomes of children's learning, such as limited mathematics and reading skills (for example, a child will learn multiplication facts 1 to 4). The focus of curriculum and instruction was a search for the most efficient ways of processing people through the management sequence. A day in one of these schools typically found children working with ditto sheets to practice examples in mathematics or reading skills or taking a pretest or posttest to measure knowledge of the skills. Teachers' time was spent checking tests or ditto sheets, giving tests, or recording test scores.

Within the technical schools, individual differences were functionally defined in relation to the rate by which a child could move through the standardized curriculum. One can begin to identify assumptions of cognition and sociality consistent with those of Locke, Bernstein's visible pedagogy, and Snedden's theory of instruction. The psychology of instruction was that a child was a deficit system, missing specific and discrete parts of knowledge that the instructional system was to correct.

A particular notion of individual responsibility came into play within this context of technical schooling. Professional responsibility was defined as searching for the efficient ways of processing people. Responsibility did not mean considering what was appropriate to teach and how to teach; rather, responsibility meant ordering objectives and keeping proper records to insure the orderly movement of children. For children, responsibility meant learning and obeying the rules of the classroom, listening to authority, and striving to master predetermined objectives. Excellence was achieved by looking busy (process) or by completing worksheets (outcomes). The criteria of excellence were applied to both teachers and students. "Good" teachers did such things as spending more time in school before and after classes to plan; "good" children looked like they were continuously working hard. High-achieving children in particular were chastised if teachers believed they did not work hard to achieve high grades.

A conception of consciousness and individuality also can be associated with this organization of instruction and this meaning of individual differences. Individuals are being taught the separability of means and ends and the segregation of bodies of knowledge from cognitive styles. The division of knowledge and self into parts with discrete and independent existence has implications for social relations itself. One can be treated with anonymity as knowledge is viewed as outside of human intervention and "objectively" detailed. Orderliness also assumes a particular rationale: it is defined as taxonomic propensities identified in social and psychological properties. The identification and ordering of the taxonomies lie not with the individual but within the institution and the occupational experts who create the systems of meaning. Justice and equality become embedded in the public rules by which one is to proceed through the institutional processes.

CONSTRUCTIVE SCHOOLING

One of the six schools organized its work and communication in a way we called constructive. The typical class day found children working with drama, music, and art, as well as social studies, science, and reading. The organization of instruction stressed that there are multiple ways that children come to know about the world and that the school curriculum should offer children many varied opportunities to consider the various contents. Throughout the day, instruction was organized to provide children opportunities to talk about their studies, to argue about their viewpoints and, on a few occasions, to challenge how teachers had planned teaching units.

The belief in multiple ways of knowing (science, art, music, drama) posed a particular viewpoint to individuality. First, teachers thought that learning developed as children interacted with their environment and from this interaction children not only learned some predefined knowledge but built and extended that knowledge through their own interests and curiosities. Knowledge thus was treated as permeable and provisional, ideas as tentative and often ambiguous. Second, excellence was defined in relation to students' responsibility and autonomy in their interactions in school, and a tentativeness and playfulness in the knowledge to be learned. But responsibility and autonomy were defined differently than in the technical schools. Each child was actively to construct or alter knowledge provided in the curriculum. The skills of reading and mathematics, for example, were taught but in relation to some general problem or activity of study. Learning phonic rules or spelling was often accomplished within a context of reading a story or writing essays and reports. It was in this context that IGE was realized. While the teachers used the team-teaching aspects of the program to respond to student abilities and interests, the instructional management systems were used marginally and made subservient to other curriculum purposes.

Individual differences in the constructive school meant responding to different individual curiosities and interests as well as to mastery or deficit in some clearly identifiable skill. Greater reliance than in technical schools was placed upon shared, cooperative educational tasks in which children had increased discretion. A developmental psychology oriented most teachers' beliefs about how children grow and learn. The emphasis upon initiative and responsibility extended to attitudes and behavior patterns, as discipline referred to inner control of children, to their attitudes toward school work, and to the consideration of social development as integrated with intellectual growth.

The emphasis upon interpersonal control in the constructive school was related to encouraging children's facility with language and responsiveness to the subtle nuances of interpersonal situations. Children frequently discussed social issues, evaluated units of instruction, and were critical of teaching which they thought inadequate. They also worked in groups to achieve certain self-organized outcomes, such as writing and acting in a play. Classroom activities encouraged flexible roles and ideas. Knowledge and work were believed to be the property of the individual developed from interpersonal relations and skepticism toward ideas was encouraged. In many ways, the conception of cognition is similar to that of Kant, and the social organization of classrooms is similar to Bernstein's "invisible pedagogy." Styles of cognition become related to the bodies of knowledge and individuality is related to community.

ILLUSORY SCHOOLING

Illusory schooling was the label applied to two of the six schools. The illusory character of the school reflected two aspects of the social conditions of classroom life. One was the lack of follow-through in teaching. Charts of management system objectives lined the school walls, children went to classes that were called reading or science; and textbooks, tests, and other materials familiar to schooling seemed in abundance. Analysis of discourse and behavior patterns, however, revealed that little teaching did in fact occur. Textbooks were passed out in class but children were not being taught the necessary skills; reading lessons were organized but little of the time was spent on teaching reading; children went through the rituals of a mathematics lesson without being taught the relevant skills.

The illusory quality of the school was related to a second aspect. The staffs of the two schools saw the children as economically poor and socially deficient because of the debilitating effects of their home life and their community. Schooling was to develop a controlled and morally correct student population. The expressive purpose of the classroom interaction was to transmit social values about the inadequacies of the children's social background. The notion of individual differences in these schools had a very particular meaning: children were seen as from poor or broken homes which did not provide adequate discipline or correct attitudes to school work, making proper learning difficult. The instructional response was to organize a safe environment for children and to teach individuals the correct moral values. Individual differences gave reference to these perceived cultural deprivations.

The imagery of illusory schooling had certain qualities related to the development of consciousness. First, it established the importance of the formal categories of school subject matter. These were knowledges that individuals should aspire to attain, as the categories of school knowledge defined how competence in society was to be judged. Second, the rituals of schooling established institutional competence in conveying the substance and skills of the subject matter. Third, that institutional competence was juxtaposed with the incompetence of the person who came to the school. Student failure became personal, the result of inadequacies of personality and community.

It is within this context that a concept of excellence emerges. For most, excellence is exhibiting the correct moral behavior in school: coming to school on time, not getting into fights, and following the procedures. For few, excellence is recognized when work is completed on time and correctly.

We can summarize the different meanings of individual differences in the following way: children in the technical schools were considered deficient in respect to a body of predefined knowledge and skills; the underlying psychology was that knowledge was held to exist outside the mind of individuals and instruction was to pace children through specific levels of information and skills. Individual differences referred to innate traits of children and the school's task of finding the most efficient instructional activities to "develop" and measure their growth. The constructive school considered knowledge as personal, and individual differences involved children in a communicative process that would enable them to develop interests that can be systematically explored and exercised to control interpersonal situations. Since children's backgrounds were seen as pathological in the illusory schools, morally correct attitudes and behaviors were taught before academic skills; individual differences were related to a moral upbringing role for the school. In each school, the practices of responding to individual differences had implications for how one was to become conscious of the world and act in it.

INDIVIDUAL DIFFERENCES AND THE
SOCIAL PREDICAMENT OF SCHOOLS

These differing views of "individual differences" are understood as we focus upon the particular social predicament of the schools. The behaviors, languages and beliefs that characterized these classrooms and schools responded to larger social contradictions, tensions, and struggles that filtered into classroom practices. For example, there was a clear relationship between "the invisible pedagogy" of constructive schooling and the professional occupations of parents; the emphasis on interpersonal control, facility with language, and personalized knowledge corresponds to the intellectual and social point of view of its professional community (university professors, lawyers, psychologists) whose position in society depended upon the creation and control of systems of communication. The illusory schools responded to a social predicament in which teachers saw the community as pathological and believed that the purpose of schooling was to establish the moral superiority and values of middle-class society. Two of the three technical schools had students from working-class, blue-collar occupations, which led the teachers and administrators to define as a school mandate the teaching of functional skills necessary for their later occupations. A third technical school involved a different social situation. Located in an affluent business community, its style of work and knowledge seemed related to an integration of certain dominant social and cultural beliefs with religious ones, as a single church dominated the social, cultural, and political infrastructure of the community. Pressures and counterpressures also existed within the schools to influence pedagogical practices to make the relations complex because multiple social interests were involved.

The interrelation of social, cultural, and professional pressures produced different social predicaments for each of the schools and influenced the differences in cognition and individuality found. We identified in the technical schools, for example, a conception of individual that is utilitarian, seemingly nonmoralistic, and built upon specialized knowledge and skills required in complex organizations. This notion is in contrast to that of a "person" in the constructive school, as well as to a third conception of the individual that underlies the illusory schools. These different meanings of individuality represent different social types that underlie everyday existence.[24] These differences respond to historical, religious, social, and economic differences in our society. What is interesting is that in the schools' response to the pressures of the IGE reform, we can begin to foreshadow fundamental points of tension and change in our society.

In each of the schools studied, individualization, human variability, and individual differences were defined as the core of the school program. The programmatic conception of individual differences, however, was psychological and technological—the treatment of human traits, aptitudes, and attitudes that seem in isolation from cultural circumstances and social location. There was a failure to consider the impact of social structure on individual development. In each of the schools studied, individualization was a social category that celebrated different styles of work and cognition and responded to different social predicaments of schools.

Conclusions

The notion of individual differences is not an abstract or administrative declaration. In the everyday contexts of schooling there are different tensions that help to produce different definitions of society and individuality. The instructional meaning of "individual differences" involves an interplay between concepts of individual and society, for one always stands in relation to the other and together they produce sets of assumptions about the role of the individual in institutional life. These different assumptions have root in larger social changes and cultural tensions, taking on concrete meaning in the daily life of schooling. The various examples of schools' responses to their social predicaments illustrate the different notions of achievement, competence, and individuality that are embedded in instructional processes to individualize. The classroom merges intellectual and moral elements in the formation of character. Locke, Kant, Durkheim, Snedden, and Dewey understood this dispositional quality of knowing when casting the problems of their inquiries, although their means of resolving the issues were not similar.

The complexity of the problem of responding to individual differences can be seen in relation to two themes underlying contemporary schooling. One theme is its missionary role to correct social and economic inequalities. There is a general social commitment that schools should provide equal opportunities for access to privileged positions in society. Schools are conceived of as objective institutions that organize, select, and evaluate children according to individual ability. The belief in equal opportunity, however, is confronted by a social situation in which there are different strata. Each has different cultural and social resources, not all of which are deemed appropriate for success in school. Special entitlements and compensatory programs, for example, are developed to provide the poor with the attitudes, sensitivities, skills, and behaviors typically found in children of other social, cultural, and economic groups. Commitment to equal treatment of individuals and commitment to redress social and economic inequities produce a tension: treat everyone alike but differently.

A second theme, schooling as a technical enterprise, provides a way of lessening the overt tensions of inequity and highlighting the meritocratic character of society. This assumption of technical purposes, however, may legitimate certain inequities found in the larger society. For example, the inclusion of scientific and technological knowledge in schools is seen by some as necessary to maintain the productive base in society. Yet the ways in which this knowledge is formulated in curriculum favor the linguistic and social competencies of middle-class culture. The school, in this instance, may reproduce the cleavages and divisions of the larger society by establishing certain styles of learning, attitudes, and behaviors as naturally superior.

It is within this context of relationship between pedagogical practices and social world that the ideas of individual differences become controversial. Schools exist within a social predicament in which the different interests, values, and inequities of society produce contradictions and tensions in the everyday practices of classrooms. To emphasize individual differences as a psychological trait is to ignore the social implications of pedagogical definitions. Individual variation is a psychological abstraction which isolates human traits, aptitudes, and attitudes from the school setting, cultural environment, and social circumstances. The focus on "management" assumes that individual differences exist apart from the social setting of schooling and that they can be "treated" in a logical and administrative fashion. Considering individualization as a technical, psychological problem may blind educators to the significance and dynamics of social structure.

The importance of the slogan, "individual differences," is, as I said in the introduction, the creation of a symbolic canopy for schooling. The slogan condenses a variety of deeply held beliefs in a manner that establishes a mood with which people can feel comfortable with institutional practices. The problem of such slogans is to understand them in terms of the concrete references and actual interests being served. Unless the label of individual differences directs attention to the relation of political, social, psychological, and philosophical aspects of our human conditions, it can obscure and mystify the meaning and implications of schooling.

In what can only be justified as an excursus from the argument in this chapter, I recognize the importance of the concern of this volume with a common curriculum and the differentiation of instruction in relation to that curriculum. I have chosen, however, to argue that any conception of teaching and learning involves a complex and profound interrelation of philosophical, social, and political elements.[25] One can argue, at an epistemological level, that there are forms of knowledge that have evolved to enable us to understand both the quality and causes of things and the feeling for the intensity of life. Science, art, poetry, and literature, for example, do provide different and complementary ways for understanding uncertainty as we act in unexpected ways and dwell in life's ambiguities and mysteries. Each perspective provides us with a vantage point for opening new horizons and showing new aspects of humanity. Each also has a sense of solitude and community by which we are to learn how to effect knowledge.[26]

The difficulty of creating a common curriculum is in its contradictions: we need to find the appropriate metaphors that enable us to understand how the play of imagination, the ambiguities of experience, the sense of the whole are interrelated to norms and patterns of communities of discourse such as science or literature. Contradiction is also embedded in the political and social circumstances of knowledge, for curriculum is realized in institutional contexts with different possibilities and pathologies. This is not to argue against the task set for this yearbook, but rather to say that this task involves a philosophical, social, and political complexity that cannot be reduced to behavioral objectives, standardized outcomes, taxonomies of thought, and psychological attributes. Such reduction is to deny what is essential to human identity.

FOOTNOTES

1. In this struggle I had the advantage of many conversations. G. P. Schedrovitsky, of the Institute of Pedagogical and Psychological Science, USSR, has one of those rare philosophical minds that could walk me through the development of the idea of personality from the Greek through Comte to the present. David Hamilton's work in pedagogical history has enabled me to understand how people in different times seek intellectual and practical resolutions to pressing social problems and transformations. In other ways, Michael Apple, Cathy Cornbleth, Fred Newmann, and Robert Dreeben, Kathey Kasten, and Jane Koehl provided comments that helped me seek clarity.

2. For the location of schooling as a social problem of institutions, see Thomas S. Popkewitz, "Educational Reform and Institutional Life," *Educational Researcher* 8 (March 1979): 3-8.

3. I use the notion of community in its general sociological sense. I am concerned with the assumptions, world views, and ideological systems that underlie everyday practices and give coherence to social practice. It is a different usage from that of educational reformers (see footnote 5) and sociologists who juxtapose community to society and articulate a sense of dislocation brought about by industrialization, such as the distinction Tonnies makes between *Gemeinschaft* and *Gesellschaft*. For Tonnies, community was a prescriptive and normative concept rather than a meta concept for considering the binding "rules" and views of a society. See Ferdinand Tonnies, *Community and Society (Gemeinschaft und Gesellschaft)*, trans. Charles Loomis (East Lansing, Mich.: Michigan State University Press, 1957).

4. See, for example, John Locke, *An Essay Concerning Human Understanding* (New York: Dover Publications, 1959) and Immanuel Kant, *Critique of Practical Reason*, trans. Lewis W. Beck (Indianapolis: Bobbs-Merrill Co., 1956). For discussion of the issue of the relation of philosophy, politics, and psychology, see Ellen Meiksins Wood, *Mind and Politics: An Approach to the Meaning of Liberal and Socialist Individualism* (Berkeley, Calif.: University of California Press, 1972) and Crawford B. Macpherson, *The Political Theory of Possessive Individualism: Hobbes to Locke* (New York: Oxford Press, 1962). The debate and nuances of the discussions extend beyond Locke and Kant into the works of Hegel, Marx, and current philosophy, social, and political theory. What could be done in this essay is only to outline certain elements of the discourse, leaving out certain of the subtleties about cognition such as those introduced by Hegel and Marx.

5. For discussion of community, see Herbert A. Thelen, *Education and the Human Quest: Four Designs for Education* (Chicago: University of Chicago Press, 1972) and Donald W. Oliver, *Education and Community: A Radical Critique of Innovative Schooling* (Berkeley, Calif.: McCutchan Publishing Corp., 1976).

6. Macpherson, *The Political Theory of Possessive Individualism,* p. 3.

7. Ibid.

8. The following discussion is based upon Basil B. Bernstein, *Class, Codes, and Control,* vol. 4 (London: Routledge and Kegan Paul, 1975).

9. Benjamin S. Bloom, *Taxonomy of Educational Objectives: The Classification of Educational Goals, Handbook 1: Cognitive Domain* (New York: David McKay Co., 1956).

10. This relationship of social, philosophical, and material conditions to pedagogical practice is persuasively argued through the historical studies of David Hamilton. See David Hamilton, "Educational Research and the Shadow of John Stuart Mill," in *The Meritocratic Intellect: Studies in the History of Educational Research,* ed. James Smith and David Hamilton (Aberdeen: Aberdeen University Press, 1980) and idem, "Robert Owen and Education: A Reassessment," in *Historical Essays on Scottish Education and Culture,* ed. H. Peterson and W. Humes (Edinburgh: John Donald, in press).

11. Emile Durkheim, *The Evolution of Educational Thought: Lectures on the Formation and Development of Secondary Education in France,* trans. Peter Collins (London: Routledge and Kegan Paul, 1977).

12. This is discussed in David Hamilton, "Adam Smith and the Moral Economy of the Classroom System," *Journal of Curriculum Studies* 12 (October-December): 281-98.

13. For discussion of Snedden, see Walter H. Drost, *David Snedden and Education for Social Efficiency* (Madison: University of Wisconsin Press, 1967).

14. Ibid., p. 166.

15. Ibid., p. 163.

16. Ibid., p. 149.

17. See, for example, John Dewey, "Individuality and Experience," *Journal of the Barnes Foundation* 2 (January 1926): 1-6.

18. Lawrence Cremin, *The Transformation of the School: Progressivism in American Education, 1876-1957* (New York: Alfred A. Knopf, 1962), p. 123.

19. See Charles Wright Mills, *Sociology and Pragmatism: The Higher Learning in America,* ed. Irving L. Horowitz (New York: Oxford University Press, 1960), and Burton J. Bledstein, *The Culture of Professionalism: The Middle Class and the Development of Higher Education in America* (New York: W. W. Norton, 1976).

20. All important social ideas have specific historical contexts which give them concrete meaning and significance as well as introducing contradictions. Liberal education, for example, originally reflected a classical belief in education for society's leaders. A shift in focus to education for freedom had the effect of democratizing the idea but located the liberal education within a specific institution, the university. In more recent years, the reinterpretation of liberal education has posed different notions of the individual relationship to the social and political order: expositions and criticism as personal engagement and intellectual relativism versus education based upon externally derived structures of knowledge and patterns of reality. See William A. Reid, "Democracy, Perfectability, and the Battle of the Books: Thoughts on the Conception of Liberal Education in the Writings of Schwab," *Curriculum Inquiry* 10 (Fall 1980): 249-64.

21. For a general discussion of this issue, see Michael W. Apple, *Ideology and Curriculum* (Boston: Routledge and Kegan Paul, 1976), and Henry A. Giroux, *Ideology, Culture, and the Process of Schooling* (London: Palmer Press, 1981), and Ulf P. Lundgren, *Model Analysis of Pedagogical Processes,* 2d ed. (Stockholm: C. W. K. Gleerup, 1981).

22. Richard H. De Lone, *Small Futures: Children, Inequality and the Limits of Liberal Reform* (New York: Harcourt Brace Jovanovich, 1979).

23. The following discussion is based upon an ethnographic study of six schools, reported in Thomas S. Popkewitz, B. Robert Tabachnick, and Gary Wehlage, *The Myth of Educational Reform: School Responses to Planned Educational Change* (Madison: University of Wisconsin Press, 1982).

24. The shifting images of individuality in society is studied in Will Wright, *Six Guns and Society: A Structural Study of the Western* (Berkeley: University of California Press, 1975). Using film as a medium for analysis, Wright argues that there has been a fundamental transformation in the social myths and social types that underlie everyday existence. The past thirty years have seen a change from the classical Western plot ("Shane") in which social relations corresponded to an individualistic conception in a market society to plots concerning the professional, such as "Butch Cassidy and the Sundance Kid." These new heroes' purpose is utilitarian, their actions are nonmoralistic, and their position is dependent upon specialized knowledge and skills required in complex organization. The underlying assumptions of the IGE program do illustrate these varying meanings. In the lived-in sites of the schools that adapted the program, different residues of individualism coexist. The transformation to the professional, with its notion of individuality, is neither complete nor without conflict and contradiction.

25. This is discussed in Thomas Popkewitz, "Whither/Wither the Curriculum Field?" *Contemporary Education: A Journal of Reviews* 1 (Spring 1982): 15-22.

26. See Thomas Popkewitz, "Craft and Community as Metaphors for Social Inquiry," *Educational Theory* 22 (Fall 1977): 310-21.

CHAPTER IV

Legal Bases of Individualization

LOUIS FISCHER AND GAIL PAULUS SORENSON

Although it has only been in recent years that educators have become keenly aware of the legal dimensions of their professional roles, various laws have always applied to them. We all live in a legal environment and each occupation, particularly a profession, is circumscribed by a set of laws peculiar to that occupation. It has been said, speculatively, that under ordinary circumstances, fish are not aware of water. Similarly, under ordinary circumstances, educators are not aware of their legal environment because they have been socialized and educated to act in ways compatible with law and with expectations based on law. However, just as our speculative analogy would have fish become aware of water in turbulence, shallows, and other special conditions, educators have become quite aware of laws relevant to them during recent decades of significant change and turbulence and perhaps pollution in their legal environment.

This chapter attempts to clarify how recent applications of legal principles and changes in law relate to individualization in schools. In order to provide perspective, some general principles will be presented first, sketching the overall relationships of public schools to various levels of government and therefore to different sources of law. Second, the chapter will indicate the difficulties courts encounter in applying legal principles while attempting to stay out of matters of educational policy. And, third, it will indicate the important but limited role that courts and the law play with regard to individualization in schools.

In a sense, the title of the chapter, "Legal Bases of Individualization," is a misnomer. As will be seen in more detail later, individualization in education is related only indirectly to fundamental legal concepts. Although the Constitution, for example, does protect indi-

---

Arthur E. Wise served as the editorial consultant for this chapter.

vidual rights such as freedom of expression and belief, and does proclaim our national purpose to treat people equally and fairly, such individualization in curriculum and instruction as results from legal influence is often the indirect result of an attempt to foster equality of educational opportunity rather than an attempt to assert an individual right for its own sake.

Despite the fact that many constitutional rights are individual rights, there is nothing in constitutional law that would proscribe grouping for just purposes; in fact, there is much that argues for treating people alike. It is only when this "equal" treatment exacerbates inequality that legal principles tending to favor individualization can be invoked. As the chapter progresses, an attempt will be made to define individualization, as this term is used in educational circles, and to explain its seemingly paradoxical relationship to the notion of individual rights. In the end, it will be suggested that individualization, like other methods, goals, and purposes of education, is largely a matter that is quite properly left to policymakers and educators.

The Sources of Law Relevant to Schools

Local control of public schools is a time-honored tradition in the United States. The ultimate legal basis of local control is ascribed to the Tenth Amendment to the U.S. Constitution, which broadly states: "The powers not delegated to the United States by the Constitution, nor prohibited by it to the states, are reserved to the states, respectively, or to the people." While this amendment does not mention education specifically, the federal and state governments as well as all levels of courts have consistently held that education is a function of the states.[1] The constitution of each of the fifty states provides for the maintenance of a system of public schools, although the state constitutions vary in the specificity of organizational structures and delegations of responsibility and authority. Forty-nine of the states further delegate most of the responsibility and authority over schooling to local governmental units, Hawaii being the sole exception.

Despite the fact that basic responsibility and authority for schooling reside with state governments, and despite the further delegation of power to local school authorities, all policies and actions of school officials must conform to the U.S. Constitution and to state constitutions as well as to federal and state laws. Courts have ruled that public school teachers, administrators, and school board members are state officials for purposes of constitutional law; therefore the prohibitions of the Fourteenth Amendment apply to their official actions. Courts have also held that the Fourteenth Amendment incorporates most of the first ten amendments, popularly known as the Bill of Rights; therefore all major provisions of the Bill of Rights apply to the public schools.[2] Private schools do not have to function consistently with the Bill of Rights or the Fourteenth Amendment, since their actions are not "state actions."[3] Thus, readers should assume that this chapter applies only to public schools.

In the field of education, as in other important areas of life, legal activity does not occur at a uniform rate. The intensity of activity will rise and diminish according to a variety of factors, including the perceived importance of schooling, the imagination and activism of lawyers and judges, sociocultural changes that affect schools, and access to courts through community legal service agencies, public law organizations, and even legislation that provides for legal fees and costs in certain types of lawsuits. The early part of our national experience saw very little court action related to schooling. The occasional suit that did appear was filed in state courts. A second period, lasting from the middle of the nineteenth century to about the middle of the twentieth, was characterized by the dominance of state law and state and local regulation of schools. As we found out subsequently, many principles, policies, and practices accepted during this period were in violation of the U.S. Constitution. *West Virginia State Board of Education v. Barnette* ushered in the third period of our educational-legal history in 1943 when, among other principles, the Supreme Court stated: "The Fourteenth Amendment . . . protects the citizen against the State itself and all of its creatures—Boards of Education not excepted. These have, of course, important, delicate, and highly discretionary functions, but none that they may not perform except within the limits of the Bill of Rights."[4]

During this third period there was considerable federal court involvement in schooling, often to the dismay of school officials who resented court-imposed restrictions on their traditional powers. This period saw widespread direct involvement by the federal judiciary, including direct supervision of schools. While such active court supervision could be found from coast to coast and in both North and

South, the best known examples came from Washington, D.C.,[5] where a racially discriminatory system was struck down by the court because of its negative effect on minority children, and from Boston,[6] where, to implement desegregation in the face of opposition by the school board, the U.S. District Court took control of the schools, appointed administrators, and supervised the hiring of teachers and administrators and the placement of students. Observers of the Supreme Court claim that the 1973 case of *San Antonio Independent School District v. Rodriguez*[7] ushered in the fourth period in the role of the federal courts vis-à-vis the schools, a period during which the role of the federal judiciary will diminish.[8]

In *Rodriguez*, where plaintiffs challenged the educational financing schema of the state of Texas, the Supreme Court rejected the notion that education is a fundamental right under our Constitution. In the words of the Court: "Education, of course, is not among the rights afforded explicit protection under our Federal Constitution. Nor do we find any basis for saying it is implicitly so protected."[9] This language, as well as other statements by the Burger Court, seems to be signaling a diminution in the role of federal courts in educational controversies. The tone of the Court is certainly different from that of the unanimous decision in 1954 in *Brown v. Board of Education of Topeka*,[10] where the Court referred to education as "perhaps the most important function of state and local governments." Its widely quoted passage goes on to proclaim: "In these days, it is doubtful that any child may reasonably be expected to succeed in life if he is denied the opportunity of an education. Such an opportunity, where the state has undertaken to provide it, is a right which must be made available to all on equal terms."[11] It is important to note, however, that even the unanimous Court in *Brown* does not assert education to be a right under the Federal Constitution and it recognizes the right to equal treatment *only where the state has undertaken* the provision of public schools. Thus, technically, there is no change in the Court's position, but the shift in emphasis and mood is clear.

No one predicts any significant decline in the near future in legal activity related to schooling. If anything, the activity will accelerate; however, a larger proportion of the cases are likely to be filed in state courts once again, with federal courts playing a lesser role.

We have already mentioned the federal and state constitutions as sources of law influencing schools. Judicial interpretations of these basic documents constitute another source, commonly referred to as case law. In addition, there are laws enacted by federal, state, and local legislative bodies, and policies, regulations, and rules promulgated by countless administrative agencies at all levels of government. All of these sources must be considered to be completely aware of our legal environment.

Law as a Source of Educational Policy

In order to understand how law influences the formulation of educational policy, including matters of individualization, it is necessary to have some conception of the theory and practice of policy-making. The courts play a limited role in this important endeavor. Our time-honored paradigm placed responsibility for creating educational policy with local school boards. Boards were to act after considering the professional advice of educators, legislatures were to provide a minimal structure for a state system of education, and the courts were to help interpret and enforce the constitutions created by the people and the laws enacted by the legislators. Such a neat separation of functions was never easy to maintain, and recent times saw the growing involvement of courts and legislatures in the creation of educational policy.

When we recognize that some levels of educational policy are inextricably connected with social policy and thus with the general welfare of the population, it becomes clear that federal and state legislatures have legitimate responsibilities in addressing educational policy issues. Recent examples of this might be the passage of PL 94-142 (the Education for All Handicapped Children Act of 1975) or the Family Educational Rights and Privacy Act of 1974, popularly known as the Buckley Amendment. Countless other pieces of legislation could be mentioned, since this source of educational regulation has increased at a pace faster than any other.[12] While school boards and educators tend to be quite unhappy with the proliferation of such legislation and regulations, their greatest resentment tends to be reserved for the courts. Judges are often accused of overstepping their proper roles and entering the arena of legislation and thus usurping power not properly theirs.

There is no doubt that in the course of exercising judicial discretion while attempting to interpret the law, some judges exceed their judicial roles and create law and policy. In their defense, however, we should note that the line of demarcation between creating and interpreting policy is not always clear. Furthermore, the very meaning of "educational policy" is often difficult to pin down. Some educational policies are so closely related to general social policies and to legal principles as to make neat, logical separations impossible.[13]

Nevertheless, judges are keenly aware of the ideal distinction between legislative and judicial roles. They have no wish to become "super school boards" and will enter the fray only when a constitutional issue is involved or the contending parties call for the interpretation of a specific law or regulation. The Supreme Court expressed its desire to stay clear of direct involvement in educational policy some time ago as follows:

By and large, public education in our nation is committed to the control of state and local authorities. Courts do not and cannot intervene in the resolution of conflicts which arise in the daily operation of school systems and which do not directly and sharply implicate basic constitutional values. On the other hand, "The vigilant protection of constitutional freedoms is nowhere more vital than in the community of American schools."[14]

Despite this reluctance and attempted self-restraint, courts have enormous influence on the shaping of educational policy. Much of this results from the ambiguities in both constitutional and statutory language that judges are called upon to interpret. The major provisions of the Constitution are all amenable to differences in interpretation; therefore the need for authoritative opinions from the courts. Consider the Fourteenth Amendment provisions that: "No State . . . shall deny any person within its jurisdiction the equal protection of the law" and "nor shall [any person] be deprived of life, liberty, or property without due process of law"; or the Fourth Amendment provision: "The right of the people to be secure in their persons, houses, papers, and effects, against unreasonable searches and seizures, shall not be violated, and no warrant shall issue, but upon probable cause. . . ." Other provisions of the Constitution could be noted where ambiguities abound, together with the many volumes of scholarly work written in attempts to clarify phrases like "due process," "equal protection," and "probable cause." Such ambiguity is a necessity in a living constitution,[15] but we also find it in statutory language. To cite but one example, the Education for All Handicapped Children Act uses ambiguous phrases like "a free appropriate" education and "least restrictive environment," whose meanings are by no means self-evident. In our system of government, the courts have the power to interpret such ambiguities; and, in the process, they inevitably influence educational policy.

Further examples could be cited; however, it should suffice for present purposes to conclude that law influences educational policy through legislative and regulatory processes and through court action. We are now ready to examine to what extent such influences bear on the idea of individualization in the processes of teaching and learning.

Individualization: An Educational or a Legal Concept?

Before the legal aspects of individualization can be meaningfully discussed, we must recognize that much confusion surrounds the notion of individualization in education. Ultimately, concern over such confusion is the justification for issuing this yearbook, but it is important to note that law is not the proper instrument by which to examine, analyze, and clarify alternative meanings and purposes of individualization. We should expect philosophy of education as well as curriculum and instructional theory to do this job.

Although individualization is an educational term and not a legal one, the individual and individual rights are very important in law. Generally speaking, individualization as an educational concept refers to means, methods, and arrangements that provide appropriate, tailor-made curriculum or instruction for a particular learner as contrasted to a group. Constitutional rights, which are ultimately individual rights, are not related to educational individualization except where impermissible bases are used for providing or withholding an educational treatment from a student. For example, if a student were erroneously classified and treated as mentally retarded based upon biased evaluation procedures, or if a non-English-speaking student were not provided with English language instruction, each could claim that his Fourteenth Amendment rights to equal protection and due process had been violated. In the first case, the individualized treatment would have been unconstitutionally provided and, in the second, unconstitutionally withheld. Thus, in an *indirect* way, constitutional rights of individuals are sometimes related to educational individualization, but they are distinct and separate concepts. While the constitutional notion of individual rights argues that each person be treated with special respect, the resulting educational application may be either a *more* individualized treatment or a *less* individualized one.

Grouping Students and the Law

Schools inevitably group students for instruction, although the criteria used for grouping may vary. Groups are formed on the basis of age, subject matter, ability, interest, involvement in athletic, musical, or other activities, or some combination of these and other factors. Such grouping decisions are not prescribed by law, but are made by educators. While many grouping decisions are beneficial or benign, student groups have often been formed based on criteria such as race, ethnicity, sex, language competence, and physical or mental handicap, which are not relevant to the particular educational purposes to be served.

Educators' practices in grouping children were generally accepted by the public until around the middle of the twentieth century when the *Brown* case successfully challenged school practices that used race as the criterion for grouping, thus segregating children. Inspired by the Supreme Court's language in *Brown*, other criteria for grouping were challenged and an extensive body of law, both case law and legislation, was generated from these challenges.

To reemphasize some basic principles, education is a state responsibility. The U.S. Constitution says nothing *directly* on the subject of student grouping. However, once a state makes schooling available to its residents at public expense, a right is created that must be available to all on an "equal" basis and no one can be denied such rights without "due process of law." Because these provisions of the Fourteenth Amendment are ambiguous, many decades and hundreds of court cases were necessary to explicate their meanings for the grouping of students in public schools.

Thus, the Constitution has important things to say *indirectly* regarding student grouping. Educators may still group for instruction, but certain criteria for grouping will come under "strict scrutiny."

These are the so-called "suspect criteria" resulting in the "suspect classification" of students on the basis of such things as race, religion, and ethnicity. This is not to say, however, that educators may never use these criteria for grouping students or that they may in no way consider such factors. It does mean that the use of such "suspect criteria" must be justified by a "compelling state interest," such as remedying the effects of past segregation, which cannot be satisfied or reached in some other way. This puts a heavy burden, indeed, on educators who propose to use such suspect criteria in forming instructional groups. Historically, the courts applied a less demanding test, the "rational basis test," to grouping for instructional purposes. This test meant that if the educators could offer some reason for the particular grouping, the courts would uphold their actions even if reasonable people could disagree on the legitimacy of the basis for the grouping. As long as *some* rational basis could be offered for the educator's actions, courts would not substitute their judgment for that of the educators. The "rational basis test" is still used by courts in connection with many educational decisions, but not when the criteria for grouping are "suspect." Then, a more stringent test, the "strict scrutiny test" will be applied. Under strict scrutiny, it is not enough to offer just any reason for a grouping decision; it must be a compelling reason on behalf of some important state interest that can be achieved only by the use of such grouping. "Strict scrutiny" would be applied by the courts whether students are included or excluded from school groupings on the bases of "suspect criteria." Thus, a decision to exclude alien children from an American history class would be just as suspect as the overinclusion of minority students in classes for the mentally retarded.

The law has treated classification based on sex and handicap differently from the foregoing "suspect" classifications, yet the "rational basis test" will no longer suffice. The Supreme Court seems to be evolving some type of intermediate standard to apply to classification based on gender, more strict than the "rational basis test" but not as stringent as "strict scrutiny." For example, sex-segregated high schools for the academically talented have been upheld by the courts so long as the curricula, facilities, and personnel were equal for girls and boys.[16] Clearly, an arrangement that is "separate but equal" is unconstitutional where race is the basis of the separation and where "strict scrutiny" is applied to examine a suspect classification. The Court, however, did not apply such strict standards to separation based on sex. Similarly, classifications based on handicap fall under this as yet undefined intermediate standard.[17]

At least some of the justices on the Supreme Court are no longer satisfied to apply the permissive "rational basis test" to gender classification.[18] While these justices urge that sex should be regarded as a suspect criterion, others have argued that pending the proposed Equal Rights Amendment, the Court should not "appear unnecessarily to decide sensitive issues of broad social and political importance at the very time they are under consideration within the prescribed constitutional processes."[19] This statement was made in 1973, in anticipation of the passage of the Equal Rights Amendment. Enactment of ERA would have made gender classification suspect, triggering strict scrutiny by the courts. Now that the time for ratification has expired, the Court will probably once again face the question of which standard to apply to sex-based classifications.

In the field of education we are not likely to face similar questions concerning the classification of handicapped children. Before the enactment of PL 94-142, the equal protection clause of the Constitution was an important legal tool with which to challenge the grouping and exclusion of the handicapped.[20] The passage of that law, however, has made the constitutional attack less necessary and perhaps more difficult to mount.[21] Thus, it is not generally the Constitution or the courts that tell educators whether and how to group the handicapped. The policy of individualized placement in the "least restrictive environment" is a declaration of social policy by Congress to remedy what Congress considered to be many decades of serious abuse, neglect, and miseducation.

The decision-making power of educators, however, is not completely preempted by PL 94-142, nor is it in any other aspect of grouping for instruction. Bureaucracies process people according to certain norms; schools, as bureaucracies, process children into groups for instruction. Whether or not the particular groups formed are educationally wise is not a decision that can be made by a court of law. The Constitution respects educators' discretion in such grouping, but requires very careful justification when "suspect" criteria, such as race or ethnicity, are the bases for grouping and requires some well-focused rationale when a "sensitive" criterion like sex is used. As a result of congressional action, special protection has been extended to the handicapped and extensive due process protections must be followed before placement decisions are made or changed.

Thus, if educators can demonstrate that their consideration of factors such as ethnicity, race, gender, or other suspect or sensitive criteria is for the educational benefit of children, they are not precluded by law from taking them into account. However, it is not sufficient to assert good intentions or to offer speculative or intuitive grounds for such grouping criteria. In light of the history of neglect, prejudice, abuse, and exclusion of* children under these suspect or sensitive categories, the law demands that educators have ample proof and compelling reasons to justify the use of such criteria in the educational placement of children.

We shall now explore several areas of concern to educators where individualization has been influenced to some extent by legal developments. These areas are the education of the handicapped, the education of limited-English-speaking children, malpractice cases, and due process in schools.

Laws Related to Exceptional Children

Recent legal developments concerning the schooling of handicapped children provide the most obvious example of individualization required by law. Yet, it is almost paradoxical that this individualization came about not through the direct pursuit of individualization but as a by-product of a long struggle for equal educational opportunities on behalf of children who historically had been excluded from school. While advocates for the handicapped were trying to convince courts and educators that total exclusion from school was not necessary—that the handicapped, like other children, could profit from an education— they succeeded in gaining both access to the "mainstream" and specialized treatment for children with handicapping conditions.

The categories of "exceptional" or "handicapped" children will be used interchangeably here, though there is some disagreement on this terminology as well as on whom to include within these designations. For our purposes we will use the definitions included in federal legislation and regulations and thus include the mentally retarded, the learning disabled, the emotionally disturbed, the speech, language, hearing, and sight impaired, and the physically and multiply handicapped. Congress estimated that over eight million children were handicapped in 1975, comprising between 10 and 15 percent of the school age population.

The key federal law related to individualization of the education of exceptional children is PL 94-142, although the Rehabilitation Act of 1973 is also very important. Section 504 of the Rehabilitation Act of 1973 would *cut off* any and all federal funds from schools that discriminate against the handicapped, while PL 94-142 makes certain funds *available* to schools that comply with its requirements. Among these requirements we find certain important features related to individualization, such as the identification and classification of students, the placement for instruction in the "least restrictive environment," the provision of an individual educational plan (IEP), the periodic reevaluation of placement and of the IEP, and various due process guarantees involving parental participation.

Each of these features of the law was enacted to correct widespread neglect and abuses of the past that led to almost wholesale misclassifications and miseducation of students.[22] Furthermore, it became clear that poor, minority, and Spanish-surnamed children were disproportionately the victims of faulty classification and labeling.[23] Such abuses were widely recognized before federal legislation was passed and a variety of separate lawsuits were brought, in different parts of the country, to secure fair and equitable education for these students.[24] These suits paved the way for the comprehensive legislative remedies at the federal level, with similar legislation now enacted in almost every state.

While there are many features of such legislation, and while there are serious disagreements concerning the educational merits of some of these features, our purpose is served by noting that PL 94-142 requires that educators pay careful attention to each individual *before* identifying, labeling, or classifying that student in any way that might be stigmatizing. Furthermore, the educational placement must be carefully considered for each individual properly identified as having some type of handicap. The requirement of the "least restrictive environment" is the guiding principle for such placement. Thus, while individualized placement decisions are mandated, children must be "mainstreamed" to the greatest extent possible. By definition, the IEP is to be constructed for each child; it is to be reviewed periodically, and appropriate adjustments or revisions must be made. Elaborate due process provisions accompany all these requirements to ensure opportunities for parental participation in both the process and substance of decisions to provide "free appropriate" education for all handicapped children. The individualization mandated by PL 94-142 illustrates how policymakers, rather than courts, can act directly to influence curriculum and instruction. The requirement of placement in "the least restrictive environment" suggests that individual differences should be accounted for, whenever possible, by individualized instruction rather than by curricular differences.

If this model makes good sense to secure individualization for the handicapped, why would it not make equally good sense to provide it for all children? This question has been raised by many parents, as well as by educators and legislators. It has resulted in legislation in the state of Wisconsin aimed at individualizing the placement of all students.[25] Most educators decry such a development as needless, claiming that the endless amount of paperwork and meetings required by such laws and regulations will suffocate the schools and consume an inordinate amount of time and money that should be used for other educational activities. While individualized placement for all children might be the ideal, it is not likely that constitutional considerations would compel such an effort in the absence of extraordinary circumstances. While a state must provide an education to all children, where it has undertaken to provide it to some, it need not provide the best possible education to anyone.

Laws Related to Limited-English-Speaking Children

Another example of individualization influenced by law arose in recent years in connection with children who spoke little or no English but who were enrolled in public schools. The most important case in this area is *Lau v. Nichols*,[26] a case involving Chinese-American students in San Francisco who attended public schools but received no special services designed to meet their linguistic needs. Once again, as in cases involving handicapped children, it is an apparent paradox that although our discussion focuses on individualization, the lawsuit was brought to secure equal educational opportunity. Sometimes, as in

Lau, treating a student the same as other students will deny equal educational opportunity by denying needed specialized curriculum or instruction. On the other hand, there are times when treating a student differently (based on race, sex, handicap, and so forth) may deny equal educational opportunity if the criteria used to determine the specialized treatment are not relevant to some legitimate educational goal. In either situation, however, it seems to be the case that to achieve equal access to education, in the sense of equitable treatment, we must often individualize the decision-making process so that it is appropriate to the particular student in a unique school situation.

The main issue in the *Lau* case was whether non-English-speaking students were denied equal educational opportunities when taught in a language they could not understand. The case was ultimately decided under Title VI of the Civil Rights Act of 1964,[27] which provides that "no person in the United States shall, on the grounds of race, color, or national origin, be excluded from participation in, be denied the benefit of, or be subjected to discrimination under any program or activity receiving Federal financial assistance." The Supreme Court held that the provision of identical educational services to all students does not satisfy the law. It ruled that students who understand little or no English are denied equal educational opportunities when English is the sole medium of instruction and there are no systematic efforts to teach that language to non-English-speaking students. Since these students "are effectively foreclosed from any meaningful instruction," schools must make special provisions for them. The Court did not specify what these provisions should be, a task properly reserved for educators. English as a second language (ESL), bilingual education, total immersion programs, or some other program might satisfy the courts, but it is up to educators to determine what plan is effective with which students.

Pursuant to *Lau*, children from other language minorities have been extended similar rights by court cases and by legislation. Controversy still surrounds the nature and extent of bilingual education for these students. It is clear, however, that the law will not allow us to ignore these individual needs and rest comfortably by providing an identical education for all children.

An interesting variation on bilingual education arose in Michigan and became known as the "black English" case.[28] Suit was brought on behalf of black students living in a low-income housing project, located in a wealthy section of Ann Arbor, near the University of Michigan. The students claimed that their language, black English, a distinct language different from standard English, constituted a barrier to learning and, thus, a denial of federal law.[29] When the court found that the teachers' lack of awareness and knowledge of black English contributed to the students' lack of progress, an order was issued to remedy the situation. The school board was ordered to develop a plan whereby teachers would become aware of language usage in the students' homes and in the community in order to be able to identify children who use black English and provide them with more effective instruction. Thus, once again, a lawsuit brought to achieve equal educational opportunities assisted in individualizing instruction. But, like the handicapped and language minority students, these students, too, sought their Fourteenth Amendment right to equal protection of the laws, to equality of educational opportunity. Individualized instruction was merely a means to the realization of this goal.

Malpractice Cases and Individualization

During recent years a new line of cases arose in connection with schooling, cases that have been labeled "consumer suits" by some but "educational malpractice" cases by most commentators.[30] If these cases had been successful, the logical extension might have suggested that schools have the duty to educate children to the full extent of their individual capabilities. Thus, if schools did not come reasonably close to fulfilling such a duty, they would be liable in monetary damages to students whom they educated "negligently."

The first, and perhaps best known, of such malpractice cases arose in San Francisco, California and became known as "the case of Peter Doe." The uncontested facts indicate that Peter Doe, a white student of at least average intelligence, graduated from high school in 1972 with average grades. Immediately after graduation his parents discovered that Peter was a functional illiterate; his reading and writing were at the fifth-grade level and he could not read job applications or fill out common forms. When, through private tutoring, his reading ability improved rapidly, Peter's parents and lawyer charged the schools of

San Francisco with negligence and professional malpractice. In the final analysis the trial court ruled against Peter Doe, the court of appeals upheld the ruling,[31] and the California Supreme Court refused to review the case.[32]

The appellate judge noted that it is not possible for courts to determine when teaching is negligent, for "classroom methodology affords no readily acceptable standards of care or cause or injury. The science of pedagogy itself is fraught with different and conflicting theories of how or what should be taught." The court then recognized that a student's learning is influenced by many factors, some of which are not controlled by the schools. Thus, it is not possible to establish causal connections between the student's injury and the school's alleged misconduct. Finally, the court was influenced by the public policy implications of holding schools liable for students' lack of progress. It was concerned with a flood of lawsuits that might follow which would burden schools and thus society in general "beyond calculation."

Subsequent cases have reached similar results. In each case, the judges were concerned with policy implications in ruling for the student claimant, with the lack of clear, agreed upon standards for specifying the duty of care educators owe students, as well as with the complexity and multitude of variables that affect learning. In the case of *Donohue v. Copiague Union Free School District*[33] in New York, the judge also noted that courts are not the appropriate forums to evaluate conflicting theories of how best to educate.

There has been recent speculation that legislative requirements of competency-based education and graduation might lead to new and successful malpractice suits. The reasoning behind this prediction is that by specifying minimum levels of competence for students at certain grade levels, educators will have established standards of care they will have to meet, and failure to meet them will constitute negligence.[34] This line of reasoning, however, does not address the two other grounds for the courts' dismissal of the claims of malpractice, namely the difficulties in establishing causal connections between alleged negligence and damages and the public policy considerations concerning the flood of suits that would follow if courts ruled in favor of the students. The judicial door to future lawsuits, however, is not completely shut. Even the New York court, which ruled against the student, noted that future cases might bring different results if they entail "exceptional circumstances involving gross deviations from defined public policy."[35]

In sum, malpractice cases do not constitute a significant example of individualization stimulated by judicial decision. Whether they will develop in that direction pursuant to legislatively mandated competency testing is highly speculative, particularly if the tort theory of negligence, which has not proven fruitful, continues to be relied upon by plaintiffs.

There is a different way in which competency legislation may impact on individualization, without relying on the problematic claim of negligently caused injury. This route to individualization depends on the requirements of widely varying state laws that mandate competency testing. One feature common to such laws is the requirement of periodic testing of student achievement at various grade levels.[36] In some states the law requires that if a student does not score at or above specified minimal levels, remediation must begin. Thus, the minimum competency testing program might trigger a process similar to the requirement of PL 94-142 for an individual education plan. To the extent that state laws or regulations contain such a requirement, a type of individualization may be stimulated by the legal requirement of competency-based education.

Due Process and Individualization

During the past two decades, the due process clause of the U.S. Constitution, as well as similar clauses in state constitutions, have been increasingly applied to schools. The relevant portion of the Fourteenth Amendment states that ". . . nor shall any state deprive any person of life, liberty, or property, without due process of law." Public schools are arms of the state; therefore, actions by teachers, administrators, and school boards are state actions for purposes of constitutional law. Courts have held that students have both a property right and a liberty right[37] in their education, and that state officials may not, therefore, arbitrarily deprive them of schooling.[38]

These principles relate to individualization not in curriculum and instruction but in matters of discipline and what might be called the nonformal curriculum. School officials may not act in a unilateral, arbitrary manner in suspending or expelling students. Furthermore, mass punishment of entire groups, a variation on guilt by association, is against the law, unless the punishment is trivial. In 1975, the Supreme Court ruled in *Goss v. Lopez* that even a short suspension, one for no more than a day, should be preceded by some modicum of due process.[39] The responsible school official must give oral or written notice to the student of the charges; and, if the student denies them, listen to his or her explanation of the events. For violations of school rules that might lead only to a short-term suspension, such a brief process would satisfy the courts. Offenses that might lead to long-term suspension or expulsion call for more elaborate due process, one that might include the calling and cross-examination of witnesses, representation for the student, written findings, and a right to appeal. Whether the simpler or the more elaborate process is involved, it is clear that some degree of individualization is called for in these disciplinary procedures whenever the deprivation is not *de minimus* or trivial.

Other Examples of Individualization Effected by Law

School records. Recent federal legislation made a significant impact on school practices related to student records. The Family Educational Rights and Privacy Act (FERPA, also known as the Buckley Amendment), passed by Congress in 1974, intended to define who may or may not have access to student records.[40] While FERPA is a significant piece of legislation for various reasons, reference is made to it here since it requires individualization related to the use and availability of students' records. Materials in such records are available only to the students, to their parents, and to relevant educators. Furthermore, if the records contain materials which the students or parents want removed, they have a right to a hearing to challenge the objectionable matter. If, after the hearing, the school officials insist on keeping the objectionable entries in the record, the students and their parents have the right to insert explanations into the files. Thus, the schools may not hinder access to student records by a blanket policy that makes them unavailable to those most affected by them.

Sex discrimination. There are school policies that are reasonable in the abstract, have a kind of face validity, yet are unreasonable when applied to particular individuals. Such policies appear in the area of competitive school athletics, where, as a general rule, it may make sense to have girls compete against girls and boys against boys. There are girls of exceptional strength, speed, endurance, and skill, however, who can compete successfully for places on boys' teams in a variety of sports. Some courts have held that schools must consider the individual and not simply lump everybody of one sex into one group for purposes of school athletics. While there is no uniform legal requirement to this effect (even Title IX allows for sex-segregated teams), some courts have extended the principle of individualization to this area of schooling.[41]

Testing. The area of standardized testing has come under legal scrutiny in recent years. Among the various issues related to such testing, a concern for individualization arises when test results might lead to a stigmatizing label being attached to a student, that is, where a liberty right is involved. Due process now requires that great care be used before such a label is attached to any student, for we are now aware of the powerful negative consequences that may follow.

A concern for individualization is also implicated where a student might be denied a present or future entitlement to the benefits of education, that is, where a property right is involved. To see how both a liberty right and a property right can be involved in an educational testing situation, imagine a student who had just been denied a diploma for failing a minimal-competency test that did not test what had been taught. The liberty interest is implicated because of the stigmatizing effect of failure, and the property interest because of the potential benefits a diploma might bring to the student. Since individuals cannot be denied liberty or property without due process, and due process is violated by fundamental unfairness, the diploma denial would be invalidated.

Special due process and equal protection concerns are often present where minority students, handicapped students, and culturally disadvantaged students are being tested. Tests must be carefully examined to assure that they are not racially or culturally biased and that necessary modifications in testing procedures have been developed to ameliorate the effect of handicapping conditions. Consideration must also be given to whether or not disproportionate failure rates for minority students can be traced to the effects of past racial segregation.[42]

While competent professionals can make good use of testing procedures designed to effectuate individualization through evaluation and remediation, history is so fraught with misuse and abuse that legal protections have been increasingly applied to protect children from denials of due process and equal protection accomplished by ill-conceived testing programs.[43]

Curriculum and the Law

To many educators it seems strange that courts have been relatively silent on matters related to the curriculum, yet so outspoken on the organization of instruction. Once again, we must refer to the basic framework of our legal system and its relationship to schooling to understand why courts speak so seldom to curricular matters. Curriculum is created by educators in collaboration with school boards, and, at times, by legislators. The only time courts enter this arena is when some individual or group alleges that a curricular decision or practice violates a right granted by the federal or state constitutions or by legislation. Illustrative examples are to be found in the well-known cases that exclude religious exercises from public schools,[44] in cases involving attempted censorship and freedom of expression protected by the First Amendment,[45] and in recent controversies related to "Scientific Creationism" which, once again, raise some perennial First Amendment questions of freedom of religion.

Aside from controversies such as these (where basic constitutional rights have been directly abridged), school boards, educators, and legislators have the power to decide all curricular matters in schools as a matter of public policy. Recognizing their lack of expertise in such matters, courts are loath to interfere with this discretion. It is in the area of instruction, even when the official curriculum was to be identical for all students, that a plethora of legal challenges were brought under the equal protection clause of the Fourteenth Amendment, while others were brought under its due process clause. Under the equal protection clause the criteria for grouping have often been questioned, and the courts have developed the various tests discussed earlier (the "rational basis test," the "suspect classification test," and the evolving "intermediate test") to determine the legitimacy of the grouping. On the other hand, the due process clause has been, and can be used in the future to challenge arbitrary and unreasonable procedures that deprive any student of an educational benefit. Some actions can be questioned under both clauses simultaneously, for example, the exclusion of female students from courses on auto mechanics. In contemporary America such exclusion is considered arbitrary, and it also involves the "sensitive" gender classification.

In sum, what seems like an overwhelming attention by courts to organization and instruction and a virtual ignoring of curricular matters is not to be interpreted to mean that somehow "the law" does not value the curriculum. Rather, our decentralized legal system and the tradition of local control of education provide only a very limited role for the courts in curricular matters. It is a limited "police" role or "negative" role that ensures that our other rights and liberties are not violated by the substance of the curriculum or by the policies and procedures of our schools. This is not to say, however, that the courts are not involved with substantive educational matters like whether or not educators are testing what has been taught and whether or not there are language deficiencies. It means only that the courts do not generally tell educators *what* to teach or *how* to remedy the deficiencies.

Another way of looking at this difference is by using the "least harm," "maximum benefit" distinction. The agencies that create educational policy and curriculum should have the maximum benefit of students as their proper concern. PL 94-142 is an example of such an effort, though legislatures are often satisfied with less than maximum benefits. On the other hand, the competency-testing movement seems to be satisfied by minimum standards and thus is more in line with the least harm principle. Since educational policymakers are free to develop curricular and instructional techniques that will provide for maximum educational benefit, they often legislate directly to provide for such things as individualization, when it is deemed appropriate and wise to do so. On the other hand, when the courts specify what educators may not do, they seem to be applying the least harm principle. This principle is suggested by the Supreme Court in the *Rodriguez* case, where, while upholding the very unequal school financing schema of Texas, the Court noted that it might well rule otherwise if Texas educational standards fell below certain minimum criteria.[46] The courts do not seek the maximum educational benefit when deciding cases; they seek only to guarantee minimal but important "fundamental rights." Whatever educational benefits may accrue from their activities are generally indirect. Their role is satisfied not by providing a benefit, but by preventing serious harm.

There is one other issue worthy of mention with regard to individualization and the curriculum. The issue of curricular exemption that arises when parents want their children excluded from some school activity provides an example of indirect judicial support for individualization where the fundamental right of parental involvement in a child's education is concerned. Courts have generally held that public schools may require all students to participate in that part of the curriculum which includes the basic subjects related to literacy and the "essentials of citizenship." Beyond those areas, the objections of parents have often been respected, particularly when the exemption claimed was based on genuinely held religious beliefs. Based on such beliefs, students have been excused from patriotic exercises,[47] from dancing in physical education classes,[48] and from sex education.[49] Here again, support for individualization of the curriculum is only an indirect result of the assertion of fundamental individual rights which are not overcome by a countervailing compelling state interest. In the "essential areas" of the curriculum, however, parental objection to the use of otherwise relevant and appropriate materials will not be supported by the courts.[50] Courts have agreed that there is a compelling state interest in the requirement that all children experience certain fundamental essentials of a common curriculum.

Conclusion

During the second half of this century, law has proliferated into every area of our lives, and education is no exception. All areas of schooling have felt the impact of court decisions, legislation, and regulations during the past two decades, with no indication that such legal activity will diminish. The idea of individualization, making the opportunities of schooling available to each individual in an appropriate way, has been influenced by law to some extent. It is most accurate to say, however, that law makes an impact on individualization only in the exceptional, unusual, or problematic situation. Thus, we saw that law plays an important role in the education of handicapped and limited-English-speaking students. Beyond those areas, constitutional and statutory provisions require some degree of individualization in disciplinary matters, such as suspension or expulsion, in the treatment of school records, in restricting access to some school-sponsored activities on the basis of sex, in making decisions concerning exempting students from parts of a required curriculum, and in standardized testing. For the bulk of school activities, however, and certainly in the areas of curriculum and instruction, the law has very little to say regarding individualization.

Grouping for instruction, a long-standing practice in schools, is a matter generally left to the discretion of educators. Courts become interested only if suspect or sensitive criteria, like race or sex, are used as bases for grouping. Such practices will be carefully examined by courts and will be upheld only if educators have adequate justification where *suspect* criteria, such as race or ethnicity, form the bases for grouping children. Where *sensitive* criteria are used, such as sex or handicap, the standard of justification is somewhat less stringent, but educators must still meet the burden of proof that the criterion is relevant to attain some specific, desired educational objective.

Courts have long held the belief, often reiterated in appellate and trial court decisions, that the ends and means of education, its goals, policies, and methods are beyond the competence of courts and judges. Such matters are for the professional judgments of educators or for the policy-making activities of school boards and legislative bodies. Since these important educational issues often involve complex moral judgments, it is often tempting for educators to avoid the highly charged controversial questions related to educational policy, curriculum, and instruction by waiting for the courts to make authoritative pronouncements on them. However, it is a sign of professional maturity to realize that the courts cannot and should not do our work for us. When complex educational issues entail legal dimensions, such as the use of suspect or sensitive criteria for grouping, the courts perform their proper function in addressing them. But when educational decisions and practices do not involve fundamental questions of legal principle, and certainly individualization is basically an educational and not a legal issue, we would do well to listen to the words of the Supreme Court: "Courts do not and cannot intervene in the resolution of conflicts which arise in the daily operation of school systems and which do not directly and sharply implicate basic constitutional values."[51] Important questions involving the individualization of

98   LEGAL   BASES   OF   INDIVIDUALIZATION

educational programs, methods, and practices are among the most fundamental questions for educational policy, and, as such, are best left to the judgment of those intimately involved in the future of American education.

FOOTNOTES

1. Dawson Hales, *Federal Control of Public Education* (New York: Bureau of Publications, Columbia University, 1954), p. 49.

2. *Cantwell v. Connecticut*, 310 U.S. 296 (1940).

3. Nevertheless, they may not discriminate on grounds of race. Furthermore, private schools that receive substantial public funds have to comply with federal and state law.

4. *West Virginia State Board of Education v. Barnette*, 319 U.S. 624, 637 (1943).

5. *Hobson v. Hansen*, 269 F. Supp. 401 (D.D.C. 1967), *aff'd in part sub nom; Smuck v. Hobson*, 408 F. 2d 175 (D.C. Cir. 1969), *appeal dismissed*, 393 U.S. 801 (1968).

6. *Morgan v. Kerrigan*, 509 F. 2d 580 (1st Cir. 1974), *cert. denied*, 95 S. Ct. 1950 (1975).

7. *San Antonio Independent School District v. Rodriguez*, 411 U.S. 1 (1973).

8. See Larry W. Hughes and William M. Gordon, "Frontiers of the Law," in *The Courts and Education: Seventy-seventh Yearbook of the National Society for the Study of Education*, Part I, ed. Clifford P. Hooker (Chicago: University of Chicago Press, 1978), pp. 338-39.

9. *San Antonio Independent School District v. Rodriguez*, 411 U.S. 1, 35 (1973).

10. *Brown v. Board of Education of Topeka*, 347 U.S. 483 (1954).

11. Ibid., p. 493.

12. The number of pages of *federal* legislation on education increased from 80 to 360 between 1964 and 1976 and the number of pages of federal *regulations* from 92 to nearly 1000 between 1965 and 1977. Joseph Califano, Secretary of Health, Education, and Welfare, as quoted in *Higher Education and National Affairs*, Aug. 25, 1978, p.1.

13. For an excellent but complex analysis of this problem, see Arthur E. Wise, *Legislated Learning* (Berkeley: University of California Press, 1979); see also, Donald L. Horowitz, *The Courts and Social Policy* (Washington, D.C.: Brookings Institution, 1977).

14. *Epperson v. Arkansas*, 393 U.S. 97, 104 (1968).

15. Shirley M. Hufstedler, "In the Name of Justice," *Stanford Lawyer* 14 (Spring/Summer 1979): 27-53.

16. *Vorchheimer v. School District of Philadelphia*, 430 U.S. 703 (1977) (4-4) (Justice Rehnquist, not participating), *aff'd*, 532 F. 2d 880 (3d Cir. 1976).

17. For an excellent analysis of this evolving intermediate standard of review, see Laurence H. Tribe, *American Constitutional Law* (Mineola, N.Y.: Foundation Press, 1978), chap. 16.

18. See Justice Brennan's plurality opinion in *Frontiero v. Richardson*, 411 U.S. 677 (1973).

19. *Frontiero v. Richardson*, 411 U.S. 677, 691-2 (Justice Powell, concurring).

20. See *Pennsylvania Association for Retarded Children v. Commonwealth of Pennsylvania*, 343 F. Supp. 279 (E.D. Pa. 1972), and *Mills v. Board of Education of the District of Columbia*, 348 F. Supp. 866 (D.D.C. 1972).

21. The Supreme Court always prefers to decide a case on statutory or other grounds if it can properly avoid a constitutional question.

22. Alan Abeson, Nancy Bolick, and Jayne Hass, *A Primer on Due Process: Education Decisions for Handicapped Children* (Reston, Va.: Council for Exceptional Children, 1975).

23. Frederick J. Weintraub, "Recent Influences of Law Regarding the Identification and Educational Placement of Children," *Focus on Exceptional Children* 4 (April 1972): 1-11.

24. *Diana v. State Board of Education*, Cir. No. 7037 R.F.P. (N.D. Cal. 1970) (Consent Decree) (misclassification of Spanish-surname students); *Larry P. v. Riles*, 343 F. Supp. 1306 (N.D. Cal. 1972) (the misuse of IQ tests with black students); *Pennsylvania Association for Retarded Children v. Commonwealth of Pennsylvania*, 343 F. Supp. 279 (E.D. Pa. 1972) (the exclusion of retarded children).

25. Wisconsin Statutes 118.15 and 118.16 reported in *NOLPE Notes* 15 (October 1980): 3-4.

26. *Lau v. Nichols*, 414 U.S. 563 (1974).

27. 42 *United States Code*, Sec. 2000d (1970).

28. *Martin Luther King, Jr. Elementary School Children v. Ann Arbor School District*, 473 F. Supp. 1371 (E.D. Mich. 1979).

29. 20 *United States Code*, Sec. 1703(f), provides that "no state shall deny equal educational opportunity to an individual . . . by the failure by an educational agency to take appropriate action to overcome language barriers that impede equal participation by its students in its instructional program."

30. See David Abel, "Can a Student Sue the Schools for Educational Malpractice?" *Harvard Educational Review* 44 (November 1974): 416-36.

31. *Peter W. v. San Francisco Unified School District*, 60 Cal. App. 3d 841, 131 Cal. Rptr. 854 (Ct. App. 1976).

32. Ibid.

33. *Donohue v. Capiague Union Free School District*, 418 N.Y.S. 2d 375 (1979). See also, *Hoffman v. Board of Education of City of New York*, 424 N.Y.S. 2d 376 (1979).

34. See Wise, *Legislated Learning*, pp. 29-30.

35. *Hoffman v. Board of Education of City of New York*, 424 N.Y.S. 2d 376 (1979).

36. See, for example, the Florida Educational Accountability Act of 1976 and California's Guaranteed Learning Achievement Act of 1971, Ch. 600, Assembly Bill No. 1483, 1971.

37. A property right is some benefit to which a student is entitled, often based upon state law. An example would be the right to a diploma, assuming all requirements had been met. It would also include the right to general, day-to-day, educational benefits. A liberty right involves the individual's interest in good name or reputation.

38. See, for example, *Goss v. Lopez*, 419 U.S. 565 (1975).

39. Ibid.

40. 20 United States Code, Sec. 1232g (Supp. 1975); Public Law 93-380 (August 21, 1974); Public Law 93-568, Sec. 2 (December 31, 1974).

41. *Brenden v. Independent School District*, 342 F. Supp. 1224 (D. Minn. 1972), aff'd., 477 F. 2d 12392 (8th Cir. 1973).

42. See, for example, *Hobson v. Hansen*, 269 F. Supp. 401 (D.D.C. 1967), aff'd in part sub nom; *Smuck v. Hobson*, 408 F. 2d 175 (D.C. Cir. 1969), appeal dismissed 393 U.S. 801 (1968); *Debra P. v. Turlington*, 474 F. Supp. 244 (M.D. Fla. 1979), aff'd in part 644 F. 2d 397 (5th Cir. 1981).

43. See, for example, *Larry P. v. Riles*, 343 F. Supp. 1036 (N.D. Cal. 1972); *Board of Education of Northport-East, Northport Unified School District v. Ambach*, 436 N.Y.S. 2d 564 (Sup. Ct. 1981).

44. See, for example, *School District of Abington Township v. Schempp*, 374 U.S. 203 (1963).

45. See, for example, *Keefe v. Geanakos*, 418 F. 2d 359 (1st Cir. 1969).

46. *San Antonio Independent School District v. Rodriguez*, 411 U.S. 1 (1973).

47. *West Virginia State Board of Education v. Barnette*, 319 U.S. 624 (1943).

48. *Hardwick v. Board of School Trustees*, 209 P. 49 (Calif. 1921).

49. *Citizens for Parental Rights v. San Mateo City Board of Education*, 124 Cal. Rptr. 68 (Cal. App. 1975).

50. Joel S. Moskowitz, "Parental Rights and Responsibilities," *Washington Law Review* 50 (1975): 623-51.

51. *Epperson v. Arkansas*, 393 U.S. 97, 104 (1968). To make this quotation completely accurate, courts should intervene only if some constitutional *or* statutory right is involved in a school policy or activity.

CHAPTER V

The Biological Basis of Variability

ROBERT ROSEN

Variability is a basic fact of life. Only at the level of elementary subatomic particles are we blessed with the assurance that any representatives of a particular class (for example, two electrons, or two protons) are absolutely identical in all their particulars. At all higher levels, however, this assurance disappears, and in fact, in many crucial situations, variability becomes the dominant fact.

This chapter is concerned with the nature of variability and the assessment of some of its consequences. Our particular point of departure is biology, although much of our discussion is perfectly general and applies universally. We feel that it is important to have a good understanding of the nature of variability because, despite its central role, it is seldom explicitly discussed, and many incorrect conclusions are based on misunderstandings of its nature and its connotations.

We thus begin with a relatively thorough discussion of the general properties of variability, which is central to all that follows. We then turn to the biological situation; we consider those forces which generate variability, and those which limit it, and the interplay between them. Any such interplay of forces generates dynamics, and indeed we argue that the underlying dynamical considerations are basic to assessing the effects of variability in any given situation.

The General Properties of Variability

THE CONCEPT OF VARIABILITY

The simple fact that we can discriminate between the systems we encounter means that there are perceptible differences between them. However, such differences do not properly constitute variability.

Paradoxically, the concept of variability depends at least as much on similarities between systems as it does on the differences between them. An appreciation of this strange but basic fact is essential for what follows, and so it must receive some consideration at the outset.

Human beings are inveterate classifiers. Consequently, almost every field of inquiry begins with some kind of taxonomy; indeed, it cannot properly be called "scientific" until some natural classification of its materials has been established. This is true in the most abstract domains as well as in the most empirical. For instance, a substantial part of pure mathematics is concerned with classifying the structures with which mathematics deals. Likewise, the physicists classify their elementary particles, the chemists have their Periodic Table, and of course the biologists have their Linnaeus.

At the root of any classification scheme is some (often tacit) notion of similarity of structure or behavior, or some commonality of descent. Any such notion generates a relation of likeness or relatedness, on which the classification is based. Systems which are sufficiently alike, or related, or similar, are placed into a common class; otherwise they are placed in different classes. For purposes of classification, then, the relation of "alikeness" overshadows any perceptible difference between systems.

Following the biologists, let us use the neutral word *taxon* to designate a set of elements which are to be classified together. Thus, for a biologist, a taxon might be a species or genus; for a chemist, a taxon might be a particular group of elements in the Periodic Table; for a physicist, a taxon might be a family of particles which obey Bose-Einstein statistics; and so forth. Thus, as we have seen, the elements in a taxon are to be counted as alike, or similar, in some basic sense. However, these elements are not in general identical; even though they are classified together, we can generally discriminate between them.

How can the elements in a taxon simultaneously be like each other, but different from each other? Essentially, the situation is as follows. In establishing any classification, we select certain features of the elements being classified and treat them as diagnostic. A taxon is then a set of elements on which these diagnostic features are constant (or better, *invariant*). Any nondiagnostic feature, then, *can* vary from one element in a taxon to another. Thus, the elements in a taxon are alike with respect to the diagnostic features, but may be different with respect to any other feature.

The manner in which one or another of the nondiagnostic or noninvariant features of our elements may change *within a taxon* is what we shall identify as *variability*. It must be carefully noted that variability depends for its very definition on the *prior* establishment of a classification procedure, or taxonomy, and refers to *intrataxon* differences between nondiagnostic features. Without this qualification, variability degenerates to mere discriminability, and is devoid of interest or implication. It should also be noted that if we change our criteria of classification, we thereby change the taxa, and hence also the notion of variability. In other words, variability is contingent on classification. We must first specify how our elements are alike; then we may inquire how they may differ.

THE CONCEPT OF "FEATURE"

In our previous discussion, we used the term "feature" to talk about the qualities of the elements being classified. Before going further, we must say more precisely what this term connotes.

The simplest and most objective kind of feature is one which we can measure through some particular observation procedure, and obtain thereby a specific numerical value. Such features are the primary objects of study in the physical sciences, where they are called observables or dynamical variables. Typical examples of such observables are position, rate, frequency, mass, energy. We shall call features of this type, which take their values in numbers, *quantitative* features.

In general, science likes to deal with quantitative features, and in particular, to base its taxonomies or classifications on them. However, the apparent precision embodied in such numbers is often quite deceptive, and rests upon a tacit underpinning of nonquantitative features. For instance, a biological taxonomist may decide whether a particular organism is an insect or an arachnid by counting its legs (insects have six, arachnids have eight). However, if asked to specify what is a "leg," we would see clearly how our apparently categorical numbers rest on tacit nonnumerical qualities. This is why it is so difficult to program a machine to classify patterns in a nontrivial way.

Nevertheless, we are going to treat all features as if they were quantitative ones, that is, as if they take their values in numbers. There are two reasons for doing this. First, such a restriction will enormously simplify our discussion, because numbers will provide a "common currency" in terms of which different features may be compared. Second, it turns out that there is not as much loss of generality in this restriction as might appear.[1]

Thus, for our purposes, a *feature* is simply a mapping or function, which associates each particular object under discussion with a corresponding number. This number will be called the *value* of the feature on the object. We will compare different objects by looking at the values which particular features assume on them.

As we saw earlier, when we establish a classification, we choose certain features as diagnostic. A taxon, then, is a set of objects or elements on which the diagnostic features are constant or invariant. The other features may assume different values on the elements which constitute a taxon; the study of variability is then simply the study of how the values of nondiagnostic features may vary within a taxon.

We need to make one further qualification before we proceed. Namely, it may happen that the value of a given feature, evaluated on a particular member of a taxon, will change with time. This may happen because of internal (autonomous) dynamical processes occurring within the element, or because of interactions (forcings) with environment, or both. In general, the study of time-varying features is called *dynamics*.

Features which do not change in time will be called *constitutive* features. Clearly, all the diagnostic features which characterize a specific taxon are constitutive features; dynamics cannot take us out of a taxon. However, there may be constitutive features which are not diagnostic, that is, which may vary within the taxon. In general, the constitutive features characterize the structure or anatomy of our systems; the nonconstitutive or time-varying features characterize physiology or behavior. A large part of the discussion to follow is concerned with the relation between variability in behavior (that is, in time-varying features) and variability in structure (that is, in constitutive features).

CONSTITUTIVE FEATURES AND DYNAMICS

We have so far partitioned the features of our systems into two classes: constitutive (time-invariant) and nonconstitutive (time-variable). Among the constitutive features, there are two subclasses: those which are diagnostic for our classification (and hence invariant in a taxon) and those which can vary from element to element within a taxon.

Since the diagnostic constitutive features which define our taxon are fixed once and for all, we need not consider them further. Henceforth, then, the term "constitutive feature" will refer to a time-invariant feature which can vary from element to element within the taxon. Further, we shall henceforth refer to a time-varying feature as a *state variable*.

As noted above, constitutive features pertain to structure or anatomy; state variables (time-varying features) pertain to behavior or physiology. Dynamics is concerned with the study of features which change in time; it is important to us because dynamics is the agency through which variability within a taxon can be modified. In turn, the central concept in dynamics is *stability*. In the present section, we shall take up some basic concepts of system dynamics, which will then be applied to the question of variability.

Let us begin with a consideration of autonomous (unforced) dynamical processes. Let us suppose that we are given a particular system in our taxon, and that the constitutive features of this system comprise a set of r fixed numbers $a_1, ..., a_r$. Suppose further that there are n time-varying features, or state variables, denoted by $x_1, ..., x_n$.

At any instant of time t, each of the state variables assumes a definite numerical value; hence at any instant we may say that the system is in the *state* represented by the n numbers $x_1(t), ..., x_n(t)$. The totality of all such n-tuples of numbers constitutes the *state space* of our system. A state of our system is thus represented by a point in the state space. If our system is in a definite state $(x_1(0), ..., x_n(0))$ at an initial instant t = 0, then as time flows, the change of state with time will be represented by a corresponding curve or trajectory in the state space.

Clearly, different initial states (that is, variability in the time-varying features of our system within a taxon) will give rise to different trajectories. Stability (or more accurately, Lyapunov stability) is concerned with the relationships between different trajectories as time increases. Specifically, will two such trajectories approach each other more and more closely as time increases, so that the initial variability is continually diminished? Or will they move further and further apart, so that the initial variability is amplified?

Such questions are approached mathematically as follows. If a quantity x_i (for example, one of our state variables) is changing in time, then it has some rate of change, or velocity; this can be denoted by the time derivative dx_i/dt. This velocity is itself a feature (generally time-varying) of the system. On what does it depend? At any instant of time, this velocity dx_i/dt will surely depend on the state of the system at the same instant. It will also depend on the particular constitutive features of the system. This dependence can be expressed succinctly by writing

$$dx_i/dt = f_i(a_1, ..., a_r, x_1, ..., x_n). \qquad (1)$$

Technically, this is a first-order differential equation. There will be such an equation for each state variable x_i. The resulting set of n first-order simultaneous differential equations comprise the *dynamical laws*, or equations of motion, governing the system. The *solutions* of such a set of equations give explicitly the system trajectories, for any initial state.

Thus, if there are systems in our taxon which share the same structural parameters a_1, ..., a_r, and initially differ only in the state variables x_1, ..., x_n, the time course of variability between these systems is governed by the stability properties of their equations of motion. We cannot of course enter further into technical details here, but it is always in principle possible to tell whether initial variability in the state variables will attenuate in time (stability) or grow in time (instability) from the equations of motion which govern the system.

If there is variability in the constitutive features a_1, ..., a_r, the situation is rather more complicated. To see this, suppose that one system in our taxon is specified by the constitutive parameters (a_1, ..., a_r), while another system is specified by a different set of constitutive parameters (a_1', ..., a_r'). Then the equations of motion for the first system are given by (1), while the equations governing the second system are

$$dx_i/dt = f_i(a_1', ..., a_r', x_1, ..., x_n).$$

The basic question is: what difference in system behavior arises from replacing (a_1, ..., a_r) by (a_1', ..., a_r')?

The study of this question is the province of *structural stability*. In particular, we ask whether the stability properties (that is, the pattern of system trajectories in the state space) of the second system are the same as those of the first system. If so, then the variability of constitutive features we have envisioned is essentially unimportant (that is, the stability properties are robust, or insensitive to such constitutive variability). If not, then this variability can result in essential differences between the behaviors manifested by the two systems. Such a basic change in dynamical behavior in the state variables, arising from constitutive variability, is essentially what is called *bifurcation*; it is presently much studied in a variety of important contexts.

Thus far, we have considered only the free (unforced) autonomous behavior of our systems. We must now consider what happens when we allow our systems to interact with environments which are themselves changing in time. Broadly speaking, this is the province of "control theory."

Technically, to describe the effect of environment on system dynamics, we must make the constitutive features of our system depend on the environmental modalities with which the system interacts. In a sense, then, the effect of an environmental interaction is to change the "anatomy" or structure of our system, and, through this change in anatomy, to affect the behavior of the state variables. Formally, this does not modify our previous discussion very much, because even though our original constitutive features $a_1, ..., a_r$ are now functions of environment, the specific form of these functions will introduce new constitutive features which are now constant. These new constitutive features characterize the "anatomy" of system and environment. From the standpoint of the equations of motion then, the only real change is, in effect, to make the right-hand sides of the relations (1) depend in general on time (through time-dependence of environment) explicitly.

The basic problem of control theory is to manipulate system-environment interactions in such a way that, even though our systems were initially different, they will nevertheless end up behaving similarly (or more specifically, come to a common state). Indeed, the following result can be established for a rather general class of systems: immediately following the establishment of an environmental interaction (that is, a forcing), the system will behave in a relatively irregular manner; this irregular behavior persists for only a limited period and is therefore called *transient*. Subsequently, the behavior comes to resemble the environmental forcing more and more closely (*steady-state* behavior). The transient period is governed primarily by the autonomous dynamics of the system (and hence ultimately by its constitutive parameters), while the steady-state behavior depends primarily on the environment. Thus, if the systems in our taxon are of such a character, variability between them can ultimately be reduced by coupling them to a common environment and waiting for the transients to disappear; intuitively, all the systems will then ultimately track the common environment, and hence behave more and more alike. (We must note, however, that the time required for the transients to disappear in a system also depends on its constitutive features).

The reverse side of this coin, of course, is that systems which are not initially different may become so through interactions with distinct environments.

VARIABILITY AND THE "REIFICATION" OF A TAXON

As we have seen, the establishment of a classification procedure creates specific taxa, and at the same time renders meaningful the concept of variability for all nondiagnostic features within a taxon. Thus, variability is a property of a *taxon*, that is, of a *set* of elements or systems. It is not yet related to a property or feature of the constituent elements in the taxon.

It is generally awkward to handle sets of things, primarily because what we observe are not the sets (these are intellectual constructs) but rather the individual elements. One way to eliminate such problems is to "reify" a set, that is, to represent it by a specific member. The question is then: how may we reify a taxon? How shall we choose a representative which will serve to embody the taxon as a whole? And, once having chosen such a reification, how shall we utilize it?

There are in effect two completely different ways in which a taxon might be reified. The first way might be called *reification through optimization*. Basically, the procedure here is to choose some nondiagnostic feature of the elements in our taxon, and look at the set of values which the feature assumes on the individual elements in the taxon. This is a set of numbers, and as such it may have a maximum (and/or a minimum). We can then choose the element of the taxon on which the maximum (or minimum) is actually attained.

This kind of procedure has been exceedingly important in mathematics, science, and technology. In mathematics, it is the basis of most "canonical form" theorems, in which an element is chosen from an equivalence class on the grounds of "maximum simplicity." For instance, in linear algebra, the Jordan Canonical Form (which represents a set of similar matrices) is the one with the smallest number of non-zero entries. In the sciences, a special status is usually accorded such representatives, in tacit accordance with the principle that the "laws of nature" generate or characterize structures which are in some sense optimal (that is, maximize or minimize something). And in technology, of course, we always strive to accomplish our goals or tasks in the most efficient, effective way.

The main difficulty with reifying a taxon through considerations of optimality is in justifying the choice of a particular feature to optimize over. Clearly, different choices will generally result in different representatives. However, let us explicitly observe that, however the choice is made, the reification will always be a member of the taxon.

The other reification procedure we wish to consider is *reification through averaging*. As before, we may begin with the set of values assumed by some feature on the elements of our taxon. However, instead of *choosing* the biggest (or smallest), we *construct* a new number, through an averaging process. In a certain sense, this number is the *mean value* which the feature in question assumes *on the taxon*. We notice explicitly that this mean value need not belong to the set of numbers of which it is the mean, that is, there need be no element in the taxon on which the feature in question actually assumes the mean value.

If we form such a mean value for *every* feature, we have in effect created a new member of our taxon, such that the value of any feature on this new member is the mean value of the feature over the entire taxon. We can choose this "mean" or "average" element, then, as the reification or representative of the taxon as a whole. The main difficulty with this procedure is that the representative we have constructed is *fictitious*; it does not exist, and very often *could* not exist. Moreover, unlike reifications based on optimality, there are no connotations of "best" or "simplest" to be associated with it. It merely provides a standard which is often convenient for discussing variability in a taxon. Unfortunately, such fictitious reifications are sometimes treated as if they were also optimal; this is a mistake which can cause no end of trouble.

Despite this, what we may call the *mean reification* of a taxon has been important in a number of different contexts. For one thing, it provides a convenient basis for talking about variability within the taxon. Specifically, given any particular feature, we may characterize the manner in which its values in the taxon are distributed about the mean value. The result is a set of numbers, which are of great practical importance because, among other things, they constitute *an alternate definition of the taxon itself*. As we noted above, the actual diagnostic features which characterize the taxon are often difficult to characterize, whereas the mean values and deviations of nondiagnostic features have a tantalizing concreteness about them. In this sense, mean reifications dominate practical taxonomy.

The properties of a mean reification are also generally utilized as indicators for how an arbitrary element of a taxon will behave in a given set of circumstances. However, as we shall see later, this can give rise to serious errors in dynamical situations.

Variability: The Biological Situation

THE THEORY OF EVOLUTION AND NATURAL SELECTION

Organisms may be studied in at least four distinct but interrelated ways: we may study their structure (anatomy) and their functions (physiology or behavior); we may also study their development (ontogeny) and their evolution (phylogeny). Anatomy and physiology study what organisms are like; development and evolution are concerned with how they got to be that way, and are characteristic of biology. More specifically, development is concerned with the personal history of individual organisms from their conception; evolution deals with the continuity of life, ultimately from its origin on the planet.

The theory of evolution has been the nucleating center around which most of modern biology has crystallized. In a sense, evolution is a necessity of thought; either life evolves or it does not. In this sense, evolution was already discussed by the Greeks. The monumental taxonomy of Linnaeus, to which we have already referred, was also most suggestive for it revealed an inherent gradient of complexity in the biosphere which could hardly be accidental. It was Darwin's great contribution to propose, and to document, a specific mechanism by which evolution could occur; he called this mechanism "natural selection."

Natural selection rests on two simple observations, both concerned with reproduction, that is, with the relation of offspring to parents. The first is that organisms tend to be like their parents. The second is that offspring are not identical with their parents (or with each other). Both of these conditions are essential for Darwinian evolution. From the second of them, we may expect that the postulated sibling variability will be translated into a differential ability to cope with the exigencies of life, and ultimately into a differential ability to leave offspring to populate the next generation. This differential ability to propagate is essentially what is meant by *fitness*. Thus, fit organisms leave progeny; unfit ones do not. Moreover, the first condition implies that the offspring of fit organisms will themselves tend to be fit. Natural selection thus envisages a continual enrichment of a population with fit organisms; over time, this enrichment constitutes evolution.

The theory of evolution thus from the outset directed attention at the hereditary mechanism, which is at the heart of natural selection. This very soon led to a rediscovery and amplification of Mendel's basic work on genetics, and subsequently to the two great syntheses of modern biology: (a) the identification of the Mendelian "linkage groups" of genes with the anatomical structures called chromosomes in the nuclei of cells, and (b) the coalescence with biochemistry (that is, with cellular physiology) which is nowadays called molecular biology.

In a nutshell, the present picture of the hereditary mechanism is as follows. The genes or hereditary factors of Mendel are to be regarded as chemical patterns in specific molecules (DNA). These patterns are then translated into other materials (proteins or enzymes) which determine the specific chemistry of individual cells (that is, they determine what reactions shall occur, and how fast they shall proceed). Since what happens in an individual cell also determines how that cell will interact with others, we can envisage this intracellular picture of genetic control modulating the intercellular interactions which characterize an entire multicellular organism.

However, it should be pointed out that the mechanism by which genes control gross features of multicellular organisms remains completely obscure. Indeed, the step from biochemistry to morphology (anatomy) and behavior is an exceedingly slippery one. The best that can be said is this: presumably, gross features (such as five fingers) are the result of many individual genes working in concert, each gene responsible for modulating one chemical reaction rate.

GENETIC VARIABILITY

As we have seen, genetic variability is in some sense the raw material on which natural selection, and hence Darwinian evolution, works. Let us therefore consider some of the sources of genetic variability.

One way to introduce genetic variability is through a reshuffling of genes which already exist. The details of sexual reproduction guarantee that such reshuffling will occur on a grand scale. For one thing, in sexual reproduction, half the offspring's chromosomes come from one parent; half from the other. There are generally many parental chromosomes, and which one comes from which parent is random. A simple computation will reveal that, just on this basis alone, the number of chromosomally different possible offspring of two parents in a species with twenty chromosomes is astronomical. Thus the simplest sexual mechanisms guarantee unlimited variability, and there are many variations of the basic mechanism which increase it by still further orders of magnitude.

In addition to the simple reshuffling of whole chromosomes which is built into sexual reproduction, there are also internal reshuffling mechanisms which redistribute the genes, both between and within chromosomes. For instance, there are crossing-over mechanisms, through which entire chromosomal segments are interchanged between sister chromosomes. There are inversion mechanisms, through which a piece of chromosome can be turned upside down relative to the rest of the chromosome. There are deletions, duplications, translocations, and a host of other mechanisms which are continually re-stirring the genetic pot, even without adding or taking away anything.

In addition to these reshuffling mechanisms, which reorganize what is already present, there are other mechanisms which constantly create new genes. In general, such mechanisms are called *mutations*.

Mutations may occur in any cell, but for evolutionary purposes, the only important ones are those which occur in the germ cells; only these are passed to the next generation. In simplest terms, a mutation constitutes a permanent alteration of the chemical pattern in DNA which is the seat of the "genetic information." Such mutations may arise through specific external agents, such as chemical mutagens or ionizing radiation, or they may occur autonomously, because the replication mechanism for "copying" DNA is itself not perfect.

Thus, already at the most elementary genetic level, there is endless variability, and therefore unlimited material on which natural selection may work. And it should be noted that the variability we have discussed is generated autonomously, without any overt environmental intervention. We shall now see what happens when environmental variation is superimposed on this autonomous variability.

EPIGENETIC VARIABILITY

Astrologers tell us that the stars impel; they do not compel. Much the same is true of the genes, at least within wide limits. For instance, the basic facts of developmental biology immediately reveal the dependence of the genome on external influences.

We have seen that according to the present picture, genetic information is expressed intercellularly; the genes within the nucleus of each cell directly affect only the chemistry of that cell. On the other hand, the cells in a multicellular organism constitute a *clone*; they are all derived from a common cell (the zygote, or fertilized egg) through a genetically conservative process of cell division. Thus, all these cells must have the same genes. Nevertheless, they can all be very different from one another. There is not much in common between a nerve cell, a gland cell, and a muscle cell; individually, they seem as different from one another as Amoeba is from Paramecium.

How is it that cells with the same genes can be so different (or so variable)? The answer must lie in *differential gene expression*; not all the genes in a cell are "on" all the time, and different cell types must correspond to different sets of genes being "on." Thus the genes themselves are under control, and at least part of this control must be modulated by the environment with which the cell interacts.

This same phenomenon can already be seen even in simple cells like bacteria. If two genetically identical bacterial cells are placed in chemically different media, the cells will become biochemically different from each other; each will manifest only those enzymes necessary to metabolize the nutrients in its particular medium. This is called *bacterial adaptation*, and it clearly shows that the expression of genes in a cell can be modulated by relatively simple environmental influences. Bacterial adaptation differs from differentiation in multicellular organisms in a number of ways (for instance, it is generally readily reversible, while differentiation generally is not), but closer investigation shows that in all cases the genes in a cell behave like a network of interacting on-off switches, very much like the neurons in the brain, and hence can exhibit relatively complicated behavioral phenomena like recognition, learning, and memory. Thus, such a genetic network must be to some extent plastic, and its properties can be shaped by environmental interactions, that is, by experience. Those properties of cells, and of cell populations, which are determined by influences outside the genome proper are collectively called *epigenetic*.

Epigenetic variability can be extremely important. For instance, it is clearly impossible for the detailed "wiring" of the neurons in the central nervous sytem to be precisely specified in the genes. Although strong biases are present which prevent gross aberrations, nevertheless the detailed neural patterns, like fingerprints, must necessarily vary from individual to individual, even if they are genetically identical (for example, identical twins). Indeed, there is strong evidence that, at least in sensory systems, the ultimate synaptic architecture is determined by environmental interactions after birth. Similar phenomena must also occur in the cortex, in connection with behavioral phenomena like learning, conditioning, short- and long-term memory, and the like, though here we begin to impinge on psychological matters.

In any case, we can conclude that epigenetic variability is as universal as genetic variability, and is at least as important in shaping the properties of individual organisms.

Forces Suppressing Variability

We have seen in the foregoing sections that there are powerful forces operating in biology which generate variability, both at the genetic and the epigenetic levels. In the present section, we are going to consider various countervailing forces which serve to limit variability. The phenomena which are actually observed in the biosphere can be thought of as arising from the interplay of those mechanisms which generate variability, and those which suppress it.

In general, the forces which act to suppress variability fall into two main classes: (a) autonomous homeostatic mechanisms, governed by concepts of stability, and (b) selection, in which the environment plays a central role. As we shall see, both of these forces are essential for an understanding of *adaptation*, a concept which, in various guises, dominates the fields of physiology, of evolution, and of learning. The present section is thus devoted to a fuller discussion of them.

HOMEOSTASIS AND STABILITY

Long ago, Claude Bernard suggested that physiology should be understood as the maintenance of the "constancy of the milieu interieur." A generation later, similar sentiments were enunciated by Walter Cannon, who coined the term "homeostasis." Starting in the 1940s, experience with control of mechanical devices culminated with the development of cybernetics and the deep study of feedback regulation.

Homeostasis is by definition the maintenance of some system quality which would ordinarily vary (for example, with changes in the environment) at a constant value. A typical homeostatic device is the familiar thermostatic regulation of room temperature in the face of ambient temperature fluctuation (and also the cognate regulation of body temperature in warm-blooded animals).

Clearly, homeostasis and stability are closely related. As we have seen, stability can be regarded as the insensitivity of a system trajectory to initial conditions, or alternatively, the resistance of system behavior to perturbations. In principle, any system can be turned into a homeostat; any system behavior can be stabilized by attaching to it an appropriate "controller."

Much of biology is dominated by ideas of stability. For instance, the stubborn independence of developmental phenomena from environmental perturbations, and the capacity of many organisms to regenerate lost parts, seemed for a long time to resist conventional mechanistic explanations, until it was recognized in the 1930s that this kind of behavior was typical of any dynamical system approaching a stable steady state. In such a case, the system dynamics guarantees that the same steady state will be reached regardless (within limits) of initial conditions, and further, that the steady state once reached will automatically resist further perturbation, that is, will behave homeostatically.

It is further true that homeostasis in a physiological system is closely related to the concept of *adaptation*. To make this clear, let us return for a moment to the control of room temperature by means of a thermostat. Typically, when the room temperature starts to change, the thermostat correspondingly manipulates the furnace dampers so as to bring the room temperature back to the setpoint. The room temperature remains thereby constant; this is the homeostatic aspect. However, the furnace dampers *move*; this is the adaptive aspect. In other words, if we watch the room temperature, we see homeostasis; if we watch the dampers, we see *adaptation*.

This example illustrates a general point; any homeostat exhibits adaptive features, and any adaptation has a homeostatic aspect. Consider, for example, one of the most thoroughly studied of such physiological mechanisms, the pupillary homeostat. This is the means whereby a constant flux of light is maintained on the retina, independent of the ambient light. Stated simply, in dim light the iris of the eye opens, while in bright light it contracts. The system is a homeostat because a certain physiological characteristic is being maintained constant. It is also an adaptive mechanism, which enables the organism to function in a wide variety of ambient conditions. If we look merely at the irises of organisms in the dark and in the light, they will appear to be in different states; this difference constitutes their "states of adaptation" to their respective environments.

Adaptation is thus a subtle concept, which can only be properly understood by taking a relatively holistic or global view. For instance, a tree growing at timberline will appear *deformed* compared to one growing at lower elevations, just as the iris of a dark-adapted individual will appear deformed compared to that of one in the light. However, in both cases, the "deformation" is to be understood as part of a larger homeostatic mechanism in which the environment, and the system-environment dynamics, must be taken into account.

In simple terms, stability, homeostasis, and adaptation are merely different ways of describing the autonomous dynamical mechanisms employed by organisms to cope with the environmental variability.

SELECTION MECHANISMS AND VARIABILITY

We have seen above that natural selection operates by exploiting genetic variability. Let us look more closely at what this entails.

To do this, we must draw a fundamental distinction between the *genotype* of an organism and its corresponding *phenotype*. Genotype pertains to the actual set of genes possessed by the organism; phenotype pertains to its visible anatomical and physiological characteristics. The two are vastly different, and the relation between them is exceedingly subtle and difficult. The genotype is, as we have seen, a set of chemical patterns in certain molecules, and it is this set of patterns which is transmitted from generation to generation. The phenotype, on the other hand, is the sum total of substantial qualities and behaviors which we perceive when looking at an organism.

The capability of coping effectively with environmental exigencies, and hence the capability of populating the next generation, comprise the essence of fitness. As such, fitness is a property of phenotypes. The effect of being unfit, however, is an effect on genotypes; the inability to reproduce effectively means that one's genes are effectively removed from the "gene pool." Thus, natural selection indirectly imposes a dynamics on genotypes, through the fitnesses of the corresponding phenotypes, and the effects of fitness on the "gene pool" from generation to generation.

If selection is strong (that is, if a "small" change of genotype produces a large change in fitness) then selection provides an extremely effective means for eliminating variability. Indeed, we may go so far as to *define* the pressure of selection on a phenotypic quality by the amount of variability it displays. Under conditions of strong selection pressure, furthermore, the resulting phenotype must in some relatively straightforward sense be *better* than its alternatives; in this way, strong selection is a way of generating structures or behaviors which are *optimal*.

Of course, each particular kind of environment, or "environmental niche," will generate its own kind of selection pressure on the organisms inhabiting it, and hence the sense in which "optimality" is to be understood will be different from niche to niche. Thus, an organism optimal with respect to one kind of niche will be phenotypically different from one optimal with respect to another niche. The perceptible differences between them constitute the specific *adaptations* of these organisms to the environmental characteristics of their respective niches. Thus, when selection pressure is strong, natural selection simultaneously (a) reduces variability, (b) generates optimal structures, (c) generates adaptations.

In effect, natural selection acts by punishing unfit organisms (by preventing or limiting their reproduction) and rewarding fit ones (by facilitating their reproduction). It is for this reason that there is an extremely close relation between the literature on evolution and that on learning, especially the literature on operant learning and conditioning. Furthermore, the relation of population genetics (that is, the study of the dynamics of "gene pools") to evolution is essentially identical to the relation between neurobiological models of learning and learning psychology.

We may also remark that, although the *mechanisms* by which adaptations are generated in physiology and in evolution are quite different, their formal properties are in all other respects similar. It is this formal similarity which justifies our use of the same word "adaptation" in such widely different contexts.

Dynamical Aspects of Variability

Let us briefly recapitulate the basic points of our discussion so far, and then draw some basic conclusions from them regarding variability and its consequences.

We have defined variability as the perceptible differences between elements or systems previously classified into a common taxon. We have agreed that these perceptible differences take the form of different numerical values assigned to specific features of our elements.

We have further subdivided these features into two subclasses: those that vary in time, and those which do not. The time-varying features are the state variables, and their time-variation constitutes behavior or physiology. The variables which are fixed in time, on the other hand, represent structure or anatomy.

We have also seen that, in biological systems, there are a number of different forces which serve to generate or amplify variability, and for each of these, there are corresponding countervailing forces which limit or attenuate variability. Thus, variability is itself a dynamical quality, but it is a quality of the taxon, and not of the individual systems in the taxon.

The forces which cause variability to grow in biological systems are:

a. Randomizing mechanisms, such as those arising from independent segregation of chromosomes during reproduction, the reshuffling of genes within and between chromosomes, and the introduction of new genes through mutation.

b. Instabilities in system dynamics, which amplify variability of initial conditions in autonomous dynamical processes.

c. Coupling to distinct or heterogeneous environmental forcings.

The countervailing forces are, respectively,

a′. Selection, which offsets genetic randomizing mechanisms through differential phenotypic fitnesses in particular environments.

b′. Stabilization, including homeostasis, which eliminates variability of state variables.

c′. Coupling to common or homogeneous environments, which (after the transients have disappeared) entrains or establishes convergence in the systems so coupled.

Except for the forces of randomization and selection, which rely essentially on the uniquely biological phenomena of reproduction, these remarks are perfectly general, and apply to any class of systems.

The actual time course of variability in a taxon is determined by the specific interplay between those forces which generate variability and those which limit it. Although a detailed study of variability from this point of view seems to present no specific conceptual problems, as far as the author is aware there have been no studies of variability *per se* from this point of view. Of course, taxonomists and evolutionary biologists have, from their various standpoints, been much concerned with variability, but in most areas of experimental biology it is regarded mainly as a nuisance, to be eliminated by stringent selection procedures before beginning an experiment. Only one author, Walter Elsasser, has treated variability from a more fundamental point of view; indeed, he elevates it to a fundamental status in drawing a distinction between biological and physical systems.[2] However, even here, Elsasser takes biological variability as a basic fact, and does not study the forces through which it is modulated.

Even without such a detailed study, we can already begin to draw some important conclusions from the qualitative analysis we have developed above. For present purposes, perhaps the most significant of them is the following: in situations dominated by autonomous stability, or by a commonality of coupling to a specific environment, initial variability of structure (anatomy) or function (physiology) cannot play a significant role, at least in the long run. For in these situations, initial variability will manifest itself entirely in the transients, and not in the long-term or steady state behavior. Of course, this conclusion must be qualified by an ability to estimate how long it will take for the transients to disappear (and this will vary from system to system); in specific situations, the transient time may be too long for practical purposes, and the systems will behave as if they were unstable. In such cases, and in situations dominated by instability, variability will be the essential feature, and unless opposed by the introduction of new countervailing forces, any initial variability will amplify as time passes.

Aside from purely empirical approaches, the general study of variability can be approached purely formally (that is, mathematically), or through the interrogation of suitably chosen model systems. For instance, a source of potentially useful model systems for the study of relationships between individual variability and education might be found in the general area of "artificial intelligence," particularly in connection with the "training" of machines like the perceptrons to recognize patterns. These are very like operant learning situations (and hence also closely akin to more general problems of adaptation in physiology and evolution). Although these machines have been studied for decades, most of the emphasis has involved the training algorithms, and the characterization of classes of patterns which such machines can recognize. To my knowledge there has not been a detailed study of the relation between initial architecture and subsequent training behavior.

It seems that there is much insight to be gained through pursuit of studies of these kinds. Without such insight, the specific relationships between variability and behavior can only remain an arena for speculation and acrimony.

FOOTNOTES

1. Although a justification of this assertion would be far beyond the scope of this chapter, those interested in details may consult Robert Rosen, *Fundamentals of Measurement and the Representation of Natural Systems* (New York: Elsevier, 1977).

2. Walter Elsasser, *The Chief Abstractions of Biology* (New York: Elsevier, 1975).

Part Two
THE COMMON CURRICULUM

CHAPTER VI

A Common Curriculum for Mathematics

THOMAS A. ROMBERG

Deliberate teaching requires choices as to what to teach.

Herbert Kliebard
Curriculum Inquiry 6 (1977)

Some mathematics should be taught to all students, but an adequate presentation of a "common curriculum" for mathematics cannot consist of a list of topics to be covered, however extensive and carefully prepared. I use the word "curriculum" as a course of study, its contents, and its organization, and my task in this chapter is to consider four questions which shape an outline for a common curriculum for mathematics. The questions to be examined are:

1. What does it mean to know mathematics?

2. Who decides on the mathematical tasks for students and for what reasons?

3. What should be the principles from which a common curriculum can be built?

4. For this yearbook, how should individual differences be considered?

What Does It Mean to Know Mathematics?

This question is not easily answered. When nonmathematicians, such as sociologists, psychologists, and even curriculum developers

---

Jeremy Kilpatrick served as the editorial consultant for this chapter.

The research reported in this paper was funded by the Wisconsin Center for Education Research, which is supported in part by a grant from the National Institute of Education. The opinions expressed in this paper do not necessarily reflect the position, policy, or endorsement of the National Institute of Education.

look at mathematics, what they often see is a static and bounded discipline. This is perhaps a reflection of the mathematics they studied in school or college rather than a sure insight into the discipline itself. John Dewey's distinction between "knowledge" and "the record of knowledge" may clarify this point.[1] For many, "to know" means to identify the artifacts of a discipline (its record). For me and many others, "to know" mathematics is "to do" mathematics.

Mathematics viewed as a "record of knowledge" has grown to be a stupendous amount of subject matter. The largest branch builds on what collectively is called the real number system, which includes the ordinary whole numbers, fractions, and the irrational numbers. Arithmetic, algebra, elementary functions, the calculus, differential equations, and other subjects that follow the calculus are all developments of the real number system. Similarly, projective geometry and the several non-Euclidean geometries are branches of mathematics, as are various other arithmetics and their algebras. Unfortunately, this massive "record of knowledge, independent of its place as an outcome of inquiry and a resource in further inquiry, is taken to be knowledge."[2]

The distinction between knowledge and the record of knowledge is crucial. A person gathers, discovers, or creates knowledge in the course of some activity having a purpose: this active process is not the same as the absorption of the record of knowledge—the fruits of past activities. When the record of knowledge is mistakenly taken to be knowledge, the acquisition of information becomes an end in itself, and the student spends his time absorbing what other people have done, rather than having experiences of his own. The student is treated as a "piece of registering apparatus," which stores up information isolated from action and purpose.[3] I do not assert that informational knowledge has no value. Information has value indeed to the extent that it is needed in the course of some activity having a purpose, and to the extent that it furthers the course of the activity. "Informational knowledge" is material that can be fallen back upon as given, settled, established, assured in a doubtful situation. Clearly, the concepts and processes from some branches of mathematics should be known by all students. The emphasis of instruction, however, should be on "knowing how" rather than "knowing what," even though in my description of a common curriculum for mathematics I shall refer to some of the concepts and procedures (the "what") of mathematics.

To appreciate what it means "to do" mathematics, one must recognize that mathematicians argue among themselves about what mathematics is acceptable, what methods of proof are to be countenanced, and so forth. Doing mathematics cannot be viewed as a mechanical performance, or an activity that individuals engage in by solely following predetermined rules. In this light, mathematical activity can be seen more as embodying the elements of an art or craft than as a purely technical discipline. This is not to say that mathematicians are free to do anything that comes to mind. As in all crafts, there will be agreement, in a broad sense, about what procedures are to be followed and what is to be countenanced as acceptable work. These agreements arise from the day-to-day intercourse among mathematicians. Thus, a mathematician engages in mathematics as a member of a learned community that creates the context in which the individual mathematician works. The members of that community have a shared way of "seeing" mathematical activity. Their mutual discourse will reinforce preferred forms and a sense of appropriateness, of elegance, of acceptable conceptual structures.[4] Furthermore, the community promotes and reinforces its own standards of acceptable work, and, as Hagstrom suggests, a major characteristic of a mathematical/scientific community is the continued evolution of its standards.[5] Not only does the range of acceptable methods vary, but in mathematics especially the standards of rigor have themselves been subject to continued modification and refinement, a point well illustrated by Bell:

How did the master analysts of the eighteenth century—the Bernoullies, Euler, Lagrange, Laplace—contrive to get consistently right results in by far the greater part of their work in both pure and applied mathematics? What these great mathematicians mistook for valid reasoning at the very beginning of the calculus is now universally regarded as unsound.[6]

Nor did Bell have the last word, for during the 1970s, mathematical logicians such as Robinson[7] and Keisler[8] found a way to make rigorous the intuitively attractive infinitesimal calculus that was developed by Newton and Leibniz and extended by those master analysts to whom Bell refers.

Given this perspective—to know mathematics is to do mathematics within a craft—what are its essential activities? Even with a superficial knowledge about mathematics, it is easy to recognize four related activities common to all of mathematics: abstracting, inventing, proving, and applying.

ABSTRACTING

The abstractness of mathematics is easy to see. We operate with abstract numbers without worrying about how to relate them in each case to concrete objects. In school, we study the abstract multiplication table—a table for multiplying one abstract number by another, not a number of boys by the number of apples each has, or a number of apples by the price of an apple. Similarly, in geometry we consider, for example, straight lines and not stretched threads—the concept of a geometric line being obtained by abstraction from all the properties of actual objects except their spatial form and dimensions. Thus, the basic concepts of the elementary branches of mathematics are abstractions from experience. Whole numbers and fractions were certainly suggested originally by obvious physical counterparts. But many concepts have been invented that are not closely tied to experience. Irrational numbers such as the square root of 2 were invented to represent lengths occurring in Euclidean geometry—for example, the length of the hypotenuse of a right triangle whose arms are both one unit long. The notion of a negative number, though perhaps suggested by the need to distinguish debits from credits, was nevertheless not wholly derived from experience. Mathematicians had to create an entirely new type of number to which operations such as addition, multiplication, and the like could be applied. The notion of a variable to represent the quantitative values of some changing physical phenomenon, such as temperature or time, goes beyond the mere observation of change. The farther one proceeds with the mathematics, the more remote from experience are the concepts introduced and the larger is the creative role played by mathematicians.

This process of abstracting is characteristic of each branch of mathematics. The concept of a whole number and of a geometric figure are only two of the earliest and most elementary concepts of mathematics. They have been followed by a mass of others, too numerous to describe, extending to such abstractions as complex numbers, functions, integrals, differentials, functionals, n-dimensional spaces, infinite-dimensional spaces, and so forth. These abstractions, piled as it were on one another, have reached such a degree of generalization that they have apparently lost all connection with daily life, and the "ordinary mortal" understands nothing about them beyond the mere fact that "all this is incomprehensible." In reality, of course, such is not at all the case. Although the concept of n-dimensional space is no doubt extremely abstract, it does have a completely real content, which is not difficult to understand.

Some mathematical abstractions have become so important that their absorption by students is taken as evidence of knowing mathematics. To illustrate, consider two types of abstractions: procedures and concepts. Procedural knowledge involves acquiring solution routines for a series of problems in a specific domain (for example, adding whole numbers, solving linear equations). Conceptual knowledge involves learning the labels used to name objects, relationships, procedures, and so forth (for example, "six" for the numerosity of a particular set, "parallel" for certain lines or planes). Some procedures and concepts from the record of mathematical knowledge should be learned by all students. However, they should acquire the knowledge through activities that give it meaning. The concepts and procedures should be formed under conditions where thought is necessary, rather than simply by means of routine and repetition.

But abstraction is not the exclusive property of mathematics; it is characteristic of every science, even of all mental activity in general. Consequently, the abstractness of mathematical concepts does not in itself give a complete description of the peculiar character of mathematics. The abstractions of mathematics are distinguished by three features. In the first place, they deal above all else with quantitative relations and spatial forms, abstracting them from all other properties of objects. Second, they occur in a sequence of increasing degrees of abstraction, going very much further in this direction than the abstractions of other sciences. In fact, it is common for branches of mathematics to feed on each other, yielding ever more abstract notions. Finally, mathematics as such moves almost wholly in the field of abstract concepts and their interrelations. While the natural scientist turns constantly to experiment for proof of his assertions, the mathematician employs only argument.

INVENTING

I have chosen "inventing" rather than "discovering" to describe this aspect of what mathematicians do even though for this chapter the distinction between the terms is not important. Discovery involves a law or relationship that already exists, but has not been perceived. Inventing involves creating a law or relationship. There are two aspects to all mathematical inventions: the conjecture (or guess) about a relationship, followed by the demonstration of the logical validity of that assertion. All mathematical ideas—even new abstractions—are inventions (like irrational numbers). Also, to assist them in the invention of their abstractions mathematicians make constant use of theorems, mathematical models, methods, and physical analogues, and they have recourse to various completely concrete examples. These examples often serve as the actual source of the invention.

However, for students who are learning mathematics, "discovering" relationships which lead to abstractions, theorems, models, and so forth, known to the mathematical community but not to the student, can serve the same purpose. In this regard, instructional activities that require "problem solving" can give students an opportunity to experience inventing. I am hesitant to use the term "problem solving" since it has become a popular catchword in mathematics education with many meanings.[9] I use it here to describe instructional activities that have three implied parts: (a) a complex task is to be solved whose solution is not intended to be obvious; (b) the concepts and procedures needed to solve the task are known by the student; and (c) the "problem" is to find a strategy (or heuristic) that can be used to connect the known ideas with the unknown. Such problem-solving activities are important, for only by this means can the variety of strategies (heuristics) common to the craft of mathematics be learned.[10]

PROVING

No proposition is considered as a mathematical product until it has been rigorously proved by a logical argument. If a geometer, reporting a newly invented theorem, were to demonstrate it by means of models and to confine himself to such a demonstration, no mathematician would admit that the theorem had been proved. The demand for a proof of a theorem is well known in high school geometry, but it pervades the whole of mathematics. We could measure the angles at the base of a thousand isosceles triangles with extreme accuracy, but such a procedure would never provide us with a mathematical proof of the theorem that the base angles of an isosceles triangle are congruent. Mathematics demands that this result be deduced from the fundamental concepts of geometry, which are precisely formulated in the axioms. And so it is in every case. To prove a theorem means for the mathematician to deduce it by a logical argument from the fundamental properties of the concepts related to that theorem. In this way, not only the concepts but also the methods of mathematics are abstract and theoretical.

The results of mathematics are distinguished by a high degree of logical rigor, and a mathematical argument is conducted with such scrupulousness as to make it incontestable and completely convincing to anyone who understands it. Mathematical truths are, in fact, the prototype of the completely incontestable. Not for nothing do people say "as clear as two and two are four." Here the relation "two and two are four" is introduced as the very image of the irrefutable and incontestable. But the rigor of mathematics is not absolute; it is in a process of continual development. The principles of mathematics have not congealed once and for all, but have a life of their own and may even be the subject of scientific quarrels. Furthermore, proving should not be seen as being independent of invention. As Lakatos has argued:

Mathematics does not grow through a monotonous increase of the number of indubitably established theorems but through the incessant improvement of guesses by speculation and criticism, by the logic of proofs and refutations.[11]

For example, non-Euclidean geometries were invented as a result of attempting to prove Euclid's fifth postulate.

Unfortunately, there is one problem associated with proofs in mathematics. The writings of mathematicians (recorded mathematics) often give a misleading view of their work. The process of invention is ignored in most published articles since only the proof of an assertion is usually presented.

APPLYING

In the final analysis, the importance of mathematics arises from the fact that its abstractions and theorems, for all their abstractness, originate in the actual world and find widely varied applications in the other sciences, in engineering, and in all the practical affairs of daily life; to realize this is a most important prerequisite for understanding mathematics. The exceptional breadth of its applications is another characteristic feature of mathematics. In the first place, we make constant use, almost every hour, in industry and in private and social life, of the most varied concepts and results of mathematics, without thinking about them at all. For example, we use arithmetic to compute our expenses or geometry to describe the floor plan of an apartment. Of course, the procedures or concepts here are very simple, but we should remember that in some period of antiquity, they represented the most advanced mathematical achievements of the age. Second, modern technology would be impossible without mathematics. Scarcely any technical process could be carried through without building an abstract mathematical model as a basis for carrying out a sequence of more or less complicated calculations; and mathematics plays a very important role in the development of new branches of technology. Finally, it is true that every science, to a greater or lesser degree, makes essential use of mathematics. The "exact sciences"—mechanics, astronomy, physics, and to a great extent chemistry—express their laws by means of abstract mathematical formulations and make extensive use of mathematical apparatus in developing their theories. The progress of these sciences would have been completely impossible without mathematics. For this reason, the requirements of mechanics, astronomy, and physics have always exercised a direct and decisive influence on the development of mathematics. In other sciences, mathematics plays a smaller role, but here too, it finds important applications. Of course, in the study of such complicated phenomena as occur in biology and sociology, the mathematical method cannot play the same role as, let us say, in physics. In all cases, but especially where the phenomena are most complicated, one must bear in mind, if one is not to lose the way in meaningless play with symbols, that the application of mathematics is significant only if the concrete phenomena have already been made the subject of a profound theory. In one way or another, abstract mathematics is applied in almost every science, from mechanics to political economy.

AN EXAMPLE: DISTANCE

To illustrate these four aspects of "doing" mathematics, let us examine the idea of distance.[12] By considering different examples of distance, it is possible to formulate concepts and procedures to solve various problems concerning the "shortest" path between two points on a surface, the geometric properties of multidimensional spaces, methods of "noise" reduction in the coding of information, and so forth.

Every child is familiar with problems of "how far" apart two or more sites happen to be. For instance, how far it is from home to school, or from home to a grandparent's house? Answers to such "how far apart?" questions inevitably vary—three blocks, two hours by car, and so forth, depending on the context. Also, there may be more than one answer to any one problem. For example, the distance by car between two points (home and grandmother's) may differ from the distance by train. Despite the differences, it is evident that all meanings taken on by the word *distance* have something in common. The first task for the mathematician is to abstract from the spatial-temporal facts about the world the fundamental properties of each of the different meanings for distance. There are three basic properties: (a) there exist two (or more) fixed points in space; (b) there is at least one "path" joining two points that is interesting (such as: shortest, requires the least effort); and (c) a measure of "how far apart" the two points are can be found.

The next problem for the mathematician is to invent a measuring procedure for some of the more interesting paths. One usually begins such investigations with the easiest cases and then goes to more complex cases. The simplest case for distance is between two points (say, M and N) on a plane surface. The simplest interesting path is the shortest path, which can be represented by a straight line, and the simplest measure is length. In fact, in practice then one uses an instrument (for example, a ruler) to estimate the length. However, in many situations, using a ruler is impractical, as in finding the height of a tall tree or the distance across a lake.[13] Also, since different lengths require different instruments, which have varying degrees of precision (but always involve some error), a more general procedure is needed.[14]

The next step for mathematicians is to define distance operationally in terms of a rule for the set of all points on a plane. If we characterize each point by an ordered pair of coordinates, say $M = (m_1, m_2)$ and $N = (n_1, n_2)$, then from the Pythagorean theorem we can develop the closed algebraic formula for the shortest distance (d) between M and N:

$$d(M,N) = [(m_1 - n_1)^2 + (m_2 - n_2)^2]^{1/2}$$

This formula then can be used as a definition of distance between any two points on a plane.

In the same manner, we can characterize the distance between two points P and Q in three dimensions in terms of an ordered triple of coordinates, $P = (p_1, p_2, p_3)$ and $Q = (q_1, q_2, q_3)$, so that:

$$d(P,Q) = [(p_1 - q_1)^2 + (p_2 - q_2)^2 + (p_3 - q_3)^2]^{1/2}$$

Although one can readily understand the properties of two or three dimensional distance, mathematicians do not hesitate to abstract beyond our temporal space to consider by analogy the distance between two points in an n-dimensional space. Thus, two points, R and S, in n-dimensions can each be represented by an ordered n-tuple of coordinates, $R = (r_1, r_2, ..., r_n)$ and $S = (s_1, s_2, ..., s_n)$ so that

$$d(R,S) = [(r_1 - s_1)^2 + (r_2 - s_2)^2 + ...(r_n - s_n)^2]^{1/2}$$

Finally, let us examine distance on a different surface; for example, the shortest distance on the earth's surface between two points, such as from Chicago to London. If we consider the earth to be a sphere of radius r, then we can define the distance between two points M and N on the surface of the sphere to be the length of the smaller arc of the great circle passing through the points M and N.

Although one could continue to examine different notions of distance, at some point, mathematicians attempt to build a more abstract definition that preserves the general properties of each of the cases. Clearly, abstracting the key features from several exemplars of an idea is an important aspect of doing mathematics. For distance, a more general definition is that of a metric space.

I have tried to illustrate in this example how mathematicians build abstract systems upon common notions in the real world. They develop new concepts (such as metric space), utilize other ideas (the Pythagorean theorem or the great circle of a sphere), and define new operational procedures in terms of quantitative and spatial concepts and procedures.

Inventing is illustrated in this example by the Euclidean n-space formulation of distance by analogy to the two- and three-space formulations. But mathematicians are more creative than this. For example, many interesting metric spaces on the plane arise out of a consideration of differently defined distances. One interesting class of metric spaces is obtained when one defines a metric d_p on the plane by the formula:

$$d_p(M,N) = [\,|x - x_1|^p + |y - y_1|^p\,]^{1/p}$$

The spaces so obtained are called Minkowski spaces. What is interesting is to change the value of p in the defining equation. For example, if $p = 1$, the set of points N for which $d_p(M,N) = r$ is a square with center M and diagonals of length 2r parallel to the coordinate axis. Also, if p approaches infinity, the set of points is also a square, but with sides of length 2r parallel to the axes (see figure 1).

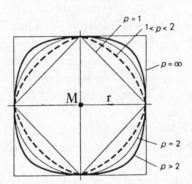

Fig. 1. Minkowski spaces for different values of p.

Source: Reprinted from *What is Distance*, p. 23, by Yu. A. Shreider by permission of The University of Chicago Press, © 1974 The University of Chicago.

These are only a few of the many examples of metric spaces mathematicians have invented. Yet no invention is accepted without also demonstrating the truth of its properties via a deductive argument.

In the above examples, I have not proved that each metric space described fulfills the four basic properties. However, mathematicians would not accept that these spaces are metric spaces without proof. Finally, the applications of the mathematical ideas about distance should be apparent, for using different definitions, scientists and engineers have developed means of measuring distance between sub-atomic particles and between galaxies (whether they are conceived to exist in a Euclidean space or some other). Applications of the idea range from space technology to plotting air traffic routes to save fuel.

In summary, I believe that to know mathematics is to do mathematics: abstracting, inventing, proving, and applying are its basic activities. The challenge to teachers is to organize a course of study which provides students the opportunity to experience these activities and thus "to know" mathematics and not just to "know the record" of past mathematical activities.

Who Decides on the Mathematical Tasks for Students and for What Reasons?

I raise this question because what is taught in schools requires deliberate choice. In the last section, I argued that the instructional activities chosen should give students experiences in abstracting, inventing, proving, and applying. But what is now taught in schools (or was taught when I was in school) bears little resemblance to this view of mathematics.

The decisions about mathematical activities in school have not been made by mathematicians. Thus, who makes the decisions? In American schools, one could argue that which tasks are assigned to students, how much time is spent with what emphasis, what is to be judged and rewarded (or punished), and so forth, are curricular decisions individual teachers make. But, it would be naive to conclude that teachers alone make the decisions about what mathematics is taught. The fact that mathematics is taught by a teacher to a group of students leads one to expect that a teacher's pedagogical principles and practices, soundly based or not, and the constraints of a particular learning situation will shape the kind of mathematics children learn and how. Thus, while teachers may be in a position to make content choices, real or imagined constraints limit such decisions. For example, Stephens has shown that elementary teachers see themselves making decisions about "my children" and not about "your mathematics."[15] Furthermore, one should not assume that mathematical inquiry will fit comfortably into the time slots of the conventional classroom, or that it will escape distortion altogether when adapted to fit the exigencies of a subject-based curriculum. The school has a wider social mandate than simply to teach mathematics, or any other subject: through what it teaches, the school helps to define and to legitimate what is to count as work by teachers and students, and what kinds of knowledge are to be valued above others. For many teachers, making content decisions is not seen as part of their job.

The actual decisions about what mathematics is taught and how it is interpreted are influenced by curriculum developers, school boards and administrators, publishers, and others interested in what is taught in schools. Given that there are over 16,000 separate school districts, each with a board of administration, over 500 publishers of educational materials, and so forth, there is no real answer to who influences curriculum decision making. However, the combined influences of these and other interest groups tend to perpetuate existing traditions about schooling, which in turn act to limit the choices available to teachers. As Popper has argued, the role of tradition in society is twofold: first, traditions create a certain social structure, and second, traditions are something which we can criticize and change.[16] Curricular traditions, such as teaching a year of geometry to fifteen-year-old students, provide regularities in the social structure of schools. The mere existence of these regularities is more important than their merits or demerits. They bring order and rational predictability into the social world of schools. To illustrate curricular traditions, I will discuss three perspectives.

THE DISCIPLINE PERSPECTIVE

Attention in schools is fixed on subject matter. Mathematics is separated from science, grammar, and other subjects. Within each subject, ideas are selected, separated, and reformulated into a rational order. For mathematics, this selection and organization has not been made by mathematicians. Seldom do they have a voice in school mathematics. Curriculum development starts by subdividing each subject into topics, each topic into studies, each study into lessons, and each lesson into specific facts. This curricular tradition is so ingrained that most educators simply take it for granted. In fact, the modern mathematics movement of the past twenty-five years really challenged only the content aims and how content was subdivided—not the discipline tradition per se—and this chapter still reflects that tradition. In fact, mathematics is so universally accepted as a part of school curricula that it is quite easy to see why little thought is given to its overall justification.

However, assuming the place of mathematics in school programs is justified, there are two serious problems within this discipline perspective. First, as was argued earlier, mathematics is too often viewed as "a record of knowledge." Second, many parents expect their children to have the same curricular experiences they had. Since they had to master a set of computational skills, they expect schools to teach their children the same things in the same way. However, as satirically narrated by Peddiwell in his classic, *The Saber-Tooth Curriculum*,[17] traditional courses such as one on "saber-tooth-tiger-scaring-with-fire" sometimes outlive their usefulness (that is, "scaring-with-fire" continues to be taught even after saber-tooth tigers have become extinct). Today's typical mathematics program is crowded with lots of "scaring-with-fire" topics. Usiskin recently did the profession a service by listing five traditional topics in algebra and geometry that should be omitted.[18] Many other topics should also be considered for omission. There is no question that the computer (and the calculator) have made obsolete the slide rule, logarithmic approximations, statistical approximation procedures, and so forth.

The adherence to curricular stability—teaching this generation of students the concepts, procedures, and values taught to previous generations—is clearly reflected in the "back-to-basics" movement, the banning of calculators from classrooms by school administrators and teachers, and so forth. However, such a position fails to appreciate that today's students will not be working in today's world but in the twenty-first century. Some of the skills needed by productive citizens then will be quite different from those emphasized in today's school. In particular, the current technological revolution brought on by the "chip" has created a whole new set of skills all should learn.

The need to challenge instructional traditions based on this technological revolution is evident with respect to the teaching of the arithmetic of whole numbers, algebraic routines, right triangle trigonometry, and even many procedures in calculus. For example, while the concepts and procedures of arithmetic are and will continue to be central to the learning of all mathematics, the tradition has been to emphasize getting students to become proficient at a set of procedural skills—finding sums of long columns of figures, doing long division with large numbers, finding square roots, and so forth. There is no question that these skills were essential in the post-Renaissance growth of business and industry. One can almost see behind the child doing sums in today's classroom a Victorian clerk poring over a ledger complete with flickering candle and quill pen. Today, small machines available to anyone can do all the calculations expected of any clerk faster and more accurately (and do a lot more as well). We need to teach students how to tell tomorrow's machines what to do. This does not mean that we no longer need to teach computational skills. Understanding the concepts and procedural skills is still needed, since computers only do what they are told to do, but extensive drill on computational skills is obsolete. In summary, the discipline tradition and how mathematics has been characterized in school mathematics need to be challenged.

THE PSYCHOLOGICAL ENGINEERING TRADITION

As a result of the vast research on individual differences, human development, and human learning, educational psychologists believe that their knowledge should influence how curricula are developed. Although it cannot be argued that current curricula are based on sound psychological principles, it is commonly assumed by many educators that they should be. Many psychologists believe that the teaching of concepts, meanings, or skills is usually done by a teacher or textbook writer in intuitive, unanalytic ways; thus, an improvement would certainly be made if psychological principles were used as a basis for curriculum development. For example, whether or not one believes in the details of Piagetian research, it is now commonly accepted by most educators that young children think differently than older children and adults and that learning proceeds from concrete experiences to abstractions that go beyond such experiences.

Nevertheless, the actual necessary connection between current psychological knowledge and classroom instruction is not clear for two reasons. First, most psychologists have related their theories to a very limited view of mathematics. Too often they have operationally defined mathematics in terms of performance on a standardized test, or have addressed a limited set of routine concepts or skills. Thus, they have focused only on getting right answers. Second, too often they have assumed that information derived in laboratory settings generalizes to classrooms. Unfortunately, learning in a classroom is not simply the sum of individual learning experiences. Classrooms are social groupings where the structure of many activities is dictated by a need to manage or control the group.

In summary, it has become commonplace to justify new programs in terms of psychological principles (or more likely to use the name of a noted psychologist—Piaget, Bruner, Gagné, Bloom, and so forth). The actual connection between the psychological notions and classroom instruction is in doubt.

CRITICAL SOCIOLOGY

This third perspective on curriculum views curricular knowledge as a mechanism of socioeconomic selection and control. The question of selection of content is seen as a form of the larger distribution of goods and services in society. One poses political questions such as:

Whose knowledge is it? Why is it being taught to this particular group, in this particular way? What are its real and latent functions in the complex connections between cultural power and the control of modes of production and distribution of goods and services in an advanced industrial economy like our own?[19]

As a result, the study of educational knowledge becomes a study in ideology that seeks to investigate what is considered legitimate knowledge by specific social groups and classes, in specific institutions, and at specific historical moments.

Although most people are likely to associate the knowledge distributed by schools primarily with the knowledge incorporated into textbooks, the sociologists of school knowledge have recognized that textbooks constitute but one of the many vehicles through which information of various kinds is disseminated. In particular, social and economic control is effectuated in schools both through the forms of discipline schools have (that is, the rules and routines that ensure order, the "hidden curriculum" that reinforces norms of obedience and

punctuality, and so forth) and through the forms of meaning the
school distributes. For example, scheduling arithmetic after recess to
quiet the students is clearly a form of social control.

Many recent studies illustrate the manner in which curriculum
content relates to the interests and ideology of some particular groups,
as opposed to that of others. For example, Anyon examined children's
work in long division in four types of schools that were using the same
mathematics text series.[20] The schools differed in terms of social class.
In the working-class school, the children's work was to follow the
steps of a mechanical procedure involving rote behavior and very little
decision making or choice. The teachers rarely explained why the
work was being assigned, how it might connect to other assignments,
or what idea lay behind the procedure to give it coherence and perhaps
meaning or significance. In the middle-class school, Anyon found that
the children's work was to get the right answer. If one accumulated
enough right answers, one got a good grade. The child had to follow
the directions in order to get the right answers, but the directions often
called for some figuring, some choice, and some decision making. In
the affluent professional school, Anyon found that the children's work
was creative activity carried out independently. The students were
continually asked to express and apply ideas and concepts. This work
involved individual thought and expressiveness, the expansion and
illustration of ideas, and a choice of appropriate method and material.
Thus, division (finding averages) became a procedure one uses to
solve problems. And finally, in the executive elite school, work was
developing one's analytical, intellectual powers. The children were
continually asked to reason through a problem to produce intellectual
products that would be both logically sound and of top academic
quality. What is important in this example from the sociology of
knowledge is the importance of establishing the ideological linkages
between a curriculum and the system of meanings and values of the
effective, dominant culture.[21] Working schools train workers, and
executive elite schools train executives. In fact, one of the traditions
which needs to be examined and challenged is how "knowing
mathematics" is operationally defined in the classrooms.

In summary, while teachers in fact decide on what is taught, they
are influenced by a set of curricular traditions. Traditions may be
explicit and recognized (like content being organized in disciplines)

and others implicit and unvoiced (like the influence of social class). Either way, such traditions undoubtedly have considerable influence on what is actually taught. And, in proposing a common curriculum in mathematics, I am both aware of such traditions and challenging some of them directly.

What Should Be the Principles from Which a Common Curriculum Can Be Built?

To consider this question, first recall that the work for students is defined by the instructional activities given them. Students are expected to listen, do assignments, complete homework, work alone (or in groups), take tests, and so forth. Tyler has argued that to build an effectively organized group of such activities, three major criteria should be met: continuity, sequence, and integration.[22] To these I would add a fourth: content integrity. By this I mean that the activities given to students should give them experiences in abstracting, inventing, proving, and applying mathematics, and at the same time, the concepts and skills they learn should form the basis for a much wider range of mathematical activities.

Obviously, no student can recreate all of mathematics. Thus, only some exemplars from various branches of mathematics should be selected. Nor should the student be exposed to the multitude of mathematical concepts and procedures in a willy-nilly fashion. They should be chosen and organized in an evolutionary manner so that new concepts and procedures can build upon (evolve from) other concepts and procedures. Thus, to engineer a common curriculum for mathematics meeting these four criteria, three principles should be followed.

PRINCIPLE 1. INSTRUCTIONAL ACTIVITIES SHOULD EMPHASIZE PROCESSES.

To know mathematics as a craft means that instructional activities should require students to actively "do" something. More specifically, at least four basic sets of processes used in mathematics can be identified: relation, representation, symboblic-procedure, and validation.[23]

Relation processes. These are used to relate objects according to common attributes. Some important relation processes are the following. *Describing* is the process of characterizing an object, set, event, or representation in terms of its attributes. *Classifying* is the process of sorting objects, sets, or representations into equivalent classes on the basis of one or more attributes. Classifying is basic to mathematics, for it requires the student to look at how things are alike; if common attributes of things are identified, then generalizations about the class can be made. *Comparing* is the process of determining whether two objects, sets, events, or their representations are the same or different on specified attributes. When comparing, the student focuses on an attribute to decide whether two things are the same or different on that attribute. *Ordering* is the process of determining whether one of two objects, sets, events, or their representations is greater than (>), equal to (=), or less than (<) the other on a specified attribute. The process of ordering gives a background for developing the natural order of numbers. *Joining* is the process of putting together two objects, sets, or representations that have an attribute in common to form a single object, set, or representation with that attribute. In the process of joining, one begins with at least two objects or sets and puts them together to make one object or set. This is most often represented with a sentence such as $5 + 7 = \square$, where the unknown is the sum. However, situations may be posed where one of the two objects or sets is unknown; these situations are represented by sentences such as $5 + \square = 12$ and $\square + 7 = 12$. *Separating* is the process of taking apart an object, set, or representation whose parts have an attribute in common to make two objects, sets, or representations each with that attribute. Separating, as well as joining, enables the children to solve problems that they will later solve symbolically with addition and subtraction. *Grouping* is the process of arranging a set of objects into equal groups of a specified size with the possibility of one additional group for any leftovers. *Partitioning* is the process of arranging a set of objects into a specified number of equal groups with the possibility of one additional group for any leftovers. Grouping and partitioning are closely related processes. Both allow students to consider problems that will be solved by multiplication or division. In grouping, one knows how many objects are in each group, but does not know how many groups there are. In partitioning, the student knows the number of groups, so he or she deals out the objects one by one, giving each group the same amount, and then counts the number in each group. When the action has been completed, in either a grouping or partitioning situation, it is impossible to tell how it was done. Both processes are represented symbolically the same way. Both grouping and partitioning are used to convert from one unit to another within a system of measurement. For example, in changing 4 meters to centimeters, the student thinks of 4 groups of 100 centimeters or 400 centimeters. Changing 20 quarts to gallons, the students think of the problem as how many groups of 4 does it take to make 20, or $\square(4) = 20$. Grouping is also the basis of place value. Students may group a set of objects by tens and represent it, for example as $3(10) + 7$. This notation is given a special name: expanded notation. The student goes from this notation to the usual notation or compact notation, 37. Grouping is also used in connection with the addition and subtraction algorithms. Partitioning is often used to build an understanding of fractions. If a set can be partitioned without any leftovers, then each group is a fractional part of the whole set. For example, if 12 cookies are distributed to 3 people, each receives one-third of the cookies.

Representation processes. These allow the student to progress from solving problems directly to solving them abstractly. Students begin by solving problems directly with the objects or sets involved in the problem. In solving many problems, they gradually learn to use physical representations, then pictorial representations, and finally, symbolic representations to help them. Representing not only includes going from the concrete to the abstract, but also includes going in the other direction. For example, students can represent the symbol 6 with six objects.

Symbolic-procedure processes. These are a great deal of what is commonly considered as mathematics. These are the procedures one uses to transform symbolic statements into equivalent statements. An *algorithm* is a finite sequence of steps one uses to close an open mathematical sentence. The common algorithms children learn (addition, subtraction, multiplication, and division of whole numbers) are examples of such procedural processes. A *sentential transformation* is a finite sequence of steps one uses to change an open mathematical sentence to an equivalent open sentence. For example: when $314 + \square = 843$ was changed to $843 - 314 = \square$, a sentential transformation was made. Such transformations are efficient in problem solving since they provide the student, as in the example above, a way of changing an unworkable problem to one in which an algorithm can be used. A *structural transformation* is a finite sequence of steps one uses to change a symbolic phrase to an equivalent phrase. For example, the phrase 3(5 + 4) can be changed to 3 x 5 + 3 x 4 because of the structural characteristic of the distributive property for multiplication over addition with whole numbers.

Validation processes. These are the processes used to determine whether a proposed proportion is true. There are three basic ways of validating: authority, empiricism, and deduction. *Authority validation* is the process of determining validity by relying on some authority. For example, if a child checks his answer to a problem by comparing it to an answer book or to the teacher's answer, he is relying on authority. *Empirical validation* involves representing a proposition with objects, pictures, or other symbols to assist in determining its validity. For example, suppose for the problem 9 □ 6, a student puts > in the box. To determine if 9 > 6 is a valid sentence, the student should represent 9 and 6 with cubes and visually show that the 9 cubes are more than the 6 cubes. Similarly, for the problem 6 + 3 = 10, the student could represent 6 and 10 with pictures and clearly show that 3 is an invalid solution. *Logical deductive validation* is the process of determining validity by a deductive argument based on agreed upon common notions, definitions, axioms, and rules of logic. This process is at the heart of mathematics.

In summary, these four basic sets of processes should be considered illustrative (certainly not exhaustive) of what it means to "do" mathematics. Each specific instructional activity should expect students to use one or more mathematical processes. In addition to processes or procedural routines such as these, there is also a set of executive routines or heuristics which should be learned. Thus, while the semantics of many activities should direct a student to use a particular process, some activities need to be provided that require the student to decide on a strategy or choose between processes. For example, to learn the strategy suggested by Polya, "If you cannot solve the proposed problems, try to solve first some related problem,"[24] students must have exposure to problems where that strategy is appropriate.

PRINCIPLE 2: INSTRUCTIONAL ACTIVITIES SHOULD BE GROUPED INTO
CURRICULUM UNITS.

Tyler's notion of integration "refers to the horizontal relationship of curriculum experiences."[25] One interpretation is that a set of activities should be related to each other to give meaning to the set. Unfortunately, during the past two decades, with "individualized" programs, this concern was not heeded. We were able to break mathematical learning into hundreds of specific behavioral objectives, but the problem was how to put them back together again so that students had an integrated knowledge of mathematics.

The problem is not new. Dewey argued for activities related to experience in his classic, *The Child and the Curriculum*,[26] and Brownell demonstrated the efficacy of meaningful instruction nearly half a century ago.[27] It is widely accepted that meaningful learning is better than rote learning. The difficulty lies in engineering a "meaningful" mathematics program. It is deceivingly easy to specify objectives, lay out or create a hierarchy,[28] and engineer a rote learning program based on that framework. The danger, as Erlwanger has shown, is that mastery of a set of objectives is no guarantee that the student can do mathematics.[29]

One answer that is emerging from current work in several areas is that activities should be grouped into curriculum units that take two to three weeks to teach. The activities should be related to a "story shell" which provides a reason for doing each activity and makes the learning clear and meaningful.

Story shell. This is not the place to go into a lengthy discussion of the research on "story shell curriculum units." But let me trace some of the argument, beginning with cognitive psychologists who have been interested in what people remember from texts they have read (that is, the relationship between reading comprehension and memory storage). Several scholars in the 1970s proposed "story grammars" (sets of rewrite rules) with two objectives: first, they are grammars for real stories, and second, they are theories about the representation of stories in memory.[30]

This line of research, although demonstrably inadequate in representing real stories, has turned out to be extremely valuable as a characterization of how to utilize planning knowledge in reading stories. In particular, Black and Bower have proposed a two-part critical path rule that predicts memory accuracy: (a) the best remembered part of a story is the critical path that provides the transition from the beginning state to the ending state of the story; (b) if the story describes the critical path at various levels of detail, then the higher (that is, the more general, less detailed) the level of statement, the better remembered it will be.[31] What is becoming clear is that the "critical path" (or "solution episode" or "story shell") is what is remembered best.

Next, relying in part on this memory research, Sternberg is currently studying learning of new vocabulary words in context (where the new words are included in a familiar story line).[32] Such learning is clearly more successful and meaningful than the rote learning of new vocabulary words. Finally, instructional research by Good and Grouws lends tangential evidence to this argument.[33] They asked teachers to spend more time explaining the content of each mathematics lesson and found that the students learned considerably more. The implication is that in explaining content, teachers put the ideas in context. Thus, a curriculum unit should have a story to tell posed in an episodic, problem, or "detective" format; and the story should fit into a larger tale (like a chapter in a good novel).[34]

Clear and meaningful activities. From personal experience in developing an elementary mathematics program, I am convinced that the creation or selection of activities within the story shell framework is also critical.[35] One could take an existing text, add a story line, expect students to read the story, and still have students answer questions on work sheets. That is not what is being proposed; instead I suggest that the following four characteristics be considered:

1. The activities should be related to how children process information. Most traditional programs fail in this regard for four reasons. First, the bulk of the developmental literature, as reviewed by Lovell, suggests that curriculum units be organized around a set of activities in which (a) "the pupils work in small groups or individually at tasks which have been provided"; (b) "opportunity is provided for pupils to act on physical materials or to use games"; and (c) "social intercourse using verbal language is encouraged since it is an important influence in the development of concrete operational thought."[36] Most programs are not organized around activities like these.

Second, if one takes seriously the notions of curricular spiralling, then one must review prior concepts and skills and get ready for others to be learned later. Most programs do not both "review" and "prepare." Third, the activities to teach concepts should differ from those to teach algorithms, problem-solving heuristics, and so forth. In most programs, one page looks like most other pages. Fourth, sequenced activities that require students to assimilate new information will differ from those that require accommodation. Again, in most programs, little attention is paid to students' methods of processing information in creating activities.

2. The reasons for each activity within the unit should be clear to each student. Too often the only reason a student sees an activity is that "it is the next one in the book" or "my teacher assigned it."

3. Ideally, every unit should include activities that expect students to abstract, invent, prove, and apply. Again, too much emphasis is placed on learning abstract concepts and procedures with the only rationale being "someday you will need this skill." Each story line should include problem-solving activities. Students should invent and argue about solutions to problems and their validity. Furthermore, the problem-solving activities should not be the word problems often seen in texts.[37]

4. The curriculum unit should be objective referenced, with tests (and observations) related to those objectives. Since part of the job of teaching is to judge the words and actions of students, the use of some behavioral objectives for evaluation purposes has proven to be helpful.

In summary, I believe it is possible to create curriculum units that are a collection of activities integrated around a story line that can give meaning to the concepts and procedures.

PRINCIPLE 3. CURRICULUM UNITS SHOULD BE RELATED VIA CONCEPTUAL STRANDS.

To develop continuity, curriculum units need to be related to each other as part of a larger story. For mathematics, one way to develop the larger story is to let history be our guide. All of elementary mathematics has been created in response to problems. Yet, few adults are aware of the story of mathematics. "No subject, when separated from its history, loses more than mathematics."[38] The story of how elementary mathematics has developed can be told via seven strands:

whole number arithmetic, spatial relations, measurement, fractions, coordinate geometry, algebra, and statistics.[39]

By strand, I mean a cognitive subdivision of mathematics that has a rich history (or story line). I have chosen to emphasize strands because, although a familiarity with number combinations and operations can develop from manual and visual experience, this of itself will take the student little beyond the level of paleolithic man. Our numeral system is the product of centuries of mathematical exploration and invention. It possesses such deceptive simplicity that it can be mechanically mastered with no reference to its history. And therein lies the danger. Because children are capable of insight and are not disposed to accept arbitrariness unquestioningly, the deadliness of uninformed teaching is immediate. Our decimal system, our rules of calculation, our arithmetical and geometric terminology—all seem natural and inevitable to anyone who has successfully mastered them by mechanical methods. To see them for what they are—a blend of logic, history, and convention—seems not only difficult, but unnecessary; to show them as such to children, almost impossible. Yet it is not only possible, but essential if the foundations of mathematical understanding are to be well and truly laid.

The *whole numbers arithmetic strand* includes counting, additive structures, and multiplicative structures. "Counting" means the assignment of numbers to sets of objects (finding out how many) and includes learning the terminology of the Hindu-Arabic numeration system. Learning "additive structures"[40] means learning to write addition and subtraction sentences to represent certain concrete numerical situations and learning the procedural rules for addition and subtraction. Similarly, learning "multiplicative structures" means learning to write multiplication and division sentences to represent certain concrete situations and learning the procedural rules for multiplication and division.

The story of how the concepts and procedures of arithmetic were developed is central to the history of mankind. The concepts of arithmetic correspond to the quantitative relations of collections of objects. These concepts arose by way of abstraction, as a result of the analysis and generalization of an immense amount of practical experience. They arose gradually. First came numbers connected with concrete objects, then abstract numbers, and finally the concept of number in general. Each of these concepts was made possible by a combination of practical experience and preceding abstract concepts. Similarly, the operations on whole numbers and the procedural rules for finding sums, differences, products, and quotients arose as a result of practical experience with joining, separating, grouping, and partitioning sets and looking for shortcuts for counting the sets resulting from those processes.

The importance of this strand cannot be overestimated. The concepts and procedures of arithmetic, which generalize an enormous amount of experience, reflect in abstract form relationships in the actual world that one meets constantly and everywhere. It is possible to count the objects in a room, stars, people, atoms, and so forth.

At the same time, every abstract concept—in particular, the concept of number—is limited in its significance as a result of its very abstractness. In the first place, when applied to any concrete object, it reflects only one aspect of the object and therefore gives only an incomplete picture of it. For example, mere numerical facts often say very little about the essence of a matter. In the second place, abstract concepts cannot be applied everywhere without certain limiting conditions. It is impossible to apply arithmetic to a concrete problem without first convincing ourselves that their application makes some sense in the particular case. If we speak of addition, for example, and merely unite the objects in thought, then naturally no progress has been made with the objects themselves. But suppose we apply addition to the actual uniting of the objects. We put the objects together, for example, by throwing them into a pile or setting them on a table. In this case, not merely abstract addition takes place, but also an actual process. The process is not arithmetical addition, and it may even be impossible to carry out. For example, an object thrown into a pile may break; wild animals, if placed together, may tear one another apart; and materials put together may enter into a chemical reaction: a liter of water and a liter of alcohol poured together produce not two, but 1.9 liters of mixture as a result of partial solution of the liquids.

The spatial relations strand includes the basic concepts of geometry. The story here is similar to arithmetic. Early man took over geometric forms from nature. The circle and the crescent of the moon, the smooth surface of a lake, the straightness of a ray of light or of a well-proportioned tree existed long before man himself and presented themselves constantly to his observation. In nature, our eyes seldom meet with straight lines, equilateral triangles, or squares. Clearly, the chief reason men and women gradually worked out a conception of these figures is that their observation of nature was an active one, in the sense that, to meet their practical needs, they manufactured objects that were more and more regular in shape. They built dwellings, cut stones, enclosed plots of land, stretched bowstrings in their bows, and modeled their clay pottery. In bringing these to perfection, they correspondingly formed the notion that a plot is *curved*, but a stretched bowstring is *straight*. In short, they first gave form to their material and only then recognized form as that which is impressed on material and can, therefore, be considered in itself, as an abstraction from material. By recognizing the form of bodies, humans were able to improve their handiwork and thereby to work out still more precisely the abstract notion of form. Thus, practical activity served as a basis for the abstract concepts of geometry.

Geometry operates with "geometric bodies" and figures. But a geometric body is nothing other than an actual body considered solely from the point of view of its spatial form, in abstraction from all its other properties such as density, color, and weight. A geometric figure is a still more general concept, since in this case, it is possible to abstract from spatial extension also. Thus, a surface has only two dimensions; a line, only one dimension; a point, none at all. A point is the abstract concept of the end of a segment, of a position defined to the limit of precision so that it no longer has any parts. Thus, geometry has as its object the spatial forms and relations of actual bodies, removed from their other properties and considered from the purely abstract point of view.

The self-evidence of the basic concepts of geometry, the methods of reasoning, and the certainty of their conclusions has the same source as in arithmetic. The properties of geometric concepts, like the concepts themselves, have been abstracted from the world around us. It was necessary for people to draw straight lines before they could take it as an axiom that through every two points it is possible to draw a straight line. They had to move various bodies about and apply them to one another on countless occasions before they could generalize their experience to the notion of superposition of geometric figures and make use of this notion for the proof of theorems, as is done in the well-known theorems about congruence of triangles.

The measurement strand involves learning to assign numbers to attributes of objects and then using the concepts and procedures from the numbers strand to solve problems of length, weight, or other properties involving measurement. This strand relates the concepts and processes of whole numbers to those of geometry. Whole number arithmetic begins with the notion that each separate object is a unit. A collection of discrete objects is a sum of units, which is, so to speak, the image of pure discreteness, purified of all other properties. Geometry, on the other hand, considers properties of a single homogeneous object, which in itself is not separated into parts, but which may nevertheless be divided in practice into parts as small as desired. Lengths, areas, and volumes have the same property. Although they are continuous in their very essence and are not actually divided into parts, they nevertheless offer the possibility of being divided without limit.

Here we encounter two contrasting kinds of objects: on the one hand, indivisible, separate, discrete objects; and on the other, objects that are completely divisible, not divided into parts, but continuous. We therefore have two properties—discreteness and continuity—and their abstract mathematical images: the whole number and the geometric extension. Measurement involves a blending of these ideas: the continuousness is measured by separate units.

The fractions strand involves learning to name fractional parts for certain situations,[41] learning the conventional symbolism for representing fractions (both common and decimal), and learning the procedural rules for operations on fractions.

Historically, the need for fractions arose out of measurement problems. In the process of measurement, the chosen unit is not ordinarily contained in the measured magnitude an integral number of times, so a simple calculation of the number of units is not sufficient. It becomes necessary to divide the unit of measurement in order to express the magnitude more accurately by parts of the unit; that is, no longer by whole numbers, but by fractions. This was the way fractions actually arose. They arose from the division and comparison of continuous geometric magnitudes. The first magnitudes named lengths, areas of land, and volumes of liquids. In the earliest appearance of fractions, we see the mutual action of arithmetic and geometry. This interaction led to fractions, as an extension of the concept of number from whole numbers to fractional numbers (or as mathematicians say, to rational numbers, expressing a ratio of whole numbers).

The coordinate geometry strand extends the interaction of arithmetic and geometry to a higher level of abstraction by developing a general procedure for the assignment of numbers to points in any space. Concepts and procedures such as naming points on a line starting at any point (the number line), going in either direction on the line (directed numbers), naming coordinates on a plane, and so forth, are to be learned in this strand.

The algebra strand incorporates the notions derived from generalized arithmetic. It deals only with mathematical operations on numbers considered from a formal point of view, in abstraction from given concrete numbers. The abstractions find expression in that magnitudes are denoted by letters on which calculations are carried out according to well-known formal rules.

Algebra, in contrast to generalized arithmetic, retains this basis, but widens it extensively. Algebra considers "magnitudes" of a much more general nature than numbers and studies operations on these "magnitudes," which are to some extent analogous in their formal properties to the ordinary operations of arithmetic: addition, subtraction, multiplication, and division. A simple example is offered by vectors, which may be added by using a parallelogram rule. The degree of generalization in contemporary algebra is such that even the term "magnitude" may lose its meaning, and one speaks more generally of "elements" on which it is possible to perform operations similar to the usual algebraic ones. For example, two motions carried out one after the other are evidently equivalent to a single motion, which is their sum; two algebraic transformations of a formula may be equivalent to a single transformation that produces the same result; and so forth. It is possible to speak of a characteristic "addition" of motions or transformations. This and more is studied in a general abstract form in contemporary algebra.

The *statistics strand* is "a body of mathematics of obtaining and analyzing data in order to base decisions upon them."[42] In this sense, statistical concepts and procedures are a natural bridge between real problems and mathematics. Data are often gathered to help decide questions of practical action. Statistics help decide what kind of information is needed; how to collect, tabulate and interpret it; and how judgments can be made on the basis of this information.

In summary, the fundamental concepts and procedures in these strands are the building blocks that enable any student to cope with many relevant problems in later life and work situations.

How Can Individual Differences Be Considered?

The common curriculum for mathematics based on the principles discussed in the last section, if expressed in terms of concepts and procedural skills to be learned, would not be much different from the curriculum appearing in most contemporary mathematics programs. My argument, however, is that students should acquire these concepts and skills differently. From related activities learned in context, they should know arithmetic and geometric ideas as abstractions from reality. They should understand that notions such as fractions or directed numbers are inventions and that to know mathematics is more than finding correct answers. Knowing mathematics includes validating and proving. Above all, as a result of their experiences, students should be able to apply mathematical ideas to a variety of mathematical and practical problems. To accomplish this, some ideas about how a common curriculum could be engineered have been suggested. This proposal is made with full realization that the design of such a program directly challenges some of the traditions of mathematics instruction in today's schools.

However, even if a common course of study for mathematics could be developed, the task is not complete, for as Kliebard argues, while the scope and sequence of a curriculum theory must first address the question of what should be taught, the second question is "who gets taught?"[43] Any mathematics is lifeless without students. Yet, "although students bring life to mathematics, they add to the instructional complexity, for they also bring to the activities the full range of their differences."[44] To consider those differences implies some sort of criterion that bears on the choice involved about who gets taught what and how they get taught. Kliebard recently has pointed out that the criteria for making such choices are based on claims about schooling from different interest groups.[45] The basic position of any interest group is that schools, teachers, and, in particular, curricular programs should take into account current knowledge about individuals and their differences. Thus, even though the common curriculum for mathematics as outlined in this paper is for all students, interest groups claim their knowledge about individuals should be considered in making instructional decisions. The interest groups are many and varied. Several have information about differences between individuals based on information from differential psychology, developmental psychology, and sociology.

Differential psychology. The first and most prevalent set of claims is based on the extensive work of a number of educational psychologists in the Thurstone tradition of distinct mental abilities.[46] From test scores and psychometric analyses these psychologists have been able to identify differential abilities, traits, aptitudes, styles, and so forth. For example, such characteristics as intelligence, rate of learning, field independence/dependence, or spatial ability have been identified and samples of students ordered from high to low on those traits. Furthermore, it is assumed that these characteristics are fixed, stable characteristics which describe intellectual differences between individuals in the same way as height, weight, stature, and so forth describe physical characteristics. Finally, it has been assumed that instruction would be more socially efficient if some of these differences were taken into account.

Developmental psychology. The second set of claims is based on information that individuals adaptively interact with the environment and gradually evolve intellectually through discontinuous stages.[47] Rather than being fixed, differences between individuals are viewed as a function of growth. Primary age children, for example, usually are at a "concrete-operations" stage, think in terms of themselves (are egocentric), and think of concrete referents near at hand. Hence, they should not be expected to reason about hypothetical, external situations. Instruction then should be tailored to their stage of development.

Sociology. From vast and various sources, sociological data indicate that children come to school having different social, cultural, and experiential backgrounds. These are differences between individuals in parental background, race, home locale, sex, and so forth. It is assumed that with these differences come differing social expectations; hence it is argued that schools should plan and carry out instruction in light of these differences.

In addition to information about differences between individuals, there are at least two sources of information about intraindividual differences based on data from social psychology and political science.

Social psychology. In contrast to the "between individuals" arguments about fixed traits, stages of development, or cultural determinants, this argument is that individuals differ in interests, likes, motivation, persistence, attitudes, attributions, and so forth. These social characteristics are transient and may change because of curricular unit, environment, teacher, membership in a group, and so on. Instruction should try to capitalize on these transient differences.

Political science. This information is based on the notion of "individualism" as an ideological construct in American history. In political thought, this involves the liberal belief in the autonomy of the individual. Cagan suggests that there are three distinct components of this belief: (a) self-determination—the individual is in control of his own destiny; (b) self-actualization—the good life is attained through acting on one's personal needs and desires; and (c) self-direction—the desire to be free from social constraints.[48] Thus, schooling should offer the student the possibility of studying different (or optional) units. It should be noted that "individualism" assumes the existence of "individual differences" but does not consider identification of those differences particularly relevant. Note that in the first four arguments it was assumed that wise adults can plan, organize, and make decisions about instruction based on information about differences. In this case, the argument is that the learner should make the choices.

Not only do the interest groups who have their claims on one of the five perspectives about individual differences base their arguments on different information; they also reach different conclusions about how instruction should proceed based on that information. One argument is that instruction should be adapted to "complement" differences. For example, if some students learn at a faster rate, they should be allowed (encouraged) to proceed through a program at a faster pace, or if students differ in spatial ability, activities should be adapted so that students with that ability can utilize it in learning and, at the same time, other adaptation should be made so that those low in spatial ability are not handicapped. This is the "aptitude by treatment" interaction argument put forward by Cronbach in 1957.[49] It is argued that this approach teaches the same mathematics to all students but in different ways. This is naive because "different ways" imply different processes; hence different mathematics is being learned even if the same concepts or procedural skills are included. Thus, the content of a two-year algebra course, as received by the student, is not the same as a one-year course even though the syllabus is the same.

A second argument is that instruction on the same mathematical units should be adapted to "compensate" for differences. This is often put forward in terms of social equity. Social, cultural, and even intellectual inequities exist, but the school should not exacerbate the inequities. For example, ability grouping is seen as social-class grouping. Thus, differential instruction based on "ability" would only further differentiate social classes.

A third argument is that different students should be taught different mathematics. In particular, the common curriculum should not be considered common for gifted or handicapped students. This again assumes that adults (teachers or counselors) are wise enough to decide who gets what mathematics. A part of this argument is that since mathematics is hierarchical, success at one level is a necessary prerequisite for further mathematical study. Thus, half the ninth graders in most secondary schools are counseled to take "general mathematics," one cannot enroll in Euclidean Geometry without passing Algebra, and so forth.

The final argument is that different students should have the option of being taught different mathematics. Mathematics, like other subjects (literature, history, science, and so forth), is seen as diverse and interconnected, but not strictly hierarchical. The diversity includes a rich array of activities or topics which all students should have the opportunity to consider and select.

Given that these perspectives and arguments (and others) exist, that they are based in part on valid information, and that some aspects of dealing with individual differences have been incorporated into the traditions of some schools, the question still remains: How should a school react to these interest groups? This is a serious, social-political question. It is a topic upon which considerable open discussion and serious debate needs to be carried out. Without such debate, schools will undoubtedly ignore the additional pressures and maintain existing haphazard traditions. Such traditions include ability grouping of students in mathematics instruction, decisions by counselors and teachers about who takes what mathematics, and so forth. However, as a result of such discussion and debate, mathematics educators, curriculum developers, and mathematics teachers, I believe, should take a more bold and radical position. A new "common curriculum" for all students should be developed. The program should have at its base a "core" program and also provide a variety of options. This proposal is based on two observations: first, the assumption that mathematics has to have a strong partial ordering when it is incorporated in a curriculum is false, and second, the assumption that our only choices are either to group students by ability or to vary the pace of instruction is based on inadequate information which tends to be discriminatory.

I see nothing inherent in many arithmetic skills to indicate that they are really prerequisites for algebra or geometry, and so forth. In fact, some are more difficult than many algebraic concepts. There is no good reason why we should teach arithmetic for eight years, algebra for two, geometry for one, and so forth. Nor is there a good rationale for students having to complete all of the units in typical courses in order to continue. Because we have traditionally organized curricula in that way does not mean it has to be that way. Robert Davis commented on this point at a National Council of Teachers of Mathematics symposium I chaired on individualized instruction. After the session, a classroom teacher asked, "What am I to do if my students can't add fractions?" He replied, "Perhaps you ought to teach them a topic in topology." The point is that mathematics is not simply a set of procedural skills to be learned in some hierarchical order. One can learn to abstract, invent, prove, and apply concepts and skills from a variety of problem situations. Thus, every student should have the opportunity to explore basic problems (for example, what is distance?). And, at the same time some students should have the opportunity to go beyond the "core" (for example, examine distance in n-dimensions). Furthermore, it is absurd that students are encouraged to stop studying mathematics as early as possible. Doing mathematics should be practiced throughout schooling experience by all students.

While differential psychologists have clearly found that individuals differ in a variety of traits, aptitudes, styles, and the like, there is little evidence to suggest that any particular trait or combinations of traits make that much difference when one is learning mathematics. I would rather argue for equity of opportunity than to group students arbitrarily. In addition, there is too much evidence that typical "ability" grouping is based on either inadequate or inappropriate data.

There is an alternative if we consider the basic elements of the common mathematics curriculum discussed earlier. In light of these observations, a compensatory modular program with options is possible. A "core" set of units encompassing the content of the seven strands outlined earlier could be developed. All students would be expected to study these units. Additional units should also be prepared

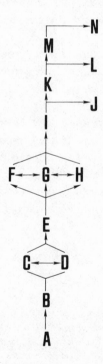

Fig. 2. Suggested sequence chart for DMP Topic 23.

Source: Thomas A. Romberg, John G. Harvey, James M. Moser, and Mary E. Montgomery, *DMP Resource Manual, Topics 1-40* (Chicago: Rand McNally, 1974), p. 68.

to give students the opportunity to go beyond the basic units. At the same time, within each curriculum unit, some students should be able to go beyond the core activities.

For example, in creating *Developing Mathematical Processes* (DMP) we decided that teachers (and children) should have options of what activities to carry out in a particular unit.[50] Figure 2 shows a sequence chart for DMP Topic 23. One begins with Activity A and moves upward, doing one activity (or more, if needed) on the central stem, until the top is reached. For example, the teacher could do Activities A; B; C or D (or both); E; one or more of F, G, and H; I; K; and M. The alternative activities (C, D, F, G, and H) provide the teacher with the opportunity to tailor instruction to "individual differences." Students who wanted to explore a topic further could do the optional activities J, L, and N. Clearly, there are many choices available in such a program.

In summation, there should be a "core" set of mathematics activities in a curriculum unit based on a strand of mathematics that all students should experience and master. The "core" becomes the basis for differential and additional study.

If all students are to know mathematics, a curriculum could be constructed so that all students have common experiences in abstracting, inventing, proving, and applying. Such a curriculum would be in structure and in spirit quite different from the programs found in schools today. It will not be easy to create such a program or to get schools to adopt it, but our children deserve to really know mathematics.

FOOTNOTES

1. John Dewey, *Democracy and Education* (New York: Macmillan, 1916).
2. Ibid., pp. 186-187.
3. Ibid., p. 147.
4. Arthur R. King, Jr. and John A. Brownell, *The Curriculum and the Disciplines of Knowledge: A Theory of Curriculum Practice* (New York: John Wiley and Sons, 1966).
5. Warren O. Hagstrom, *The Scientific Community* (New York: Basic Books, 1965).
6. Eric T. Bell, *The Development of Mathematics*, 2d ed. (New York: McGraw-Hill, 1945), p. 153.
7. Abraham Robinson, *Non-standard Analysis* (Amsterdam: North-Holland, 1974).
8. H. Jerome Keisler, *Elementary Calculus: An Approach Using Infinitesimals* (Boston: Prindle, Weber, and Schmidt, 1971).
9. Jeremy Kilpatrick, "Stop the Bandwagon, I Want Off," *Arithmetic Teacher* 28 (April 1981): 2.

10. Learning to invent or to discover is not simply explaining a set of rules to be followed. It truly is an art. Readers interested in this topic should see Jacques Hadamard, *The Psychology of Invention in the Mathematical Field* (New York: Dover, 1954); George Polya, *How to Solve It* (Garden City, N.Y.: Doubleday Anchor Books, 1957); or Wayne A. Wickelgren, *How to Solve Problems* (San Francisco: W. H. Freeman, 1974).

11. Imre Lakatos, *Proofs and Refutations* (Cambridge: Cambridge University Press, 1976), p. 5.

12. This example draws heavily on Yu. A. Shreider, *What Is Distance?* (Chicago: University of Chicago Press, 1974).

13. For these cases, properties of similar triangles and angles (trigonometry) can be used to find the distances.

14. This is one distinguishing characteristic between mathematics and its applications, particularly engineering. Mathematicians are not concerned with the instruments for making the estimates; engineers are.

15. W. Maxwell Stephens, "Mathematical Knowledge and School Work: A Case Study of the Teaching of Developing Mathematical Processes" (Doct. diss., University of Wisconsin, 1982).

16. Karl Popper, *Conjectures and Refutations* (London: Routledge and Kegan Paul, 1949).

17. J. Abner Peddiwell [pseud.], *The Saber-Tooth Curriculum* (New York: McGraw-Hill, 1939).

18. Zalman Usiskin, "What Should NOT Be in the Algebra and Geometry Curricula of Average College-bound Students?" *Mathematics Teacher* 73 (Summer 1980): 413-24.

19. Michael W. Apple and Philip Wexler, "Cultural Capital and Educational Transmissions," *Educational Theory* 28 (Winter 1978): 35.

20. Jean Anyon, "Social Class and the Hidden Curriculum of Work," *Journal of Education* 162 (Winter 1980): 67-92.

21. Raymond Williams, *The Long Revolution* (London: Chatto and Windus, 1961).

22. Ralph W. Tyler, *Basic Principles of Curriculum and Instruction* (Chicago: University of Chicago Press, 1959).

23. Thomas A. Romberg, "Needed Activities Basic to the Learning of Mathematics" (Paper presented at the National Institute of Education Conference on Basic Skills and Learning of Mathematics, Euclid, Ohio, November 1975).

24. Polya, *How to Solve It*, p. 31.

25. Tyler, *Basic Principles of Curriculum and Instruction*, p. 55.

26. John Dewey, *The Child and the Curriculum* (Chicago: University of Chicago Press, 1902).

27. William Brownell, "The Place of Meaning in the Teaching of Arithmetic," *Elementary School Journal* 47 (January 1947): 256-65.

28. Such as that proposed by Robert W. Gagné, *The Conditions of Learning* (New York: Holt, Rinehart and Winston, 1965).

29. Stanley Erlwanger, "Case Studies of Children's Conceptions of Mathematics," *Journal of Children's Mathematical Behavior* 1 (Summer 1975): 157-281.

30. See, for example, George P. Lakoff, "Structural Complexity in Fairy Tales," *The Study of Man* 1 (1972): 128-90; Jean M. Mandler and Nancy S. Johnson, "Remembrance of Things Passed: Story Structure and Recall," *Cognitive Psychology* 9 (January 1977): 111-91; David E. Rumelhart, "Notes on a Schema for Stories," in D. H. Bobrow and A. Collins, eds., *Representation and Understanding: Studies in Cognitive Science* (New York: Academic Press, 1975), pp. 211-36; Perry W. Thorndyke, "Cognitive Structures in Comprehension and Memory of Narrative Discourse,"

Cognitive Psychology 9 (January 1977): 55-110; Teun A. van Dijk, *Text and Context: Explorations in the Semantics and Pragmatics of Discourse* (London: Longman, 1977); Nancy L. Stein and Christine G. Glenn, "An Analysis of Story Comprehension in Elementary School Children," in *New Directions in Discourse Processing*, ed. Roy Freedle (Norwood, N.J.: Ablex Publishing Corp., 1979), pp. 53-120.

31. John G. Black and Gordon H. Bower, "Story Understanding as Problem Solving," *Poetics* 9 (June 1980): 176.

32. Robert J. Sternberg, Janet S. Powell, and Daniel B. Kaye, "Teaching Vocabulary-Building Skills: A Contextual Approach" (Paper presented at the Conference on Computers and Cognitive Science, Madison, Wis., November, 1981).

33. Thomas L. Good and Douglas G. Grouws, "Experimental Research in Secondary Mathematics Classrooms: Working with Teachers," Final Report, NIE Grant (Columbus, Mo.: University of Missouri, May 1981).

34. There are several examples of Instructional Units that have story lines. Martin Covington and colleagues studied general creative thinking and problem solving using mystery problems following a story line. See Martin V. Covington, "Promoting Creating Thinking in the Classrooms," in H. J. Klausmeier and G. T. O'Hearn, eds., *Research and Development toward the Improvement of Education* (Madison, Wis.: Dembar Educational Research Services, 1968).

Also, several experimental mathematics programs created excellent topics with these characteristics, such as *Stretchers and Shrinkers* developed by UICSM (University of Illinois Committee on School Mathematics), *Minnemast Units* developed by the Minnesota Mathematics and Science Teaching Project, or some topics from *Developing Mathematical Processes* developed by the Wisconsin Research and Development Center. See Joseph R. Hoffman, *Stretchers and Shrinkers* (New York: Harper and Row, 1970); James H. Werntz, *Minnemast Units* (Minneapolis: University of Minnesota, 1968); and Thomas A. Romberg, John G. Harvey, James M. Moser, and Mary E. Montgomery, *Developing Mathematical Processes* (Chicago: Rand McNally, 1974, 1975, 1976).

35. Thomas A. Romberg, *Measurement: An Instructional Approach for Primary School Mathematics, Summary Report.* (Madison: Wisconsin Research Center for Education, 1982).

36. Kenneth R. Lovell, "Intellectual Growth and Understanding Mathematics," *Journal for Research in Mathematics Education* 3 (May 1972): 176.

37. For some excellent examples, see Usiskin, "What Should NOT Be in the Algebra and Geometry Curricula of Average College-bound Students?" pp. 415-16.

38. Harold E. Wolfe, *Introduction to Non-Euclidean Geometry* (New York: Henry Holt, 1945), p. vi.

39. I suspect few mathematics educators would disagree with these seven strands; many might have expected some others. Let me comment on two, problem solving and computer literacy, which I did not include. Problem solving was not included because problem-solving activities should be included in most curriculum units. Dealing with it separately would falsely separate strategies from concepts and procedures where they can be used. Problem solving should be learned from problem situations imbedded in the context of the "story shell" of each instructional unit.

Computer literacy poses a more difficult problem. All students should learn to communicate with and use computers. Such instruction is the responsibility of schools but should not be considered as another part of mathematics. On the other hand, the use of computers in mathematics is important, but it needs to be considered as a tool to solve problems in many of the units within the seven strands.

40. I have chosen this label based on Vergnaud's work with students and their understanding of various arithmetic situations. See Gerard Vergnaud, *L'enfant: la mathématique et la réalité* (Berne: Peter Lang, 1981).

41. For a good discussion of the "situations" in which fractions are used, see Thomas E. Kieren, "On the Mathematical, Cognitive, and Instructional Foundations of Rational Numbers," in Richard A. Lesh, ed., *Number and Measurement* (Columbus, Ohio: ERIC, 1977).

42. W. Allen Wallis and Harry V. Roberts, *Statistics: A New Approach* (Glencoe, Ill.: Free Press, 1956).

43. Herbert Kliebard, "Curriculum Theory: Give Me a 'For Instance'," *Curriculum Inquiry* 6 (1977): 261.

44. Thomas A. Romberg, "Organizing for Individualization: The IGE Model," in F. Joe Crosswhite and R. E. Reys, eds., *Organizing for Mathematics Instruction* (Reston, Va.: National Council of Teachers of Mathematics, 1977), p. 1.

45. Herbert M. Kliebard, "Education at the Turn of the Century: A Crucible for Curriculum Change," *Educational Researcher* 11 (January 1982): 16-24.

46. Ann Anastasi, *Differential Psychology* (New York: Macmillan, 1953).

47. Jonas Langer, *Theories of Development* (New York: Holt, Rinehart and Winston, 1969).

48. Elizabeth Cagan, "Individualism, Collectivism, and Radical Educational Reform," *Harvard Educational Review* 48 (May 1978): 227-66.

49. Lee Cronbach, "The Two Disciplines of Scientific Psychology," *American Psychologist* 12 (December 1957): 671-84.

50. Romberg et al., *Developing Mathematical Processes*.

CHAPTER VII

A Common Curriculum for the Natural Sciences

HUGH MUNBY AND THOMAS RUSSELL

Yearbooks of the National Society for the Study of Education in 1932, 1947, and 1960 reveal three major themes in arguments about the science curriculum: students should know something of the body of scientific knowledge, should study science to develop skills of problem solving, and should study science to develop some of the attitudes attributed to scientists and to the climate in which science may continue to prosper.[1] Given the increasing extent to which ours is a culture influenced by and dependent upon science and its technological applications, the good of the individual and the further development of the culture are said to require the study of science. The focus of this yearbook on the idea of a common curriculum coupled with concern for individual differences invites a break with traditional arguments and calls for a novel analysis, one which also attends to the way schools operate at the present time.

What is taught in schools is closely related to what is written in textbooks, but the basic characteristics of our textbooks do not change. Content has been updated to keep pace, to some extent, with the development of new knowledge in the sciences, but textbooks are at their best in presenting statements of fact and interpretation which are to be learned by students for later use in responding to teachers' questions, both verbal and written. That this tradition persists may be related to two of the fundamental but unspoken aims of teachers' work—the preparation of students for the next level of education, and the provision of equal opportunity for all students to achieve access to the next level of education. In this context, the idea of providing for individual differences appeals to most teachers but, when given opportunities to reflect on their actual success in doing so, many teachers readily admit that they achieve only limited results, far short of the ideal. This is hardly surprising; it is extremely difficult for one individual to respond continuously and creatively to the differences presented by a collection of thirty students.

The most common adaptations to individual differences are ones that relate to ways in which students differ in the pace of their learning. Schools also typically provide separate tracks or levels in each subject at the secondary level, when student differences in achievement have become so significant that they provide an apparent basis for grouping students by ability. Unfortunately, the science curriculum for "less able" students is often a diluted version of the one prepared for students who aspire to enter postsecondary education. In elementary schools, where many teachers work with one group of children for most or all of each day in the school year, there is greater opportunity to adjust content to student characteristics, yet frequently all children are expected to master the same content, if at all possible. The provision of the same book to each student is the most tangible support for this contention.

These manifestations of the conventional approach to thinking about the core curriculum and individual differences exemplify how the traditional way of coping with individual differences flounders in the context of classroom life. The problem lies at the heart of the traditional conception because, from a logical perspective, there is nothing about the idea of a common curriculum that requires all students to master the same body of knowledge, yet it is only too easy to assume that "common curriculum" implies a core curriculum or a single curriculum. The provision of a single curriculum to all students seems to be a prescription for ensuring that at least some educationally relevant differences are ignored. Over the course of the past seven decades, quite distinct trends are apparent in the "emphasis" which has been given to science subjects.[2] Further relevant differences are available in the ways in which textbook authors view and present science, frequently in response to the activities of the 1960s in the development of science curricula. But *experiencing* these differences, though educationally relevant, is beyond the reach of students simply because textbook choices are made at the level of school and school district, rather than at the classroom level. Therefore students have essentially no choice in the way science is presented despite their individual differences. This shows a serious sterility in the assumption of a common core, and presses more urgently for a novel perspective on the problem of individual differences and the core curriculum.

An Alternative Conceptualization of a Common Curriculum

When the focus of talk about individual differences shifts from the student to the curriculum, we witness a switch in attention from instructional procedures to common or core curriculum. Unfortunately, the switch has led many to interpret the common or core curriculum within a comfortable and customary context in which one assumes that the "core" is something that devolves straightforwardly from discussions about what science knowledge (both content and process, in the conventional terminology) is really fundamental to all the areas of science that a student might later encounter. We find this way of viewing the "core" both unwise and unproductive. It is unwise because it is adopted with the expectation that there is such a core, and we have reservations about this expectation as a result of our finding that there have been few substantial changes in science curricula over the last five decades despite the extraordinary changes and advances in science itself and in our understanding of science. It is unproductive because we see that the most favored manifestation of individualization is a pacing and diluting of the so-styled "core." All this returns us to the beginning of the cycle and to the question: "What shall be the core?"

A break in the cycle is needed. We suggest that the most promising approach lies in abandoning the traditional context that has given the above meaning to the phrase "the common or core science curriculum." The way out that we advance here came to us from our manipulating three concepts provided by the editors of this yearbook, who suggested that appropriate educational experiences are those which enable people to live rational, moral, and authentic lives. The more we wrestled with these terms, the more we came to see that one could not expect *rational, moral,* and *authentic* lives to be a consequence of educational experiences *unless the experiences per se were rational, moral, and authentic.* Or, to put it conversely, we can expect dismay, disgruntlement, and disillusionment from students who gather from schooling the implicit message: "Do as I say, not as I do!" Out of this line of thinking came the realization that the terms rational, moral, and authentic could be shaped into a conceptualization that holds promise for offering a novel perspective on individual differences and the common curriculum.

The conceptualization is not easily represented by a diagram, because we are not speaking of a new model for curriculum thinking. Yet, figure 1 is helpful for it foretells the overall direction of the argument, in which the three central concepts are applied to three aspects of the science curriculum: first, to science, education, and science education; second, to the science teacher and the teacher's context; and third, building on the analysis of the previous two aspects, to the individual student.

CENTRAL CONCEPTS

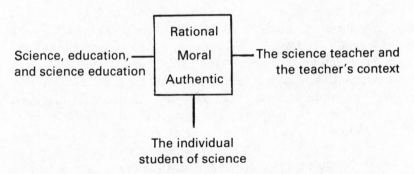

Science, education, and science education —— Rational / Moral / Authentic —— The science teacher and the teacher's context

The individual student of science

Science, Education, and Science Education

The first step in our argument is to use the notion of rationality as a way of showing that science has *limits*, and that these are important to consider when it comes to talking about the common curriculum. The thrust of the argument is to challenge the familiar view that rationality is inexorably linked to science. Here it becomes necessary to prick conventional balloons and to establish that there is nothing especially scientific about "scientific processes" and "scientific thinking." The distinctive essence of thinking in science is to be found in quite different quarters.

THE LIMITS OF SCIENCE

Discussion here can begin with the notion that science is a strictly rational enterprise. Now, while this is true, it is only a part of what is the case, and it is significant to note that conveying part-truths may not be authentically educational. Specifically, if science becomes portrayed as the sole route to rationality, then we run the risk of being inauthentic about science. There is a good deal packed into these statements which needs close examination, so it is helpful to step away from science and look at it from three different perspectives: Pepper's work on world hypotheses, Roberts' work on explanatory modes, and Toulmin's view of the nature of science.

In *World Hypotheses: A Study in Evidence*, Pepper developed the thesis that all human knowledge is built upon six distinct assumptions or world hypotheses: formism, mechanism, contextualism, organicism, mysticism, and animism.[3] The first four of these have a conception of evidence which allows us to see that they give rise to legitimate knowledge, in twentieth-century eyes. The differences among these world hypotheses lie in the sorts of rules which govern what counts as evidence, as a sufficiency of evidence, as argument, and as an appropriate knowledge claim. Recent discussions of Pepper's hypotheses are readily available elsewhere,[4] but a few examples will help to show the legitimacy of each and their idiosyncrasies. In science, typically, it is very important that arguments end in generalizations explaining all events which are of an identical character. We are not satisfied with a theory that explains an event at one time but cannot repeat the explanation at another. Neither, of course, are we satisfied unless explanations are couched in terms of cause and effect, with a very close temporal relationship between the two. In this way, we see that science, particularly physical science, is built upon the powerful metaphysical model of a machine, thus permitting us to construct the universe as if it were a machine, with all the predictability, generalizability, cause and effect, and power that goes hand in hand with the machine metaphor. That is the stuff of mechanism, and once its basic metaphysical postulate is adopted, then the rationality of the epistemological system is in place. Rationality, of course, refers to a system of rules, and the system that the physical sciences have adopted flows inexorably from the mechanistic viewpoint. All well and good, but there *are* other ways of obtaining knowledge, and these rely upon other world hypotheses.

Take history as a case in point. The rationality of the discipline of history flows from the metaphysical stance of contextualism, which urges that to understand an event one needs to examine the full context in which that event occurred. The purpose of history is to do just that, not to seek generalizations about the way in which all humans behave under precisely identical circumstances. As soon as we begin to talk in that style, we are slipping into mechanism and the discipline of psychology is invoked, particularly behaviorism. This is not to suggest that there is something wrong with behaviorism, in principle. The point is that Pepper's treatment of world hypotheses allows us to see why we have different approaches to knowledge and even different answers to the same sorts of questions. In psychology itself, for example, there are several distinctive branches which are not so much at odds with each other but rather stem from distinctive metaphysical positions. Piaget's work, with its familiar insistence upon development, is basically an extension of the growth metaphor that characterizes the organicist hypothesis. Its rationality is secured here, and not in a mechanistic view of development that is equally though differently rational.

It is worth spending time with Pepper's work to begin to see that a strict adherence to the viewpoint that science *is* rationality can be rather misleading. And, although there is evidence that science does get presented this way in schools to some extent,[5] we are not making that claim. Instead, our claim is a logical or analytical one: if science gets presented as the epitome of rationality, then it is being misrepresented. Put another way, such a portrayal is *inauthentic* both to science and to education. And this statement leads directly to showing something of the utility of the conceptualization that we are advancing here to deal with the problem of individual differences and the core curriculum: an inauthentic representation of science is clearly at odds with the attempt to provide for authentic lives. Basic to the requirement of an authentic science education is the requirement that science not be presented as the zenith of man's rationality.

Science, we know, explains. But science is not the *only* system that explains. Roberts makes this very clear by pointing to alternative systems for explaining, which he calls explanatory modes.[6] The significance of his work for present purposes lies in the way that he talks of the personal or psychological satisfaction that must come to us from an offered explanation if it is to fulfill the "whys" that we ask. For many events, scientific explanations satisfy, but only to a point. When faced with very distressing circumstances, such as personal tragedies, scientific explanations may not suffice and we may be surprised to find ourselves turning to other sources or explanatory modes for satisfaction and peace of mind. It is almost as if science runs up against its limit at such times, and that is precisely what Roberts presses: science is limited as a way for humanity to explain its predicaments, and other explanatory modes are appropriate depending upon the circumstances. The consequence of Roberts' treatment is the realization that science in schools can be misrepresented (or represented inauthentically) if it is not presented in the context of being a *limited* explanatory system. We find Pepper and Roberts helpful in recognizing the inauthenticity and the limited view of rationality present in the pervasive assumption that science offers the most direct route to rational thinking.

THE MEANING OF SCIENCE

The next step of this argument requires that we give careful attention to the rationality within science, and here we need to examine two phrases that appear to have accompanied discussions about the science curriculum for many years: the "scientific method" and "scientific processes." We find that neither phrase is very useful for talking about a common core in science, and this is because they turn out to have little to do with science exclusively. Put another way, there appears on examination to be nothing within these phrases that does not belong equally to all disciplines and areas of inquiry. These arguments have been advanced at length elsewhere;[7] the treatment here is necessarily brief.

It is particularly evident in statements of objectives for science curriculum materials that much importance is attached to having youngsters acquire scientific processes, yet when we ask what these might be it becomes evident that they are the sorts of things that can be called logic-wielding and puzzle-solving. To make this plain, it is helpful to look at an example of a test item which professes to measure these things. This item comes from the Psychological Corporation's *Processes of Science Test:*[8]

Several similar rosebuds were selected for an experiment. Half the buds were placed in a liter of tap water; the other half were placed in a liter of similar tap water in which aspirin had been dissolved. The most general hypothesis the experiment was designed to test was that aspirin

(A) will purify tap water.
(B) has an effect on rosebuds.
(C) improves the appearance of rosebuds.
(D) has the same effect on water as do rosebuds.

When we set this item alongside one from the Watson-Glaser *Test of Critical Thinking*,[9] we see a notable similarity.

A report of the U. S. census states that during 1940 there were approximately 1,656,000 marriages and 264,000 divorces granted. Conclusions:
(A) Getting a divorce is a quick and easy matter in the United States.
(B) If the above ratio still holds true, then about six times as many people get married each year as get divorced.
(C) The divorce rate in the U. S. is much too high.

Basically, a knowledge of the content of science is not called upon to answer such items. Instead, a familiarity with logic and general algorithms for solving problems will do the trick. Indeed, a very considerable amount of what gets touted as scientific processes is no more than a contemporary version of Mill's canons,[10] and it is significant to note that despite the title of his work, Mill was dealing with rigorous inquiry generally, of a sort that would apply to history, sociology, literary criticism, and so on, just as much as it would apply to science. This is particularly apparent in the following, which appear among a list of fallacies allegedly relevant to the study of inquiry in biology:

Assuming that events that follow others are caused by them.
Drawing conclusions on the basis of nonrepresentative instances.
Drawing conclusions on the basis of very small and fortuitous differences.[11]

It is our conclusion that nothing *unique* to science is being conveyed by the notions of scientific processes and the scientific method. To be sure, we would want students to be proficient logic-wielders and problem-solvers, but the acquisition of these skills is the responsibility of schooling generally, not the common science curriculum exclusively. However, this conclusion does not leave us without anything to say about the basis of scientific thinking. What is *basic* to the logic of *science* is the way it uses language to construct a unique reality, and it is this uniqueness that sets science apart from other disciplines, which themselves have unique ways of employing language to construct realities.

Consider a brief episode in a recorded grade four science lesson, at the moment when the teacher is advancing a biological classification system in which "people" are classified as "animals." One of the girls in the class, Lucy, objects strenuously to this. "People aren't animals, they're humans," she insists. For a while, the teacher and Lucy remain at verbal loggerheads, until the teacher puts her foot down: "That's enough. People are animals," and essentially closes the discourse. Now, no amount of talk about inadequacies in the logic-wielding and puzzle-solving capabilities of Lucy or her teacher can come close to explaining why these two cannot agree. This is not surprising, for the source of the bitter exchange lies in a problem of language and not of logic. Simply, we have here two category systems, not one. First, there is Lucy's rich and highly useful system for sorting out the significant elements of her perceptual world. Second, there is the teacher's (or rather biology's) highly structured system for ordering things that matter to biologists in a way that is convenient to them. As often happens, some terms in these two separate systems happen to coincide, but that does not mean that the term here, "animals," has the same meaning in each system. It clearly does not. Of course, what the teacher seems to have missed is that Lucy is working with her own language system, and it is no wonder that the child is upset. The teacher could have averted this awkwardness in her lesson by attempting to show the youngsters what science (and other viewpoints) do. She could have established that we, as humans, need to talk about the world we experience, and that we talk about it in different ways according to the needs we have. Thus, in science, a language is used to construct the world along highly specialized lines, because science needs that type of precision. Some terms in science, though familiar to the context of everyday speech, have a different context, and that gives them a different meaning.

Within this understanding of what science does with language lies the heart of what we find *distinctive* about scientific thinking. Science constructs the world using language in a special way, and employs rules about the generalizability of its constructions, their predictive power and explanatory force, and their necessary public testability. Toulmin makes the plainest case for this view. In discussing the principle of rectilinear propagation of light, he makes sure that we do not fall into the language trap of thinking that someone looked and "discovered" that light travelled in straight lines in the same way that one might *discover* footprints in the sand. Toulmin argues:

The discovery that light travels in straight lines—the transition from the state of affairs in which this was not known to that in which it was known—was a double one: it comprised the development of a technique for representing optical phenomena which was found to fit a wide range of facts, and the adoption along with this technique of a new model, a new way of regarding these phenomena, and of understanding why they are as they are.[12]

Highly significant here is the emphasis on "a way of regarding," "a way of understanding." Science is *a* way, not *the* way, of understanding phenomena. With its systematic structures and internal consistencies, it is a powerful way of understanding. Yet, for all of this, science is still just a way of constructing the world. It can be very misleading if we fail to make it clear to youngsters in our teaching and textbooks that science is a construction of experience invented and tested by ourselves, not handed to us on a platter by Mother Nature.[13] Basically, *when we omit this message we leave the way open for the belief that science has really found out what is what in the natural world*. That naive view is an unsatisfactory consequence of science education, because it is an inauthentic view of science. Accordingly, our answer to the question about what is basic to an understanding of scientific thinking has to be that science is a way of using language to construct a highly organized and powerful way of looking at the world and understanding it. Other areas of human inquiry construct reality too, but the constructions are different because they are undertaken with different ends in mind and generated with different constructs and rules. That is why we have separate disciplines. (And we might add that it would be very helpful if youngsters could be encouraged by their education to understand that point also.)

None of this is intended to suggest that the nature of physical reality is decided upon. Instead, as we will see shortly, it becomes very important to our position that ultimate decisions about the nature of reality be left to the judgment of the child. For now, it suffices to say that, if the above authentic view is not provided in youngsters' educational experiences with science, then the opportunity for them to make judgments for themselves on the matter is quickly preempted—a further inauthenticity in education.

SCIENCE IN SOCIETY

We cannot escape from the fact that, once we ask youngsters to adopt, if only for the duration of a course, the scientific perspective on the world, then we and they are involved in moral issues. They have been asked to act, and requests of this kind raise issues of an ethical and moral nature. There is more, for science itself is not conducted in a sphere which is hermetically sealed from the rest of the human condition. Science is a part of life, and its cousin, technology, has a propensity for taking substantial bites from our world. The purposes of science education in a science-dependent society deserve very thorough analysis. Here we limit our discussion to the topics of scientific literacy and student attitudes to science.

Arguments for more or better science education have often been supported, in recent decades, by reference to the importance of "scientific literacy." Karplus sees this literacy as "a functional understanding of scientific concepts," which he explains in this way:

To be able to use information obtained by others, to benefit from the reading of textbooks and other references, the individual must have a conceptual structure and a means of communication that enable him to interpret the information as though he had obtained it for himself.[14]

Arguments based on scientific literacy often stress the importance, in a culture pervaded by and dependent upon science and technology, of a citizenry which has a "functional understanding" so that decisions taken by politicians and at the ballot box may be "informed" and so that support for science will continue.

Champagne and Klopfer have relied exclusively on the idea of scientific literacy when suggesting a way for the science education community to respond, with political pressure, to imminent and substantial reductions in U. S. government spending for education.[15] They argue that economic stability requires a scientifically literate work force. Then, arguing ideologically, they note that U. S. society (a) seeks the well-being of its members, (b) requires citizens who can participate in decisions on science-related social issues, and (c) takes pride in being a world leader. The points are familiar ones. In this instance, scientific literacy is invoked in the name of responding to a perceived crisis closely related to the well-being of the science education community itself.

We find it essential to notice three features of arguments that invoke scientific literacy in support of suggestions for improving science education. Scientific literacy appears to be a very versatile goal which, when achieved, is thought to bring many desirable states in its wake. Also, the arguments tend not to analyze in detail the unique features of "scientific literacy." Finally, the term "literacy" has a distinctly *moral* force in our culture, because illiteracy is so unquestionably an undesirable state. The moral force associated with the term "literacy" may, in fact, account for the frequent lack of detail and the high desirability associated with the more specialized term, "scientific literacy."

Our central point is that the very term "scientific literacy" invites an unquestioningly positive response; it is difficult, at first, to imagine arguing against scientific literacy. Those who invoke this phrase undoubtedly recognize that some training is required before one may read and write the language of science, and that ours is a culture in which certain advantages accrue to those who have a "functional understanding of scientific concepts." Yet it seems equally important to ask whether those who use the term "scientific literacy" intend to bring to their arguments some of the moral force of the term "literacy." Why, for example, do we not hear calls for "musical literacy," or "historical literacy"? The language of science is definitely a specialized one, yet scholars in disciplines other than science know that their disciplines also differ in important and distinctive ways from common sense and everyday knowledge.

Arguments about the need for scientific literacy call attention to a moral dimension of science education which is, in our view, distinctly and unfortunately underdeveloped. Perhaps it is the potential of scientific knowledge to be used to alter our environment (in increasingly threatening ways, at times) which drives part of the need to speak of scientific literacy. We notice, also, that the literature of science education contains very little about the distinctly ambivalent attitude to science which exists in our culture: we enjoy the power of science when it works for the comfort and pleasure of the majority, yet we deeply fear the uncontrolled power of the discipline.[16] To talk simply of scientific literacy seems very much to underestimate the moral dimension of science education.

It is evident that much of this moral dimension ultimately involves the taking of moral decisions by students, and this point is revisited later. Undoubtedly, another significant component of the moral dimension comes from the decisions taken by teachers concerning what they will include in or exclude from classroom study and discussion. In short, and to foreshadow a view we elaborate later, it is unlikely that the notion of scientific literacy can make much headway without taking account of the science teacher's personal context.

Although much of the current thinking on the place of moral decisions in science education appears to acknowledge that, ultimately, it is the student who will take the decision, this is not so clearly seen in the literature of measures of student attitudes to science. Indeed, sketching the argument rather briefly, the literature on measuring student attitudes to science seems to be preoccupied with the development of increasing numbers of instruments, without much thought being given to whether or not the items of these instruments actually do measure attitudes to science, and with virtually no thought being given to the significant moral questions which surround what otherwise seems a simple and straightforward matter: improving youngsters' attitudes to science.[17] In our view, one question appears central: "Is it morally defensible to attempt a systematic change of youngsters' attitudes to science?" On the surface, and certainly following smoothly from the strictly (but inadequate) rational view of science, there is nothing wrong with having people come to like science. Indeed, that idea may not even arise as something that could be right or wrong. But when we learn to view science as a way of constructing experience, and a way that is accompanied by limitations, then we have to ask why we should encourage anyone to adopt such a perspective, and presumably, enjoy it.

Perhaps we have fallen into the trap of expecting our science courses to "significantly improve student attitudes toward science" as a result of perceived implicit pressure from curriculum evaluation. After all, if a course has the potential for improving these attitudes, then we have the potential for measuring the improvement. This thinking can result in the generation of interminable instruments upon which children indicate in various ways their likes or dislikes for science and its components. This approach to curriculum evaluation, which assumes that educational outcomes of even the most complicated sort can be measured, is a close relative of the strictly rational view of science that we have already argued to be inauthentic and excessive. A quick example makes the point. An item from one attitude instrument states: "I wouldn't like to pursue a science research project." If a student indicates agreement, then the typical inference is that he has a negative attitude to science, and if disagreement, then a positive attitude. Unfortunately, neither response tells us very much about *why* the decision was made. That is, whether a student likes or dislikes science is made to seem more important than the fashion in which he came to that view. So long as we are satisfied that students have gained an adequate understanding of science, then whether or not they like science remains, as always, a matter of personal preference. And, if our understanding of the concept of education is correct, then attempts to alter personal preferences do not fit, but are better seen as miseducational.

Accordingly, it looks very much as if there is a serious moral issue lying at the root of thinking about attitudes to science, just as a moral issue lies beneath the language of "scientific literacy." In the latter, exhortations about scientific literacy have the potential for making moral decisions on behalf of students, while the concern for positive attitudes toward science appears to preempt the place of personal preference. And, of course, when it comes down to issues at the science, technology, and society interfaces, the significance of moral judgments and their authorship is inescapable. We find that these matters are best considered by attending to what we refer to as the authenticity of education.

AUTHENTICITY IN SCIENCE EDUCATION

It should be apparent we have refrained from making a model of the three concepts rational, moral, and authentic because the concepts are interactive and do not feed linearly from one to the next. So it is that our discussion of the excessively rational view of science reveals this view to be inauthentic, thus providing the understanding that depicting an inauthentic view of science in teaching or in texts constitutes an inauthentic science education experience. Similarly, the above discussions about the likely immorality of deliberately moving to alter someone's attitude shows the clear linkage between the moral and authentic concepts in education, because deliberately changing attitudes is antithetical to authentic education. In this section, we need to expand on our view of authenticity in education so that we can point again to the matter of the common core, though in a way that is independent of considerations of content as such.

Komisar has argued that *teaching* is an inauthentic human encounter, "a service masquerading as a gift" though lacking gift features and not waiting upon "client demand or acquiescence." "It is thrust upon minds not fit out to welcome, avoid or even appraise it. Imagine . . . trying to make a mind aware so it can choose whether to become so."[18] First glance would suggest that, in teaching, the teacher holds all the aces, leaving the students with few of the prerogatives that we normally possess in social discourse, not the least of these being to disagree and to disengage. Yet it is equally apparent that one prerogative remains in the province of the student, that of deciding whether to accept or reject, silently, what is being purveyed. It is at this point that we need to introduce into the argument some considerations about how we might wish decisions about truth and falsity and the adoption or rejection of viewpoints to be taken by students. Presumably, decisions of this sort can be taken in several ways, ranging from the toss of a coin, through a reliance upon ill-considered beliefs, to a thoroughgoing analysis of all pertinent details. We are of the view that the last of these is the most defensible approach to the making of judgments, and the capacity for making judgments in this way has been referred to as being "intellectually independent." Essentially, being intellectually *independent* means possessing all the resources—assumptions, alternatives, evidence, and arguments—that are necessary for judging a claim independently of the "say-so" of others. And the condition of intellectual independence is not applicable just to knowledge claims, but pertains equally to value positions, views of science, and views of the nature of reality.[19]

The implication here is that, if there is any determination for teaching to be conducted in a manner that is congruent with our aspirations for rational, moral, and authentic encounters, then it must make provision for students to make their judgments from a position of knowledge. In its ideal form this requires that classroom discourse contain arguments, evidence, alternatives, and so forth, of the sort which we normally associate with rational discourse, and that these requirements become the responsibility of the students as well as the teacher.

Anything less than this can be the cause of considerable inauthenticity in science education. If students are denied access to the support for a scientific theory, if they have no way of knowing why a portion of reality is thought to be adequately represented by one model rather than by another, if they are presented with one moral position in the absence of alternatives, and if they are forced to adopt the scientific worldview without the option of at least examining alternatives, then the experience loses some of its integrity, tends toward inauthenticity, and leaves the phrase "Do as I say, not as I do" ringing stridently.

The Science Teacher and the Teacher's Context

The approach to the common science curriculum that we are advancing is clearly more than a matter of rearranging the "paper curriculum"—the content of textbooks, course outlines, laboratory work, and examinations. Our argument makes the case that if individual differences are to be accommodated within a common science curriculum then the only way this can be done is by presenting an authentic account of science and by teaching in an authentic manner. These ideas become the *context* of any science that is taught. But the concept of context has another and equally important side to it, and this refers to the teacher's setting. Here, then, we need to examine the way in which shortcomings of this setting may impede the fostering of the qualities of reason, morality, and authenticity through students' study of a common curriculum in science.

It is often noted, correctly, that teachers have considerable autonomy within the confines of their classrooms. We have little evidence about how fully teachers utilize or test the limits of that autonomy; teaching can also be a surprisingly lonely occupation. These points deserve mention because they contrast with the very significant ways in which teachers' work is constrained. In addition to the normative pressures exerted by parents and students, teachers are more formally influenced by administrative decisions and practices with respect to the curriculum and with respect to supervision procedures. In each of these two broad domains, traditions have persisted through most of this century, although various schools of thought have produced variations over time. The following discussion treats these elements of the teacher's context in terms of the concepts rational, moral, and authentic. As in the discussion on science, we are concerned that rationality has been applied overzealously to contextual matters.

CURRICULUM

The most recent wave of curriculum revision, during the 1960s, was particularly significant in the natural sciences, at both elementary and secondary levels. Personnel of the curriculum projects appeared to take a rational view of the science teacher, a view so exclusively rational that it seemed to be assumed that changes in teaching practices could be made as easily as, say, turning on a light switch, once a directive had been given to teachers to adopt a particular new curriculum. Significantly, this rationality ignores the science teacher as an *individual*; most curriculum decisions are taken by committees of teachers, at the school and school district levels. Yet new materials must be used by teachers as individuals, and individuals choose, select, even reject. So, when the 1970s began to produce studies of the extent to which curricula had been adopted as intended by developers, we soon heard teachers referred to as "stone-age obstructionists" or, more generously, as "pragmatic skeptics,"[20] presumably because they were not "rationally" following rational implementation plans. The term "pragmatic skeptic" reflects, at least partially, the realities that teachers had become skeptical of "new" curricula and that teachers are obligated to make a given program work. The concepts of morality and authenticity remind us that teachers must remain true to themselves, at least partially, and must also be able to preserve some sense of a personal concept of education in their relationships with their students. There is more to the matter than rationality and "what works."

We may explore these issues further by turning to the teacher's relationship to the educational researcher, which closely parallels the teacher's relationship to the curriculum. The researcher is often seen as the developer and disseminator of educational theory and, in turn, theory is commonly regarded as something to be put into practice directly by a teacher—a further extension of the rational approach. Roberts has shed important new light on this issue by arguing that curriculum materials and theoretical statements from research are *not* meant to tell teachers what to do. "The potential contribution is one of conceptual enrichment, rather than direct influence on action."[21] Put another way, research can be seen as enhancing the potential for sound professional judgment. Roberts stresses the significance of the *context* in which teaching occurs: "Teachers inevitably have to modulate the materials they select when they are confronted with the particularities of their individual pupils in their own unique situations."[22] Furthermore, educational research modeled on scientific research assumes a theory of change which is exclusively rational,[23] yet experience tells us that contextual considerations are highly significant in the formation and maintenance of teaching practices. By using science as a model, we may have achieved some degree of respectability but paid the price of irrelevance. Research *is* irrelevant unless one can see similarities between one's personal teaching context and that of the research being considered.

Just how great the gap can be between theory and practice is apparent in the work of Argyris and Schön, who suggest the value of separating theories of action into espoused theories (the principles one says one does follow in a situation) and theories-in-use (the principles implicit in one's actual behavior).[24] Their studies of professional behavior indicate that it is common, even normal, to find significant discrepancies between espoused theories and theories-in-use. Also, reducing or eliminating such discrepancies is neither easy nor something which follows readily from simple awareness of the discrepancies. Science teachers like to joke about the expert who lectures to them on the virtues of the "discovery method," yet the joke seems no laughing matter when we begin to realize that every teacher probably displays discrepancies between what he or she thinks is being done and what students experience the teacher to be doing. It is, most immediately, a matter of authenticity: to say that "the words and the tune don't go together" puts it rather well.

From arguments such as these, we conclude that the relationship of curriculum developers and researchers to science teachers has been an excessively rational one, deficient in terms of significant contextual considerations including those indicated by the terms "moral" and "authentic." We do not seek to assign blame. However, recognizing this feature of the science teacher's curriculum context helps us to understand why teachers have found it difficult to attend to all curricular prescriptions, including attending to individual differences in students. Those in authority, by either expertise or position or both, have not established a relationship with teachers, on matters of curriculum, which could be characterized as strong on the dimensions of morality and authenticity.

SUPERVISION

We do not find major differences between the curriculum context and the supervisory context in which most teachers work. To observe a teacher at work in the classroom and then make judgments and prescribe changes is, in its crudest form, to ignore the context of the teacher and to take an exclusively rational view of how practices may be changed. Of course, many of the individuals who perform official duties of supervision do so with some significant knowledge of the teacher's classroom context, but the act of supervision is set within a tradition which has little or no capacity for incorporating contextual details into the procedures and results of supervision. "Clinical supervision" makes important moves in the direction of recognizing contextual features, yet it has remained a minor movement in the field of supervision and it tends not to gain the support of those who set supervisory policies.[25]

In considering the possibility that a supervisor may prescribe changes in teaching practices on the basis of findings from process-product research on teaching, Fenstermacher has suggested terms which highlight the potential neglect of the teacher's rationality.[26] He draws a contrast between "conversion" and "transformation," noting that it is only too easy, yet rationally and morally problematic, to omit opportunities for the teacher to interpret research findings in the light of personal beliefs. It is not only the teacher's personal beliefs but also the teacher's own understanding of the context of his or her teaching that must be brought to bear on decisions to attempt to change teaching behavior. The tradition of supervisory practices has neglected these contextual features, much as the traditions of curriculum development and research have neglected the context in which the individual science teacher works. These traditions, which are deeply embedded in today's educational setting, have their definite strengths, but they are not well suited to the challenge of meeting individual differences, whether among teachers or among students.

We have argued that traditions in curriculum and supervision have been excessively rational in their views of how theoretical principles influence practice and, correspondingly, have been neglectful of the context of the work of individual teachers. Brief reference to items of recent research that attend to teachers' context adds substance to our position. Olson, who studied eight teachers attempting to use the materials of the Schools Council Integrated Science Project, found major gaps between existing practices and the demands of the new materials. His conclusion that the teachers were making adaptations to maintain their customary practices explains many of the difficulties that innovations have faced in the past.[27] With respect rather than criticism for teachers' work, Olson has helped to reveal contextual features that are significant in any scheme for modifying educational practice.

The case-study findings of Stake and Easley[28] stress the central and critical place of the science teacher and the emphasis which the science teacher gives, in practice, to skills and information derived from text-books. This emphasis has long been criticized, but we find it much more important to understand it as a practical compromise by teachers who must resolve many, often conflicting, pressures. No matter how much the "paper curriculum" makes noises about individual differences, what really counts is the curriculum-in-use, and that is always a consequence of the teacher and the teacher's context.

The Individual Student

The failings of conventional approaches to the common core should by now have become clear. Driven most frequently by the perceived need to keep a watchful eye upon entrance requirements for university science, the typical approach is to view the common core as consisting of a common science content wrapped up in scientific method, scientific processes, and a general encouragement to enjoy science, all as preparation for science courses at the succeeding level. When this view is confronted with the demand to be responsive to the individual (and real) differences presented by a classful of students, the view necessarily stumbles, falters, and dies. It meets its end mostly because its conceptualization is inadequate to the real and chalkface task of dealing with *context*. What we have argued in this chapter is that an entirely fresh approach to the problem is needed—one that is true not only to the context of the individuality of teacher and student, but also one which heeds and preserves the special integrity of science education itself. For this reason, we have fashioned our arguments around the idea of a rational, moral, and authentic education in science. As we have shown, the articulation of these concepts is helpful to gaining a purchase on what is truly central and unique to science: that science provides *a* (not *the*) way of constructing reality. Pushed further, the concepts show us something of the necessary character of educational discourse: it must be conducted so as to provide for intellectual independence.

Significantly, these two results of the analysis of science education point to the *context* of science education, and this becomes the key to altering the traditional view of the common core. In the view of the common core that we are pressing, what is common is *context*. That is, the question "What should all youngsters gain from some education in science?" is answered by pointing to what we have said about the nature of science and about intellectual independence, and not by arguing endlessly about what theoretical content of science is most basic.

It is also important to our case that we declare why we think arguments about basic or core content are unproductive. It is not that we jettison content considerations, but that we cannot see the fruitfulness of talking about science content without an understanding of the context (again) in which it is to be delivered. Here the context is two-fold. First, there is the context represented by the teacher of science. As we have shown, the traditional view of the common core carries the notion of rational science right into the heart of curriculum implementation, and makes the appallingly naive assumption that if a teacher (or any other professional) is told what to do, absolute compliance will result. Again, the problem is one of failing to attend to context. Teachers hold perspectives on what is valuable to learn in science, and these perspectives are bound to make a difference to what gets taught, and to the emphasis that different parts of the curriculum receive. Second, there is the context presented by the individuals and the class they compose. Unsurprisingly, the teacher's understandings of the students, their abilities, interests, and aspirations will influence his or her selection of content and the emphasis that it receives. It is at this point precisely that our conception for dealing with the common core and individual differences bears fruit.

Our conception of the common core involves two components: context (of science and education), and *variable* content. The idea that something that is variable can be core may seem disturbing at first, but it proves to be the only way to proceed without doing violence to the notion of individuality. We have argued that whatever science content a student studies, he or she should experience that content in ways which identify the limits of science and the special role of language and concepts in science. That much should be *common*. In addition, every student should be offered the opportunity to *choose* among a number of different ways of approaching the science content to be studied.

Traditionally, at the high school level, we have provided a single choice for students whose exceptionalities are not extreme. Students who require a slower pace and students who are not bound for university are offered a "diluted" version of the material designed for those who do seek university entrance. This is a very limited choice, if it is a choice at all, and it implies a very limited range of educationally significant differences: university-able, and university-unable. It also implies that there may be only the single approach to science in the school curriculum, namely, that which prepares students for studying science at the next level. But the domains of natural science may be approached interestingly and productively from a wide range of perspectives, all of which are candidates for the school curriculum.

Some of these alternative perspectives exist in the significant curriculum options of the marketplace, thanks in part to the developmental projects sponsored by the National Science Foundation during the 1960s. The Biological Sciences Curriculum Study developed three separate versions of high school biology, organized around the perspectives of biochemistry, ecology, and levels of biological complexity.[29] In high school physics, *The Project Physics Course* set out to reduce the mathematical aspects and emphasize the "humanistic" aspects of science;[30] in part, this is done by including significant amounts of historical material. *PSSC Physics* does not attempt to "cover" all of physics, but instead emphasizes the development of the conceptual schemes which are central to the discipline of physics.[31] So-called "traditional" textbooks continue to provide a comprehensive treatment of physics with generous reference to everyday applications.

At the elementary level, projects such as the Elementary Science Study, the Science Curriculum Improvement Study, and Science—A Process Approach generated significantly different approaches to the study of science.[32]

We are of the view that the commercially available alternative approaches to the study of science in the elementary and secondary schools only scratch the surface of the possibilities for meeting individual differences by providing genuine choices for students. Alternatives need also to be offered which honor Layton's view that there are different *sciences*.[33] If we follow this view, then we see that it is unrealistic to speak of the science curriculum as if there were *a* science. Layton sees several sciences whose distinctiveness lies not in the subdisciplines to which we have become accustomed but in the way in which science appears as important in different lines of work and inquiry. Thus we can see the science of high technology as different from the science of medicine. Our suggestion is that if *real choice* is to be available to *students*, then teachers need to be encouraged to generate quite novel approaches to science. We see the possibility of the following sorts of approaches being made available to students in schools: high technology science, surgical science, industrial science, scientific research and ethics, science and pollution, engineering science,[34] health care science, mathematical modelling and science, the science of music, architectural science, nuclear science, science and societal safety, and so on.

The list of possibilities like these is virtually limitless. But we need to end, not only because our space is limited, but also because the thrust of our argument is that *teachers* ought to make these sorts of choices. We have chosen not to make detailed recommendations, ones which could be attempted without close attention to underlying rationales and to the unique features of each teacher's working context. We hope that the new perspectives we have suggested will guide the development of contextually appropriate modifications, respectful of individual differences and of the discipline of science. As we have said, the traditional conception of the common core carries with it a view of curriculum implementation that ignores the essential contextual features confronting the science teacher and assumes that the teacher will comply with the perceived inherent rationality of a designated core. Our perspective on the core is quite different. It takes account of what is authentic in science education, and then attends to the teacher's context. Educationally significant individual differences, says our perspective, are met best by (a) providing students with genuine choices among alternative approaches to a given science subject at a particular grade level, and (b) encouraging teachers to develop those alternative curricular approaches which are in concert with their views of what is important about science for the individual students they teach.

FOOTNOTES

1. *A Program for Teaching Science*, ed. Guy M. Whipple, Thirty-first Yearbook of the National Society for the Study of Education, Part I (Bloomington, Ill.: Public School Publishing Co., 1932); *Science Education in American Schools*, ed. Nelson B. Henry, Forty-sixth Yearbook of the National Society for the Study of Education, Part I (Chicago: University of Chicago Press, 1947); *Rethinking Science Education*, ed. Nelson B. Henry, Fifty-ninth Yearbook of the National Society for the Study of Education, Part I (Chicago: University of Chicago Press, 1960).

2. Douglas A. Roberts, "Developing the Concept of 'Curriculum Emphases' in Science Education," *Science Education* 66 (April 1982): 243-60.

3. Stephen C. Pepper, *World Hypotheses: A Study in Evidence* (Berkeley, Calif.: University of California Press, 1942).

4. Douglas A. Roberts, "The Place of Qualitative Research in Science Education," *Journal of Research in Science Teaching* 19 (April 1982): 277-92; Brent Kilbourn, "World Views and Science Teaching," in *Seeing Curriculum in a New Light: Essays from Science Education*, ed. Hugh Munby, Graham Orpwood, and Thomas Russell (Toronto: OISE Press, 1980).

5. Michael W. Apple, *Ideology and Curriculum* (London: Routledge and Kegan Paul, 1979).

6. Douglas A. Roberts, "Science as an Explanatory Mode," *Main Currents in Modern Thought* 26 (1970): 131-39.

7. Hugh Munby, *What Is Scientific Thinking?* (Ottawa: Science Council of Canada, 1982).

8. Biological Sciences Curriculum Study, *Processes of Science Test* (New York: Psychological Corp., 1962).

9. Goodwin Watson and Edward M. Glaser, *Critical Thinking Appraisal* (New York: World Book Co., 1952).

10. John Stuart Mill, *Philosophy of Scientific Method* (New York: Hafner Publishing Co., 1950).

11. A. Dreyfus and E. Jungwirth, "Students' Perception of the Logical Structure of Curricular as Compared with Everyday Contexts: Study of Critical Thinking Skills," *Science Education* 64 (July 1980): 309-21.

12. Stephen Toulmin, *The Philosophy of Science: An Introduction* (New York: Harper and Row, 1960), p. 29.

13. Hugh Munby, *What Is Scientific Thinking?*; idem, "Some Implications of Language in Science Education," *Science Education* 60 (January 1976): 115-24; Thomas Russell, "Analyzing Arguments in Classroom Discourse: Can Teachers' Questions Distort Scientific Authority?" *Journal of Research in Science Teaching*, in press.

14. Robert Karplus, "The Science Curriculum Improvement Study," *Journal of Research in Science Teaching* 2 (December 1964): 296.

15. Audrey B. Champagne and Leopold E. Klopfer, "Actions in a Time of Crisis," *Science Education* 66 (July 1982): 503-14.

16. George Basalla, "Pop Science: The Depiction of Science in Popular Culture," in *Science and Its Public: The Changing Relationship*, ed. Gerald Holton and William A. Blanpied (Boston: D. Reidel Publishing Co., 1976); Thomas Russell, "What History of Science, How Much, and Why?" *Science Education* 65 (January 1981): 51-64.

17. Hugh Munby, "An Evaluation of Instruments Which Measure Attitudes to Science," in *World Trends in Science Education*, ed. C. P. McFadden (Halifax, Nova Scotia: Atlantic Institute of Education, 1980); Hugh Munby, "Thirty Studies Involving the Science Attitude Inventory: What Confidence Can We Have in This Instrument?" *Journal of Research in Science Teaching*, in press.

18. B. Paul Komisar, "Is Teaching Phoney?" *Teachers College Record* 70 (February 1969): 407-11.

19. Hugh Munby, "Analyzing Teaching for Intellectual Independence," in *Seeing Curriculum in a New Light*, ed. Munby, Orpwood, and Russell.

20. Walter Doyle and Gerald A. Ponder, "The Practicality Ethic in Teacher Decision-Making," *Interchange* 8, no. 3 (1977): 1-12.

21. Douglas A. Roberts, "Theory, Curriculum Development, and the Unique Events of Practice," in *Seeing Curriculum in a New Light*, ed. Munby, Orpwood, and Russell, p. 85.

22. Ibid.

23. Thomas Russell, "Teacher Education Research and the Problems of Change," in *Seeing Curriculum in a New Light*, ed. Munby, Orpwood, and Russell.

24. Chris Argyris and Donald A. Schön, *Theory in Practice: Increasing Professional Effectiveness* (San Francisco: Jossey-Bass, 1978).

25. Robert Goldhammer, *Clinical Supervision* (New York: Holt, Rinehart and Winston, 1969); Morris L. Cogan, *Clinical Supervision* (Boston: Houghton Mifflin, 1973); Brent Kilbourn, "Linda: A Case Study in Clinical Supervision," *Canadian Journal of Education* 7 (1982): 1-24.

26. Gary D Fenstermacher, "A Philosophical Consideration of Recent Research on Teacher Effectiveness," in *Review of Research in Education 6*, ed. Lee S. Shulman (Itasca, Ill.: F. E. Peacock, 1978).

27. John Olson, "Teacher Influence in the Classroom: A Context for Understanding Curriculum Translation," *Instructional Science* 10 (September 1981): 259-75.

28. Robert E. Stake and Jack A. Easley, Jr. (Codirectors), *Case Studies in Science Education*, Vol. I: *The Case Reports*; Vol. II: *Design, Overview and General Findings* (Washington, D.C.: U. S. Government Printing Office, 1978).

29. Biological Sciences Curriculum Study, *Biological Science: A Molecular Approach*, Blue Version, 4th ed. (Lexington, Mass.: D. C. Heath and Co., 1980); *Biological Science: An Ecological Approach*, Green Version, 3d ed. (Chicago: Rand McNally and Co., 1973); *Biological Science: An Inquiry into Life*, Yellow Version, 3d ed. (New York: Harcourt Brace Jovanovich, 1972).

30. F. James Rutherford, Gerald Holton, and Fletcher G. Watson (Directors), *The Project Physics Course* (New York: Holt, Rinehart and Winston, 1970).

31. Uri Haber-Schaim, Judson B. Cross, John H. Dodge, and James A. Walter, *PSSC Physics* (Lexington, Mass.: D. C. Heath, 1976).

32. For a brief comparison of these three elementary science curricula, see Donald Kauchak and Paul Eggen, *Exploring Science in the Elementary Schools* (Chicago: Rand McNally College Publishing Co., 1980), pp. 332-35.

33. This view was suggested by David Layton, Director of the Centre for Studies in Science Education, Leeds University, during a colloquium at Queen's University, July 1982.

34. Donald A. George, *An Engineer's View of Science Education* (Ottawa: Science Council of Canada, 1981).

CHAPTER VIII

A Common Curriculum for Language and Literature

MARGARET J. EARLY

It is possible to conceive of a common curriculum for language and literature that is adaptable to the widest range of individual differences and still provides every learner with the essential knowledge and skills for leading "rational, moral, and authentic lives," provided that we limit such a conception to goals and themes. I begin this chapter by explaining why a curricular model in language and literature is usually stated in goals and themes. I shall look at the influences on the curriculum in English (that is, language and literature), referring to curricular models that have been recommended over the years, especially those emanating from the National Council of Teachers of English.

To define the curriculum in English in terms of goals and themes is to argue that what students should learn in English classes is how to use language in understanding themselves and others. Such a broad goal must be further specified in terms of *process*, as in learning how to send and receive messages; *attitudes*, like respecting another person's language; and *appreciations*, like enjoying a short story. Specifying *themes* as well as *goals*, the curriculum maker suggests the range of ideas that students might encounter in using language to understand themselves and others and offers an assortment of texts that relate to these themes. But specifying themes is as far as most curriculum makers will go; they hold back from specifying works of literature. *Topics* may be included as ways of organizing the uses of language skills. *Concepts* may be listed, such as understanding how literature reflects cultural traditions, but specific technical vocabulary assigned to any grade level is likely to be avoided.

Courtney Cazden served as the editorial consultant for this chapter.

Defined in these terms, so that there are no universal requirements as to what is to be read, listened to, written about, or discussed, an English curriculum can be adapted to a wide range of abilities without sacrificing major goals and central themes. Students who are different in every respect—backgrounds, aptitudes, interests, aspirations, abilities—can learn how to use language, choose books and films, respond to literature, raise questions, make decisions, order their priorities, and assess their values. The educational experiences leading to these goals can be based on language lessons and literature selected to match the developing abilities of the learners. In matching readers with books, for instance, or writers with assignments, teachers can respect students' interests and abilities. Even within restrictions imposed by concepts to be learned (such as how dialogue reveals character or how words change in meaning), English teachers still have considerable luxury of choice.

When the high school existed chiefly to prepare students for entrance to liberal arts colleges, the curriculum in English usually was restricted to studying the books that were the bases for the college entrance examinations. In the first decade of the 1900s, a group of English teachers, working through the National Education Association, protested the attempt by colleges to control the English curriculum through the issuance of the book lists, and out of this committee was born the National Council of Teachers of English (NCTE) in 1911. By 1917, the Hosic report on the *Reorganization of English in Secondary Schools* offered pages of titles of modern works as well as classics from which teachers might choose reading matter to suit their students. The idea that there is no set canon of literary works that would dictate the content of the English curriculum in elementary and secondary classrooms thus began to influence curriculum theorists almost from the first decade of this century. The idea did not take hold rapidly, however. It was not until teachers began to realize how few high school graduates entered college—in 1950, 20 percent was the national norm—that they began to move away from what they perceived to be a college-oriented curriculum. The no-set-canon theory had little effect on most elementary teachers, who tended to ignore "literature" in favor of "reading skills," and it had little effect on curriculum theorists who said that elementary schools open to all children should be more concerned with process than with content in any case.

Over the years English teachers have had reason to welcome a curriculum that imposed few requirements and allowed the widest choice of texts. One reason is the changing composition of the high school population, which in 1910 represented less than 10 percent of the age group and in 1980 more than 75 percent. At the same time that the high school has become the common school attended by almost everyone, it remains a preparatory school for more than half its students. In the 1980s, for example, about 60 percent of high school graduates are expected to enter college. However, far from suggesting a return to a set list of books as a core for curriculum development, these statistics emphasize the need for centering on goals and themes and permitting teachers to choose several texts that convey a particular theme, assigning them to students at different levels of literacy who can thus move toward common goals along different paths.

Curricular theories that depend on teachers making choices of materials have been recommended in the professional literature on teaching English for almost as long as English has been recognized as a school discipline. The first problem these theories encounter is teachers' reluctance to choose. Freedom of choice leads to confusion. "What is English?" the teachers ask, echoing Archibald MacLeish, who received no satisfactory reply when he put that question to the head of the English Department at Harvard, whose ranks he was about to join. "Give us national guidelines for English curricula," they say to their professional organizations, as they did in 1977 in a sense-of-the-house motion at the business meeting of the National Council of Teachers of English. "Where are the textbooks?" asks the novice teacher. "Is there not a literary heritage to be transmitted to the young?" "Are there not master works that can be identified for each grade level?" "What are the questions on the SAT, the state-mandated competency exams, the school district tests, the end-of-term reviews, the mastery tests?"

Answers to these questions come from textbook publishers and testmakers as well as from educational theorists and writers of curriculum guides. Teachers shape these answers into "what to teach" according to what they believe about how children learn and what teachers are supposed to do to assist that learning. And if the curriculum is equated with what happens in the classroom, then the curriculum is also influenced by how classes are scheduled, how students are assigned to classes, and how they are grouped for instruction within the classes. All these influences must be considered as we test the question of whether teachers can adapt a curriculum stated in terms of common goals and themes to the needs of students who represent a wide range of abilities.

Influences on the English Curriculum

EDUCATIONAL THEORIES AND PHILOSOPHIES

A reasonable procedure for determining the goals of a common curriculum, especially those related to language acquisition and development, is to identify the life needs of the learner; specify objectives based on those needs; arrange learning experiences leading to these objectives; measure the results and, on the basis of these results, plan future learning sequences. From the early years of this century to the present time, this method of organizing the curriculum has been urged on English teachers. To accommodate the different needs and abilities of students within the same classroom, different learning experiences have been arranged around common topics or problems or themes.

An "experience curriculum" for kindergarten through grade twelve, issued by the National Council of Teachers of English in 1935, is a good example of the application of this general curricular theory to the teaching of English.[1] The experience strands were drawn from life needs: social conversation, telephoning, interviews and conferences, social and business letters, listening to radio broadcasts, and enjoying films. All instruction, the writers advised, must be related to real situations. "Classroom experience that is itself real and is as close as possible to the reality of extraschool and postschool life, without deception or pretense, must be the actual basis of any realistic curriculum."[2] In 1939, *Conducting Experiences in English* advised teachers to individualize instruction through the use of contracts and through topical or thematic units which permitted students to work at their own pace on different materials all related to a central theme.[3]

From World War II to the launching of Sputnik, theories from life adjustment education significantly affected the curricular models that the National Council of Teachers of English presented as successors to the so-called "experience curriculum." For example, the second of the five volumes produced by the Commission on the English Curriculum, *The English Language Arts in the Secondary School*, listed the physical, mental, and emotional characteristics of adolescents in one section, the language characteristics in another, and cross-referenced teaching and learning activities to young people's needs as shaped on the one hand by their changing physiological and psychological nature and, on the other hand, by the complex and rapidly changing society in which they lived.[4] Although influenced by the psychological theories of the 1940s and 1950s, which emphasized developmental stages, the NCTE curriculum writers were limited, according to Applebee, in their understanding of the concept of growth, since they had no theory of cognitive or moral development from which to draw. They could only describe what the student might be like at a given time and suggest activities appropriate to that "static delineation."[5] Nevertheless, the volumes were well received by the profession and had considerable use in teacher education in the decade in which they appeared.

The launching of Sputnik in 1957 is generally credited with the demise of the life adjustment curriculum and the beginning of the search for the "new" English. Of course, Sputnik is only a convenient and arbitrary marker on the time line; the shift to an academically oriented English curriculum had earlier prodding from critics of the schools like Albert Lynd (*Quackery in the Public Schools*), Arthur Bestor (*Educational Wastelands*), and Rudolf Flesch (*Why Johnny Can't Read*), many of whom united to form the Council on Basic Education in 1956. During the subsequent decade, academicians in English and psychology moved into the lower schools with their theories and research. "School people turned to the studies of Jean Piaget to learn how children developed, to the works of B. F. Skinner to discover how children could be controlled, and to the theories of Jerome Bruner to discover how children could be taught," writes Glatthorn, crediting Piaget and Bruner with the greatest impact on the school curriculum.[6] During this time Glatthorn, who later served as director of the NCTE continuing Commission on the English Curriculum, was a high school English teacher and principal very much involved in developing and using curricula. It was a time, he says, when curriculum leaders believed that "the theories and research of the academicians, rationally applied, could be used to develop 'teacher-proof' curricula, based upon the structure of the discipline."[7]

Humanitarian philosophies dominated the curriculum proposals of the next ten years, beginning with the Dartmouth Seminar in
the summer of 1966, which brought together fifty specialists in the
teaching of English from England, Canada, and the United States, and
ending with the back-to-the-basics movement of the mid-1970s.
Miller forecast a "revitalized English curriculum," which would avoid
the arid and often artificial literature study of the academic period and
would educate the moral imagination.[8] In the late 1960s and early
1970s, curriculum theory backed away from the prior emphasis on
structure in language and language development and again focused
attention on students. Characteristic of the "student-centered curriculum" were concern for the student's own language, use of im-
provisational drama, the primacy of informal discussion as the instructional mode, and the encouragement of imaginative writing. At the
elementary level, the best setting for the student-centered curriculum
was said to be the open classroom. At secondary levels, the elective
system emerged as the vehicle for delivering curricula to serve
students' interests.

We turn now to the recent past and to the present. Glatthorn's label
for the period, "privatistic conservatism," is an attempt to capture two
moods at large in society and also in education: concern for self (this is
the "me generation") and a resistance to change. Summing up, Glatthorn says that aside from a "widespread" renewal of interest in mastery
learning, some attention to the gifted, and much talk about what is basic
in English, the current period finds most English teachers either "sitting
back and waiting" or "cautiously refining older practices."[9]

This summary treatment of the influence of educational theories
and philosophies on curriculum treatment owes much to the perceptions of others, mostly Glatthorn. Glatthorn acknowledges his debt to
Applebee, whose sources are largely the written documents produced
by a very small percentage of the elementary and secondary teachers
who are teaching language and literature. Many of the sources referred
to are the curricular recommendations of committees and individuals in the National Council of Teachers of English. I believe these
sources yield an accurate account of what educational theories have
been influential at the leadership level. But how accurate a picture do
we have of what is happening in the hundreds of thousands of

elementary and secondary classrooms where the curriculum in language and literature is what happens from day to day, indeed from minute to minute?

INSTRUCTIONAL MATERIALS

To hazard a guess about what is actually taught in language and literature we must turn to sources other than those we have thus far examined. The recommendations of scholars and national committees influence classroom practice only indirectly and with considerable dilution as they move through the instructional hierarchy to the teacher in the classroom. Curriculum writers at state and local levels incorporate many facets of recommended programs into their documents, thus moving them a step nearer to actual use. But what Goodlad defines as the *formal* curriculum,[10] issuing from a state education department or local school district, is often ignored, or read and forgotten. There may be some effect on the actual curriculum, but not nearly so much as there is when curricular recommendations from the leadership are translated into commercially published instructional materials. For example, at a NCTE meeting in the early 1960s, a publisher heard Paul Roberts extol structural linguistics as the way to teach grammar and thus improve writing and speaking, contracted with him for a series of textbooks for kindergarten through grade twelve, and within a few years (and for a short time) in many schools across the country the curriculum in language was the Roberts English Program.[11]

Moffett's student-centered curriculum, which was first described in a professional text and then translated into instructional materials for elementary classrooms, is a different example.[12] Leaders in the field credit Moffett with bringing significant synthesis to English education and having far-reaching influence on teachers' thinking. Undoubtedly his ideas have impressed teacher educators in English, especially at the secondary level, who cite his *Teaching the Universe of Discourse* as essential reading for future teachers.[13] But publication of instructional materials that implement Moffett's ideas has not made them the actual curriculum in many of the nation's schools. One reason may be that the teachers most likely to use them prefer to devise their own similar materials; another reason is that many language arts supervisors judge the program too complex and its materials too numerous for many teachers to handle.

Other examples might be cited to help us estimate the power of publishers' influence on the curriculum as it is taught. Many textbook series in language and literature that faithfully interpret the curricular theories of leaders in academic and professional circles do not win the approval of language arts consultants, teachers, or state and local education board members who constitute textbook committees. For instance, an attractive paperback series for grades seven through twelve,[14] which implemented Northrop Frye's theories of literature, achieved only limited sales before being withdrawn. Publishers only "dictate the curriculum" when they give textbook committees what they want. To be sure, publishers spare no expense in trying to convince these committees and teachers in general that they want what the textbook editors and their author-consultant teams have devised. But it is inaccurate to credit publishers with major influence on the curriculum even in the case of elementary reading instruction, which depends so heavily on basal reading series. If Dick and Jane reappear decade after decade in only slightly new guises, the publishers are responding to teachers' invitations.

Nevertheless, textbooks and instructional materials (including the study guides that many paperback publishers and distributors now provide for fiction and nonfiction titles on their lists) remain one of the best clues to what the curriculum is in language and literature. Recognizing this, in his history of the teaching of English[15] Applebee turns to two analyses of literature anthologies: Olson's doctoral dissertation covering the forty years between 1917 and 1957[16] and Lynch and Evans's book focusing on seventy-two texts in use between 1958 and 1962.[17] It is unfortunate that more up-to-date studies are not available; new studies would include the many single texts-with-guides, which replaced anthologies in many literature courses in the late 1960s, and also the newly revised anthologies that made a strong comeback in the late 1970s.

In the earlier period studied by Olson, anthologies gradually appeared that reflected, somewhat palely perhaps, the recommendations emanating from NCTE conventions and publications: a gradual shift in the 1930s and 1940s from studying literature by types and chronology to organizing selections in topical and thematic units, with concern for life adjustment emerging in the 1950s through units on human relations, the family, understanding self and others.

Written from the perspective of college English professors and published at the peak of enthusiasm for academic elitism, Lynch and Evans's analysis of anthologies in use at the end of the progressive era helped to hasten the passing of that era and undoubtedly influenced the revisions in next editions already underway when this "trenchant and detailed critique" made its appearance.[18] Since their purpose was to attack and reform the teaching of literature, Lynch and Evans went right to the mark, acknowledging that the actual curriculum is more nearly like the textbooks than like the curriculum guides.

TEACHING PRACTICES

Can teachers and students give us a better idea of the actual curriculum than what we can infer from guides and instructional materials? Perhaps. But Goodlad warns us that the teachers will give us a *perceived* curriculum, what they think they are teaching in response to what they identify as students' needs; and the students will describe what they think they are learning, providing what Goodlad calls an *experiential* curriculum. The two perceptions frequently do not agree.[19] We need to keep these caveats in mind as we look at a recent study that provides data related to what is being taught in English. Nevertheless, for whatever they are worth, insights into teaching practices are essential if we think of curriculum not simply as stated goals and themes but also if we ask how and whether these are implemented in classrooms.

In a recent publication Purves reports data obtained in 1970 from American elementary and secondary teachers who participated in an international study of achievement in reading and literature.[20] Summarizing responses to questionnaires on which teachers identified instructional practices, Purves notes that the variety of activities diminishes greatly as the student passes from elementary to junior to senior high school. "Whole class instruction becomes the order of the day in senior high school and that instruction is dominated by recitation and discussion. The aim of instruction becomes focused more clearly on historical and critical approaches to literature, on what might be termed the academic approach.''[21] Note that these findings come in the middle of an educational era frequently described as open, liberal, humanitarian, and romantic-radical.

Adapting a curriculum of common goals and themes to individual differences among students can hardly be accomplished without small-group instruction and contracts. In Purves's survey, 51 percent of elementary teachers, 21 percent of junior high, and 13 percent of senior high teachers reported they used within-class ability grouping frequently. The slightly higher percentages reported for small-group work without regard to ability suggest that group discussions are probably based on common, not differentiated, readings. Individualized or programmed packets, which imply that the nature of the work being done is quite different from one student to another, are used frequently by less than a third of elementary teachers, about a fifth of teachers in junior high, and only 12 percent of high school teachers. Unfortunately, however, this analysis does not tell us whether the students already had been divided into tracks within each of which students were studying subject matter different from that studied in other tracks.

With respect to the literature curriculum, it is safe to make the inferences that Purves does when the data show that 61 percent of high school teachers frequently assign histories of literature and handbooks of critical terms, and even larger majorities (84 percent and 73 percent) report the frequent assignment of biographies of authors and critical essays on literary works. Biographies of authors are almost as popular with elementary and junior high teachers, and half of the latter also claim to assign histories of literature and critical essays. There is little evidence in these data that a curriculum of common goals and themes is in widespread use.[22]

The Purves study also sheds light on teachers' use of goals in literature courses. Secondary teachers ranked in order of importance eight goals of instruction and then rated twenty questions designed to elicit students' responses. Relating data from these questions with data on instructional practices, Purves concludes that teachers' goals probably affect the kinds of materials they assign, but goals may not be related to students' needs. He suspects that teachers' goals and critical stance and thus their instructional practices are more influenced by their preservice education than by their students' needs. Goodlad's data suggest, however, that teachers teach as they were taught through their sixteen or more years of schooling.[23]

In secondary schools (including middle schools) the chief means of recognizing, if not providing for, individual differences has been to form classes on the basis of intelligence or, more often, past achievement (usually in reading), or on a combination of scores on reading and intelligence tests. Elective systems recognize individual differences also, but usually with students' interests added to ability and achievement as the basis for forming classes.

Elective programs are a means of organizing the curriculum (as instructional practices are a means of delivering the curriculum), but there can be no doubt that organizational and instructional techniques influence and sometimes determine what is taught. Indeed, in some situations elective programs have permitted students to determine the content of their own curricula and for that reason have been cited as one of the factors responsible for declining SAT scores.[24]

Such criticisms, the certifiable weaknesses in many elective programs, and the shift away from appealing to students' feelings may explain why the heyday of the elective movement seems to have passed. Applebee's data support this conclusion, even though in 1977 department heads were retaining electives for most seniors. They were also responding to criticisms of the system, however, by imposing more constraints, weeding out unsuccessful courses, adding basic courses, providing more guidance and less free choice.[25] After 1977, the decline of the elective movement gained such momentum that a doctoral study appearing in 1980 could view it historically.[26] As one evidence of its demise, Christenbury notes that, whereas the *English Journal* carried eleven articles on electives in 1976, by 1978 the category was deleted from the journal's subject index. Since electives offer an additional, and in many ways an effective, means through which secondary teachers can achieve a curriculum in language and literature that is responsive to individual differences, it is worth examining the strengths and weaknesses of an idea that caught the enthusiasm of so many English teachers in one decade and lost favor so rapidly in the next.

The one strong advantage that an elective system has over the traditional omnibus packaging of the curriculum is its flexibility. In schools of sufficient size this flexibility permits closer matching of the content and level of instructional materials to students' interests and abilities than is possible through administrative grouping. Almost as important, it permits teachers to offer courses appropriate to *their* knowledge and interests. That the idea of an elective system is in harmony with a curricular theory that addresses individual differences can be seen in its philosophical underpinnings: (a) choice is an important element in human motivation; (b) motivation is essential to learning; (c) students can recognize their needs and, with help, choose instruction that meets those needs; (d) many kinds of content can serve the development of skills and appreciations; (e) teachers are competent to determine course content; (f) sequence in the study of language and literature is relatively unimportant; (g) interest and ability, not age or years of schooling, should determine the makeup of classes.

To be sure, these assumptions are debatable, some more than others, and in any case must be modified to meet the conditions of a particular school: the size and diversity of the student body; the competence of the English faculty; the availability of support services (for example, guidance counselors, reading specialists, administrative assistance, media specialists, aides); budget for books, nonprint media, and course development. So many different kinds of schools experimented with elective programs, and modifications were so various, that we cannot describe *the* elective system which critics attacked. We can only note common characteristics. Some were nongraded; some were phased or leveled, thus imparting a measure of sequence; students in some programs were closely guided in their "choices"; most electives were centered on literature and many substituted paperbacks for hardbound texts and anthologies; courses were scheduled for a semester or a period of six or nine weeks.

Many of the flaws cited by critics of the elective systems sprang from inadequate and hasty implementation, from too much enthusiasm and too little experience. Many were correctable; others were more fundamental. Variety and change, introduced as antidotes to student apathy, inhibited teachers' chances to get to know the learning characteristics of their students. Increased course loads and accompanying preparation time led teachers to cut down on writing assignments and to spend less time in evaluating students' performances and their own. When courses in writing were introduced to counter the effects of literature dominating the curriculum, the process of writing was often isolated from purposes for writing that can be stimulated by literature. Other serious charges leveled against elective programs were (a) lack of balance either in total offerings or in individual students' choices; (b) reduced opportunities to assess students' learning; (c) insufficient evaluation of course offerings; and (d) less attention to individualizing instruction within classes. Flaws of lesser significance but greater mischief were often cited: students choosing courses to be with their friends or popular teachers, and course descriptions that were more attractive than truthful.

Many elective programs died because teachers' enthusiasm waned as they realized the amount of time and degree of expertise needed to correct weaknesses in the system. At the same time that teachers were losing the courage of their convictions, the mood of the country was swinging toward academic conservatism and colleges that had given lower schools the model of elective education were taking the lead in reinstating core curricula.

The elective system is not itself a curriculum, but since it offers schools of the right size and makeup many opportunities to deal effectively with differences in students' interests, abilities, aspirations, and backgrounds, it seems worth retaining as one type of delivery system. Maybe, given a new label and new twists and given sufficient time for careful tinkering, it will rise out of the ashes. Certainly, if we learned nothing else from the decade of the elective, we learned that English teachers can be seized by an idea and can respond to it with dramatic swiftness. We are confident that they will do so again when they find workable ways to serve students' varying styles of learning.

Three Recent Curricular Models

In 1978-79, the Commission on the English Curriculum of NCTE agreed on three curricular paradigms that could be applied at each of five instructional levels (prekindergarten to grade five, the middle school, senior high school, and the two- and four-year college) and asked individual teachers and instructional leaders to describe each in brief independent essays.[27] The three paradigms thus described are labeled the process or student-centered model, the heritage or traditional model, and the competencies model. Working under the Commission's definition of curriculum as "goals, contents, and teaching-learning procedures," the writers tend to pay less attention to content and more to goals and procedures and to display considerable overlap among the three models. More nearly critiques of teaching-learning procedures than ideal or perceived curricula, the essays nevertheless offer examples of current thinking on what might constitute a common curriculum in English.

THE COMPETENCIES MODEL

At the elementary level, the writers on this model limit their discussion to language arts skills. One assumes, however, that these authors are reserving time and probably a different approach for literature. They list competencies needed by the teacher: ability to diagnose and prescribe, to identify obstructive behavior and analyze reasons for it, to shape behavior through positive reinforcement, to provide immediate reinforcing feedback and opportunities for success, to maintain an environment conducive to work, to encourage self-monitoring, and to keep records. Since competency-based programs and behavioral objectives are readily obtainable, instead of detailing content and goals the writers list sources such as the National Diffusion Network Exemplary Programs and the Exemplary Center for Reading Instruction. While they espouse mastery learning, they urge that "subjective judgment should be a central and essential part of evaluation."[28]

At the middle school level, we are told, "literature competencies [for example, responding to, interpreting, valuing, and evaluating literature] help to define what has long been the most amorphous part of the English curriculum." The writer stresses the need for traditional selections in a broadly defined competency curriculum in order to develop students' abilities to "draw upon their literary and cultural heritage."[29]

In presenting the competency paradigm for the senior high school, Clapp, director of language arts for the Buffalo Public Schools, applies the systems approach to the contents of traditional curricula chiefly through adding preassessments and postassessments based on "careful behavioral analyses" that include evaluating attitudes, feelings, and values as well as skills in listening, speaking, reading, and composing.

While she admits that record keeping is "demanding for both teacher and student," she believes it proves motivational since it allows students to perceive their needs and their progress.[30]

When Clapp illustrates the competency approach in a unit centered on *Our Town* and in an elective titled "The Community: A Force That Shapes Human Lives," she describes a variety of instructional techniques that are found also in the descriptions of the other paradigms in this collection. Remembering how few secondary teachers in the Purves study reported using these techniques with high frequency, I wonder how much enthusiasm teachers have for a systems approach which asks them to make extensive assessment, keep detailed records, and hold frequent individual conferences. But Clapp avers that there is an "undeniable demand" for competency systems (presumably on the part of teachers).

THE HERITAGE MODEL

Mandel's introduction to the heritage model is perhaps the best statement of its purposes and directions:

In the heritage model, the underlying assumption is that the way to acquire skills and knowledge is to submit to something larger than oneself, that is, to the culture. By culture I mean traditions, history, the time-honored values of civilized thought and feeling (including the time-honored resistance to these values) and the skills that make it possible to share in one's culture and to pass it on. For the heritage teacher, there is value in surrendering one's ego-bound sense of relevance to a more informed or enlightened sense of what truly endures.[31]

At the elementary level, the old heritage model, which was text-centered and developed text-related skills, must be reformed so that the learner becomes the center of an education that "coordinates oral communication, language development, exploration through literature, and personal growth and experience."[32] The curriculum is organized around thematic units based chiefly but not exclusively on literature, and in all units "focus [is] placed on talking—questioning, seeking, hypothesizing, evaluating." In her recommendations for a balanced literature program, Evertts sets four requirements: (a) "no form or genre of literature is omitted"; (b) selections should represent many cultures; (c) personal reading lists must be unique to groups and individuals; (d) literary quality must be the criterion for selections teachers share with large groups.[33]

Addressing the heritage model at the middle school, Hodges says it offers excellent opportunities for matching the goals of the curriculum to students' needs, interests, and capabilities, provided teachers know both the developmental processes of the learners and the nature of language. Like other contributors to this collection of curriculum models, he states the goal of English instruction is "to produce adults who are competent in communication and who display and appreciate the functional and aesthetic uses of language."[34] Although he sees no way to make the heritage model "teacher proof," he clearly supports the use of commercially prepared texts to be supplemented by a wide range of teacher- and student-selected materials.

LaConte sees the heritage model in the senior high school organized into thematic units that "consider the themes of the literature of the past as inextricably connected to those of the literature of the present."[35] All instruction in language, literacy, and media skills is integrated in units designed so that students explore questions related to "thematic polarities" that "delineate a range of human behavior that has been of literary concern through the ages" (for example, loyalty and treachery).[36] He proposes a six-year sequence in which six polarities, subdivided into thematic questions, are explored each year. This scheme does not imply thirty-six different issues, since it is possible to trace some of the same polarities through a span of years, developing thematic questions of increasing maturity and intellectual challenge. He would assign not only contemporary literature but "the best of older British, American, and world literature," thus avoiding the "crash survey courses commonly taught in the last years of high school." LaConte acknowledges that to implement this paradigm teachers must start from scratch, but its flexibility and open-endedness would permit teachers to match meaningful content to adolescents' abilities and their need to understand the human condition.

THE PROCESS MODEL

The three essays on process, as one would expect, focus even less on content than do the essays on the competency and heritage models. Stressing strategies (both teaching and learning) and attitudes (both teachers' and students'), they may be a trifle more polemical than the other essays since, as McPherson points out, it is the process model which is currently under attack; traditional and competency-based programs are not.[37] While the two other models as interpreted in this collection can also claim to be student-centered, the process paradigm is the one that can be most closely identified with the student-centered curriculum which Moffett (and others) specified in the wake of the Dartmouth Conference of the mid-1960s. Modified to accommodate what teachers can do and what society expects of secondary schools, the process model presented by the Stanfords for the senior high school looks rather familiar in its format and examples (units on "You and Others" and "Grammar and Usage," for instance). "After identifying the current level of student skills, the teacher needs to design activities to move students to the next level," the Stanfords write. They then present a sampling of communication skills areas (ability to talk to different people in different situations, to listen effectively, to recognize emotional content and connotation of a message) and list levels of skills for each one, phrased like behavioral objectives.[38]

The process paradigm for grades six through nine presented by Watson is much less specific than the Stanfords' and emphasizes how a process-oriented teacher thinks about "language, literature, learners and learning." The tone is romantic: "When students are encouraged to share their world and to tell about their lives in their own preferred language, the entire class can only become richer and wiser." The teacher is "an incurable kid watcher," understanding that "if care and attention are given to the process (the risk-taking, the hypothesizing, the miscuing) by which learners make sense of their world, the results of such endeavors will be meaningful, important, and satisfying for both teacher and learner." The curriculum, in Watson's view, is a series of invitations that learners may accept or refuse, and she offers just four examples of activities: reading to students, students reading, improvisation, and writing.[39]

Applying the process paradigm at the elementary level, Stauffer describes activities, especially for learning to read, that might be found in traditionally oriented classrooms, but he rules out "skillbook activities" and emphasizes "functional communication of messages generated by the learner."[40]

Mandel underlines the striking differences between competencies models and process strategies, though both stress the developmental potential in learners. "Whereas a competencies model can fairly clearly state behaviors expected to occur . . . a process approach focuses more on watchfulness, the observation of what is developing at a given moment of instruction and then the harnessing of its energy."[41]

In presenting these three models, the Commission's purpose is to help teachers recognize their own dominant approach, develop new strategies within that approach, and "branch out into the use of other models in ways that might not have seemed feasible or even apparent before."[42] But I suspect that many teachers will be as much frustrated as helped by this collection, which offers more choices of style than they can handle and less direction on content than they want. Unsure teachers will fall back on the curriculum provided by the instructional materials available, chiefly texts today but increasingly the "courseware" for computers and other electronic hardware, which we were promised in the 1960s and will probably arrive in the 1980s. If the process model, which seems to have the solid support of researchers and theorists, is to win the support of teachers also, it must be translated into widely available and easily used materials. In the meantime, the heritage model that has survived in one form or another the progressive, academic, and romantic movements will be refurbished for the 1980s. We could do worse.

A Guide for Developing an English Curriculum for the 1980s

As demonstrated by the three curricular models summarized in the preceding section, the view of the current NCTE Commission on the English Curriculum is that local committees of teachers and consultants, not a national organization, should specify the details of the curriculum that unfolds in particular classrooms. How specific should be the written curriculum produced by local committees? This section, which carries the title of a useful NCTE publication written by Glatthorn, draws on that publication to suggest that even at the local level the degree of specificity should be modest. Glatthorn's guide, which is intended for instructional leaders, directs them to produce the "heart of the curriculum" and to leave room for substantial contributions by the classroom teachers. I summarize his advice in the following paragraphs because I believe it speaks to curriculum theorists as well as to practitioners and because it supports my view that a "common curriculum" in language and literature can be common only in its goals and themes. Moreover, as a local committee uses Glatthorn's guide, a practicable amalgam of the Commission's three curricular models is likely to emerge.

Glatthorn's recommendations are meant to accommodate seven current developments in education that he perceives as determining the conditions under which curricula in all subjects may be developed or revised. These seven developments are: (a) a stable teaching staff that will exert increasing authority over the curriculum; (b) tight budgets precluding large-scale curriculum projects; (c) continuing technological change; (d) the need to take "realistic cognizance of state mandates"; (e) increasing knowledge about the processes of teaching and learning; (f) the need to be responsive to a public that will continue to express dissatisfaction with the schools; (g) a growing divergence between recommended curricula and what actually takes place in classrooms.[43]

Since funds are limited, the process of curriculum development should be "simple, fast, inexpensive, and focused," should begin with what teachers think is actually being taught, and should result in diminishing the differences between what is recommended, what is perceived, and what is practiced. The "heart of the curriculum" turns out to be a mastery curriculum. This is composed of all the skills and concepts which need to be sequenced, which teachers can be held accountable for teaching, which can be packaged in mastery learning units, and which will determine the selection of instructional materials. The mastery curriculum should "never require more than 60 to 75 percent of the total time available." The remaining time is given over to "organic learning," which is determined by the teacher and the students and "embraces all those skills, concepts, and attitudes which can be mastered without such careful sequencing, planning, and delineation."[44]

What is written by the planning team and handed to the teacher is the mastery curriculum contained in a notebook and organized into eight major sections: reading and study skills, literature and media, composition, grammar and language, word study and vocabulary, speaking and listening, critical and creative thinking, and spelling, punctuation, and usage. For each of these sections, a teacher's notebook when first received would contain a summary of the pertinent research; course objectives for one grade only; a brief list of available materials. Teachers may add to the notebooks as they see fit: lesson plans, units, journal articles, updated research notes, and so forth.

Glatthorn would have teachers individually or in groups develop the curriculum from this point through *focused* units, in which all concepts, skills, and objectives relate to a single area of the discipline such as vocabulary development, and integrated *thematic* units linking concepts, skills, and objectives from reading, writing, speaking, and grammar. Either all mastery concepts and skills are assigned to focused units or all of them are included in integrated units; a third alternative is to divide them between focused and integrated units. Although Glatthorn presents cons as well as pros in discussing mastery learning, he clearly states his belief that "mastery learning can be used to good effect in English."[45]

Glatthorn's guide describes "the process and form of curriculum work in English" and eschews considerations of content. I have given it this much space because I know from experience, my own and that of teachers with whom I have worked, that he has described a workable plan for organizing a curriculum. It is more flexible than this tight summary suggests, but obviously it appeals to people who find comfort in structure and who believe that learning to use language proceeds in an orderly fashion. These are teachers who see themselves as helping students most in that orderly process when they can assess their needs and recommend next steps. I think most teachers welcome the structure Glatthorn insists on because it makes it possible for them to use the freedom he leaves them for choosing content.

I find Glatthorn's structured approach congenial to my view that the curriculum in language develops processes of reading and writing, ways of learning and thinking as well as attitudes and values, and that the curriculum in literature serves those ends through a wide diversity of works in print and on film. In accordance with these views, it seems reasonable to suggest that before graduating from high school all students should have had planned experiences with the following goals related to language and literature.

Literature

Reading, listening to, viewing, and discussing certain literary classics, works of contemporary literature, works by authors whose ethnic identity is similar to their own, works from popular culture for purposes of comparison and motivation, folklore of their region that also displays regional dialect

Learning to respond personally to literature

Understanding how American language and literature reflect cultural values

Understanding the language and literature of other cultures

Accepting and appreciating the language and literature of ethnic groups besides their own

Developing ability to interpret literary works

Increasing their appreciation of literature

Language Study

Understanding the function and characteristics of language

Understanding the relationship between changes in society and changes in language

Studying the history of the English language

Valuing their own individual uses of language

Eliminating traces of sexism and racism in their language

Understanding the nature and use of nonverbal communication

Oral Language

Using oral language extensively in their classrooms

Learning to communicate effectively and appropriately

Writing

Using writing to communicate effectively in a variety of situations

Using writing to learn and for self-expression

Reading

Developing skills of comprehension at literal and interpretive levels

Reacting critically to what is read

Using reading to learn

Listening

Developing habits of listening attentively

Learning to listen critically

Mass Media

Developing skills for evaluating and criticizing mass media

Using Language in
   Reasoning logically
   Stating problems clearly and accurately
   Retrieving, evaluating, and applying information to solve problems
   Thinking creatively, finding innovative solutions
   Reflecting on personal values
   Discussing or writing about ideas and problems of personal
      relevance and importance
   Discussing socially relevant problems
   Studying the local community
   Communicating successfully as a citizen, consumer, worker[46]

Other Perspectives on English Curricula

The discussion thus far has omitted several curricular plans, theories, and notions which have either proved their value in influencing the teaching of English or give promise of shaping curricular models still to be developed. This section will pay brief attention to (a) a developing model that has roots in the past but has taken on a newish-sounding label, the response-centered curriculum; (b) suggestions that have been made for developing curricular strands based on students' raising questions; (c) a notion that casts language study as the basis for the whole school curriculum; (d) a proposal for an English curriculum directed at finding meaning in life; and (e) the question of whether or not study of nonprint media should constitute a fifth part of the language arts, equal to reading, writing, speaking, and listening.

THE RESPONSE-CENTERED CURRICULUM

As early as 1938 Rosenblatt argued that the student's response rather than the content of the work of literature must be the focal point of concern in the teaching of English. While *Literature as Exploration*[47] is not a curriculum model, it "deals at length with the proper role of and approach to literary studies"[48] and clearly anticipates "process teaching" and "student-centered" curricula. Rosenblatt prescribes neither method nor content, although she proposes that the exchange of ideas in group discussion is a major vehicle for refining responses. She sees literature serving a central role in helping individuals to understand themselves and the "various superstructures of ideas, emotions, modes of behavior, moral values, that that particular society has built up around the basic human relationship."[49]

Rosenblatt's ideas expressed in *Literature as Exploration* and over the years in journal articles (now collected in one volume[50]) have been continuously influential, reaching teachers not only directly but through professional texts on teaching English, methods courses, and the "editorial apparatus" in students' anthologies. An attempt to communicate the response-centered curriculum directly to teachers in a kind of "how to do it" manual appeared in 1972, edited by Purves. The manual offers "notes" on film, talk, drama, responding through visual symbols, writing, and evaluation, demonstrating that the response-centered curriculum can embrace not only literature but other traditional content of the English curriculum as well.[51] Also under Purves's general editorship, anthologies for grades seven through twelve were published in the 1970s, making not only content but quite specific lesson plans available to any teachers who were looking for this approach in a standard textbook format.

The importance of centering curriculum on the cultivation of students' responses is a powerful idea frequently addressed by scholars and researchers, but not yet embraced by many teachers (though the increased use of small-group work encourages the hope that more of them are inviting students to discuss their reactions to literature at least some of the time). What prevents the response-centered curriculum from becoming part of the actual curriculum is that it still lacks definition in operational terms. Teachers need to know what to expect (and how to absorb the unexpected) and how to elicit, interpret, and evaluate responses. Perhaps a place to begin is to analyze the domain of response and to isolate those types of responses that are most easily developed. One such category of response is the question, and teaching students the art of questioning has been recommended from time to time as a major element that should help to structure the curriculum in English.

RAISING QUESTIONS

Inquiry and discovery are, of course, hallmarks of the process paradigm and can be traced to the early decades of this century when the "scientific method" touched virtually every subject in the curriculum, even literature. Most recently, Postman has proposed once again that "study of the art of question-asking [be made] one of the central disciplines in language education."[52] Arguing persuasively, if sweepingly, Postman asserts that because "all our knowledge results from questions," teachers of every subject "must show the young how questions are productively formed in speaking their subject, in listening to their subject [including rules that] govern what is and what is not a legitimate question."[53] He claims that the ability to ask probing questions can be tested and taught, although he excuses himself from the responsibility of producing a textbook (or a curriculum) that might implement his suggestions.

Like Postman, I know of no inclusive curriculum based on question-asking either for English teaching or for the whole-school instructional program, but I learned from the first methods course I took that reading teachers should elicit questions from children, not just answers, for comprehension is a process of getting one's questions answered.[54] Predicting and hypothesizing, which are forms of question-asking, are familiar concepts in recent professional texts on reading and literature. In *Reading and Learning from Text*, Singer and Donlan outline a year-long procedure through which teachers transfer question-asking from themselves to their students.[55] Fillion has recently described a plan for teaching question-asking as the central response mode in reacting to literature.[56]

POSTMAN'S "LANGUAGE EDUCATION IN A KNOWLEDGE CONTEXT"

Although he eschews the common slogan "language across the curriculum" and refuses to acknowledge any progress in teaching reading and writing in content fields, Postman is obviously arguing for a goal that many educators have sought to implement for the last several decades. (Postman wants nothing to do with persons who might divide language learning into "skills," "competencies," or "strategies.") He calls question-asking an "intellectual tool" and suggests two others as basic: understanding the role of metaphor and the process of definition. I have cast the latter two also as "tools" because Postman wants students to learn how to use them, but he believes that improvement of the student's uses of language requires increased knowledge of subject matter, knowledge that cannot be separated from the language in which it is expressed.[57]

GLATTHORN'S "CURRICULUM OF MEANING"

Postman's concern that students learn not only knowledge but how that knowledge is conveyed takes us back to Glatthorn, who ends his guide to curriculum making with an outline of what he would include in a "curriculum of meaning." Minimizing discrete skills that are not sufficiently generalizable, he would concentrate on a "few cognitive processes of high transferability" with the aim of helping "young people to make sense out of their lives."[58] He would stress the relationship between language and meaning, writing as a way of knowing, critical reading and critical viewing, "mastery units in critical and creative thinking," and integrated thematic units "examining issues grounded in the human condition." Closer to what teachers are now doing, less grandiose than Postman's exhortations, Glatthorn's recommendations point to a common curriculum in which skills and knowledge are developed sequentially, using process teaching and contemporary media as well as traditional literature as the vehicles.

STUDYING THE NONPRINT MEDIA

Most writers on the curriculum in language and literature accept nonprint media as vehicles for content, and most curricula list them as resources along with books and magazines. Students learning to use media as an additional tool of expression, from first graders making filmstrips to middle-grade students producing videotapes and adolescents making films, is fairly commonplace in schools with access to funding sources. Given tight budgets and the desire to cut frills, however, the prospects seem not very bright for expanding the study of media until it becomes the "next language art,"[59] or the new discipline ("information environments") that Postman proposes should be sequenced through the elementary and secondary grades. Some of the content Postman specifies is scattered through some curricula now (for example, the history of language, the uses of computers), and at least one high school textbook is available,[60] but an actual curriculum in the study of media would require additional faculty—a media education department—and scheduling outside of the English curriculum in junior and senior high schools. The beginnings of media education can be accommodated in elective systems but probably not in the present restricted systems. In the meantime, media electives should be encouraged, but not as substitutes for English courses.

Until electives make a comeback, I see elementary and secondary English teachers doing for the study of nonprint media about as much as they have done over the years for reading the newspaper—a focused unit or two here and there. It is not enough; is it better than nothing?

Issues to Be Faced in Planning English Curricula

1. *Can English teachers plan a common curriculum in language and literature without involving the whole school staff?* The question is adaptable to elementary schools: should there be a curriculum for reading and writing that is independent of the curricula for social studies, science, and the arts? My answer to both questions is, "no." To say that curriculum planning must be schoolwide seems to imply expensive large-scale curriculum projects that few school boards are willing to afford these days. Yet it is at the local level that curriculum planning must be done if it is to reach into classrooms. What can be accomplished short of mounting a large-scale curriculum project? Since questions affecting the curriculum are the daily concerns of instructional leaders (administrators, consultants, department heads) and work on the curriculum is always in progress, "large-scale projects" may be unnecessary and artificial. It is, for example, a curricular matter when graduates of a high school complain that they are unprepared for reading and writing assignments in college. What needs to be examined, if these complaints are to be taken seriously, extends far beyond the English curriculum.

The first step in such an examination would be to review the school's current curriculum documents for all subjects, not English alone. (In many schools these may not exist or may be in various stages of development or disrepair.) The curriculum team might follow up an examination of documents with a brief questionnaire to all teachers asking for estimates of time now spent on reading and study skills, critical thinking, media study, writing, grammar and language, vocabulary development, speaking and listening, and the conventions of language (spelling, punctuation, usage). The survey would permit teachers in every subject to consider their responsibilities for language education, to study what the English staff believes should be included in a common curriculum in language and literature, and to make decisions about allocating goals not presently being taken care of. English teachers might find that media study, critical thinking, and study skills figure more prominently than they thought in their colleagues' perceived curricula. An across-the-board survey of the present curriculum would also broach the questions that follow.

2. *Should responsibility for the humanities rest with the faculty in language and literature?* Since literature is only one of the humanities, that question seems both presumptuous and superfluous; nevertheless, it must be asked. But it must be answered by whole school faculties as they consider where in the total curriculum the humanities presently reside. Often, but not always, English teachers take the lead in developing humanities courses, which are usually elective in the senior high school and are interdisciplinary (one course fused from two or more), correlated (English and social studies taught separately, for instance, but covering the same periods of history), or isolated. Copeland discusses a great variety of approaches, noting that NCTE organized the first national humanities conference for teachers in 1966 and continued to sponsor annual meetings through 1972, when the National Association of Humanities Education, founded in 1968, took over.[61] Perhaps that is a good pattern for school districts to follow: begin with the English faculty but develop an interdisciplinary humanities faculty.

3. *Is a common curriculum in language and literature possible and desirable?* I began this chapter with an affirmative answer to this question. After a fleeting examination of curricular models that have been recommended to English teachers through the years, I repeat that affirmation. So long as we think of the curriculum in language and literature as goals to be achieved and themes to be addressed, but not as specific works to be studied, we can say, yes, every student capable of graduating from high school should engage in learning experiences structured around these common goals and themes. But while the goals are common, the specific learning experiences cannot be, not just because students are different but because teachers and schools and communities are different. Which books are to be read, what stories are to be listened to or dramatized, what levels of usage are to be spoken and written, what activities are to be engaged in—curricular questions

of this kind are for the teachers, students, and parents of a particular place (and time) to decide.

Such a recommendation invites problems but not chaos. The goals of a proposed common curriculum should provide sufficient structure to guard against whimsical choices of content. All too frequently teachers have dodged curricular decisions by seeking packaged programs— basal reading series, for example, at the elementary level, anthologies and multitext units devised by publishers for the secondary level. While there have been signs of teachers taking control of the curriculum (for example, teacher centers and the spread of elective systems) current trends suggest a setback. Instructional technology flourishes, and coincidentally teaching suffers from a bad press; so the call for teacher-proof curricula grows louder. As the teaching staff matures and stabilizes with fewer new teachers entering the field, the advantages of maturity and stability may be diluted by apathy and stagnation. Experienced teachers who are more capable than newcomers of making curricular decisions may shirk the responsibility because they lack self-confidence, are denied the right by consultants and administrators, or are distracted by extracurricular concerns ranging from union politics and personal pleasures to making ends meet, raising single-parent families, and earning another degree. Thus, publishers may continue to furnish the vehicles of the common curriculum for reading, the language arts, and literature, making it more common than we intend.

While most teachers at present exercise little control over the curriculum, most parents and most students remain completely unheard from in the planning that affects how curricular goals will be reached. Frequently, however, a minority of voices outside the schools have much to say about the content of English curricula, especially what is read. Those voices sometimes belong to parents seeking to censor not only what their own children read but what is accessible in school libraries as well as classrooms. Censorship is at risk when parents are not involved in thinking about the content of the curriculum, and admittedly the risk may be worsened rather than ameliorated by their involvement. Nevertheless, I recommend that teachers, parents, and students all have voices, not necessarily equal ones, in selecting content for literature and language study. The community must be considered in making choices for classrooms and libraries, and curriculum planners can respect parents' values without yielding to censorship. "Choosing" becomes "censoring" at the point that one community, or one group within a community, attempts to inflict its choice on others. That happens, of course, and the attempts are often successful because the publicity surrounding a censorship case in one town alerts administrators and teachers and, worse still, publishers across the nation so that the novel attacked on Long Island disappears from library shelves in California and is dropped from the latest anthology or newest packaged unit. Censorship would not be nearly so virulent if curricula in literature and language were based on common goals and themes rather than on common readings. With a list of literary works illuminating the same theme, the teacher can offer alternatives to a book that is objectionable to one student's parents without depriving other students of the right to read it.

Urging curriculum planners to take into account the values of the communities they serve is not to condone censorship or the closed societies from which it springs. For thousands of years teachers have had to fight censorship and they will continue to do so. However, they may avoid many disputes, win some that are unavoidable, and limit the spread of censorship if they ask parents to join them in selecting the best vehicles for reaching goals that parents can understand because they have been explained in laymen's language and demonstrated through good teaching and successful learning. Adjusting the content of curricula in language and literature to the values and mores of the local community is an essential recognition of the principle of individual differences and one test of the soundness of a "common curriculum."

4. *Does adjusting content to individuals' varying interests, abilities, and prior experiences negate the idea of a common curriculum?* That is, is the curriculum still common if one group of ninth graders reads *The Pigman* and another reads *Huck Finn*? Or if one twelfth-grade class reads and writes about *Hamlet* and another views *Macbeth* on film and responds to it through discussion and role-playing? I believe it is, if all of these students are learning to respond personally to literature, to interpret literary works, and to reach, through their diverse experiences, these and other goals.

Nevertheless, there must be limits in the interpretation of goals if we are to hold on to a common curriculum that enables almost all students to acquire knowledge and skills leading to "rational, moral, and authentic lives." The goals listed on pp. 205-207 can be adapted to every grade level if interpreted through appropriate lessons and readings to fit students' current levels of development. For example, the last goal on that list—communicating successfully as a citizen, consumer, worker—requires different interpretations at the sixth grade and the twelfth grade levels, but at no level should it mean excessive attention to "survival skills," which in many courses today threaten to displace literature of any but the most frivolous kinds. In fact, learning how to read texts in history, mathematics, and science, as well as biographies, reference works, and other nonfiction leads more surely to consumer skills than completing workbook exercises based on labels, recipes, and how-to-do-it manuals.

A crucial and perennial problem faces curriculum planners in language and literature when they select content to suit students of varying backgrounds, aspirations, and abilities. It is the problem of balance referred to in the preceding paragraph. The curriculum gets out of kilter when, as today, there is so much attention forced on reading and writing skills that literature and the development of personal values go by the board. On the other hand, when the emphasis on personal relevance dominates, the content swings too heavily toward the popular and contemporary, and students miss learning how to read relevant literature from the past.

To some extent the problem of balance might be alleviated if English teachers at every level could concentrate on literature and humanistic values and distribute the teaching of language skills and concepts among all the other subjects of the whole curriculum. Many of the goals commonly listed for English curricula are also appropriate to the "content subjects." A truly common curriculum in language would be taught by every teacher in secondary schools and in every subject in elementary schools. When that kind of common curriculum is achieved, it will be easier to maintain balance and quality in the English curriculum, giving every student ample opportunity to engage in writing and reading without neglecting either the study of literature, the uses of reading for personal satisfactions, or the development of aesthetic uses of oral language and the appreciation of aural modes.

A Conclusion

The concept of a common curriculum in language and literature does not violate our commitment to students' differences. Freedom in the choice of content permits teachers to help students move toward similar goals along various paths and at different rates. The idea of a common curriculum in English—defined in goals and themes rather than specified content—goes back nearly fifty years to *An Experience Curriculum* (1935). It remains an ideal curriculum, however. It will not be widely implemented until teachers gain more confidence in selecting various content for different levels of interest and ability and in delivering it in thematic units not only within English as a school subject but in all school subjects whose concepts are conveyed in language.

FOOTNOTES

1. W. Wilbur Hatfield, *An Experience Curriculum in English* (New York: D. Appleton-Century, 1935).

2. Ibid., p. 134.

3. Angela M. Broening, *Conducting Experiences in English* (New York: D. Appleton-Century, 1939).

4. National Council of Teachers of English, Commission on the English Curriculum, *The English Language Arts in the Secondary School* (New York: Appleton-Century-Crofts, 1956).

5. Arthur N. Applebee, *Tradition and Reform in the Teaching of English: A History* (Urbana, Ill.: National Council of Teachers of English, 1974), pp. 168-69.

6. Allan A. Glatthorn, *A Guide for Developing an English Curriculum for the Eighties* (Urbana, Ill.: National Council of Teachers of English, 1980), p. 7.

7. Ibid.

8. James E. Miller, Jr., "Literature in the Revitalized Curriculum," in *The English Curriculum in the Secondary School, Bulletin of the National Association of Secondary School Principals* 318 (April 1967): 25-37.

9. Glatthorn, *A Guide for Developing an English Curriculum for the Eighties,* p. 9.

10. John I. Goodlad, "What Goes On in Our Schools?" *Educational Researcher* 6 (March 1977): 5.

11. Paul Roberts, ed., *The Roberts English Series for Grades 1 to 12* (New York: Harcourt Brace Jovanovich, 1964-66).

12. James Moffett and Betty Jane Wagner, *Student-centered Language Arts and Reading, K-13,* 2d ed. (Boston: Houghton Mifflin, 1973).

13. James Moffett, *Teaching the Universe of Discourse* (Boston: Houghton Mifflin, 1968).

14. Northrop Frye, Supervising Editor, and Will T. Jewkes, General Editor, *Literature: Uses of the Imagination, A Literature Series for Grades 7-12* (New York: Harcourt Brace Jovanovich, 1972-74).

15. Applebee, *Tradition and Reform in the Teaching of English,* pp. 171-74.

16. James W. Olson, "The Nature of Literature Anthologies Used in the Teaching of High School English, 1917-1957" (Doct. diss., University of Wisconsin, 1969).

17. James J. Lynch and Bertrand Evans, *High School English Textbooks: A Critical Examination* (Boston: Little, Brown and Co., 1963).

18. Applebee, *Tradition and Reform in the Teaching of English*, p. 171.

19. John I. Goodlad, *A Place Called School* (New York: McGraw-Hill, 1983).

20. Alan C. Purves, *Reading and Literature: American Achievement in International Perspective* (Urbana, Ill.: National Council of Teachers of English, 1981).

21. Ibid., p. 24.

22. Ibid., table 10, p. 25.

23. Goodlad, *A Place Called School*.

24. Willard P. Wirtz, *On Further Examination* (Princeton, N.J.: College Entrance Examination Board, 1979).

25. Arthur N. Applebee, *A Survey of Teaching Conditions in English* (Urbana, Ill.: National Council of Teachers of English, 1978), p. 291.

26. Leila Mayo Christenbury, "The Origin, Development, and Decline of the Secondary English Elective Curriculum" (Doct. diss., Virginia Polytechnic Institute and State University, 1980), *Dissertation Abstracts* 41A (December 1980): 2421.

27. Barrett J. Mandel, ed., *Three Language-Arts Curriculum Models: Pre-Kindergarten through College* (Urbana, Ill.: National Council of Teachers of English, 1980).

28. Betty C. Mason, Sara W. Lundsteen, and Paula S. Martinez, "Competency-Based Approach to Language Arts: Pre-Kindergarten through Grade Five," in *Three Language-Arts Curriculum Models*, ed. Mandel, p. 33.

29. Donna Townsend, "Competency Paradigm: Grades Six through Nine," in *Three Language-Arts Curriculum Models*, ed. Mandel, p. 73.

30. Ouida H. Clapp, "Competency Paradigm: Senior High School," in *Three Language-Arts Curriculum Models*, ed. Mandel, p. 110.

31. Barrett J. Mandel, "Introduction," in *Three Language-Arts Curriculum Models*, ed. Mandel, pp. 8-9.

32. Eldonna L. Evertts, "A New Heritage Approach for Teaching the Language Arts," in *Three Language-Arts Curriculum Models*, ed. Mandel, p. 35.

33. Ibid., pp. 43-44.

34. Richard E. Hodges, "The English Program, Grades Six through Nine: A Heritage Model," in *Three Language-Arts Curriculum Models*, ed. Mandel, p. 88.

35. Ronald LaConte, "A Literary Heritage Paradigm for Secondary English," in *Three Language-Arts Curriculum Models*, ed. Mandel, p. 130.

36. Ibid., pp. 131-32.

37. Elisabeth McPherson, "Language Arts in the Community College," in *Three Language-Arts Curriculum Models*, ed. Mandel, p. 202.

38. Barbara Stanford and Gene Stanford, "Process Curriculum for High School Students," in *Three Language-Arts Curriculum Models*, ed. Mandel, pp. 138-54.

39. Dorothy J. Watson, "Process Paradigm: Grades Six through Nine," in *Three Language-Arts Curriculum Models*, ed. Mandel, pp. 91-100.

40. Russel G. Stauffer, "Process-Oriented Instructional Activities: Pre-Kindergarten through Grade Five," in *Three Language-Arts Curriculum Models*, ed. Mandel, pp. 47-60.

41. Mandel, "Introduction," p. 8.

42. Ibid., pp. 10-11.

43. Glatthorn, *A Guide for Developing an English Curriculum for the Eighties*, pp. 16-18.

218 A COMMON CURRICULUM: ENGLISH

44. Ibid., p. 32.

45. Ibid., p. 100.

46. Adapted from "Comprehensive Criteria for a Syncretic English Curriculum," in Glatthorn, *A Guide for Developing an English Curriculum for the Eighties*, pp. 117-19.

47. Louise Rosenblatt, *Literature as Exploration*, 3d ed. (New York: Modern Language Press, 1976).

48. Applebee, *Tradition and Reform in the Teaching of English*, p. 123.

49. Rosenblatt, *Literature as Exploration*, p. 223.

50. Louise Rosenblatt, *The Reader, the Text, the Poem: The Transactional Theory of the Literary Work* (Carbondale and Edwardsville, Ill.: Southern Illinois University Press, 1978).

51. Alan Purves, *How Porcupines Make Love* (New York: Wiley, 1972).

52. Neil Postman, *Teaching as a Conserving Activity* (New York: Delacorte Press, 1979), p. 154.

53. Ibid., p. 155.

54. Frank Smith, *Understanding Reading*, 2d ed. (New York: Holt, Rinehart and Winston, 1978).

55. Harry Singer and Dan Donlan, *Reading and Learning from Text* (New York: Little Brown and Co., 1980).

56. Bryant Fillion, "Reading as Inquiry: An Approach to Literature Learning," *English Journal* 70 (January 1981): 39-45.

57. Postman, *Teaching as a Conserving Activity*, p. 165.

58. Glatthorn, *A Guide for Developing an English Curriculum for the Eighties*, p. 106.

59. Deborah R. Ruth, "The Next Language Art: Views of Nonprint Media," in *The Teaching of English*, ed. James R. Squire, Seventy-sixth Yearbook of the National Society for the Study of Education, Part 1 (Chicago: University of Chicago Press, 1977), pp. 96-125.

60. Marshall McLuhan, Kathryn Hutchon, and Eric McLuhan, *City as Classroom: Understanding Language and Media* (Ontario: Book Society of Canada, 1978).

61. Evelyn Copeland, "Humanities in the Schools," in *The Teaching of English*, ed. Squire, pp. 145-57.

CHAPTER IX

A Common Curriculum in Aesthetics and Fine Arts

H. S. BROUDY

Introduction

A common curriculum in arts education means that a pupil population will be exposed to the same content. This limits the great variety of available materials in the several media and imposes an obligation to justify the limitation. On what principle does one justify such a narrowing of the offerings, especially in the light of the commitment of the school establishment to individual differences? Clearly, it is the principle that the selected contents are too important for any pupil to miss or to be left to individual choice. One can imagine, however, a collection of items each of which is valuable and yet which taken together do not constitute a design—a string of unmatched jewels, so to speak. Accordingly, the construction and justification of a common curriculum in the arts require a coherent set of aims and functions of the arts in education. This, in turn, requires a theory as to the role of art in experience, and particularly in educated experience.

If room in the curriculum is limited and financial resources scarce, then not only does arts education have to make a case for a particular curriculum design, but for inclusion in the general education curriculum at all. This brings to mind the question asked by Herbert Spencer in his 1859 essay, "What Knowledge Is of Most Worth?"—a question that generation after generation of school people never tire of asking, presumably because the answer is elusive.

Stanley Madeja served as the editorial consultant for this chapter.
I am indebted to the Spencer Foundation for assistance in preparing this essay.

Spencer listed the following human activities: (a) those ministering directly to self-preservation, (b) those which secure for one the necessities of life, (c) those which help in the rearing and disciplining of offspring, (d) those involved in maintaining one's political and social relations, and (e) those which fill up the leisure part of life and gratify tastes and feelings.

The arts have been classified in our culture under (e). Of course, if the arts do not require knowledge, as some of their advocates aver, then there is no point of arguing about where they fit in the rankings. Are the items arranged in ascending or descending order of importance? As means of survival, activities making up "the leisure part of life" would come last, but in the order of ends and quality of life, the order might be reversed. Which order does a public school use to determine its priorities?

Idealistic rhetoric favors the priority of ends, the quality of adult life. This is all very well for those pupils whose other four classes of needs are taken care of outside of school, as indeed they are for the children of the well-to-do. For other children, schooling for means ranks with, and perhaps ahead of, education for ends. Accordingly, aesthetic education cannot stake its claim entirely on the quality it brings to living after the means of life have been secured. And it would be indeed odd for any value domain to be so unique that it had no effects on other value domains and would not be affected by them. The intrinsic experience of the aesthetic values is unique, but its distinctiveness lies not in its independence of other domains of existence, but rather in its peculiar power to create images of their distinctively human import.[1]

In view of the title of this volume, the common curriculum is to be constructed in the light of individual differences. Here we encounter controversy as to what shall be denoted by the term. Should it be confined to the contents of instruction, the process, or both? In this essay, I have chosen the first meaning. The choice entails another, as to what shall vary with individual differences, for contents and process can both be varied. As indicated in the closing remarks of this chapter, I have chosen to argue for varying the process and have indicated a few ways of doing so. These are not arbitrary choices, but rather are grounded in the practical difficulty of taking the vast array and dimensions of individual variations literally as guides to content selection.

Some Political Considerations

The case for arts education in the public school is not improved by the close association of the fine arts with "filling up the leisure part of life." The segments of the population with large amounts of leisure are the very rich and the chronically unemployed. It is not the leisure of the latter that Spencer or the art world has in mind.

The "fine" arts have always been classed among the "finer" things in life and cherished by the "finer" elements in the population, namely, the elites. This connection is accentuated by the association of the arts with expensive museums, concert halls, and the high price of famous paintings. The public school presumably would extend these satisfactions to all people; it would democratize the aesthetic values. But can instruction in the arts "democratize" the cultural and financial elitism?[2]

Perhaps it cannot by itself, but the art world today does offer its riches to virtually all social classes. Shopping malls have become art galleries; opera and the dance are now available through radio, records, and television. There is no dearth of community choral groups, chamber music, and theater. Unfortunately, mere availability is no guarantee of acceptance, especially if the works of art require some form of disciplined perception, perception in the manner of art. For the individual to go beyond the popular art objects that do not require formal instruction, the school has to make some contribution, just as it has to discipline the mind to go beyond commonsense science, commonsense history, and commonsense anything else.

1. The role of the arts in the public school curriculum, especially in a curriculum with a common content prescribed for the total school population, is in some respects a political question because it touches on the values of the school's constituencies. The public may favor a common curriculum in the arts if it promotes accepted sentiments toward the family, the community, the nation. It may be hostile to such a curriculum if it challenges and endangers them. We are familiar with such considerations in the attempts to ban books, plays, and paintings, let alone films. To be sure, biology and psychology, not to mention social studies, run a similar risk, but art has traditionally claimed absolute freedom to create objects without regard for conventional values and to ignore the mores of any social class. If, as is generally believed, middle-class citizens are the bulwark of the public schools, which art is taught and with what emphasis becomes a

political question indeed. If, in addition, prominent advocates of the arts and arts education abjure and abuse all claims to objective standards in the arts, the citizen feels free to regard this curriculum issue as a political issue, or at least an ideological one in which his tastes have as much right as anyone else's.

2. Political considerations also loom when the difference of interests—imagined or real—arise between art specialists in one medium and those in another; between arts specialists and artists, on the one side, and classroom teachers, on the other. Once these groups are organized formally (as members of the Music Educators National Conference, the National Association of Art Education, and analogous organizations of teachers of dance, theater, and other media) the differences become more than academic. Art teachers, for example, are belittled for lack of talent by practising artists, but arts supervisors overawe the classroom teacher who makes no claim to talent and therefore would like to be excused from any responsibility in teaching the arts. Art teachers, for their part, can point out that the good artist may not be a good art teacher; artists may regard anything other than standard studio training as misguided amateurism.

3. Inasmuch as study of the arts, despite a century of advocacy in their behalf, is still largely peripheral at the elementary level and elective on the secondary one—albeit some states (for example, Missouri) have established some requirements—the arts program, and therewith the arts specialist, is the first to be curtailed or abolished in times of financial retrenchment. The employment prospects of the arts specialist would be greatly improved if the arts program were established firmly in the curriculum, as firmly as language, arithmetic, history, or geography. But if this should come about, the general classroom teacher would have to be given the same role in teaching the arts as in other areas, especially at the elementary level. After all, elementary classroom teachers give instruction in a wide range of subjects without having qualified as specialists in them. To permit it in the arts would be tantamount to admitting that in some sense no special talent is needed to teach them. So the specialists are between the Scylla of surrendering some of their mystique and the Charybdis of precarious employment.

4. A common curriculum in the arts means not only that for the

relevant school population there will be in some sense a uniform program of instruction, but also that there is something common to all the arts that can be extracted and taught to that population. Aside from the fact that "uniformity" as a putative threat to creativity is anathema to the arts establishment, there is also a widespread reluctance to "mix" the various arts media. The very term "arts education" raises hackles. Artists are so steeped in the techniques of their particular medium that they are suspicious of any "talk" about art in general.

This problem is not peculiar to the arts. There is a curriculum called "general science" that tries to distil a content or process common to the several sciences. For example, the hypothetico-deductive method of reasoning is common to all the empirical sciences. However, scholars are wary of such generalizations and abstractions because they tend to scumble the distinctive differences of phenomena, modes of inquiry, and standard problems of each discipline. So general science curricula tend to end up with a little of each of the sciences.

Because the arts also are not reducible to a general art or a single master art, the common curriculum must either be a little of each for everybody, or concentrate on one medium and hope that something transfers to the others, or it has to find something that applies or is applicable to all the media without trying to reduce their differences. It is the latter option for which this essay is trying to make a case.

5. The art world includes many constituents: artists, collectors, entrepreneurs, managers, impresarios, and other deliverers of cultural services. It also involves state and local arts councils, national endowments of the arts and humanities, and countless private foundations and organizations, all sincerely intent on fostering the arts in school and out. Proponents of school programs reflect this diversity of interest and support. Hundreds of exemplary programs are described as being enthusiastically received by pupils, teachers, and parents.[3]

It remains to mention another constituency, namely, the colleges of fine arts on the university campus. One might think that these schools or colleges would be interested in preparing teachers of the diverse arts for the public schools. Some are, some are not, even when such programs are housed in their administrative units. In some universities the preparation of arts supervisors and offerings for teacher certification in this field are under the jurisdiction of the college of education. It is fair to note, however, that the faculties devoted to the training of artists and those attending to the preparation of personnel for the public schools constitute different constituencies.

Rationale for a Common Curriculum in the Arts

A common curriculum finds its raison d'être in the supposition that there are some school learnings that no member of the school population can afford to miss. There is more than one way of determining what these learnings are. One is to inventory the tasks that everyone in the society has to perform more or less regularly and which, presumably, require some sort of formal instruction. In our society these tasks range from changing tires on an automobile to voting. Another is to seek out the minimal set of concepts and skills that can function in the greatest variety of situations. Still another is to adopt some ideal of human existence and prescribe the learnings necessary and sufficient to produce it. The first approach may be called justification by frequency of use, the second by generalizability, and the third by the need for the liberal studies to actualize the human essence or form.

A common curriculum in the arts may have some difficulty in making the frequency-of-use argument, if the use is restricted to experience with official works of art, that is, objects put forward as works of art. These are not encounters of the daily kind even in the most culturally sensitive communities. Visits to the theater, museums, and concerts are still special affairs and not, like television, absorbed while eating or drinking. Frequency of use can be claimed, however, if we refer to aesthetic experience rather than to one species of it, namely, experience with works of art. Everyday aesthetics validates frequency of use, albeit the users rarely use "aesthetic" to describe it. For example, we may not go to the museum often, but we make aesthetic judgments about the aesthetic properties of the faces, gestures, speech, clothing of people every day, perhaps every waking hour.

A similar qualification has to be made in the claim to generalizability. The arts do not constitute a logical hierarchy with some concepts more general and more inclusive than others. Works of art can be classified by media, styles, periods, themes, and the like. Aesthetics formulates theories about the nature of art and principles for making and justifying judgments about it. However, a common curriculum in the arts has to give primary attention to the direct encounter with aesthetic objects, natural or contrived, for the sake of the experience itself, and not merely to illustrate concepts or principles. The aesthetic attitude and the aesthetic object are not simple counterparts of the scientific attitude and the scientific object, and this distinctiveness of the aesthetic experience pervades the arts curriculum. The broad uses of art education are grounded in the generic use of the imagination, that is, the power to create and construe images as vehicles of human import, or as some would put it, as images of human feeling. If it can be shown that this function is ubiquitous, functioning in all forms of experience, then the claim to generalizability can be sustained.[4]

As to membership in the liberal studies, a good deal depends on the meaning of "liberal." It may mean the class of courses usually included in catalogues as "humanities," or general nonscientific culture courses, or some version of what used to be called the "classical studies." If these meanings have anything in common, it is the implicit claim that there is an ideal of man, sometimes called the human essence, which should constitute the steady and ultimate goal and guide of education. These are the studies of "man as man," not as this or that member of a vocation or occupying this or that status in the social order. The arts certainly qualify as "liberal" studies in the usual meaning of the term, although only a classical view of art—and fine art at that—makes this claim explicit. It is debatable, however, whether the standard studio pattern of professional art training sees itself as a "liberal" study; the artist as a craftsman, a skilled artisan, is a durable tradition. Courses in art appreciation are more likely to make this claim. In Aristotle's view, liberal studies were those cultivated by persons free from the constraints of economic and social obligation. This ties the arts to leisure (*schola*). However, if considerable leisure is to be the portion of all classes, as in the ideal society it would be, then the onus of snobbish elitism is removed, and it can be argued that studies undertaken solely for the enrichment of leisure are indeed "liberal."

The claim of art to be a vehicle for insight into the good life or into the nature of the human condition implies the promise that like the other humanities the study of art or the appreciation of "great" art will make human beings better human beings. That among the great villains of the world, it is not at all unusual to find beneficiaries of first-rate humanistic schooling, including a fondness, sometimes a passion, for fine art, should make us wary of claiming too much for art as the road to the improvement of mankind.[5]

The rationale for a common curriculum in the arts, one may conclude, will have to argue its claims in all three modes of justification: frequency of use, generalizability, and as a liberal study. The argument, it seems to me, should be addressed to a hypothetical school board made up of citizens who are "friends of the arts" and who, on the whole, are friendly to the public schools. They should not be rednecks or belligerent philistines, but persons who are knowledgeable and critical of how best to use the resources of the school. Such a board has a right and perhaps a duty to get answers from advocates of a common, required curriculum in the arts to the following questions:

1. Is the aesthetic (everyday and artistic) experience so distinctive that it will not be covered in other subjects of the common curriculum? This query has been the theme of formal aesthetics ever since that discipline was born, and any claim of aesthetic education to a place in the general education curriculum has to indicate that distinctiveness. My own answer, I believe, is shared by many of these theories, namely, that its distinctiveness lies in the making and perceiving of objects as images of feeling. Aesthetic objects convey meaning by images rather than concept. "The threatening sky" is an aesthetic statement, not a scientific one; it relates the appearance of sky to the human import of rain and storms. It is one visage of "threatening."[6]

It is in this sense that aesthetic objects by their appearance enable us to "understand" the countless (and for the most part nameless) nuances of human feeling, that is, by presenting a "portrait" of anger, resentment, joy, elation, and the like that we recognize. Feelings do not float about waiting to be perceived, but a solitary tree on a barren plain may be a portrait of loneliness objectified for our perception and in this limited sense understood. A thousand images could portray loneliness and yet not resemble each other, as do the members of the same species of plants or animals. The words "understand," "portrait," and the like are used figuratively, not literally. If, on the morning after a devastating ice storm has made all electrical appliances unusable and interrupted a host of normal activities, one can still concentrate on the peculiar glisten of the ice on the branches of a tree nearby, one has achieved the aesthetic attitude. In that moment one has "distanced" the storm and disengaged its appearance from the cognitive and practical considerations that attend it in normal life.[7]

2. Yet even if the distinctive values of aesthetic experience are understood and appreciated, the hypothetical board cannot avoid asking how this mode of experience affects other strands of life. What is its relation to language, to concepts, to judgments, to the economic, social, moral, and intellectual values? The art-for-art's-sake advocates of education in the arts who are impatient with this question must realize that the board cannot inject into a common curriculum a strand of experience that has no effect on other strands of life. Such a strand might be an interesting oddity, but would hardly make a strong claim on the public purse or that portion of it devoted to education.

However, *aesthetic* experience is not rare at all, albeit art masterpieces are rare, as is artistic talent.[8] Aesthetic judgment is extraordinarily, almost frighteningly, relevant to everyday living. In a modern technological society the instruments—the technology—are the works of the intellect, but their products are sold to the public by means of images, as indeed nearly everything else is. Objects are made enticing not only by their usefulness but also by the images of prestige, importance, wealth, and general well-being that they display. Candidates for political office must project an image of leadership and virtue. Judgments of persons are based pretty much on the image of feeling conveyed by standardized appearances. These, in turn, have been absorbed from the popular arts. Most of us forecast the weather by the appearance of the sky, and a physician does not ignore the way a patient "looks." So, however we construe general education, aesthetic education has a place in it, provided we think of it as cultivation of our sensitivity to images of feeling, and not as synonymous with the acquiring of performance skills.

3. Granted that the aesthetic experience is distinctive and relevant to all other values, and that the perception of import-bearing images is not a part of other subjects of the curriculum, does it necessitate formal instruction? Could it not be picked up in the ordinary commerce with the cultural surround? Is not popular art picked up this way? The answer is the one given for formal instruction in any field, namely, that there is a body of expertise and scholarship, together with exemplary works, that are not picked up informally. If the arts have such

knowledge and exemplars, then formal instruction in them is required. However, if no difference between the "popular" and "serious" arts is recognized, then the board would rightly be skeptical about devoting curricular time and pedagogical resources to teaching what young people are bound to acquire anyway and almost anywhere.

4. If it is granted that some formal instruction in the arts is desirable for the entire school population, then the board can still ask whether it ought to be undertaken by the public school. Could not the museums and the community symphony do it? Could not visits to the studios of "real" artists become an instructional activity? Or could not artists-in-residence from time to time provide the school population with sufficient insight into what art *really* is? Could not the rich pool of talent, amateur and professional, in the community provide the needed instruction? In exposure to art and artists the school cannot hope to compete with other community agencies. Indeed, the more such resources a community commands, the less likely, on the exposure theory, is the board to use its resources for arts education.

5. Is the proposed program multimedia or confined to one or two? Traditionally, literature, some poetry, music, and "drawing," varying in amount and emphasis, constituted the arts curriculum. In recent years, dance, theater, film, weaving, ceramics, and architecture have drawn increasing attention from both public and teachers.[9] What principle should govern the selection? Where art education is elective, this is not a serious problem; in a common curriculum, it becomes central. Does a proposed program take account of this problem?[10]

6. Is the program teachable to the total school population or does it require special talent on the part of the learner as well as of the teacher? Programs that require special aptitudes traditionally have been excluded from the required general education curriculum. Why should not arts education be included in the extracurricular program that is tailored to the specialized interest of pupils?

7. Does a proposed program provide a graded sequence of content and approach that might guide the design of the curriculum for kindergarten through grade twelve? If so, what is the principle of the design?

8. Is the proposed program feasible? Can the classroom teacher in the elementary years participate in it after the manner of such participation in the teaching of the other subjects? At the secondary

level, is there a way of utilizing the skills of the several specialists in team teaching? Is there a vocabulary or approach that will enable them to communicate and organize (not necessarily integrate) their efforts?

9. Finally, are the results of the program in some way assessable? Are there signs (not necessarily measurable) of growth that can be observed? Are there standards that could be used to judge that growth?

These questions are relevant and proper to ask any candidate for admission to a program of general education and especially to membership in a common curriculum that in some sense will be required for a given school population. These questions are in order when dozens of arts education programs vie for funds and publicity. In the politics of arts education few programs even try to answer these questions. Instead, the board is likely to be offered testimonials from enthusiastic sponsors. Very often these testimonials are as genuine as the enthusiasm, but they are not always relevant answers to the relevant questions.

Curriculum Content

The contents of the curriculum can be classified as (a) skills of aesthetic impression or the skills of perceiving aesthetic properties, (b) the skills of performance or the making of objects that have aesthetic properties, (c) knowledge about the arts, and (d) criticism (enlightened appreciation).

SKILLS OF AESTHETIC PERCEPTION

The following properties characterize objects viewed aesthetically, whether encountered in nature or contrived by the artist: (a) sensory patterns formed by sounds, colors, gestures, textures, or combinations of these; (b) formal properties or design that give shape and character to the pattern of sensory qualities; (c) technical properties pertaining to skills of performance in the medium; (d) expressive properties by virtue of which an image is perceived as an image having human import. The systematic exploration of these properties may be called "aesthetic scanning."

Sensory properties. Sensory properties are presented as stimuli to the eye, ear, touch, sense of movement, taste. An aesthetic object has a sensory surface, either directly stimulating one of the senses or, as in literature, indirectly. Even though we speak of an elegant mathematical equation when there is no manifest sensory image of the ideas expressed by it, I would argue that an idea cannot be perceived as beautiful or elegant without *some* sensory shape, real or imagined. Psychologists speak of imageless thought, and given sufficient familiarity with the concepts of a science, we can perhaps dispense with images in thinking, but to contemplate them as aesthetically expressive, as images bearing human import, it seems to me, does require sensory imagery.

We can talk about sounds, sights, and movements in the language of psychology or physics using frequencies, wave lengths, color wheels, stimuli, and nerve paths, but for a sensory content to become aesthetic requires that it be perceived as carrying on its face a quality that can be described in human terms. When we speak of colors as warm-cold, tingling-languorous, sharp-dull, we are drawing attention to the colors as images of feeling tone, and feelings are intimations of human import. Sounds made by voices or instruments are perceived aesthetically as warm-cold, sharp-dull, lazy-propulsive. And it is not at all odd to speak of sounds, colors, shapes, lines, movements, and gestures as sad-glad, bright-dull, kind-threatening. Because some sensory properties, however simple, already are potentially expressive,[11] there may be an unlearned vocabulary of feeling out of which responses to aesthetic objects are built.

Formal properties. The sensory properties are unified by some pattern or design. Gestalt psychology insists that we always perceive wholes, that the mind tends to find form in whatever it perceives and to impress form where it does not find it. For the artist, the form, the organization, the design are perhaps the most important parts of the creative task. For the perceiver, the form or design is the most important clue to perception and comprehension, for form is the principle of intelligibility. Hence works of art that have no readily discernible form seem to the perceiver to have no form at all, that is, to be unintelligible. In such cases the perceiver may break the whole work into many fragments each of which does have a familiar form. Or one may reject the object as "crazy." This is the familiar reaction to very modern music. It is not that this music lacks form; on the contrary, it may utilize a very complex organization of sound, but the form is unfamiliar to many, if not most, symphony hall patrons.

A useful summary of the formal aspect of art is given by DeWitt

Parker.[12] The most general principle of form, he argues, is that of organic unity (unity in variety), that is, where each of a diversity of parts finds meaning in the whole and the whole finds its meaning in the relationship of the parts. The organs of the body afford a familiar example. The ideal of organic unity imposes on the work of art of the obligation to contain nothing that could be omitted without perceptible loss of unity. This is a severe demand on the artist, but it is a fundamental principle of criticism. To achieve unity in variety or organic form, Parker lists the following: principle of the theme; thematic variation, balance; hierarchy; and evolution. To discern how each of these principles is exemplified in the aesthetic object is a target of aesthetic perception, and this skill, like that of becoming increasingly sensitive to the sensory properties, is teachable at virtually all school ages.[13]

Technical properties. By the technical properties are meant the procedures or methods by which the aesthetic properties are produced. Although not always perceptible in the finished object, they have a place in aesthetic pedagogy simply because pupils are almost always interested in how "it was done or made." These properties belong more logically to the knowledge section of aesthetic education, because techniques play so important a part in the study of stylistic problems. For example, the differences in the size and instruments of an eighteenth-century and a modern orchestra are factors in the way eighteenth-century music is heard. Artists are often identified by their techniques, and some forms of art die out because the technical skills involved in their production are lost as, for example, in certain types of ceramics.

Expressive properties. The expressive properties of the aesthetic object are produced by the expressive properties of the sensory and formal ones. But the expressive properties of the objects as a whole may not be simply their sum. The expressive quality of the rose is not merely the sum of the appearance of its petals, stem, and so forth. Given a different arrangement of petals, the total effect might be quite different from the conventional arrangement. The image, if unified, will have a pervasive expressive quality of its own.

Aesthetic objects are expressive of (a) moods, (b) dynamic states, and (c) ideas or ideals. The first are describable by such terms as gay-sad, bright-dull, hopeful-dejected, and countless other pairs. When given pairs of opposites to designate moods or dynamic states, there is usually a high uniformity of response. By dynamic states are meant high or low energy levels, for example, strong-weak, peace-conflict, peaceful-dangerous. Ideas or ideals are often attributed to aesthetic objects when they are said to express integrity, nobility, cruelty, sublimity, tragedy, sacrifice, and the like.

These expressive characteristics, it should be reiterated, are to be perceived by the observer as being *in* the aesthetic object: the melancholy is perceived as being *in* or *of* the music or the poem or the dance or the painting.[14] This imputed objectivity is important pedagogically because those participating in the perception can be asked to point to what is perceived; they do not at this juncture have to state or justify their attitudes toward or interpretations of the object. That belongs to criticism.

It may be asked why aesthetic perception should require formal instruction. It is, after all, a very primitive form of apprehension; the very young child, one may suppose, natively and naively perceives much of the world aesthetically. However, this innocence of the eye, ear, and touch soon gives way to the demands of the adult world that the child use appearances as clues to relational thinking, theoretical and practical. Good thinking requires *abstraction* from the concrete particularity of the object; aesthetic perception requires the *apprehension* of this particularity. Good action requires relating objects and actions to each other in the light of some goal or as causes and effects; the aesthetic perception, on the contrary, asks that attention be concentrated on the appearance in its own right. Hence, the innocent eye (if it ever did exist) loses its innocence fairly early in the game. And so our perceptions become selective, noted as tokens of our interests and not as expressive properties of the object.

This has a two-fold consequence. One is that in daily life the aesthetic properties of objects and persons are skimmed over or become stereotyped clues to practical inference. For example, the appearance of the man who passes on the street is translated into "He's a salesman" or "He's a banker" or "He's an actor." A quick glance at a woman may be translated by immediate inference into, "She didn't buy those clothes on a secretary's salary." We literally look and listen *through* the multitudes of human beings who pass in and out of our field of perception. Conversely, we forget that our own bodies, clothes, voice, gesture, and demeanor constitute an expressive aesthetic image, and the image may or may not do us justice, let alone be "interesting to perceive," as D. W. Gotshalk liked to put it.[15]

The loss of the ability to adopt the aesthetic attitude toward objects is most noticeable in the presence of works of art, objects designed to be perceived as aesthetic objects, and not as signs or causes of something other than themselves. We become awkward and disoriented when confronted with works of art, and especially when the works are not familiar and we have not learned the conventional things to say about them.

It is for this reason that any common curriculum in this field must begin with the restoration and training of aesthetic perception. The paradigm for such perception is found in the way the artist perceives the image he creates.[16] Perception is the pivot between the making of images and the critical appreciation of them. Perception in the manner of art, so to speak, guides the making of images that are expressive in the manner of art, on the one hand, and lays the groundwork for informed judgments about the aesthetic merits of such images, on the other.

Pedagogically, the perceptional approach, or what has been called aesthetic scanning of the aesthetic properties, commends itself because it can be taught at all levels and with all objects, natural or contrived, that have a perceptible surface. It requires no special talent and provides a common vocabulary for the discussion of the aesthetic properties in all media. This enables the classroom teacher to participate in arts instruction and makes it possible for a monospecialist (a specialist in one art medium) to scan aesthetically in other media. Aesthetic scanning, therefore, can be regarded as a general approach to aesthetic education, for it is directed toward the perception of the properties that all aesthetic objects exhibit in one medium or another without fusing or confusing the media.

There is evidence that teaching aesthetic perception is possible at all age levels and in all the standard media. Children take to it readily; art specialists in one medium can learn to scan aesthetically in other media. Methods for carrying it on have been used in workshops and classrooms.[17]

SKILLS OF PERFORMANCE

In addition to the skills of aesthetic impression (proper perception) there are the skills of aesthetic expression—the making of images of feeling. Traditionally, music and drawing (art) and occasionally some creating writing have been prescribed at the elementary level for this purpose. At the secondary level, performance courses are not usually required but are available as electives. There was a time when all young ladies of good family were expected as part of their general education to paint in water colors and play the piano or the harp. Later, the working classes were persuaded to purchase pianos for their children so that they too could share in the accomplishments of the upper classes. Performance competence has been and still is the standard goal of arts education, so one takes even mild exception to it at one's peril.[18]

Opportunity for manipulation and experimentation with the materials of the various media should be available to the pupil, especially during the elementary grades, because the expressive potentials of a medium depend on its special characteristics in producing sounds, movements, colors, shapes, and the like. Without such first-hand familiarity, it is virtually impossible to put oneself in the place of the artist and his problems. However, the primary purpose of this instruction or exposure or experimentation is not a high level of technical competence. It is far more reasonable to expect the educated layperson to perceive in the manner of the artist than to perform like one. It cannot be repeated too often that these remarks are in no way intended to restrict the opportunities for specialized training in the arts. However, specialized training of any sort by definition need not be prescribed for everyone.[19]

During the early years, from kindergarten through grade four, it seems natural for the children to make the objects that they perceive and want others to perceive aesthetically, that is, in the manner of art. Children at this age are already immersed (one would hope) in fairy stories, rhymes, songs, poems, and other products of the imagination. They are at home in the world of make-believe. But even young children need not be restricted to baby art. In one project produced by the Educational Research Council of Greater Cleveland, materials for use in the early grades were selected with an eye to artistic quality, and field tests in a number of schools showed a high level of acceptance of many instances of mature art in painting, poetry, and music.[20]

The skills of performance are the sticking point in the controversy between arts education specialists and those who favor a more general approach. For many specialists, artists, and critics, art education that is not baptized and fully confirmed in a performance skill is a sham and an illusion. The notion that there might be a difference between arts education for the consumer and for the producer does not impress them; for them, a good consumer goes through the same training— albeit somewhat shorter—as the good producer, even though one does not make a career of it. Little wonder that playing in the band or singing in the school glee club or taking part in the class play is so often regarded as the proper process, product, and proof of education in the arts.

There comes a time in the life of the child when the making of expressive images is frustrated by lack of technical skill. Either the technical skill is acquired by talent and industry or the activity is abandoned. Schooling in performance ceases to be part of general education and becomes a species of special education. To insist that every pupil achieve high competence in a performance skill or to keep on trying to do so from kindergarten through grade twelve makes little sense for most of the student body. To provide such training for those who feel the need for it and are willing to devote the energy to become proficient makes all the sense in the world.[21]

ENLIGHTENED CHERISHING

If grades kindergarten through four are devoted pretty much to the skills of aesthetic impression and expression so that children feel at home in the various media, then the subsequent grades can gradually shift emphasis to knowledge about the arts and to the enlightened appreciation of them. The skills of impression provide import-bearing images for understanding and appreciation. What in the earlier grades had to be taught and practiced explicitly now should function tacitly. Deliberate and systematic aesthetic scanning is now habitual except in the presence of aesthetic objects that resist perception. Knowledge about a work of art often leads the eye and ear to what had been overlooked, and in this way enriches and enlarges perception, but can never displace it as the primary form of aesthetic experience. Knowing about the formal characteristics of a Beethoven concerto, for example, may alter our hearing of it, but whatever counts in the concerto as a musical image must be heard.

I use the term "enlightened cherishing" to cover both knowledge about the arts and the use of that knowledge to justify preferences in the arts. As to the knowledge component, one might expect by the end of grade twelve: (a) some understanding of the historical development of the several arts; (b) familiarity with stylistic characteristics of certain periods; (c) familiarity with exemplars of styles, themes, periods; and (d) familiarity with some of the more frequently cited theories of art or philosophies concerning the nature and function of art.

Knowledge about the arts is generated and validated in the same way as knowledge in other academic disciplines. Over the centuries scholars have investigated virtually every aspect of every major art and many minor ones. It is the business of each disciplinary guild to scrutinize, criticize, and correct the work of its credentialed members. "Good" knowledge about the arts is certified in the same way that "good" physics or "good" biology is, namely, by the judgment of the guilds devoted to the respective disciplines. The curriculum problem is to select from this body of knowledge materials that constitute a reasonably logical and workable sequence.

There is no lack of materials for a grade seven through twelve sequence. The organization of the materials can take many, many forms: by themes (freedom, democracy, and so forth), by periods (early Greek, Renaissance, Modern, and so forth), by styles (abstract, romantic, surrealist, and so forth). Because the field is so voluminous and the possible approaches so varied, a uniform principle of selection is as important, if not more so, as the particular item selected. If, for example, grade seven uses the theme organization, grade eight the organization of stylistic periods, and grade nine wants to proceed with a straightforward historical account, chaos will and often does ensue. A common approach is almost imperative for a common curriculum.

In selecting materials, whatever the approach chosen, we should seek items that yield, to paraphrase a colloquialism, the biggest bang for the pedagogical buck. Exemplars in the various arts are items of this kind. Exemplars are useful not only for knowledge about the arts, but also for enlightened cherishing of them. Before discussing the criteria for an exemplar, a few words about interpretation, taste, and criticism are in order.

An aesthetic judgment takes the form: This painting (sculpture, building, musical composition, dance) is good because it has the following aesthetic properties; how good depends on the degree to which it has these properties. To fill in the definitions of aesthetic properties and the estimate of degree requires aesthetic principles of the form: "All good works of art have properties A, B, C . . . N." These principles are the subject matter of formal aesthetics and the philosophy of art. Should formal aesthetics be included in the curriculum of general education in grades kindergarten through twelve? Formally and systematically probably not, because they lean so much on technical issues in philosophy and art criticism. Furthermore, current work in aesthetics has more to do with the logical requirements for discourse about works of art than about art itself. Any issue of the *Journal of Aesthetics and Art Criticism* will demonstrate what is meant. So will the current anthologies on aesthetics. If, perchance, a school enrolls pupils who can take this kind of literature, more power to them and to a curriculum including such materials.

For more modest schools and students, however, an informal acquaintance with some of the major historical theories about the nature and purpose of art and the justification that some important critics have given for their judgment about the exemplars being studied are more productive. This, of course, can and should be supplemented by reading and discussion of criticism in current periodicals. One important test of the success of the program is whether the high school graduate can read such material with a modicum of confidence and understanding.

Among the expected outcomes of education in the arts are some things called "good taste" and "good judgment" in matters pertaining to the aesthetic domain. It is fashionable, however, to deny that there are defensible grounds for either. *De gustibus non disputandum est* is taken as a warrant for asserting boldly, "I know what I like" and that preference is immune from criticism, in justification whereof the disagreement among critics is cited as evidence. Are then these locutions meaningless or self-contradictory? Not at all.

When people speak of "good taste" they can mean the preferences of the "good" or "right" people, where "good" and "right" denote some elite group. It may be a social elite that justifies both its taste and judgment by a claim to inherent superiority of birth or wealth. If the elite group is an intellectual or artistic one, then its taste carries the implicit claim of connoisseurship, that is, the possession of experience and standards that are grounded in principles. Nevertheless, there is difference between taste and judgment. The former is spontaneous and more or less habitual; the latter—good judgment—is always a reasoned response that answers the question, "Why *ought* one to like this and not that?" Accordingly, it is not meaningless or self-contradictory to say "I like X, but it is not good art" or "X is good art, but I don't care for it." We can refuse to dispute about tastes, but not about judgments. Enlightened cherishing covers both good taste and good judgment insofar as they are influenced by knowledge and reflection on experience.

The school should be wary of what it promises. Habits take time to develop, and the school is far from being the most potent factor in the process. Good judgment calls for broad experience and keen analysis. A more realistic promise is that given systematic instruction in proper perception and basic knowledge about the arts, the pupil will in time acquire in embryonic form the criteria and habits of preference that are not merely conventional, but are in some sense defensible on aesthetic principles.

Related to appreciation as an expected outcome of art study is what might be called sensitivity to the meanings of works of art. This expectation follows from the belief that art captures the deeper meanings of life, and that these meanings are not always apparent to the naive observer. Some works of art do try to express ideas and ideals. Classical art tries to do so by dealing with "great" themes and personages. Historic events (Washington crossing the Delaware) are commemorated in works of art, and few Americans can resist the emotional impact of seeing the Statue of Liberty as they return from journeys across the Atlantic. Thus, patriotic songs, plays, monuments, and paintings can and often do enhance patriotic sentiments. The popular arts demonstrate this power over attitudes daily in every phase of life. The serious arts are supposed to plumb deeper and more significant levels of meaning and feeling.[22]

Not a little of the support for a program of arts education in the schools comes from those who ascribe to art this power over attitudes, but it also stipulates a selection from the realm of art works that will enhance the values cherished by a particular constituency of the schools. And at this point the schools run into trouble, what can be serious political trouble.

Art as the product of the artist's imagination is not limited to any set of beliefs or values. Art can celebrate the values of an era or undermine them. Fortunately, the school does not have to conduct a plebiscite on which art to choose for instruction. It can validate its choices by relying on a consensus of the learned in the arts and in education, as it does (if it is wise) in other subjects of instruction. There are, as will be noted shortly, exemplars that embody that consensus, both with respect to artistic merit and the values they express.[23]

The claim that schooling in the arts should improve the ability to interpret and grasp the significance of a work of art also needs some qualification. The responsibility for conveying meaning or significance falls primarily on the work of art, not on the perceiver. Given proper scanning of the aesthetic properties, and a reasonable familiarity with styles, conventions, conventional symbolisms, and technical characteristics of various art forms and periods, the "real" meaning of the work should be directly accessible to the perceiver. It should not require an elaborate historical, logical, or psychological interpretation. Such outside help is justified only if it makes perceptible what has been obscured by factors external to the work itself.

Nevertheless, works of art do vary in the degree to which they match the needs and resources of the perceiver. Although it is likely that all members of the species experience the same fundamental emotions—anger, fear, joy, jealousy, and the like—they do not experience them with the same degree of subtlety and complexity. Adolescent love is not seventy-fifth anniversary love, despite efforts of some current best sellers to persuade the elderly to the contrary. The possible variations in these moods and emotions are precisely the stuff that art converts into images of sound, color, gesture, and motion. Folk art or popular art thus serves to express the standard images of the emotions, and it may be argued that it is from these popular arts that most of us learn what the emotions are supposed to "look" and "sound" like. These stereotypes of both the emotion and its aesthetic expression unite the members of a generation and cut them off from generations who do not share them.

When, however, love and anger and joy take on strange and subtle variations, their expressive stereotypes in the popular arts may not adequately express them. Presumably the serious arts try to provide nonstereotyped expressive adequacy, so that mismatches between felt emotions and images of them can be expected. The arts are expected to expand and subtilize the emotional life by creating images in which these emotions are recognized. In turn, the more complex images may reveal to the perceiver subtlety and complexity not hitherto suspected.

While on the subject of interpretation, it is relevant to note how aesthetic criteria are used by the public to interpret events. Assassinations of famous persons by random bullets fired by random persons responding to more or less random impulses create suspicion that a great conspiracy more aesthetically suited to the importance of such events is being concealed by the authorities. The account of the event has to be aesthetically right or it leaves us uneasy about its factual rightness. Historic events tend to be shaped by time and art into legends that are more believable and believed than the official facts. Life requires dramatic structure to be interesting, and drama calls for conflict, suspense, and a resolution that is at once surprising and inevitable. "Once upon a time" is the universal signal that a dramatic event is about to be disclosed. Journalists use the term "story" for the facts they report, and the more like a story the account is, the more interesting to the reader, listener, and viewer. Truth about human affairs may be stranger than fiction, but it has to conform to the structure of fiction to be believed.

EXEMPLARS

The task of selecting the content and structure for a *common* curriculum becomes discouraging by virtue of the volume and variety of materials and the way in which the literature has classified them. Some texts treat each art separately; some discuss them together; some treat the materials historically, some by the themes with which they deal, some by stylistic trends.

Then there is the task of deciding on the sequence in which the materials are to be presented for instruction. This essay envisions a combination of the skills of perception and manipulation in the major media to be emphasized from kindergarten through grade six, with knowledge about and appreciation of the arts to be dominant in grades seven through twelve. Grades ten through twelve might concentrate on interpretation and criticism.

One way out of this embarrassment of riches is to organize instruction around a set of exemplars in the various media, especially in grades seven through twelve. By an exemplar is meant what is sometimes called a classic, or an item commonly included in the lists of "great" books, paintings, musical compositions, literature, drama, architecture, sculpture. The term "exemplar" denotes an example of a class of products, on the one hand, and an ideal example, on the other.[24]

Exemplars have survived critical scrutiny over long periods of time and represent in an unusually clear and vivid way (a) the fruition of a trend or period, (b) a transition or bridge between periods, summarizing a passing era and ushering in a new one, (c) a new trend not fully appreciated in its time. Avant-garde art claims to be in this genre, and some of it does serve the prophetic role although much more does not. These characteristics endow an exemplar with great educative potential, a big "bang" for the pedagogical "buck."

The exemplar approach is compatible with many types of organization. If the curriculum is to be organized by historical periods, exemplars can be chosen in the various media for each period; if the principle of organization is great themes (freedom, good and evil, the profane and the sacred) there are exemplars for each theme in each period, and the same holds if the organization is by stylistic periods (classical, modern, baroque, romantic, and so forth). Which exemplars are chosen depends on the grade level, the principle of organization, and their pedagogical potential for a wide variety of learnings. There can be a standard minimum set of exemplars that are covered by all pupils in the course of their schooling, or there can be alternate sets that exemplify analogous characteristics.

One further factor favors the use of exemplars in general education, and particularly general education in the arts. The exemplars are beacons that mark significant items in the memory bank of a civilization. What a community remembers in common serves as a set of lenses through which the world is seen and understood. Without them a community cannot exist. Exemplars are powerful signals for eliciting common images, concepts, and sentiments. Much of what is meant by the term "educated mind" is the sharing of this imagic-conceptual store by way of the exemplars.

The use of exemplars as the chief targets of instruction, especially in grades seven through twelve, entails two requirements: (a) that the list of exemplars to be studied be relatively short, and (b) that each be studied intensively over fairly long periods of time. The reason for this is that the exemplar is not being studied for the sake of getting information—the kind that program notes provide—about it or to memorize the encomia heaped upon it. Rather, the goal is perception of an image that conveys human import in an important and usually complex way. It takes time to "see" or "hear" as the artist has seen or heard that image, especially if that artist lived in a culture now strange to the pupil.

The dirty work of curriculum construction—the choice of design, exemplars, and sequence, the production of materials for pupil and teacher use, and instruments of evaluation—can be done by the teaching staff, committees, consultants, or left to the enterprise of textbook publishers. As a reward, this dirty work can and should bring together teachers, art specialists, artists, scholars, and critics—no mean reward.

Individual Differences and the Common Curriculum

The curriculum described above, it seems to me, meets the putative demands of the hypothetical intelligent board of education that has to decide on whether the arts have a place in the curriculum for general education.[25] It does not posit any skill or understanding that is prima facie unteachable to any pupil in the normal range of scholastic aptitude. The contents of the curriculum cannot be picked up informally from the cultural surround and cannot be acquired without formal tuition. Furthermore, although the community delivers many cultural services including access to the arts, it can be argued that opportunities to enjoy the fruits of art are not equivalent to learning how to do so. The participation in the cultural resources of the community is a test of aesthetic education, not a substitute for it. The curriculum tries to show in what respects the various arts have common properties: the sensory, formal, technical, and expressive; and that the scanning of these properties can be taught systematically. It defines the respective roles of the classroom teacher and the art specialist. The curriculum covers the skills of impression and expression, knowledge about the arts, and some familiarity with the principles by which critical judgments about the merits of art works are rationalized.

Finally, growth in sensitivity to aesthetic properties can be assessed. Informally, progress can be noted in the increased readiness to identify and describe aesthetic properties; in the range of properties identified, and the awareness of the distinctions between what is perceived, understood, and judged. The informal evaluation gains a good deal of reliability from one of the rules of aesthetic scanning, namely, that anything may be said about an object provided one is willing to identify the properties of the object that are being asserted. This rule inhibits using the object as a stimulus to free associations outside of the object.[26]

I have construed the common curriculum to mean a uniform program of studies, and the use of exemplars as central in these studies smacks strongly of pedantic traditionalism. Above all, does not such a curriculum blatantly ignore individual differences and the school's obligation to respect them?

Several responses can be made to this criticism. One is that individual results of learning will be variable despite all efforts for uniformity. Individual differences do not entail different curricula, but rather the possibility of variation within a uniform design. One such variable is the abstraction level at which the material is taught; another is the time spent on a given unit. Homogeneous grouping for instruction, provided it is based on achievement status in the subject matter and not on IQ, and provided it is adjusted frequently and freely, goes a long way to meeting relevant individual differences.

If it is argued that uniform curriculum inhibits the teacher's need to vary motivational strategy to meet classroom exigencies, then it should be shown that the curriculum is beyond the learning capacity of the pupils and the ingenuity of the teacher, or that some other curriculum will achieve the same goals with more effective motivation.

Finally, within the general design of the curriculum there is ample opportunity for pedagogical variation and adjustment. The range of objects chosen for training in perception is almost unlimited. And the same may be said for the experimental manipulation in the performance skills. As the instruction shifts to the higher grades and the study of exemplars, how these are to be perceived, analyzed, judged is not determined a priori by the curriculum committee. The consensus of the learned is more an agreement on criteria of evidence than on particular conclusions.

Given a common approach and design, there is ample room for variation. Just as for a musical theme, there is almost no limit on relevant variation, so given a well-structured design and rationale for a curriculum there is no inherent necessity for mindless uniformity. It is when there are variations but no theme or when many variations of many themes compete for attention that there is no hope for unity in variety, for the form that makes everything intelligible, including a curriculum.

FOOTNOTES

1. For a more detailed discussion of the several value domains and their relations, see my *Building a Philosophy of Education*, 2d ed. (Englewood Cliffs, N.J.: Prentice Hall, 1961. Reprint edition, Melbourne, Florida: Robert E. Krieger Publishing Co., 1977).

2. As one example of the intricate relationship among the arts, money, politics, and diverse forms of "elitism," see Edgar B. Young, *Lincoln Center: The Building of an Institution* (New York: New York University Press, 1981).

3. See American Council for the Arts in Education, *Coming to Our Senses: The Significance of the Arts for American Education* (New York: McGraw-Hill Book Co., 1977). For an excellent critique of this volume, see Ralph A. Smith, "The Naked Piano Player: Or, What the Rockefeller Report *Coming to Our Senses* Really Is," *Journal of Aesthetic Education* 12 (January 1978): 45-61. The article is also illuminating on the new "policy-making complex in cultural and educational affairs." An example of the attitude of the professional artist toward "innovative" programs is expressed in the fear of one critic of the Rockefeller report lest the public get the idea that art is pleasurable because it is "easy." "I have too much admiration for those who dance, sculpt . . . to want anyone to think that what they do is easy or even enjoyable in a limited sense." Hence, it is understandable that Bart Teush, Director of Undergraduate Studies in Theater at Yale, took exception to the implications that lying on the floor and moving is "doing ballet," that working with baking dough is "sculpture." From a letter to the *New York Times*, June 12, 1977.

4. It is noteworthy that ordinary terms take on special meanings when used in the aesthetic context. Thus "knowledge," which ordinarily means a system of concepts, in art and aesthetics takes on the meaning of "emotive knowledge." Art is "cognitive" but in the same sense that it apprehends a revelation of human feeling in an image. Similarly, to say that art deals with emotions does not mean what it means in the statement "psychology deals with the emotions." Art, it is said, presents emotions not as had but as recollected in tranquility.

5. It has been suggested that the rationale might include the claim that the arts curriculum might lead to employment opportunities after schooling, for example, the television industry, the entertainment field, and the graphic arts industry. I do not include this claim in my rationale because unless the arts curriculum is more specialized

and technical than *general* education can "require," it will not contribute very much to vocational skills.

6. I have tried to explicate this view in my *Enlightened Cherishing: An Essay on Aesthetic Education* (Urbana, Ill.: University of Illinos Press, 1972. Distributed by Kappa Delta Pi, Lafayette, Indiana). Perhaps the most familiar aesthetic theory that espouses this view is that of Susanne K. Langer in *Philosophy in a New Key* (Cambridge, Mass.: Harvard University Press, 1942).

7. This is the concept of psychical distance discussed in Edward Bullough, " 'Psychical Distance' as a Factor in Art and an Aesthetic Principle," *British Journal of Psychology* 5 (June 1912): 87-118.

8. I have tried to give numerous examples of this elsewhere, but even a cursory study of work origins indicates how fundamentally the meaning of words is rooted in images. Indeed, virtually all but the most mechanical symbol-coding system rely on the imagic background of the users to give meaning to usage. For example, what is one to do with "We worked around the clock," if the imagery is absent? What will happen to this expression when clocks do not have "hands" that move around a "face?"

9. For data on this point, see H. S. Broudy and Edward Mikel, *Survey of Aesthetic Attitudes of Key School Personnel* (St. Louis, Mo.: CEMREL, 1978).

10. Ibid. Tables 4 and 5, pp. 24-26, indicate the degree of confidence of teachers and arts specialists to work in areas other than their specialty.

11. A view urged by Rudolph Arnheim, *Art and Visual Perception* (Berkeley: University of California Press, 1954).

12. DeWitt Parker, "The Problem of Esthetic Form," in *The Analysis of Art* (New Haven: Yale University Press, 1926). Excerpted in Melvin Rader, *A Modern Book of Esthetics*, 4th ed. (New York: Holt, Rinehart and Winston, 1973), pp. 250 ff.

13. The task is facilitated by the relative ease with which the formal as well as the sensory properties are manipulatable by the pupil. A set of lines or shapes or colors can be put into many designs. With the use of overlays, slides, and other blessings of modern technology, aesthetic scanning can be as subtle, flexible, and creative as the teacher cares to make it.

14. Of course there is a library of debate as to whether these properties do inhere in the object or are contributed by the observer. But on either view, in aesthetic perception they must be perceived as being *in* the object: their origin is irrelevant for perception, however relevant it might be for aesthetic theory or interpretation. This is the principal of phenomenological objectivity as distinguished from ontological objectivity.

15. Delman W. Gotshalk, *Art and the Social Order*, 2d ed. (New York: Dover, 1962). Important as scenic beauty is to make America beautiful, most of the objects that could make the daily scene aesthetically tolerable are persons. There may be such a virtue as aesthetic charity, which bids us to present ourselves to our fellows as objects interesting to perceive.

16. Anyone wishing to test these observations need only try to copy any work of art in any medium. All of a sudden details have to be noted; nothing the artist put into the work can be skipped. The details, of course, produce the aesthetic properties.

17. The most detailed account of such attempts is to be found in the reports on the Aesthetic Eye Project, which was carried out under the direction of Dr. Frances D. Hine. Especially impressive is the volume entitled *Teacher to Teacher Talk*, a detailed account of programs in kindergarten through grade twelve initiated by the members of the Aesthetic Eye Project workshop in their classrooms. The three volumes dealing with this project, written by Frances D. Hine, Gilbert A. Clark, W. Dwaine Greer, and Ronald Silverman, are entitled *The Aesthetic Eye: Generative Ideas*, 1976, *Teacher to Teacher Talk*, 1977, and *Final Report, The Aesthetic Eye Project*, 1976, and were

distributed by the Office of the Los Angeles County Superintendent of Schools, 9300 Imperial Highway, Downey, Calif. 90242. Other projects using the aesthetic scanning approach include the HEART program in Decatur, Illinois, under the direction of Nancy Roucher, and a number of in-service workshops conducted by Carol Holden of the Elementary Education Department at the University of Illinois, Champaign/Urbana, whose article, "Which Looks Faster, Red or Blue?" *Instructor* 85 (December 1975): 29-33, shows how "you can help children respond to art." Aesthetic scanning is also used in the curriculum units, *Treasures of Tutankhamun* and *Times of the Jaguar: The Arts and Cultures of Ancient Mexico*, produced by the Southwest Regional Laboratory under the direction of W. Dwaine Greer. The materials were assembled in student packets and widely used in the schools of Los Angeles County in connection with the respective exhibitions at the Los Angeles Museum.

18. It was reported to me that exhibitors of art supplies at a convention of art teachers had warned some of them that Broudy would "take the crayons away from children."

19. A set of materials that function in both the skills of impression and expression for general education has been developed by CEMREL in St. Louis. These materials have been field tested in a wide variety of classroom situations.

20. Educational Research Council of Greater Cleveland, *Humanities for All Program* (Cleveland, Ohio: Educational Research Council of Greater Cleveland, 1967).

21. One solution, of course, is to make a clear distinction between curricular requirements for promotion, credit, graduation, and similar bookkeeping purposes and extracurricula activities that are desirable and desired by students but are not required. An elective curriculum evades this difficulty and does not need this compromise, but a common curriculum by its unavoidable exclusions cannot do without it. As a matter of fact, schools and colleges do *require* many things of students for which no credit is given, for example, immunization against certain diseases, attendance at assemblies, not to speak of the observance of all sorts of rules. Failure to meet such requirements may earn a discredit. The distinction between requiring a certain mode of instruction and requiring certain behaviors is itself a reflection of one important meaning of general education, namely, development of the functions of the mind conducive to cognition. Performance skill in an art is not usually regarded as a form of cognition or indispensable to it; neither is it a behavior required for the preservation of the student or the institution. Therefore, it falls more naturally into the class of highly desirable extracurricular electives.

22. Nobody understands this better than totalitarian regimes. Unlike liberal societies in which art is likely to be regarded as a delightful refinement of life but not ideologically important, totalitarian rulers take art seriously and manage in a remarkable way to insult and respect the artist at one and the same time.

23. Of course, this is a high-handed denial of political relevance to certain curriculum questions, and may itself stir up a political storm. Yet there is a significant difference between the authority of vox populi and the internal validation of propositions within a logical system of ideas, such as a discipline purports to be. Thus, while what physics is *good* for is a political question, what *good* physics *is* has nothing to do with the will of the people, some contrary ideologists notwithstanding.

24. Exemplars as a strand of the curriculum of general education is explored in some detail in H. S. Broudy, B. Othanel Smith, and Joe R. Burnett, *Democracy and Excellence in American Secondary Education* (Chicago: Rand McNally, 1964. Reprint edition, Melbourne, Florida: R. E. Krieger Publishing Co.), chap. 13.

25. There have been many programs put forth as candidates for a general curriculum, for example, the CEMREL projects, the programs sponsored by the Alliance for the Arts, various versions of artists in residence, and many, many more, among those

listed in *Coming to Our Senses*. I am suggesting that all of these should meet the criteria I
have tried to meet.

26. There have been a number of attempts to construct objective tests for aesthetic
scanning. One such test was devised for use with the HEART Program in Decatur,
Illinois, to which reference has been made. See also, Eleanore Bregand, "Development of
a System for Raising the Levels of Aesthetic Perception in the Visual Field for
Elementary Students" (Doct. diss., University of Redlands, 1978).

CHAPTER X

A Common Curriculum in the Social Studies

CHARLOTTE CRABTREE

The theme of this yearbook poses a timely and complex challenge for the social studies curriculum. What should be its essential, core learnings for all students in the schools? Social studies educators currently are turning considerable attention to this question. Its resolution depends, ultimately, upon what we hold to be the central purpose of this field.

Traditionally, social studies education has been concerned with developing the knowledge and values believed essential for participation in a free and democratic society. Its central goals have been integrally bound to the democratic-liberal tradition of schooling, which places its faith in the worth and dignity of each individual, values freedom of inquiry and expression, and espouses independence of thought and participatory action, widely exercised by an informed and enfranchised citizenry.

On this theory of society and schooling, goals in the social studies have emphasized more than knowledge of the structure and processes of constitutional, representative government and of one's civic rights, privileges, and participatory responsibilities. Knowledge has been sought also of the basic values and ideals of the society embodied in the Declaration of Independence, the Constitution, and the expanded Bill of Rights. Knowledge has been sought, too, of the long-term historical and contemporary processes through which these values, institutions, and procedural arrangements have evolved. Beyond knowledge, this view of social studies education has sought commitment to these values and enlightened inculcation of them on the

John Jarolimek served as the editorial consultant for this chapter.

premise that this was the fundamental purpose for which the public schools were founded. The widely accepted central responsibility of the social studies, in sum, has been to engage each new generation of American youth in what Butts has termed "the regeneration of a sense of democratic political community."[1]

If practice did not entirely reflect these goals in mainstream social studies, it clearly did not do so in the case of separately tracked, "slow-learning" students, for whom the curriculum has been a sharply constrained, minimally involving diet, abstracted from these larger goals. For these students, the generally shared aim has been the development of citizens who will be "employed, law-abiding, nondisruptive" members of society. Simplified content in United States history and government, emphasizing patriotism, famous citizens, national holidays and national symbols, together with stress upon personal responsibility in family and community, has been found by Curtis to constitute the most prevalent program for these youth.[2]

A host of forces has brought all these purposes, for all students, under sweeping review, and subjected the means by which these ends were most commonly sought to broadside attack. Traditional teaching methods, developed prior to the widespread disillusionment that pervades society today, have been widely judged to be neither effective in achieving their purported ends nor comprehensive enough to serve well the national need. For separately tracked, slow-learning high school students, the curriculum has been challenged for its unexamined assumptions and personally limiting outcomes that are inconsistent even with the traditional purposes of social studies education.

Today students from all income levels and from all ethnic groups bring into the classroom the social disorders of our time, the disillusionment and social conflict that bear witness to a pervasive crisis in the values and institutions of modern societies.[3] As Husén has lately demonstrated, these are not problems encountered in American schools alone.[4] They pervade western society and the industrialized nations undergoing the wrenching strains of postindustrial change. Metcalf argues persuasively that these problems do not fall neatly into personal or societal contexts.[5] Personal disorders and behavior crises, he demonstrates, are better understood when examined in the context of the larger social, economic, and technological tensions of our time.

In this milieu of disillusion and discontent, teaching that piously expounds on values as ideals in unexamined classroom discourse and texts risks further reinforcing the alienation of youth who have already experienced discrepancies between these ideals and the social, economic, and political realities of their world. For separately tracked, slow-learning students, who have been found to be disproportionately representative of minority and low socioeconomic status groups in the society, the curriculum has been further assailed for its failure even to address those social and economic realities for which their knowledge is first-hand.

What, then, should the social studies be about? In the case of mainstream social studies, the last twenty years have seen enormous developmental work, engaging some of the best minds among its many constituencies. These large-scale efforts, though largely aborted in the sense of effecting major changes in the schools, have nonetheless left pervasive influences upon mainstream social studies in significantly expanded social science content, textbook emphases, electives, and minicourses.[6] If the task of the two preceding decades was to generate wide-ranging alternatives to conventional school programs, it is the widely acknowledged task of the present to bring new unity out of diversity, to assure that attention is given to priorities, and to keep in sight the central purpose of the field: its unique contribution to the civic education of all children and youth.

This chapter addresses these issues, with specific attention to the following tasks: (a) defining a basic core of social studies learnings within the framework of a potentially unifying organization of the field; (b) examining the appropriateness of these learnings for all students, and (c) considering how the schools might best assure that these learnings will be accessible to all.

Toward a Basic Framework for Social Studies Education

Finding a framework for a new unification of the social studies is widely agreed to be the major challenge confronting the field today. This was the task addressed in two recent position statements of the National Council for the Social Studies: the 1979 "Revision of the NCSS Social Studies Curriculum Guidelines," and the 1980 "Essentials of the Social Studies."[7]

BASIC GOALS OF THE SOCIAL STUDIES

The first of these statements defines the basic goal of social studies education as the preparation of "young people to be humane, rational, participating citizens in a world that is becoming increasingly interdependent." Central to this goal is the concept of participatory citizenship—the centering concept of the field, though one not exclusively the responsibility of the social studies. Other subject fields, the institutional structure of the school, and extracurricular activities all contribute to this basic objective. By widespread agreement, however, the social studies bears a special responsibility in citizenship education, but one more comprehensively defined than has historically been the case.

Assuming responsibility for this central goal, the social studies at once assumes responsibility for a relatively broad and demanding range of learnings: (a) skills of rational analysis and decision making required for informed participation in the political, social, and economic life of the nation; (b) basic historical and social scientific knowledge needed to bring informed perspective to that task; and (c) understanding of the nation's highest ideal, human dignity, and of those basic substantive and procedural values expressed in the Constitution and the Bill of Rights which give operational meaning to that ideal. Given the central mission of the social studies, these learnings are closely interrelated. The test of what knowledge is of most worth—hence "basic" to the field—rests largely on the contribution that knowledge makes to bringing broad perspective and informed analysis to the affairs with which citizens must cope. Participatory action that is uninformed by tested knowledge and unguided by disciplined processes of rational analysis and responsible decision making is strongly censured for its potential for unanticipated and costly consequences in the lives of citizens and in the social, economic, and political well-being of the nation. Participatory skills, therefore, are closely linked in social studies education to basic knowledge and to skills of analysis and decision making. But even these rational processes, unless leveraged by a basic commitment to human dignity and to the basic substantive and procedural values of the democratic political community, carry no guarantee that participatory action will be humane or serve the well-being and improvement of the human condition. Knowledge, participatory skills, rational analysis and decision making, and basic values are all interrelated in the criterion of responsible citizenship to which the social studies directs its central efforts. Together, these four domains define the basic learnings of the field.

A BASIC FRAMEWORK FOR SOCIAL STUDIES EDUCATION

A political perspective on social studies education. In what settings, with what specificity, are these basic learnings to develop? In part, they are centered in political education to prepare students for participation in the political system at all levels—local, state, and national.[8] These learnings will need to incorporate not only under-standing of *political institutions* in the society, but also new social science knowledge concerning *political processes*, including the breadth of the formal and informal undertakings by which multiple agencies participate in the making, judging, and influencing of political deci-sions at all levels of civic life. Finally, this view of social studies education requires learnings about the *political culture*—the beliefs and norms (the rules of the game) on which political processes rest, and the core values and ideals that define the normative framework of the nation.

A comprehensive perspective on social studies education. Important as this political perspective on social studies learnings is, it is nonetheless insufficient as an organizing framework for social studies education today. The political system is inextricably interlocked with the social and economic systems of the nation and increasingly of the world as well. At the same time, it is influenced by important historical antecedents. What is needed is a comprehensive plan of social studies education, capable of integrating the many purposes of this field. This plan would need to incorporate critical learnings about the social, political, and economic systems of the nation. It would need, also, to incorporate three broad perspectives on these systems. First of these is a *historical perspective*, to allow for basic understandings of the emergence of the "collective consciousness" of the nation and of the antecedents and comparative analogies of the problems besetting present-day society. Second is a *spatial or geographic perspective*, needed to allow for consideration of critical human and resource distributions in the world today, and the consequences of their increasingly complex interactions in the social, economic, and geopolitical problems confronting the nation and the world. Finally, there is need for a *global perspective* to allow for consideration of the increasingly worldwide character of the problems confronting citizens today at every level of national life.

Given these three basic systems, and the perspectives bearing upon them, an integrative framework for basic social studies learnings can be proposed. Figure 1 illustrates these dimensions, centered vertically in the three participatory systems in which all learners are integrally involved from birth and horizontally in four basic perspectives on each: a systems perspective, social-scientific in its content, and illuminating these systems individually and in their interactions; a historical or time perspective; a geographic or spatial perspective; and a global or humankind perspective. Subsumed within each of these learning perspectives are the four basic learning domains with which the social studies are centrally concerned: knowledge (K); cognitive skills of rational analysis and decision making (CS); attitudes, including basic values (A); and participatory skills (PS). What remains is to flesh out these multiple cells of the framework in order to define the essential core learnings for which the field is uniquely responsible.

PARTICIPATORY SYSTEMS	LEARNING PERSPECTIVES			
	Systems Perspective	Historical Perspective	Geographic Perspective	Global Perspective
	K CS A PS	K CS A PS	K CS A PS	K CS A PS
Political System Social System Economic System				

Fig. 1. A basic framework of social studies learnings

Essential Learnings in the Social Studies

Determining what knowledge, attitudes, and cognitive and participatory skills are of most worth in social studies education requires consideration anew of the enormous changes in every major domain of national life: in social values, in political processes, in social institutions, in economic and technological developments, and in the nation's changing relationships within the world community. Determining appropriate goals for all students also requires an understanding of the developmental processes in childhood and adolescence, and of the interests, personal knowledge, present needs, and developmental tasks that influence what students can incorporate with comprehension and meaning. Learning is an interactional process, and neglecting either of these two basic considerations—learner and society—in curriculum planning inevitably limits the goals that might be achieved.

For the social studies, these developmental considerations are critical. The scope of learnings incorporated in figure 1 is simultaneously expansive across at least four dimensions. It envisions students moving at once (a) spatially from here to far away; (b) temporally from now to times past; (c) interculturally from the familiar to the unfamiliar; (d) systemically from the first interactions of young children within the social system of the family to increasingly complex understandings of the social, economic, and political systems in their many interactions and linkages. Students at different levels of development are more or less ready for these obviously demanding learnings; indeed, there is some reason to believe there are optimal times for engaging in activities leading to one or another of them. These considerations are specifically addressed later in this chapter, together with some of the accommodations for individual differences that must be made if these learnings are to be available to all students.

KNOWLEDGE

Understanding the political system. An important aspect of the young child's developing world is his or her strong feeling of membership in the political system. Important consequences have been found to follow from this early sense of belonging, including attitudes of basic loyalty, support, and love for the political community, that is inculcated within school and beyond. This basic sense of affiliation is an important base on which to rest later political learnings, including understandings of political processes in the nation and insights into the nature and significance of conflict in a democratic society.

Social studies programs have historically been premised on the value of consensus in a pluralistic society. Emphasizing the significance of shared norms, the schools have traditionally focused upon the consensual and the conforming to assure social cohesion and common purpose in a nation of immigrants. Given the hierarchically organized institutional structure of schools, it is not surprising that this emphasis became linked in time to consensus and conformity to rules in the school as well. From the students' earliest years in school, conflict and dissent have tended to be discouraged and restrained. Conflict and dissent are judged not only to be threatening and dysfunctional in the quest for order in classrooms and corridors; when carried by analogy into the political system, they are also seen as dysfunctional to the development of social cohesion and tranquility in the society at large. Much less frequently have students found equivalent value placed on the enlightened discussion of alternative and dissenting viewpoints that are openly elicited and examined in the mediation of conflict that inevitably occurs.

Whether a consequence of these schooling norms, or of an emphasis in textbooks and instruction on a largely benevolent and harmonious political system,[9] American students have been found to subscribe to a naive, unrealistic, and idealized view of that system. They view the political system as consensual and conflict-free. When compared to European students of similar age, American students exhibit low tolerance for dissent.[10] In the eyes of many teachers and their students, good citizenship is conforming and passive, and abhors open expression of controversy and dissent.

Such views reflect important misunderstandings of the political processes of the nation and of the significance of political conflict. While some have argued that democracy depends upon the adherence of its political elites to the procedural norms of the society and can safely permit the relative passivity of an unknowledgeable and intolerant mass citizenry, recent trends in the political life of the nation have given reason to reexamine this view.

American politics has undergone tremendous change in the last twenty-five years. Citizens who have increasingly withdrawn from involvement in organized political parties have also undergone dramatic losses in their trust in and respect for all governmental and social institutions. Some traditional mediating functions of political institutions are breaking down. Two such functions historically performed by the major political parties (forging consensus across the wide-ranging interest groups affiliated within the party and insulating masses of citizens from direct influence on policy formation) have weakened. New patterns of activism have emerged.[11] Large and volatile groups of citizens, negative in their feelings toward governmental institutions, and unaffiliated with organized political parties, are mobilizing on highly personalized, single issues on which feelings often run high and on which compromise is often perceived to be difficult to achieve if not ideologically impossible.

Under these conditions, the ability of citizens to understand and tolerate political conflict is more important than ever.[12] The social studies must assure that youth develop understanding of the nature of conflict and compromise in a democratic society and of democratic procedural norms, the survival of which cannot be entrusted to the stewardship of political elites alone. To address these concerns, the social studies must help youth to understand the nature, sources, functions, and inevitability of conflict in a free society.[13] It must engage them as well in analyses of the permissible limits that must be placed upon the expression of conflict, and provide them with an understanding of those political institutions and processes of the constitutional system through which conflict on public issues can be mediated and resolved.

Traditionally, students have been introduced to the political processes of the nation through studies of the Constitutional Convention, which produced the basic institutions and principles by which the United States is governed today. These learnings, essential in their own right, should be supplemented with new understandings of policy-making processes engaged in at all levels of government, and of policy-influencing processes engaged in by citizen, special interest, and political action groups. Students should also understand some correlates of these processes, such as the recent decline in the influence of political parties and the major changes in the allocation of power in Congress. Through these studies students should acquire insights into the functions and distributions of power and political advantage in the society. They should also acquire understanding of basic processes of constitutional choice and consent. These are processes engaged in by groups at all levels of political decision making, including students' own organized political activity in school and community. They are processes that can be carried out with greater or less adherence to basic democratic norms, and with greater or less support from the group's constituencies, depending upon how participants structure the group, define its rules (including its collectively binding decision-making processes), and distribute the costs as well as the benefits incurred in achieving the group's considered goal.

Understanding the social system. To understand the political system requires that students understand the social system as well. The two are closely related, with the concept of society central to the structure of political thought. To understand the sources, inevitability, and legitimacy of political conflict in a free society, for example, requires understanding of those basic substantive values that assure pluralism in the society: the central value given to the worth and dignity of the individual, and the values of freedom and individual choice. Understanding these social values, students will understand the legitimacy rendered pluralism in the society, both in the widespread diversity among religious, interest, ethnic, and racial groups in the nation, and in the viewpoints, interests, and cultural values each chooses to espouse.

Basic learnings concerning the social system also include understandings of (a) the social institutions by which the social life of the community is organized; (b) the nature of social relationships within and between groups, large and small; (c) factors contributing to changing roles and role expectations; (d) factors contributing to social class differences, and to status, mobility, power, and prestige within society; (e) and processes of social continuity and change, of organization and disorganization in the social life of communities. These learnings provide insights immediately relevant in the everyday lives of children and youth, as well as insights into complex and persistent social issues, viewed both in historical and contemporary perspective.

Basic learnings concerning the social system also include insights into the close relationships between society and the law. Students should discover that important controversies not resolved within the institutions of the social system regularly make their way into the political system and the judiciary for ultimate resolution. A century and a half ago, Alexis de Tocqueville noted this close relationship in American society between public controversy and the law: "Scarcely any political question arises in the United States which is not resolved, sooner or later, into a judicial question."[14] Every major social issue of the last quarter century, Gross has observed, whether civil rights, equal educational opportunity, abortion, or criminal justice, has been found to chart its course through the legal system.[15]

To understand why this is the case, students need to understand that within every public social issue on which multiple interests come to bear, different values that are inherent in the normative framework of the nation come into conflict. Resolving controversy on social issues of public importance is not simply a matter of deferring to the law. As the supreme law of the land, the Constitution has been described by Supreme Court Justice Powell as a "charter of principles and concepts, not a Code Napoleon."[16] The law, in the words of Oliver Wendell Holmes, "cannot be dealt with as if it contained only the axioms and corollaries of the book of mathematics."[17] While assuring basic guarantees, the Constitution leaves their interpretation open to review—and that interpretation is not self-evident. Students should understand that interpretations rendered by the courts are the result of human decisions, influenced by powerful forces within the society, including "the felt necessities of the time, the prevalent moral and political theories, intuitions of public policy, avowed or unconscious, even the prejudices which judges share with their fellow men."[18]

Understanding the Constitution, Gross suggests, requires searching analysis of those public issues and controversies, past and present, that are ultimately resolved on constitutional grounds. The relationship of the law and of the social life of the nation is symbiotic. If the interpretation of the law is influenced by forces within the social life of the nation, the law contributes, in turn, to shaping "the goals and values . . . indeed the whole character and ethos of the society."[19]

This relationship between the law and basic social values can be observed by students if they examine, for example, the profound implications of rulings on civil rights over the last thirty years, as well as rulings on other basic issues addressed in numerous cases reaching the Supreme Court. Examining public issues neither requires that students reach, nor authorizes teachers to advocate, specific judgments on the issue at hand. These value judgments must remain the province of individual choice, and are not the business of the school. But helping students to acquire basic understandings of the processes at work here, and those skills of rational analysis and warranted decision making by which students ground their personal value judgments on defensible arguments and hold them with enlightened conviction, are responsibilities the school can accept.

The business of the law, students will discover, is not unlike the business of the citizen engaged in clarifying personal positions on controversial issues of importance in the social life of the nation: addressing the clash of counterbalancing social values and interests inherent in the issue, and clarifying, evaluating, and resolving priorities among them. These processes, inescapably part and parcel of civic life in a free nation (whether attended to by the schools or not), may reveal to students yet a higher insight, a discernment "that the profoundest reality and the most demanding morality lie not in particular judgments or results, but in the process of moving toward them."[20]

This more complex vision of the society makes heavy demands on the schools. It suggests that what is needed is not simple, personal belief systems that cannot stand the test of realistic appraisal of society as it is. Rather, the development of a more complex, realistic, and functional network of understandings, analytic skills, and basic values is required. On these learnings, students are more likely to confront social and political realities in the nation with comprehension. They are more likely, moreover, to address their civic responsibilities with a firmer grasp of the fundamental values at stake, and of the range of political and judicial processes at their disposal as citizens confronting controversy in a free and pluralistic state.

Understanding the economic system. If any issues are widely perceived to impinge directly upon the quality of life of the individual, they are the issues arising within the economic system. These issues cut across all socioeconomic classes in the society, and regularly confront political decision makers in the form of demands. From various interest groups come demands for wage, price, or credit controls; demands for controls on free trade or for price supports; demands for a guaranteed minimum income for all American citizens, or for jobs in the public sector; demands for greater freedom from governmental regulation, or for greater government controls in the interest of pollution control or worker protection. When economic demands engage the processes of public policymaking, their solutions hold far-reaching consequences for the political, social, and economic life of the nation, and for its relationships abroad. Informed voting, whether with one's dollars, the ballot, or with time devoted to political advocacy on these issues requires a basic and comprehending grasp of economics on which to rest one's decisions.

Implicit in these economic issues is the need for two classes of economic learnings.[21] One class includes *substantive learnings* that illuminate the basic economic problem confronting all societies (scarcity and choice); the operation of economic systems; problems in resource allocation and income distribution (microeconomics); and problems in achieving the broad social goals of freedom, economic productivity and efficiency, stability, growth, security, and equity in income distribution (the domains of macroeconomics). A second class includes *process learnings* necessary for effective economic analysis and decision making, useful in one's personal life and in contemplating the pervasive, continuing economic problems that citizens collectively address when these issues enter the political system and become the concern of representative government and its regulatory agencies.

Developing historical perspective. Of the disciplines offering students insight into the interrelationships among the three basic systems just considered, none has played a more central or enduring role than history. Its significance rests on the broadly integrative understanding it develops of the social, economic, and political life of the nation, within the historical continuity and sweep of human experience. We live today with the consequences of human decision making of times past. The decisions in which we acquiesce today just as surely will cast their shadows and influence the opportunities and constraints facing generations to come. It is the special function of history to provide insights into the complex web of causes and events which, unfolding over time, give meaning to the unique event. These historical insights and perspectives can both broaden and enrich, in deeply personal ways, students' understandings of self and society.

Determining how the study of history can fulfill and not extinguish this broadly humanizing vision of purpose has captured the attention of the field throughout the last twenty years.[22] Emphases have expanded to incorporate (a) broadly integrative social histories, engaging students in comprehensive understandings of the whole of American society, in much of its diversity, complexity, and humanity; (b) studies admitting pluralism and dissent in the experiences of multina-

tional ethnic and racial minorities, women, and labor in the nation; and
(c) studies incorporating a world view, including understandings of
nonwestern nations whose present and future destinies are increasingly
and irreversibly interlocked with our own. To these emphases should
be added the history of today's scientific and technological developments, and of the social dislocations and changes that have accompanied major technological revolutions in the past. For young people
caught up in this bewildering period of postindustrial technological
change, and its accompanying social ramifications on a worldwide
scale, history can, through analogies and comparative study, yield
important insights and the invaluable perspective of time on the
problems of the present.

Developing geographic perspective. Geographic perspectives bring
to students the essential orientation of space, an orientation uniquely
enriching one's sense of self and of one's place in the universe. Like the
perspective of time, the perspective of space is broadly integrating,
developing understandings of linkages between self and planet earth,
between societies, and between their social, economic, and political
activities and their environments. Basic geographic learnings for all
students, therefore, should include understandings of planet earth, of
spatial orientation upon the earth, of spatial patterns in the distributions of social and physical environments locally, regionally, and
worldwide, and of major patterns of interaction between man and
environment within and between regions throughout the world.[23]

These understandings develop as students examine important
environmental and land-use issues in their immediate communities and
in the world today. They also develop through studies in cultural
geography, economic geography, historical geography, and political
geography. Each approach emphasizes relationships between particular populations, their cultural beliefs, traditions, and technologies, and
the opportunities and constraints in the resources available to each in
the environment (situation and site) each occupies. Beyond these basic
understandings, students should understand that these relationships
undergo change as a consequence of new technologies, new belief
systems, changing market demands, as well as environmental altera-
tions. In all of these emphases, students should develop insights into
inescapable relationships between man and environment: between the
fragile, exhaustible, and already ravaged resources of the planet, and

the imperatives that must be faced today on a worldwide scale if oceanic, atmospheric, biotic, agricultural, fresh water, and energy resources are to be available to generations yet to come.

Developing global perspectives. A final perspective the social studies can bring to students' understanding of their own and others' societies is that of a global world view. We stand today, as a nation, at the confluence of two major global forces: (a) the emergence of technological, social, and economic problems profoundly affecting all upon the planet, challenging not only the quality of human life but the very ability of life to survive, and transcending the resources and power of any one nation to solve alone; (b) the simultaneous emergence of worldwide systems of economic, technological, and social relationships, touching deeply the lives of individual citizens and transcending national institutions and jurisdictions.

In part, these developments signal the importance of an international perspective in social studies education. This perspective, state-centric and geopolitical in its conceptual orientation, would support students' learning of significant international affairs in the world today, of the role of the United States as a major world power, of comparative governments and political ideologies, of origins of international tension and conflict, and of conflict mediation between nations.

Beyond these learnings, however, are others not adequately addressed through an international or geopolitical focus alone. Becker, Torney, and others have lately joined in considering the dimensions of a world-centered or humankind perspective on the affairs of the planet.[24] Such a perspective recognizes that all people in today's world, despite their differences, share common problems requiring international efforts for their solution; and that increasingly all people are interrelated through worldwide systems of economic, technological, and social relationships whose development presages, in the thinking of many analysts, the gradual emergence of a "global society." Joining these considerations with international and intercultural understandings holds the possibility of enriching and enlarging the scope, depth, realism, and humanity of students' world view. The affairs of the nation inevitably interconnect with the affairs of the world, and a citizenry sensitively informed of growing complexities in that world is

both better prepared to address those problems and to analyse
undertakings proposed in response to changing global imperatives.

The social studies are centrally concerned with those values that
constitute the normative framework of substantive beliefs and procedural guarantees expressed in the nation's fundamental documents.
These values undergird the nation's constitutional order. They provide the framework on which cohesion across all groups in a pluralistic
society fundamentally depends, and within which value conflicts
inherent in public issues and controversy can be clarified. The recently
adopted *History-Social Science Framework for California Public Schools,
Kindergarten through Grade Twelve*, has drawn upon the scholarship of
R. Freeman Butts to differentiate between values judged to promote
cohesion in the political community and values judged to promote
pluralism and the protection of individual rights.[25] Among the first
Butts has included equality, justice, truth, authority, responsibility,
participation, respect for persons and property, and personal obligation for the public good. Among the second, he includes freedom,
privacy, diversity, human rights, and due process.

The California framework advises that students should have
opportunity to acquire understanding of these values, and of the
rights, privileges, and responsibilities they convey.[26] It suggests that
they should also be engaged in open examination of controversial
public issues and violations of these ideals in public life.[27] The critical
analysis in classrooms of significant, value-laden public issues and
public controversy may be among the school's most effective methods
for assisting students to grasp fundamental insights into these basic
values and norms of their society. It provides the opportunity for
students to develop the higher reasoning skills needed to arrive at and
test the validity of their personally held value judgments on the issue at
hand. These ends Scriven has held to be "especially critical in moral
matters, since conclusions [accepted] without understanding of the
arguments for them are rejected as soon as they conflict with inclina-
tions." Moral analysis in particular and value analysis in general "are
extremely complicated disciplines in which the cognitive methodology
is not that of physics or mathematics or literature, but that of the

law."[28] The skills prerequisite to this task are considered in the following section, in the context of a third major goal of the social studies.

Basic skills are a critical component of the social studies, permitting students independently to derive data, to generate and refine their social understandings, to resolve value conflicts inherent in public issues, and to bring reasoned judgment and decision-making skills to their more effective participation in society. The skills involved in these operations are generally considered to be of three kinds: basic study skills, skills of rational analysis and decision making, and interpersonal skills involved in effective social participation.[29] The first two are considered here; participation skills are treated in a subsequent section.

Basic study skills. The social studies share an interest with many fields of the curriculum in developing students' basic study skills, and gives special emphasis to the skills involved in searching, locating, categorizing, retrieving, and communicating basic information:

1. Locating specific information in a variety of sources: in texts, encyclopedias, dictionaries, almanacs, government and historical documents, journals, newspapers, maps, globes, charts, graphs and tables, as well as in community resources, oral history sources, and microfiche, electronic and computer resources.

2. Extracting and interpreting information from these sources. Inherent in these skills are the abilities to decode the symbol system employed, and interpret meaningfully the data each conveys.

3. Categorizing, organizing, and retrieving these data, through development of file systems, economic graphs, historical time lines, data retrieval charts, outlines, and maps.

4. Communicating effectively, orally and in writing.

Skills of rational analysis and decision making. The social studies also share with many fields of the curriculum an emphasis on basic critical thinking skills that are essential to productive inquiry, rational analysis, resolution of issues, and problem solving. Involved are skills in:

1. Defining a problem, its assumptions, and its terms; identifying the sources of the problem or conflict, and the range of interests involved.

2. Predicting or hypothesizing possible explanations, courses of action, or solutions.

3. Observing to acquire specific information or data relevant to the problem, issue, or decision-making task.

4. Differentiating between facts and the inferences or deductions asserted by the data source.

5. Evaluating data critically, including the authority of the data source, its relevance and timeliness, its evidence of bias, distortion, and "loaded" words or images, and the demonstrated accuracy of its facts.

6. Classifying or grouping data obtained according to rational criteria relevant to the problem, issue, or decision-making task.

7. Comparing, through contrastive analysis, to identify critical likenesses and differences, trends in the data, patterns of spatial interaction, or possible causal relationships.

8. Formulating inferences and conclusions, and evaluating whether each is warranted by the evidence and by the logic of the argument.

Particularly important to the social studies are competencies in decision making. While decision making incorporates most of the basic skills considered above, it goes beyond those skills in requiring reasoned choice between value-laden alternatives, and the ability to anticipate and evaluate the consequences of these choices. Included are skills in:

9. Predicting and evaluating the consequences (costs and benefits) of alternative conclusions or proposals for actions.

10. Selecting a decision and acting upon it.

11. Monitoring its consequences, evaluating those effects, and on the basis of those judgments formulating revised definitions of the problem or revised choices for action.

PARTICIPATORY LEARNINGS

The social studies goals that are probably the most difficult to provide for are those in the domain of participatory learnings. These goals may also be the most important. Basic to the concept of a democratic society is its dependence upon a responsible, ethical, participating citizenry. Threatening to the fiber of a democratic society is a citizenry widely doubting its political efficacy in influencing policy decisions, distrusting the morality and motivations of its leadership, and disengaged from personal involvement in the political processes of the state. When these attitudes are joined, in students, with disillusionment and distrust in the major institutions of the society, the schools are faced with enormous challenge.

Civic participatory competence and commitment rests fundamentally upon the attitudes one holds: attitudes *toward self*, one's self-worth and one's efficacy in assuming responsibilities within the democratic system; attitudes *toward others*, particularly those prosocial, empathic, cooperative predispositions that allow one to view a situation from another's perspective and to take into account multiple viewpoints and interests in working toward common goals and conflict resolution; attitudes *toward the political system*, including warranted trust, identification, and support for democratic procedural norms and civil liberties; attitudes *toward the abstracted "common good,"* incorporating freely chosen commitment to the core values of justice, equality, and freedom of choice as guiding principles of action.

Because attitudes are among the most difficult of learnings to influence or change in the schools, it is important that these constraints be recognized. Political and participatory attitudes, attitudes toward self and others are all influenced by multiple factors outside the influence of the school.[30] Attitudinal development and change, however, have been observed to occur, not so often through programs of direct intervention as through the favorably mediating effects of the climate of classrooms and schools, the quality of the interpersonal relationships which the activities of the school foster, the quality of the participatory experiences in group decision making and problem solving the school encourages, and the opportunities provided for reflecting upon those experiences and clarifying, in that context, one's developing value system.

Perhaps more easily developed are some skills required for citizens' effective political participation.[31] Developmental studies in the High School Political Science Curriculum Project at Indiana University and in the Citizenship Development Program at the Mershon Center at Ohio State University have emphasized students' acquisition of the skills involved in such roles as *informed observer* (keeping government accountable); *support group participant* (engaging in fund raising and "get-out-the vote" efforts); *citizen advocate* (using skills of stating and defending a position, and influencing others through interest groups engaged in lobbying and media communication); and *citizen organizer* (assuming leadership roles, clarifying goals, mobilizing resources, and organizing groups for political action). These skills provide relevant preparation for students' present and future participation in society and may favorably influence their concepts of personal political efficacy, their anticipated future involvement, and the significance they correspondingly attach to social studies education in the school. The ability of teachers to provide practice in these skills, however, depends in large measure upon the opportunities the school provides for students' participatory involvement and the linkages it fosters within the larger community. These requirements are considered further later in this chapter.

Individual Differences and Common Learnings in the Social Studies

The learnings just considered are obviously comprehensive in scope and challenging in their complexity. How realistic is it to assume that they can be acquired by all students possessing at least modest, but apparent learning abilities? Two basic assumptions are at the heart of the argument to be presented. The first assumption is that these learnings, for the most part, develop sequentially, dependent upon important developmental changes occurring throughout childhood and adolescence. Students' cognitive functioning, moral reasoning, political thinking, ideology formation, social learning (including social role taking and empathy), as well as those socioemotional developmental tasks influencing conformity to authority, autonomy, efficacy, risk taking, and responsible decision making have all been found to undergo important developmental changes in early and middle childhood and in early and later adolescence.

For the social studies, these developmental considerations are critical. Basic goals in the social studies cut a broad swath across all these developmental functions, and can be expected, therefore, to be facilitated or constrained, at any time, by the stage of still developing capabilities learners bring to these tasks. One essential consideration in curriculum planning, therefore, is to provide for developmentally appropriate sequence and continuity of learnings, through a well-articulated curriculum plan, across the years of childhood and adolescence.

A second assumption is that social studies teaching can and must take into account considerable individual variability within age groups, and make accommodation for it. While all youth undergo these developmental changes, the pace and timing of these developing capabilities differ dependent upon intraindividual factors as well as upon the experiences students have undergone in childhood and adolescence in their particular home, school, and societal milieu. Qualitatively defined developmental changes occurring through childhood and adolescence are consistently reported to occur within a span of years; age-graded implications are necessarily tenuous and misleading, due to considerable individual variability in the onset and pace of these changes.

Yudin's research on abstract reasoning skills in adolescence, for example, found the greatest development of an "ideal" reasoning strategy—one integrating all previous and current information on a problem—occurring between ages twelve and fourteen for students of average intelligence.[32] For students of below-average intelligence, that developmental surge in reasoning and capability came later, between ages fourteen and sixteen. These individual differences in the onset and rate of important developmental changes do not suggest different goals and objectives for different populations of learners. Rather, they require a variety of instructional accommodations to take into account the present developmental level, interests, and readiness of each, the optimum pace at which instruction should proceed, and the nature of support students individually require. As Good and Stipek have observed in an earlier chapter in this volume, what teachers need in order to accommodate individual differences among their students are better understandings of student developmental levels, and the ability to observe, to derive sensible hypotheses and strategies for accommodating individual differences, to monitor their effects, and to alter their hypotheses and strategies accordingly.

PROVIDING FOR SEQUENCE AND CONTINUITY IN LEARNINGS

A significant research literature now demonstrates the importance of the childhood years to a number of social learnings. These years are a time of increasing cognitive organization, with an increase in social role-taking ability and a decline in cognitive egocentrism being among the most important developmental changes underway. The relatively low rejection of groups and higher attitudinal flexibility found to be characteristic of middle childhood have led Torney to suggest that this may be a critical period in attitudinal development and particularly timely for the development of intergroup and intercultural perspectives as bridges to global understanding.[33] Children's demonstrated ability to profit from geographic studies[34] suggests a related approach to developing for all children beginning levels of intercultural and global understanding. Necessarily centered in early childhood in studies of the immediately accessible data base—home, neighborhood, and community—these geographic studies can be effectively extended, over succeeding years, into well-developed, in-depth culture studies centered in selected regions from throughout the world.

Children can also acquire important learnings concerning the economic system in the context of experience-based approaches in which they carry on economic activities in their own classroom "minisocieties" and cope with real problems encountered in economic analysis and decision making.[35] Under these conditions, children can master and apply a broad range of economic concepts and decision-making skills. When interviewed about these personally involving approaches, children report heightened feelings of ability to cope, not only in the minisociety in which they are immediately engaged, but in the economic problems of the real world, some of whose dimensions they seem clearly to understand and whose challenges excite rather than overwhelm them. These are sound bases indeed on which to extend, in secondary school, understandings of macroeconomics, and more complex skills in economic analysis and decision making.

Important foundations also exist in childhood and early adolescence for the development of basic skills involved in issues analysis and decision making. Children clearly cannot take on the insightful analysis of major social, economic, and political issues that transcend their experience base or the scope of their cognitive understandings. Macro issues have their equivalents, however, in micro issues in the everyday lives of children and youth. Through social problem solving and role playing on issues immediately within children's comprehension and range of interests, basic analytic and decision-making capabilities can be practiced and enhanced, and the foundation laid for approaching broader social issues with a heightened sense of personal efficacy and confidence in oneself as a "problem solver" and "decision maker."[36]

Later childhood may also be an important time for supporting the development of somewhat more elaborate and adequate understandings of the political system. There is evidence that young children's strong feelings of basic trust in the benevolence of the political system and its leaders decline significantly from their third through sixth year of schooling, while at the same time their feelings of political efficacy significantly increase. These findings seem to suggest that older children have begun to test earlier held beliefs against their increased experiences and understandings of their world.[37] Young children's fragmented understandings of the political system, their belief in the immutability of its laws, and in the basic threat posed by any criticism or change in any part of that system give way only gradually, however, to more adequate conceptions of the political system as a whole, and of its accommodations of pluralism, diversity, and change.

Adelson and O'Neil have found in preadolescent children a frequent and pervasive inability to speak in terms of a coherent, abstractly perceived political system.[38] "Government" and "society" are abstract concepts. An understanding of them requires a sociocentric orientation, and the ability to grasp systemic networks of obligation and purpose, of political processes and their collective consequences, all linking people to one another in organized social interaction. Newer "experience-based" approaches to political education take these constraints into account, and stress political decision-making activities immediately relevant in the everyday lives of children in their schools and communities.

Adolescence, Adelson has observed, is a "watershed era in the emergence of political thought," a period of transition from concrete to hypothetico-deductive analytic reasoning, during which the adolescent's grasp of the political world emerges "recognizably adult."[39] These are years during which a student's historical perspective undergoes important development. Temporal causal antecedents acquire significance and alternative futures—the hypothesized consequences of alternative choices—are taken into account. Because of considerable individual variability in these changes, which emerge as early as ages eleven and twelve and continue to undergo significant development at least through ages seventeen and eighteen, the later years of high school may be a critical time for most students for emphasizing and elaborating upon the more complex historical and political learnings: understanding, for example, of the fundamental principles expressed in the Declaration of Independence, the Constitution, and the Federalist Papers, and in the institutions and processes of democratic government; understanding of the nature of and limitations on delegated authority in that system; understanding of the legitimacy of conflict and the means for resolving political conflict.

All these understandings require complex thought. To accept others' rights to express opinions and take positions in strong conflict with one's own, for example, requires a complex group perspective— an ability to comprehend simultaneously laws shared by the larger society and the permissibility of variable norms and values of subgroups within it. With less developed cognitive and moral reasoning capabilities, older elementary school children can acquire important insights into attributes shared widely as well as those specifically distinguishing subcultures; they can acquire recognition of the values of minority rights, free speech, and due process. Until cognitive processes permit the development of the more complex cognitive structures described above, however, students are likely to display considerable difficulty in accepting the legitimacy of conflict and in applying the protection of those basic values to those whose expressed beliefs do not wholly conform to their own concepts of what constitutes "good Americans." Principled thinkers, operating at higher levels of cognitive and moral reasoning complexity, are significantly more likely to understand and endorse the legitimacy of partisan political conflict.[40]

Bringing considerations of the nation's constitutionally defined normative values (substantive and procedural) to the clarification of public issues and to ethical decision making are similarly demanding outcomes. Kohlberg has defined the moral reasoning capabilities required for these tasks of principled judgment at Stage 5 in his conceptualization of moral development.[41] Earlier research reported that at age thirteen most adolescents in the United States have attained the level of conventional morality, employing moral reasoning processes at Stage 3 (a "good boy-nice girl" orientation) or Stage 4 (a law-abiding "law and order" orientation in which informed consent is given to constitutional government, and right action is judged in terms of dutiful observance of the law, respect for authority, and maintenance of the established social order).[42] Studies in which a revised scoring system for moral reasoning was used, however, reveal large samples of high school students reasoning primarily at a preconventional Stage 2 (an "instrumental-relativist" orientation, in which action is pragmatically taken, largely to satisfy one's own needs) or at conventional Stage 3.[43]

Seldom before age sixteen do students demonstrate those principled reasoning processes defined by Kohlberg at Stage 5 (a "social contract" orientation in which right action is defined in terms of general individual rights, and standards are critically examined and consensually agreed upon by the society). Stage 5, as Kohlberg has defined it, corresponds to the "official morality" of the U.S. Constitution and government, and incorporates commitment, for example, to the values of individual rights and due process, and to constitutionally contracted, rational processes of peaceful change in the law. Kohlberg has estimated that this stage will only develop if students' cognitive development has reached the stage of formal operations, permitting students to comprehend abstract issues.

Ability to engage in these higher levels of moral reasoning appears to be related to higher, more abstract levels of conceptual functioning and ego development.[44] Research reported by Oja suggests that adults have largely stabilized at Stage 4 on Loevinger's scale of ego development, with significantly fewer achieving the higher conceptual and ego development stages associated with higher stages of moral reasoning.[45] Consistent with these findings, Stage 4 appears to be the modal level of moral reasoning attained by adults in the United States, and is judged by Kohlberg to be a reasonable goal for all high school students to attain by graduation.[46]

Whether or not one assumes the "invariant stage" model these developmental theorists have proposed, it seems reasonably apparent that the higher levels (stage 5-equivalent) of values development and moral reasoning espoused in citizenship programs in the social studies present an unattainable goal for most students before their senior high school years, and may be found to constitute a difficult, possibly even unattainable, goal for many students even then. These difficulties in meeting the psychological requirements for a stable democratic regime have been emphasized over the years by a number of political analysts, in their examination of the continuing threats to democracy posed by cognitive and moral development insufficient to maintain the long-term commitment required to sustain such a regime.[47] How the schools, and the social studies in particular, can effectively contribute to students' development of these more advanced modes of principled socio-moral reasoning and civic behavior is a question that elicits perennial hope and recurrent despair; it is one currently under considerable study and analysis.

PROVIDING FOR INDIVIDUAL DIFFERENCES

Holding a developmental view, teachers at all levels of schooling will assess students' present state of readiness, interest, and instructional need, within any of these learning domains, and adapt accordingly. A growing literature in "mainstreaming" in the social studies provides teachers some assistance in the kinds of adaptations required to meet the needs of a wide range of ability levels and learning styles in the classroom.[48] These guidelines consistently recommend that teachers provide a wide range of multisensory experiences and varied activities that accommodate multiple paths to learning.

Large-group social studies teaching that relies basically upon a single text, enlivened for the most part only by teacher lectures and discussion in a "closed" recitative style, has been found to be highly alienating to advanced, "high-track" high school students.[49] It has also been judged clearly dysfunctional for students with a range of learning problems, including low motivation, short attention span, memory problems, language problems, and reading deficiencies. To address these problems, teachers must be able to identify where students stand with respect to the instructional goals toward which they are working, and to marshall an appropriate variety of instructional resources and strategies in adapting classroom activities to this range of abilities. Among the adaptive responses currently being recommended for slower-learning students are some with a long tradition in the social studies: the use of projects, activities, and problems relevant to students' interests and needs as the integrating focus of instruction; and, to support students' productive participation in these activities, the use of a variety of simpler reading materials and illustrated reading resources supplementing the basic text; taped editions of class texts and other reading materials, available at "listening centers" in the classroom; a variety of visual and other media resources available in "viewing centers"; and the use of structured role playing, simulations, and a variety of "hands-on" manipulatives, as well as "first-hand" community resources.

A recent and well-designed experimental research demonstrates just how effective an adaptive approach that is responsive to individual differences can be with slow-learning high school students. The study yields evidence that, given these accommodations, these students can engage in and profit from considerably more sophisticated studies than those usually offered them.[50] Experimental subjects from 225 slow-learning students in this study were engaged in the critical analysis of some relatively complicated social issues confronted in their local community. Students were assisted in defining the issue, and in obtaining data through a wide variety of briefly written, interesting materials, tailored to their reading capabilities, as well as selected newspaper articles, government documents, field studies, and inter-views with resource persons. They were supported in analyzing these data, and encouraged to develop a proposed plan of action on the problem.

Students demonstrated important learning outcomes. Compared with students in traditional remedial or slow-learner classes, these students became significantly more interested in social issues, their scores on dogmatic thinking were significantly reduced, and their critical thinking scores improved significantly. In addition, they expressed belief that societal conditions could improve, and that citizens could affect such changes in their communities. After reflect-ing upon their experiences, the students urged that studies such as these be a regular part of their school programs. This is one study, of course, and replication is required. But the results are consistent with implications drawn earlier from Yudin's research, and with the persua-sions of those who have urged that separately tracked slow-learning students, as much as those mainstreamed in social studies, can and should share more fully in a common core of significant social studies learnings.

PROVIDING SUPPORT WITHIN A TOTAL EDUCATIONAL ENVIRONMENT

The complex learnings proposed in this chapter present a challenge not only to the skills of the curriculum planner and the teacher. They pose a challenge also to the total educational environment, including the organizational features of the school, the "climate" generated within classrooms and schools, and the relationships fostered between home, school, and community. In the growing research literature that examines the effects of high schools in developing students' understanding of and support for democratic values, it is the quality of the instructional climate that appears, with remarkable consistency, to yield important effects. In study after study, critical instructional characteristics have tended to be associated with students' lower authoritarianism, lower political cynicism and alienation, increased political efficacy, and positive attitudes of political trust, political interest, and support for democratic values. Among those characteristics are the willingness of teachers to discuss sensitive issues in class; the frequency of exposure to controversial issues, provided such exposure is offered under conditions of an "open" classroom climate; the teachers' encouragement of expression of opinion; the range of viewpoints encouraged by the teacher; the openness of students' expression of opinion; and support for students' decision-making opportunities in the school.[51]

The last of these, student decision-making opportunities in the school, is dependent, in large part, upon institutional arrangements beyond the control of the teacher alone. To provide such opportunities may require nothing short of important modifications in the authority structure of the school. For most students, Patrick notes, the school environment is the first, and for many years, "the most salient form of external authority with which they have direct experience."[52] For those adolescents who bring to school a low sense of efficacy in the political system, and who perceive little likelihood that they will be significantly involved in that system in years to come, the organizing arrangements of schools may be particularly important. If schools, through their regulatory systems of hierarchic managerial control, continuously deny students significant participatory decision-making experiences, they may only confirm predispositions to low political confidence, apathy, and withdrawal from democratic processes. Schools that have provided more effectively for students' active, participatory involvement in decision-making processes have been found, with considerable consistency, to be associated with students' attitudes of political trust and interest, and with student support for democratic norms.[53]

Providing these participatory opportunities presents an enormous challenge to the institutional arrangements of schooling. Schools are bureaucracies, and the trend nationwide is toward increasing rather than decreasing consolidation, with all that implies for hierarchically distant and centralized managerial control. Providing the institutional changes required to support students' learning of basic democratic processes and values involves nothing short of reducing the inherent conflict between the centralized, vertically ordered managerial arrangements the bureaucratic system puts in place, and the more flexible, interpersonal, participatory requirements these more complex curriculum goals and their pedagogical processes demand.

A number of recent proposals have demonstrated how, even within present organizational structures, schools might develop considerably improved opportunities for participatory involvement. Massialas and Hurst, for example, have shown how the elementary school might become a laboratory for participatory decision making with important links to community participation.[54] Wasserman has described three projects undertaken to implement Kohlberg's concept of the "Just Community School," two of them in alternative schools within large comprehensive urban high schools.[55] Husén, addressing the problems of alienated youth and new imperatives in education for the world of work, has envisioned new arrangements engaging parents and students in genuine decision making related to smaller units within the comprehensive high school, and to participatory opportunities within a network of activities in cooperating schools, work places, and community institutions.[56] In all these proposals, emphasis is placed upon support structures likely to sustain the participatory involvement of students, and thus to facilitate attitudinal, decision-making, and participatory learnings that are difficult to achieve but are essential to students' more effective transition into and participation in society. To the degree these outcomes are judged important, proposals for institutional reform merit the most serious consideration.

Basic changes in the arrangements of schooling are not likely to be rapidly forthcoming. As Remy notes, precedents for such change are limited, and their effects not yet well studied.[57] It seems reasonable to anticipate, however, that significant changes in the institutional constraints now widely operating upon some of the most critical of social studies learnings, may be the best hope for the improved civic education of all children and youth.

FOOTNOTES

1. R. Freeman Butts, "The Revival of Civic Learning: A Rationale for the Education of Citizens," *Social Education* 43 (May 1979): 359-64.

2. Charles K. Curtis, "Citizenship Education and the Slow Learner," in *Building Rationales for Citizenship Education*, ed. James P. Shaver, Bulletin no. 52 (Arlington, Va.: National Council for the Social Studies, 1977), p. 77.

3. David C. Schwartz, *Political Alienation and Political Behavior* (Chicago: Aldine Publishing Co., 1973); Samuel Long, "Urban Adolescents and the Political System: Dimensions of Disaffection," *Theory and Research in Social Education* 8 (Winter 1980): 31-43; James D. Wright, *The Dissent of the Governed: Alienation and Democracy in America* (New York: Academic Press, 1976).

4. Torsten Husén, *The School in Question: A Comparative Study of the School and Its Future in Western Societies* (Oxford: Oxford University Press, 1979).

5. Lawrence E. Metcalf, "Developing and Applying Humane Values," in *Issues in Secondary Education*, ed. William Van Til, Seventy-fifth Yearbook of the National Society for the Study of Education, Part II (Chicago: University of Chicago Press, 1976), p. 99.

6. See, for example, John D. Haas, *The Era of the New Social Studies* (Boulder, Colo.: ERIC Clearinghouse for Social Studies/Social Science Education and Social Science Education Consortium, 1977); Richard E. Gross, "The Status of the Social Studies in the Public Schools of the United States: Facts and Impressions of a National Survey," *Social Education* 41 (March 1977): 194-200, 205; John Jarolimek et al., "The Status of Social Studies Education: Six Case Studies," *Social Education* 41 (November-December 1977): 574-601.

7. "Revision of the NCSS Social Studies Curriculum Guidelines," National Council for the Social Studies Position Statement, *Social Education* 43 (April 1979): 261-73; "Essentials of the Social Studies," *Social Education* 45 (March 1981): 162-64.

8. See, for example, Richard C. Remy, "Making, Judging, and Influencing Political Decisions: A Focus for Citizen Education," *Social Education* 40 (October 1976): 360-65.

9. See, for example, Jean Anyon, "Elementary Social Studies Textbooks and Legitimating Knowledge," *Theory and Research in Social Education* 6 (September 1978): 40-55; Thomas E. Fox and Robert D. Hess, "An Analysis of Social Conflict in Social Studies Textbooks," Final Report, Project No. 1-I-116 (Washington, D.C.: U.S. Department of Health, Education, and Welfare, 1972).

10. Judith V. Torney, A. N. Oppenheim, and Russell F. Farnen, *Civic Education in Ten Countries* (New York: John Wiley, 1975); Lee H. Ehman, "Implications for Teaching Citizenship," *Social Education* 43 (November-December 1979): 594-96.

11. Schwartz, *Political Alienation and Political Behavior*, pp. 231-46; Everett Ladd, Jr., *Where Have All the Voters Gone?* (New York: Norton, 1978).

12. Janet Eyler, "Citizenship Education for Conflict: An Empirical Assessment of the Relationship between Principled Thinking and Tolerance for Conflict and Diversity," *Theory and Research in Social Education* 8 (Summer 1980): 11-26.

13. Lewis A. Coser, *The Functions of Social Conflict* (New York: Free Press, 1956); Charles N. Quigley and Richard P. Longaker, *Conflict, Politics, and Freedom*, Teachers ed. (Lexington, Mass.: Ginn and Co., n.d.).

14. Alexis de Tocqueville, *Democracy in America*, ed. Richard D. Heffner (New York: Mentor Books, 1956), p. 126.

15. Norman Gross, "Teaching about the Law: Perceptions and Implications," *Social Education* 41 (March 1977): 168-69.

16. Lewis F. Powell, Jr., "The Myths and Misconceptions about the Supreme Court," *American Bar Association Journal* 61 (November 1975): 1347.

17. Quoted in Gross, "Teaching about the Law," p. 168.

18. Ibid.

19. Charles E. Silberman, *Crisis in the Classroom* (New York: Random House, 1970), p. 42.

20. Paul A. Freund, *On Law and Justice* (Cambridge, Mass.: Belknap Press of Harvard University Press, 1968), p. v.

21. See, for example, James D. Calderwood, John D. Lawrence, and John E. Maher, *Economics in the Curriculum: Developmental Economic Education Program* (New York: John Wiley and Sons, 1970); W. Lee Hansen, G. L. Bach, James D. Calderwood, and Phillip Saunders, *Master Curriculum Guide in Economics for the Nation's Schools: Part I. A Framework for Teaching Economics—Basic Concepts* (New York: Joint Council on Economic Education, 1977); Lawrence E. Leamer and Paul A. Smith, "Integrating Economics and Political Science," in *Analyzing Government Regulation: A Resource Guide*, ed. John F. Bibby, Leon M. Schuss, and George G. Watson (New York: Joint Council on Economic Education, 1978).

22. See, for example, *Teaching American History*, ed. Allan O. Kownslar, Forty-fourth Yearbook of the National Council for the Social Studies (Washington, D.C.: The Council, 1974); Margaret Stimmann Branson, ed., "Teaching American History," *Social Education* 44 (October 1980): 453-85; Mark M. Krug, *History and the Social Sciences* (Waltham, Mass.: Blaisdell Publishing Co., 1967), chaps. 1, 2, and 10.

23. See, for example, *Focus on Geography: Key Concepts and Teaching Strategies*, ed. Phillip Bacon, Fortieth Yearbook of the National Council for the Social Studies (Washington, D.C.: The Council, 1970); Jan O. M. Broek, Henry L. Hunker, Raymond H. Muessig, and Joseph M. Cirrincione, *The Study and Teaching of Geography* (Columbus, Ohio: Charles E. Merrill, 1980).

24. James M. Becker and Maurice A. East, *Global Dimensions in U. S. Education: The Secondary School* (New York: Center for War/Peace Studies, 1972); Richard C. Remy, James A. Nathan, James M. Becker, and Judith V. Torney, *International Learning and International Education in a Global Age*, Bulletin No. 47 (Washington, D.C.: National Council for the Social Studies, 1975).

25. California State Department of Education, *History-Social Science Framework for California Public Schools, Kindergarten through Grade Twelve* (Sacramento: California State Department of Education, 1981), pp. 7-8.

26. See the many volumes and multimedia resources (*On Freedom, On Authority, On Justice*, for example) of the project on Law in a Free Society, Charles N. Quigley, Director, under development by the State Bar of California, in cooperation with the Schools of Law of the University of California, at the Center for Civic Education, Calabasas, Calif. See also, Charles N. Quigley, *Your Rights and Responsibilities As an American Citizen: Civics Casebook and Teaching Guide* (Lexington, Mass.: Ginn and Co., 1967).

27. Donald W. Oliver and James P. Shaver, *Teaching Public Issues in the High School* (Logan, Utah: Utah State University Press, 1974): Maurice P. Hunt and Lawrence E. Metcalf, *Teaching High School Social Studies: Problems in Reflective Thinking*, 2d ed.

(New York: Harper and Row, 1968): Fred M. Newman and Donald W. Oliver, *Clarifying Public Controversy: An Approach to Teaching Social Studies* (Boston: Little, Brown and Co., 1970); *Values Education: Rationale, Strategies, and Procedures*, ed. Lawrence E. Metcalf, Forty-first Yearbook of the National Council for the Social Studies (Washington, D.C.: The Council, 1971).

28. Michael Scriven, *Student Values as Educational Objectives*, Publication 124 (Boulder, Colo.: Social Science Education Consortium, 1965), pp. 17-18.

29. See, for example, Barry K. Beyer, *Teaching Thinking in Social Studies*, rev. ed. (Columbus, Ohio: Charles E. Merrill, 1979); June R. Chapin and Richard E. Gross, *Teaching Social Studies Skills* (Boston: Little, Brown and Co., 1973); *Developing Decision-Making Skills*, ed. Dana G. Kurfman, Forty-seventh Yearbook of the National Council for the Social Studies (Washington, D.C.: The Council, 1977).

30. Lester Milbrath and M. L. Goel, *Political Participation: How and Why Do People Get Involved in Politics?* 2d ed. (Chicago: Rand McNally, 1977); Robert D. Hess and Judith V. Torney, *The Development of Political Attitudes in Children* (Chicago: Aldine Press, 1967); *The Political Character of Adolescence: The Influence of Families and Schools*, ed. M. Kent Jennings and Richard G. Niemi (Princeton, N.J.: Princeton University Press, 1974); Wright, *The Dissent of the Governed*, pp. 126-200.

31. Judith Gillespie and Stuart Lazarus, "Teaching Political Participation Skills," *Social Education* 40 (October 1976): 373-78; Remy, "Making, Judging, and Influencing Political Decisions"; Fred Newman, *Education for Citizen Action: Challenge for Secondary Curriculum* (Berkeley, Calif.: McCutchan Publishing Corp., 1975).

32. Lee W. Yudin, "Formal Thought in Adolescence As a Function of Intelligence," *Child Development* 37 (September 1966): 697-708.

33. Judith V. Torney, "Psychological and Institutional Obstacles to the Global Perspective in Education," in *Schooling for a Global Age*, ed. James M. Becker (New York: McGraw Hill, 1979), p. 68.

34. Charlotte Crabtree, "Sequence and Transfer in Children's Learning of the Analytic Processes of Geographic Inquiry," *Journal of Experimental Education* 45 (Fall 1976): 19-30; Marion J. Rice and Russell L. Cobb, *What Can Children Learn in Geography? A Review of Research* (Boulder, Colo.: ERIC/CHESS and Social Science Education Consortium, 1978).

35. Marilyn Kourilsky, *Beyond Simulation: The Mini-Society Approach to Instruction in Economics and Other Social Sciences* (Los Angeles: Educational Resource Associates, 1974); Marilyn Kourilsky, "Economic Education: Making the Most of the Curriculum," *Social Studies* 72 (March/April 1981): 87.

36. Fannie R. Shaftel, Charlotte Crabtree, and Vivian S. Sherman, "Problems Resolution in the Elementary School," in *Problem-Centered Social Studies Instruction: Approaches to Reflective Teaching*, ed. Richard E. Gross and Raymond H. Muessig, Curriculum Series no. 14 (Washington, D.C.: National Council for the Social Studies, 1971), pp. 12-35.

37. Allen D. Glenn, "Elementary School Children's Attitudes toward Politics," in *Political Youth, Traditional Schools*, ed. Byron G. Massialas (Englewood Cliffs, N.J.: Prentice Hall, 1972), pp. 51-63.

38. Joseph Adelson and Robert P. O'Neil, "Growth of Political Ideas in Adolescence: The Sense of Community," *Journal of Personality and Social Psychology* 4 (September 1966): 295-306.

39. Joseph Adelson, "The Political Imagination of the Young Adolescent," *Daedalus* 100 (Fall 1971): 1013-50.

40. Janet Eyler, "Citizenship Education for Conflict: An Empirical Assessment of the Relationship between Principled Thinking and Tolerance for Conflict and Diversity," *Theory and Research in Social Education* 8 (Summer 1980): 11-26.

41. See, for example, Lawrence Kohlberg, "Moral Stages and Moralization: The Cognitive Developmental Approach," in *Moral Development and Behavior: Theory, Research, and Social Issues*, ed. Thomas Likona (New York: Holt, Rinehart and Winston, 1976), pp. 31-53; Lawrence Kohlberg and Carol Gilligan, "The Adolescent as a Philosopher: The Discovery of Self in a Postconventional World," *Daedalus* 100 (Fall 1971): 1051-85; Lawrence Kohlberg, "Revisions in the Theory and Practice of Moral Development," in *Moral Development: New Directions for Child Development*, ed. William Damon (San Francisco: Jossey Bass, 1978).

42. Lawrence Kohlberg and Richard Kramer, "Continuities and Discontinuities in Childhood and Adult Moral Development," *Human Development* 12, no. 2 (1969): 93-120.

43. Reported in Edwin Fenton, "A Response to Jack R. Fraenkel," in "The Cognitive Developmental Approach to Moral Education: An Exchange of Views," *Social Education* 41 (January 1977): 58.

44. Edmund V. Sullivan, George McCullough, and Mary Stager, "A Developmental Study of the Relationship between Conceptual, Ego, and Moral Development," *Child Development* 41 (June 1970): 399-411; Stuart T. Hauser, "Loevinger's Model and Measure of Ego Development: A Critical Review," *Psychological Bulletin* 83 (September 1976): 928-55; O. J. Harvey, David E. Hunt, and Harold M. Schroder, *Conceptual Systems and Personality Organization* (New York: John Wiley and Sons, 1961).

45. Sharon N. Oja, "A Cognitive-Structural Approach to Adult Ego, Moral, and Conceptual Development through In-Service Education" (Paper presented at the annual meeting of the American Educational Research Association, San Francisco, 1979).

46. Lawrence Kohlberg, "This Special Section in Perspective," in "The Cognitive Developmental Approach to Moral Education," ed. Edwin Fenton, *Social Education* 40 (April 1976): 213-15.

47. Harold D. Lasswell, "Democratic Character," in *The Political Writings of Harold D. Lasswell* (Glencoe, Ill.: Free Press, 1951), pp. 465-525; Richard M. Merelman, "The Development of Political Ideology: A Framework for the Analysis of Political Socialization," *American Political Science Review* 63 (September 1969): 750-67.

48. *Mainstreaming in the Social Studies*, ed. John G. Herlihy and Myra R. Herlihy, Bulletin no. 62 (Washington, D.C.: National Council for the Social Studies, 1980).

49. Mary H. Metz, *Classrooms and Corridors: The Crisis of Authority in Desegregated Secondary Schools* (Berkeley: University of California Press, 1978), pp. 73-88.

50. Charles K. Curtis and James P. Shaver, "Slow Learners and the Study of Contemporary Problems," *Social Education* 44 (April 1980): 302-09; Charles K. Curtis, "Citizenship Education and the Slow Learner," in *Building Rationales for Citizenship Education*, ed. Shaver, pp. 83-91.

51. Lee H. Ehman, "The American School in the Political Socialization Process," *Review of Educational Research* 50 (Spring 1980): 108-12; idem, "An Analysis of the Relationship of Selected Educational Variables with the Political Socialization of High School Students," *American Educational Research Journal* 6 (November 1969): 559-80; idem, "Change in High School Students' Political Attitudes as a Function of Social Studies Classroom Climate," *American Educational Research Journal* 17 (Summer 1980); 253-65.

52. John J. Patrick, "Political Socialization and Political Education in Schools," in *Handbook of Political Socialization: Theory and Research*, ed. Stanley Renshon (New York: Free Press, 1977).

53. Deven J. Metzger and Robert D. Barr, "The Impact of School Political Systems on Student Political Attitudes," *Theory and Research in Social Education* 6 (June 1978): 48-79; Lee H. Ehman and J. A. Gillespie, *The School as a Political System*, Final Report, Grant NE-G00-0163 (Washington, D.C.: National Institute of Education, September

1975); Richard M. Merelman, *Political Socialization and Educational Climates* (New York: Holt, Rinehart and Winston, 1971); Simon Wittes, "School Organization and Political Socialization," in *Political Youth, Traditional Schools*, ed. Massialas, pp. 103-22.

54. Byron G. Massialas and Joseph B. Hurst, *Social Studies in a New Era: The Elementary School as a Laboratory* (New York: Longman, 1978).

55. Elsa R. Wasserman, "Implementing Kohlberg's 'Just Community Concept' in an Alternative High School," *Social Education* 40 (April 1976): 203-7.

56. Husén, *The School in Question*, pp. 121-22, 149-81.

57. Richard C. Remy, "Social Studies and Citizenship Education: Elements of a Changing Relationship," *Theory and Research in Social Education* 6 (December 1978): 40-59.

Part Three
APPLICATIONS TO POLICY
AND PRACTICE

CHAPTER XI

Policy Implications of Individual
Differences and the Common Curriculum

MICHAEL W. KIRST

The Policymaking Context

The essence of educational policymaking is the authoritative allocation of competing values. Often this competition is intensified by
scarce resources, different stakeholder interests, and conflicting ideologies. Curriculum policy is an excellent area to explore policymaking,
as any recent examination of the newspaper attests. Philosophical
differences are exemplified by the creationist trial in Arkansas, the
agitation of business groups to teach the free enterprise system in
Arizona, and the mothers in San Jose (California) protesting the
cutbacks of high school electives caused by the five-period day.
Federal, state, and local authorities must decide which of these values
will receive formal sanction. Ultimately, teachers in separate classrooms will make the final allocation by deciding, for example, how to
teach evolution or whether to stress the free enterprise tradition.

From a curriculum standpoint, policymakers face the age-old
question of deciding what knowledge is of most worth. This allocation is necessary because school time and resources are limited. As
Early observes in chapter 8 of this volume, the reservoir of content for
instruction in English is so fluid, various, broad, and deep that many
teachers are confused by the question, "What is English?" As Early
suggests, one type of policy decision is currently prevalent regarding
the English curriculum—"sit back and wait" for the confusion to clear
while teaching whatever content is in current use. Often these issues
are resolved through capitulating to recurrent cycles. This year's

---

Some of the conclusions in this paper are based on the writer's experience as
President of the California State Board of Education from 1977-1981.

emphasis on back-to-basics gives way to next year's concern that electives need to be reinstated to prevent dropouts. Periods of disarray in such areas as social studies, which Crabtree highlights in chapter 10, are followed by core curricula with standard formats for citizenship training. A policymaker, such as a department chairman or a legislator, must strike some balance between the conflicting claims of advocates for a more rigid common curriculum and advocates for individualization of instruction. These policymakers find that there are no undisputed goals or established teaching technologies to resolve this conflict. Consequently, the policymaking process is pervaded with politics and pressures. The pedagogues cannot provide the answers.

The authors in this yearbook analyze the conflicting concepts and argue their personal viewpoints. They are aware of the need to incorporate both common and individualistic elements. But since we cannot simultaneously maximize the common and the individualistic, someone in authority must make the ultimate decision. In recent years a rich literature has grown up around the interaction of value conflicts and technical expertise during curricular policymaking.[1] Theories from political science have been applied to policy matters pertaining to the curriculum from a historical and current events perspective. Case studies of innovations like the new mathematics illuminate curricular policy making as a field of study.[2] In chapter 9 of this volume, Broudy analyzes the weak political position of the arts compared to other subject areas with more common concepts. My task in this chapter is to highlight issues and solutions surrounding the inevitable need to balance attention to individual differences with concern for a reasonably common curriculum.

My focus is on broad educational policies and general content decisions that are outside the classroom. Before turning to these matters, it is useful to comprehend how the teacher is a crucial maker of curriculum policy. Even in such a seemingly low-conflict subject as elementary school mathematics, the teacher is not simply an implementor of educational policy. For instance, teachers decide whether computation drill is more important than problem solving. As scholars newly opening this perspective have concluded:

In this semiautonomous role, teachers are better understood as political brokers than as implementors. They enjoy considerable discretion, being influenced by their own notions of what schooling ought to be as well as persuaded by external pressures [such as state textbooks and district curriculum guides] . . . This view represents a middle ground in the classic sociological contrast between professional autonomy and bureaucratic subordination. It pictures teachers as more or less rational decision makers who take higher-level policies and other pressures into consideration in their calculation of benefits and costs.[3]

In a real sense, by definitely allocating public resources in such matters as choosing which students will get what kind of curriculum content, the teacher takes on a political role. The teacher then plays a similar political role in regard to school board and administrative curriculum decisions. Thus, questions in elementary mathematics about what will be taught, to whom, and for how long, are matters that teachers often decide. There are some pressures, however, from students (what has worked in the past with them predisposes the teacher to its reuse) and from external sources including standard policies of local school districts. Externally, a varied urban environment, as compared to a small rural homogeneous site, is much more likely to free the teacher in making such decisions. It is much easier, for example, to use bilingual materials in Los Angeles than in a conservative rural area of Monterey County, California. Policies regarding statewide adoption of texts by centralized state authorities are another kind of external factor affecting teacher discretion. And Hawley has pointed to factors of organizational rigidity or receptivity within the school itself that create expectations in teachers about how power is to be used.[4]

Much of the preceding suggests an organizational structure for schooling characterized by "loose coupling." This is the tendency of educational organizations to disconnect policies from outcomes, means from ends, and structure or rules from actual activity.[5] Such a nonstructure puts the teacher's behavior beyond the control of the formal authorities, such as superintendents or principals, who themselves constitute no command structure with straight lines and precise directions for teaching policy. In such disjointed relationships, one would not expect overwhelming impact from program innovations originating outside the locality.

We have just begun to probe this expectation. By 1980, there was growing interest in evaluation studies "from the bottom up" rather

KIRST285

than in those from "the top down" that had characterized the 1970s. Longitudinal studies were just beginning, such as a thirteen-year impact analysis of Title I of the Elementary and Secondary Education Act. That analysis showed that over time federal efforts to target more dollars to low-income students were indeed successful.[6] Federal objectives were gradually embedded in districts' standard operating procedures, and so the potential for impact upon the teacher exists. If found, it may be that the loosely coupled system is not as uncoupled as the literature suggests. Indeed, a survey of classroom reforms over our history finds that lasting changes, if they are structural or organizational, create a new clientele and are easily monitored.[7] Vocational education, Carnegie units, and driver training are good examples. Innovations that tend to disappear, however, rely solely on the teacher to use different methods (individualized instruction) or work harder (team teaching).

Thus, the role of teachers in local governance is much more than trade union politics and collective bargaining. We need more knowledge of the teacher as a pivotal curriculum screen between external influences and the student, and as a political agent within the classroom in both manifest and latent terms. Teachers will then be better understood as one of the set of local political actors in the conversion of private preferences and curriculum policy.

The Need for Better Macro-Curricular Policy

Economists make a distinction between macro and micro policy. Macro policy includes federal fiscal and monetary policy, such as money supply and budget practices, while micro policy stresses the economic decisions of individual firms or consumers. In curriculum policy, a macro analogy would be the application of Tyler's major criteria for curriculum organization, such as continuity, sequence, and integration. A micro policy would include Romberg's recommended characteristics for a curriculum unit in mathematics or Good's analysis of rewards for particular pupils. In the context of decision making by a local school board, a macro decision would be an explicit policy on the problem of balance among language, literature, and composition in the language arts program for kindergarten through grade twelve. Key arbiters of macro decision alternatives have been colleges with their admission requirements expressed in course units, such as four years of

English. In this volume, discussion of the "common curriculum" is more oriented to the macro perspective and consideration of individual differences is oriented to the micro context. The feature of macro curriculum policy stressed in this chapter includes the configuration and structure of the overall context that a student actually experiences.

In my view, there has been a deterioration in the *quantity* and *quality* of macro-curricular policymaking, with the exception of minimum competency specifications and testing. Universities, school boards, local administrators, federal and state authorities, and curriculum coordinators have not given sufficient priority to the major macro issues discussed in this volume. Many problems of public education are, of course, beyond the control of educators, but public education is, nonetheless, particularly vulnerable to public perceptions that its standards, rigor, and quality have slipped. At the heart of this slippage, it is alleged, is a watered-down curriculum and the lack of sufficient time spent by students on challenging academic material. Three of the major reasons put forward to explain the debasement of our school curricula are: (a) an overattention to the legitimate needs of those in the bottom band of the achievement distribution, which has caused neglect of the college-bound and has lowered the instructional center of gravity; (b) a preoccupation with process, technique, procedural accountability, finance, and governance, with a consequent inattention to what content should be taught; and (c) a lack of emphasis on the usefulness and relevance of our common cultural heritage and on other common concepts such as those discussed in this volume in the chapters by Early and Broudy. Specific examples of these problems are not hard to find, as the next sections demonstrate.

Higher Education and the Common Curriculum

University curriculum has lost all sense of its coherence, integration, sequencing, and priority. The consensus around the concept of collegiate general education was shattered in the 1960s. General education was replaced by a smorgasbord of electives and distribution requirements that leave students to wander through a disconnected maze. Since the university curriculum has no common core and is unfocused, the high schools have no curricular standard or core around which to orient their macro policy.[8] This problem is exacerbated by the minimal university entrance requirements. For example, the largest university system in California (the California State University and College System, which awards 53 percent of the baccalaureate degrees received in that state each year) has no explicit course requirements for admission. Admission is based solely on grade point average (GPA) and scores on the Scholastic Aptitude Test. Moreover, an "A" in photography or typing counts the same as an "A" in English or physics in computing the GPA for university admissions. The system provides no clues about what knowledge it believes most worth knowing. In a much publicized "innovation," the system voted to require four years of English and two years of mathematics for admission, beginning in 1984.

As a result of minimal requirements for admission, the University of California spent $5.3 million for instruction in basic skills at the high school level during 1979-80, and employed the equivalent of 280 full-time persons for this purpose. Despite this investment, 3,500 students could not be accommodated in remedial courses. As the universities provided more remedial work in basic skills, the need to learn academic skills in high school became less urgent. Again, the concept of a common curriculum for the secondary school was clouded by the overlap between university remedial courses, community college duplication of the eleventh and twelfth grades, and unclear signals from colleges about proficiencies required for admission.

Several years ago, President A. Whitney Griswold of Yale reported that an otherwise able and promising youth from a midwestern city applied for admission to Yale, but was not considered. The academic part of his last two years of high school consisted only of two years of English and one of American history; the rest was made up of two years of chorus, two years of speech, one each of typing, physical education, journalism, and marriage, family, and personal problems, along with several other similar courses. This type of high school transcript has now become commonplace. Our curriculum policymakers have no clear conception of what balance and integration ought to be. Continuity is also lacking, as evidenced by the very light academic loads taken by many high school juniors and seniors. In order to make the last two years of high school more rigorous, the

University of California will require all freshmen entering in 1984 and after to have had at least seven academic courses during their junior and senior years of high school.

Universities can have a powerful impact on high school curricula if they promulgate a logical and consistent pattern of courses for their own graduates designed to have a cumulative impact on students' intellectual development. But few university presidents, trustees, or academic senates are willing to reexamine macro-curriculum policy for all college graduates. The balance has tilted too much toward individual choice. Moreover, we have no models like the University of Chicago's interdisciplinary approach of 1947 or the Harvard "Redbook" of post-World War II. I am not advocating a strict return to these concepts, but some rethinking of the current situation is imperative. The movement in the 1970s was in the other direction. In 1967, 90 percent of a sample of 271 higher education institutions in the United States (including two-year colleges) required a course in English composition for graduation. By 1974 the percentage had dropped to 72 percent. The situation with respect to mathematics and foreign language is even more striking. During the same period, the percentage of institutions requiring two years of foreign language study dropped from 72 percent to 53 percent, while the percentage of institutions requiring at least one mathematics course dropped from 33 percent to 20 percent.[9] It is very difficult for the secondary schools to require common curricula when their collegiate counterparts do not require any common academic pattern for admission or for graduation. There is probably no ideal course pattern, but it would be beneficial if college faculties would periodically reexamine their curricula and think about the purposes of undergraduate education. The College Entrance Examination Board's 1981 announcement of basic academic competencies and curriculum[10] is a graphic example of both major points in this section: (a) the potential of colleges to establish a common curriculum in lower education, and (b) the neglect of the secondary curriculum by higher education in the past fifteen years.

State versus Local Curricular Control

Most states do *not* prescribe detailed common curricula. There may be minimal graduation requirements and typically schools are required to offer courses in such areas as English or physical education. But local school boards have considerable flexibility in prescribing courses of study, graduation requirements, and curricular offerings. States exert powerful influences, however, where there are statewide texts and a standard minimum competency examination. Because of dissatisfaction with local standards and test results, the states have recently been taking back their delegation of curriculum policy to local school boards in all the above areas.[11]

Decker J. Walker examined the issue of state versus local role in macrocurriculum policy and advocates even more state control.[12] In his experience, local school boards rarely consider overall curriculum policy. Their curricular discussions consist of staff presentations on specific subject areas, but not on how the parts fit together or on overall emphases. Local boards react to lobby groups, such as creation scientists, sex equity groups, and environmentalists.

These lobbying groups usually want to add subjects. Although it is imperative that the high school curriculum retain an extensive offering of elective courses to capitalize on student interests, these courses should be extensions of a core, or general education curriculum. Schools have been pressured into developing instructional courses in drug abuse, sex education, moral education, energy, career education, ethnic studies, parenting, environment, and so on. Indeed, the weakest lobbies are in such established subject areas as English and mathematics. Rarely do educators or the public ask what is to be excluded when these new curricular foci are introduced, or where they should be placed in the total pattern of instruction. A comprehensive high school in suburban Chicago, for example, has 252 courses. Educational reform in the 1980s should not, and because of limited funds cannot, simply add new layers and functions around existing ones. What is needed is a balancing of functions, a realism in claims, and a focus on a core curriculum that schools can actually implement. As Broudy cautions in chapter 9, however, core curriculum notions must recognize the particular nature of artistic experience and not limit art education to concepts.

The structural bias present at the local level is sufficient reason, Walker submits, to believe that the public interests can be better served by appropriate state action. He contends that local curriculum considerations are too particularistic to the local setting, and do not assess what content students are actually experiencing. At the local level, accountability for curricular decline over a period of years is not fixed, and curricular matters get low priority in policy deliberations. The single variable that best predicts student achievement on a standardized test is whether or not the students have had a chance to study the topic. Many legislators believe that the public interest in making sure that students study "crucial" curriculum content can be served better by state rather than local action. For example, California state officials contend that science receives too little time in kindergarten through grade six (about 40 minutes per week). In California, Governor Brown has advocated three years of mathematics and two years of science for *all* high school graduates. Implementation of such state requirements might include:

Variances. Blanket state requirements can be softened by allowing local districts variances to develop substitutes for required courses, and to permit individuals who probably should not take a particular required course to take something more appropriate. For example, applied science courses taught in the vocational education sequence could meet the state science requirement.

Incentives. Incentives for local districts to increase achievement could be used. Effort is much less constricted and much freer when schools are pulled to achieve. One possibility is to award high-achieving districts additional funds that could be used to expand their curricular programs. School improvement program funds granted in this manner enable teachers to see themselves in a different light—as curriculum developers. They might cause principals to change their focus from athletics and management to budget and curriculum issues.

Promotion. Above all, if state standards are to have the desired effect, the target population must see value in taking required courses. There must be a convincing rationale to study important subjects. It will require effort on the part of everyone involved in the student's school experience to stir interest and pique attention. State standards need to be soundly developed and carefully field-tested for three to five years in volunteering districts, Walker contends. Results will show up on tests and can be evaluated. Data would also be available on the impact of students' choices as to what subjects they take and how they spend their time.

A Revitalized Local Role in Curriculum

An alternative to increased state assumption of curricular policy would be a revitalized local role. The California State Board of Education has devised a curriculum review handbook and urged that local school boards should use it.[13] Since state assumption of school finance has already severely limited local flexibility, the Board was reluctant to restrict local control further in one of the few policy areas left. The State Board's concern was galvanized by a field review of secondary school curricula. The Board discovered that secondary schools rarely have an integrated coherent program. Instead, secondary schools tend to be a collection of classes and teachers, and to a large extent the classes offered are dependent upon the skills and preferences of the faculty. Most schools and districts have adopted goals and objectives. Very few of them, however, have made an effort to operationalize these goals and objectives into student outcomes, and then to design a program or curriculum to achieve the desired outcomes. The more capable students in a typical secondary school will usually succeed in spite of this condition. These students usually enjoy the benefit of significant amounts of adult support, both teacher and parental, and they may even be able intuitively to perceive "wholeness" from the various parts.

Less capable students are sometimes completely bewildered by the randomness of it all. Unfortunately these students are usually the ones who receive the least adult support. Is it any wonder that they drop out in disproportionate numbers? State money to improve secondary school curricula is interpreted and implemented as a series of disjointed miniprojects. Talk of providing balance, integration, and continuity falls on deaf ears.

What is actually taught in specific classes, regardless of course titles, is even more dependent upon the skills, interests, and preferences of individual teachers. In many schools a given class, say English II, will be taught by several teachers and in spite of the common course title, what is actually taught may vary significantly from class to class, the district course of study (if one exists) notwithstanding. Early's chapter highlights how little empirical evidence we have about what content is covered in English.

Within a given school, the quality of instruction varies extremely from teacher to teacher. In spite of this, many teachers do not receive in-service training, even when they are required to teach subjects for which they have had little preservice training, or for which they received preservice training more than fifteen or twenty years ago. North Carolina estimates that 44 percent of its current physical science teachers have been diverted into science from other fields.

While few educators will argue against these observations, most discussions about curriculum tend to ignore them. Instead, we challenge the validity of the assessment instruments or focus on symptoms such as attendance, violence, and vandalism; or we propose solutions (for example, tougher graduation standards, independent study, instructional television) before fully conceptualizing the problems. At best, most discussions about curriculum address only a portion of the problem, such as a single subject (mathematics), teacher evaluation, or graduation standards, with scant attention to overall curricular configuration and structure.

A Local Curriculum Policy Framework for Secondary Education

While the chapters in this volume are major steps forward, they are not specifically designed to aid the deliberations of local school boards. Even superintendents may have difficulty translating the conclusions in these chapters into specific curricular recommendations. The main audience would be the subject matter supervisors and college professors. I have listed below a series of questions that include elements of common curriculum and individual differences for secondary schools, which is a major area where common curriculum declines. This type of question will help frame and orient the deliberations of local boards and superintendents regarding a common curriculum. Before making decisions on content, local policymakers should comprehend the current content and how various types of students flow through the curricular options and variations. The subject-by-subject approach tends to overwhelm the lay person or lead away from macro-curricular issues that are most neglected. The details and elements of the English curriculum, for instance, should be considered after the following questions are researched and debated. These questions provide some specifics to Early's call for curriculum mapping and small-scale local planning.

Although the questions are not complex, they are rarely asked by school boards or superintendents, nor are the data collected by local school authorities. Subject matter supervisors and department chairs rarely consider overall issues that transcend their subject specialties or how the courses from many subjects fit together. In effect, these questions are a prelude to consideration of the issues raised throughout this volume. They address the challenge that Crabtree raises at the end of her chapter. Moreover, they provide a bridge for local school boards to consider specific subject areas like mathematics. After collecting data on the issues and deliberating on their consequences and adequacy, local policymakers can then move on to a consideration of issues subject by subject.

CATEGORY I: STUDENT ACCESS AND AVAILABILITY OF COURSES

1. What courses and subjects are being offered (particularly in advanced content areas)? How and why have course offerings changed over the past five to ten years?

2. What are the trends in enrollments for courses by student subgroups over five or ten years? Why have enrollments in some subjects increased or decreased?

3. What courses are required for graduation? What courses are recommended? Are these graduation standards pervaded by minimum concepts?

4. What are the criteria for student access to courses? Do students and others know these criteria? What do students see as barriers to taking particular courses? Do some students miss out on elements of the common curriculum because certain courses cannot fit into their schedules?

5. When and how do students select or become assigned to courses, sequences, and tracks? Why do they take the courses they do? Especially, why do they *not* take advanced courses?

6. How much is course access affected by scheduling, number of periods per day, electives, and work experience programs?

7. What information is provided to students about the relationship between courses, sequences, requirements and college and job entrance? When and how is this information provided? Is it provided prior to high school? What characterizes the student's process in planning courses?

8. What are sources of information and influences on students'

planning of courses? How are parents involved in this planning process? Are they aware of curricular choices and consequences?

9. Do students and parents feel well informed and confident about getting information? Are they satisfied with courses and their qualifications to choose them? How do they assess the planning process?

10. Are students tracked, laned, or otherwise grouped? How many tracks are there and what characterizes them (courses, students)? What effect does tracking have on instruction, content, student self-image, aspirations, and so forth?

11. Do courses in all tracks prepare students for advanced coursework, or is the track a barrier to advancement?

After discussing findings from these questions, local policymakers can move to a set of general questions for each subject area. Each department should prepare a self-study based on this type of question. Such a self-study would substitute for the usual ritualistic presentations to the school board by the various subject areas.

CATEGORY II : NATURE OF COURSES AND COURSE CONTENT

1. How consistent is course content across teachers and schools in terms of (a) materials covered (texts, topics), (b) number of assignments (writing, reading), and (c) entrance and exit criteria?

2. How do policies or views regarding the common curriculum and individual needs influence the findings in answer to the above question?

3. Why do teachers teach the particular courses they do?

4. How do teachers and others assess adequacy of course content, difficulty, and achievement? Is there periodic analysis of these matters?

5. How much do teachers modify their courses to accommodate student characteristics? What are the student characteristics that most affect teacher planning?

6. Are courses sequential or otherwise articulated or coordinated? Is there an organizational structure to support this coordination? Do students, teachers, and others see connections and continuity in sequences?

7. Do students experience instructional continuity in skills and subject matter? Do they get instruction in missing areas when needed? What barriers do they see to getting the content, receiving assistance, and achieving good grades?

8. What screening or entry and exit criteria are used to determine students' mastery of content and access to appropriate instruction? Who decides what courses fit into various tracks? What specific content fits into the tracks?

9. Are remediation, special assistance, and lower-track courses designed to provide students with skills for more advanced work? Or are they dead ends?

These questions provide a stimulant and framework for discussions of common curriculum and individual differences. The focus of this yearbook can be woven into the deliberations the questions engender. Note how individual differences are explored as part of the question of how different types of students work their way through the secondary curriculum. In large high schools with 200 or more courses, we need to explore the students' paths through the content before we can assess whether a common curriculum is being implemented or feasible. This curriculum issue seems most urgent at the secondary level in view of recent trends in achievement scores.[14]

Goodlad raises the difficult question of how local educational authorities and teachers can aggregate the time and resources to deliberate and answer these questions.[15] They cannot make much headway in faculty meetings or weekly meetings for two hours or so. Local boards argue that funds do not exist to employ teams of teachers and consultants during the summer. Goodlad proposes strategies for implementing serious, sustained overall curriculum development. First, the staffs of several schools must be employed an added month. Second, a local, county, or state research agency must help conduct the assessment outlined above. Third, a composite group of federal, state, university, intermediate (county), and local agencies must each play a role. Given the current passive role of the federal government in curriculum matters, the states will often have to lead in stimulating curriculum concern, assessments, and technical assistance. Universities and intermediate offices can help in developing prototypes and by field-testing curriculum units developed elsewhere.

While this is an ambitious strategy that requires new interagency linkages and resources, the alternative is a continuation of the current drift and deterioration of overall curriculum policy. Concern is rising from a variety of perspectives. For example, an Urban League report stressed that "emphasis on basic and limited curriculum may be leading to a decline in black performance on higher-order intellectual skills such as problem solving." "Mechanistic" and narrow approaches to curricula deprive minority students of the opportunity to excel because they "are marched lock-step through curriculum offerings based on behavioristic models of learning which are appropriate only for the most elementary kinds of learning."[16]

Vermont has added proficiency in such areas as problem solving, classifying and organizing, making reasoned judgments, and research skills for all high school graduates.[17] But Vermont state officials say there are no suitable texts on the market. California has influenced text manufacturers to upgrade the level of the content of texts by specifying requirements prior to statewide adoption. By 1984, mathematics texts will contain many more problem-solving tasks and give much more emphasis to problem-solving processes.

Curriculum Policy and the End of Reform by Addition

In the 1980s school improvement can no longer rely primarily on costly additions and added functions such as Title I of the Elementary and Secondary Education Act, bilingual education, education for the handicapped, school breakfasts, driver training, and so forth. In the past two decades there has been a rapid increase in the use of instructional specialists, such as specialists in remedial reading, and of classroom aides. New organizational structures, such as "pull-out" programs or added departments (driver education), were the dominant intervention modes. Categorical grants and state mandates were designed to be additive to the prior school structure.[18]

The decline of federal aid, the recession, and the impact of tax limitations on state revenues, and the loss of faith in categorical strategies will change the mode of school improvement. Reformers will focus once again on upgrading the core of schooling—classroom teachers and curriculum. Specialists and aides will be reduced in a push to do more with less. One way to increase school output with the same (or fewer) resources is to maximize curriculum content, classroom coverage of content, and time on task in preferred instructional directions. As long as the United States could add more school resources and expand school time, these issues were less urgent. But curricular content and coverage can be altered without necessarily increasing total resources. Low priority or repetitive content can be deleted and teachers can cover more *within existing time*. This may involve changing state laws, as evidenced by the law suit brought by the Worcester (Massachusetts) schools to stop a state law requiring physical education. California reduced its state financial aid for driver training and the governor proposed three years of mathematics and two years of science for all students.

Future fiscal and demographic trends will provide impetus for more intense scrutiny of common curriculum and individual differences. Much of this effort will focus on the secondary school where enrollments will decline six times faster during the 1980s than at the elementary level.[19] The rapid growth of immigrant populations from 1982 to 1992 will cause further debate about the balance and integration of the language curriculum. In short, the 1980s will be a period when the issues considered in this volume will receive a higher priority and more attention from policymakers at the state and local level than has been the case in the past fifteen years.

The political and public opinion forces favoring curricular specialization and pluralism at the expense of a common core are deeply embedded in our society. Many students and parents are oriented to short-term and local employment needs. They want stress on auto mechanics, electronics, graphics, and secretarial skills. The popularity of magnet schools with such emphases as performing arts, science, languages, health, intercultural issues and urban studies is indicative of a large-scale desire for specialized study. So far, the common curriculum for each of these magnet-school emphases has not received much attention. Indeed, the American economy is increasingly specialized, and students are worried about high rates of youth unemployment. Photography and marketing courses may not appeal to core curriculum advocates, but they appear to have more immediate job payoffs.

Another powerful force for curricular pluralism is the need to provide special courses or content for target groups in a desegregated setting. Remedial work is needed for disadvantaged and limited-English-speaking students. But these students should not be segregated. Rather, courses like business mathematics or English should satisfy the needs of a broad range of students, including the target groups. Even though schools in the United States may be swinging back to a common curriculum at all levels of education, there could be a backlash if the deep forces for proliferation are not recognized.

Pluralism is not caused by myopic educators; the educators reflect societal demands, and these shift back and forth.

There is no political consensus concerning a value hierarchy of different subjects. At the college level, many students and professors do not believe that one must study the liberal arts *before* electronics or public administration. Curricular priorities do change, as evidenced by the demise of theology and rhetoric in the core and the acceptance of science. The large number of different course contents called English seems quite agreeable to teachers and parents. But in an era of fiscal constraint, we cannot afford specialized courses, with their small enrollments, for everyone. The comprehensive high school is supposed to provide a depth program for every student interest or need, but it is unlikely that this can be afforded in our specialized economy. Educational policy makers will be confronted with difficult choices, and it is unlikely that either pluralism or a common core will dominate the outcome.

FOOTNOTES

1. See Jon Schaffarzick and Gary Sykes, eds., *Value Conflict and Curriculum Issues* (Berkeley, Calif.: McCutchan Publishing Corp., 1979).

2. See Frederick M. Wirt and Michael W. Kirst, *Schools in Conflict: The Politics of Education* (Berkeley, Calif.: McCutchan Publishing Corp., 1982), chap. 7.

3. John Schwille et al., "Teachers as Policy Brokers," in *Teaching Policy*, ed. Lee Shulman (New York: Longman, 1982).

4. Willis D. Hawley, "Dealing with the Organizational Rigidity in Public Schools," in *The Polity of the School*, ed. Frederick M. Wirt (Lexington, Mass.: Lexington Books, 1975).

5. Karl Weick, "Education Organizations as Loosely Coupled Systems," *Administrative Science Quarterly* 21 (March 1976): 1-14.

6. Michael W. Kirst and Richard Jung, "The Utility of a Longitudinal Approach in Assessing Implementation: A Thirteen Year View of Title I, ESEA," *Educational Evaluation and Policy Analysis* 2 (September-October 1980): 17-34.

7. David B. Tyack, Michael W. Kirst, and Elisabeth Hansot, "Educational Reform: Retrospect and Prospect," *Teachers College Record* 81 (Spring 1980): 253-69.

8. See Lewis Mayhew, *Quality in Higher Education* (San Francisco: Jossey-Bass, 1982). As an antidote to this problem, the College Entrance Examination Board's "Project Equality" presented recommendations for preferred patterns of college preparation. See College Entrance Examination Board, *Preparation for College in the 1980s: The Basic Academic Competencies and the Basic Academic Curriculum* (New York: College Entrance Examination Board, 1981).

9. Robert Blackburn, Ellen Armstrong, Clifton Conrad, James Didham, and Thomas McKune, *Changing Practices in Undergraduate Education* (Berkeley, Calif.: Carnegie Council on Policy Studies in Higher Education, 1976), pp. 15-16.

10. College Entrance Examination Board, *Preparation for College in the 1980s.*

11. See Wirt and Kirst, *Schools in Conflict.*

12. Transcript of a hearing before the California State Board of Education, January 10, 1980.

13. California State Department of Education, *Curriculum Review Handbook* (Sacramento, Calif.: California Education Department, Instructional Services Unit, 1981).

14. Michael W. Kirst, "Loss of Support for Public Secondary Schools: Some Causes and Solutions," *Daedalus* 110 (Summer 1981): 45-68.

15. John I. Goodlad, "Curriculum Development Beyond 1980," *Educational Evaluation and Policy Analysis* 3 (September 1981): 49-54.

16. Reported in *Education Week*, January 26, 1982, p. 6. The Urban League report is entitled *State of Black America.*

17. Ibid.

18. See Tyack, Kirst, and Hansot, "Educational Reform: Retrospect and Prospect."

19. See Michael W. Kirst and Walter Garms, "The Political Environment of School Finance Policy in the 1980s," in *School Finance Policies and Practices*, ed. James Guthrie (Cambridge, Mass.: Ballinger, 1980), pp. 47-78.

CHAPTER XII

Individuality, Commonality, and Curricular Practice

JOHN I. GOODLAD

This chapter addresses four questions. First, what general characteristics of individual differences among learners appear to be particularly significant for curriculum planning? Second, what considerations appear to call for balance in accommodating individuality on one hand and providing some commonality in curricula on the other? Third, what appears to be the current state of practice in elementary and secondary schooling with respect to these dual concerns? Fourth, what are some promising directions for adjusting apparent deficiencies and imbalances?

This chapter comes after most of the central issues pertaining to commonality and differentiation have been discussed and the relevant literature cited. Consequently, I endeavor to refrain from elaborating on these issues and to choose references particularly relevant to the points I seek to make. However, revisiting some themes is virtually unavoidable.

Individual Differences

Three aspects of individuality in particular call for attention in curricular practice. The first of these is the developmental differences among learners of the same age. These are pronounced among five- and six-year-olds coming to school for the first time. Given equal time to learn school fare, children progress at markedly different rates. Indeed, even given more time, some children continue to lag far behind those who advance most easily and rapidly. By the time students enter the junior high school, differences in academic attainment are so great that many administrators and teachers see little promise or practicality in grouping them randomly for instruction. Consequently, a common practice is to accommodate these differences by separating students into high-, middle-, and low-track classes.

Second, boys and girls coming into elementary schools already demonstrate different modes or styles of learning. Some take readily to symbols such as letters and numbers. Others relate more naturally to building and manipulating. Conventional wisdom suggests that some people are more hand-oriented than head-oriented in how they learn and what they do. Some critics of schooling maintain that the teaching is overly head-oriented, disadvantaging those who might progress successfully in academics if given greater opportunity to learn them through emphasis on manual and kinesthetic activities. Individual differences are met best, they maintain, not through those organizational arrangements which essentially accept the inevitability of gross differences in achievement but through creative pedagogy designed to capitalize on different learning styles.

The third major aspect of individuality pertains to differences in interests, goals, and life styles. Some of these individual differences, too, are pronounced by the time children enter the formal educational system. Interests can be ignored as irrelevant to a predetermined school curriculum; they can be used as vehicles to get to this curriculum; or they can be cultivated as the roots of lifelong pursuits. Preoccupation with what stance to take regarding the recognition of students' interests has led to alternative, usually conflicting, ideologies regarding the curriculum.

Although arguments for or against a common curriculum often interweave these three aspects of individuality, it is possible to sort out the relationship between each one and the curricular debate flowing from it. Educators and others who extrapolate recommendations directly from observed differences in learning rate and accomplishment usually argue for a common curriculum in the early years and an increasingly differentiated one in the later years, the later years coming at least by the senior high school grades. They would accommodate these differences by means of achievement grouping or continuous progress plans such as nongrading in a common elementary school curriculum.[1] Many would carry these arrangements into the secondary school while recognizing the necessity for curricular differentiation. Conant, for example, based some of his recommendations for the comprehensive high school on the assumption that courses in the "hard" sciences and mathematics, beyond the introductory ones, would be taken only by the most able students.[2] Vocational education courses frequently are proposed as alternatives to the more advanced classes in the academic subjects.

Some people are unwilling, however, to accept differences in learning rates as irrevocable "givens." They do not regard curricular differentiation as inevitable and argue for more powerful, sometimes varied, pedagogical interventions. Carroll has provided a model of the components to be manipulated, all of which—even the way he defines ability and aptitude—imply a potential for modification through instruction.[3] The model is basic to Bloom's concept of mastery learning and the strategies he proposes for reducing the ratios of the difference in achievement among learners engaged in a common curriculum without slowing down those who initially take most readily to academic work.[4] There will come a time, he says, when we will not classify students as good, poor, fast, or slow learners. Bruner's heuristic, "We begin with the hypothesis that any subject can be taught effectively in some intellectually honest form to any child at any stage of development,"[5] would become more than a thesis; it would be a description of reality. The benefits of a common curriculum would become commonly attainable.

But, others argue, is not a commonly encountered set of learnings a denial of individual uniqueness? Schools are all too common in what they do. The result is a squeezing out of what does not conform to the ways of schooling, a denial of what does not fit the mold, and, all too often, alienation of those who come to see themselves as not conforming, sometimes to the point of perceiving themselves as having little worth. These critics maintain that individual interests and talents should be cultivated as ends and not merely exploited as means to achieve uniform goals for all. A society such as ours provides many opportunities for the utilization of this diversity.

The Case for Both Diversity and Commonality in Curricula

Except for some persons at the extreme edges of the debate, those who argue for a common curriculum and those who favor differentiation share some common ground—namely, that everyone must learn the fundamental processes of reading, writing, and figuring. During the past thirty years, criticism of the schools has fueled two distinct "back-to-basics" swings. Each has followed perceived overemphasis on individual differences, personal development, and the like. The swing back, in each instance, has been accompanied by little disagreement on the necessity of schools teaching the fundamentals.

The strip of shared ground diminishes in size, however, as agreement is sought regarding what is fundamental. During the 1970s, some legislatures sought to have the curriculum include what was sufficiently fundamental to support with state funds. Usually, they ended up with a broad set of goals encompassing most ways of knowing and all major domains of knowledge, including the arts. In a comprehensive inquiry entitled "A Study of Schooling," my colleagues and I analyzed goal statements in documents sent to us by all of the fifty chief state school officers.[6] We found explicit commitments in virtually all states to four broad goal areas: academic, social and civic, vocational, and personal. Nowhere did we find assertions that these were for some students or schools but not others. The implication is, rather, that the elementary and secondary schools of all states are to provide a broad, comprehensive program of studies for all students.

What these documents do not make explicit, however, is either the balance of attention to each subject to be experienced by each student or the variability of choice to be made available in seeking, for example, to develop individual talents. One would expect small schools to be sharply restricted in the choices available and that all schools would need to make decisions regarding what is most important to know and, therefore, to provide. The guiding criterion, presumably, if we take the state goals seriously, is that the things most worth learning are worth knowing by everyone. Optionality, to the degree provided, should not detract from commonality but extend beyond.

But this still leaves us with the issues of what and how much is to be encountered commonly and of how much of what is to be generally common is to be specifically common. One can argue persuasively that all citizens should understand something about the history of their country, but what is this "something" and must everyone encounter all of it? If "some" is enough, when does *just* some become not enough?

It begins to become obvious that the answers to these and related questions are relative; they never will be answered absolutely or finally. The best we can hope for is that the questions always will command our attention and that school programs are the result not of omission but of decisions of commission. It is my view that these questions have a relatively low place in decisions of educational policy and practice and that the answers are as much or more the product of omission than commission.

Rational processes of curricular decision making should be guided by a conception of why we have schools—of what schools are for. Schools should do what the rest of the society does not do well and what individuals and society very much need. Schwab reminds us that homes and families cultivate individuality: in language, values, goals, habits, level of self-esteem, and the like. The school, he argues, must be somewhat countervailing in assuring common awareness of the wider political and human community. The ideal to be sought is a kind of balanced tension between the centrifugal tendencies of homes (differing in ethnicity, national origin, religion, and social class) and the centripetal tendencies of schools (pressing toward greater homogeneity).[7] In the United States today, the growing diversity of homes, the increasing complexity of life, and the high entry levels of most vocations combine to raise the floor of what must be accomplished commonly in schools.

Simultaneously, our increased knowledge of individual differences and individuality demand more creative, sophisticated, professional approaches to engaging learners in common curricula extending beyond elementary education. If knowledge is to be increasingly democratized—that is, extended to larger percentages of the population for longer periods of time—then it simultaneously must be increasingly humanized—that is, rendered in such way as to be learnable. In effect, increasing the commonality of curricula calls for increasing the uncommonality or diversity of pedagogy.

A Review of Current Practice

There is growing evidence to suggest that practice in schools, especially at the secondary level, is virtually the opposite of what I am suggesting above as desirable. That is, pedagogy is quite uniform and becomes more so as curricular diversity increases at junior and senior high levels. Kirst, in the preceding chapter, calls for state policies to control what he perceives to be a chaotic curriculum brought about through a relaxation in college and university entrance requirements and an elective system run rampant. The heads of several studies of high schools now underway have signaled their preliminary concern with curricular diversity.[8]

The findings of "A Study of Schooling" reveal both extraordinary lack of variety in pedagogy and persistent patterns of both commonality and uncommonality in the curricular encounters of students, this overall picture becoming more pronounced with progression upward from elementary to secondary grades. Based on observations in 887 secondary classes (with two to three complete observations in each), we conclude that the teachers used, on the average, only two different techniques and grouping configurations. The students were either listening to the teacher or working on assignments in large groups or as a total class.[9] These same procedures were very much in evidence, also, in the 129 elementary classes we observed (for two or three full days each), except that classes at the primary level almost consistently were divided into groups (usually three) for reading and mathematics. Primary and, to a lesser degree, upper-elementary teachers interspersed their talking or lecturing and monitoring of seatwork with two or three alternative procedures.

Lacking at all levels were the kinds of activities and teacher behaviors one tends to associate with awareness of and attention to individuals as persons and learners. Just under 2 percent of the instructional time spent by the secondary teachers in interacting with students involved corrective feedback (and only a fraction of this small percentage involved some guidance as to what to do about errors). At the elementary level, this average percentage increased to less than 3 percent. Teacher-student interaction, almost all of which was initiated by teachers, was overwhelmingly neutral in regard to affective tone. Students seldom were singled out for doing a good job, for contributing to class morale, or for scolding. We estimate that, overall, neutral (or flat and unemotional) affect characterized the classroom environment over 95 percent of the time.

Conspicuously absent from or at least grossly underrepresented in classes, especially above the primary level, were activities associated with students' own goal setting, problem solving, collaborative learning, autonomous thinking, creativity, and the like—behaviors identified over and over in the state documents previously mentioned. Only occasionally was there a class or group delving curiously into the characteristics of another culture or excitedly anticipating the outcomes of an experiment, conditions we so readily and idealistically attach to studies in the social and physical sciences. The methods in mathematics and the language arts were those most commonly displayed in the social studies and science classes. Indeed, the major differences were in the subject matter of the textbooks used, but not in the format and the kinds of questions to be answered at the end of the chapters or in teachers' quizzes.

It appears that, if there is anything about schooling that justifies the cliché "a school is a school is a school," it is the pedagogy commonly in use. If there is anything in common that students take away from their experience in schools, it is most likely to be a mental picture of how classrooms are conducted. Because the class-to-class variation in the techniques of instruction is so unvarying, it is likely that graduates carry away, too, an overlapping image of both what is and what should be. At any rate, students appeared passively content, generally reacting quite favorably to the "telling" mode of their teachers, a conclusion supported by our earlier study of the first four grades.[10] Also, data gathered in "A Study of Schooling" add up to the observation that teachers teach very much as they were taught through sixteen or more years of student life. Their professional education and subsequent experience appear not to jar them loose from equating the way teaching is with the way teaching should be.

There appeared to be a rather comfortable fit between certain pedagogical and curricular commonalities. We examined the contents of courses of study, textbooks, and teacher-prepared instructional materials used by our sample of 1,350 teachers. Three characteristics, in particular, caught our attention. First, the courses of study or curriculum guides tended not to sort out threads of common emphases, whether in the form of student behaviors or concepts and principles inherent in the subject fields, from topics likely to prove useful in developing these emphases. In other words, a concept such as interdependence was not differentiated from the topics one might choose from the social and natural sciences for purposes of teaching such a concept. There were not inferences to suggest that teaching interdependence might be something commonly expected of the schools, whereas choice of the topics for so doing might vary with location of the community and resources available.

Second, all types of curricular materials generally neglected or downplayed long-term curricular continuity. Topics followed topics by grades and shorter intervals but the threads connecting them—what curriculum specialists refer to as "organizing elements"—were obscured or missing. Compounding the first characteristic—namely, the confusion of ends and means or the nondifferentiation of examples and basic concepts, skills, and values—was a specification of topics to be covered. Implicitly, the nature of the courses of study and instructional materials encouraged the mode of teaching we found to dominate.

If the implication had been that students were to inquire into the nature of energy, for example, and might study magnets, batteries, air movement, or the actions of streams and waterfalls as alternative means to gain insight, we might have found teachers beginning with students' interests and past experiences instead of with the topics laid out for them. If students are required to learn about magnets, why pretend that they might exercise choice among alternative topics? And why not get the information across as quickly and directly as possible? Support of the assumptions imbedded in both questions gives credence to a theory of teaching and a set of teaching practices which dominate staff development programs today and go largely unchallenged.

The third characteristic of these curricular materials pertained to the clear fit between this topical specification and organization of what was to be taught, the exercises to be performed on concluding a topic or a segment of it, and teachers' quizzes. Rarely were students called upon to integrate information derived from many sources (in an essay, for example). Rarely were they called upon to read extensively beyond the textbook or for other than purposes of attaining specific information. The acquisition of rather easily tested information becomes a dominant "good," reinforced by teaching method, course of study, instructional material, and testing. Indeed, even the research on time on instruction and time on task and the relationship of these and other factors to student achievement tends to support and conform to this interlocking paradigm. The net impact appears to be a highly uniform set of expectations and activities for all students. But these tend not to be what primarily attract the attention of those persons seeking greater curricular variability, even though they are potentially powerful ammunition for their cause.

Variability sought in the name of providing for individual differences often pertains to curricular content, and here we found both considerable uncommonality and cause for alarm. There was substantial school-to-school variability in the use of time and distribution of the teaching staff to subject fields. And there was substantial within-school variability regarding the courses taken and content experienced by secondary-level students. Rather than assuaging my concerns about schools' provisions for individual differences among students, these curricular differentiations raised serious questions in my mind about the degree to which our schools assure equity regarding students' access to knowledge.

Curricular differences among elementary schools appeared to be a concomitant of efficient time utilization. We added up and averaged for each school the total time each class was in an instructional mode or setting for the various subject fields. (We recognize that classes vary in the degree to which this time is divided among handling routines, disciplining the class, or instruction and formal learning. But our intent here was simply to get an overall quantitative measure). School-to-school differences proved to be surprisingly great: from a low of 18.6 hours a week at Newport to a high of 27.5 at Dennison. The average number of hours for children to be in an instructional setting for our sample of elementary schools was 22.4.

It is clear from our data that all of these schools placed a high value on mathematics and language arts (reading, spelling, writing, and so forth). On the average, these subjects combined took up an average of 54 percent of class time. The remaining 46 percent was distributed among social studies, science, physical education, and the arts. Dennison, with 27.5 hours available, was able to give generous attention to social studies and science—about an hour to each daily. But Newport, with only 18.6 hours available each week, devoted less than two hours of this to social studies and just over an hour, or about 13 minutes daily, to science.

It appears that elementary school children could experience in common the entire array of subject fields implied by the goals cited previously. Even an average instructional week produced in our sample an average of 90 minutes in the language arts and 54 minutes in mathematics each day. Children did not necessarily experience less time in these subjects when the total work week was shorter but, obviously, something had to give. Equally obvious, when school and home cooperated to get the children to class on time and when school personnel stayed close to the amount of time scheduled for recess and lunch and kept clean-up time to a minimum, ample time for all subjects opened up. Curricular inequities resulted in part from school-to-school differences in the management of time. These inequities are evidence of a gap between practice and our rhetoric regarding the desirability of a reasonably common curriculum at the elementary school level.

At the secondary level, we examined the distribution of teachers to subjects as an indicator of curricular commonality or uncommonality. We added up the courses offered in each subject and, after adjusting for number and length of class periods, converted the total into full-time teacher equivalents (F.T.E.s). One could argue from the averaged results that the curricula of our schools were well balanced, except for a deficiency in the teaching of foreign languages. The percentages of F.T.E.s distributed to the several subjects at the junior high level were as follows: 22 percent to English, 17 percent to mathematics, 14 percent to social studies, 13 percent to science, 11 percent to vocational education, 11 percent to the arts, 10 percent to physical education, and 2 percent to foreign languages. The senior high average distribution was as follows: 24 percent to vocational education (a doubling over the junior high allocation), 18 percent to English, 13 percent to mathematics, 13 percent to social studies, 11 percent to science, 9 percent to physical education, 8 percent to the arts, and 4 percent to foreign languages.

We might quarrel with the marked gain for vocational education at the expense of all other subjects except foreign languages. But a greater concern arises when one looks at the data school by school. Let me use only the senior highs to illustrate. At Euclid, 41 percent of the teachers were in vocational education—just slightly less than the total for English, mathematics, science, social studies, and foreign languages. At Newport, teachers in these five fields totaled 62 percent of the teaching force, as contrasted to only 13 percent in vocational education. School-to-school differences in the distribution of teachers to each academic subject were not this extreme but they were substantial, with the percentage of teachers allocated to science, for example, at one school being double the percentage at another.

One would like to believe that marked school-to-school curricular differences resulting from the allocations of teachers were the product of careful, rational decisions. For example, one might expect an urban school serving a low socioeconomic community to stress vocational education, particularly in the senior high school years. Neither Fairfield nor Euclid, with 42 percent and 41 percent, respectively, of their teachers allocated to vocational education, is an urban school serving a low-income group. Rosemont High, with the lowest family income in our sample, is an urban school. Its vocational education program takes up 21 percent of the teaching force—slightly below average for the sample and half the Fairfield and Euclid allocations.

I failed to find in the schools visited either awareness of and concern about the vital issues of teacher allocation and its impact on the overall curriculum or a process of analyzing data regarding the curriculum of individual students. Principals, counselors, and teachers with whom I talked often were puzzled about my questions regarding school practices and arrangements which might make it difficult for some students to gain access to various curricular alternatives. This was the case even in schools where members of the staff expressed satisfaction and even pride over their interest and success in providing for individual differences. For example, I frequently encountered principals, counselors, and vocational education teachers who took pride in the preparation for and placement in jobs of students lacking an academic bent. "How long might students delay," I asked, "before beefing up vocationally oriented curricula with the academic courses generally required for college admission?" "Not later than the end of the sophomore year," I was told, unless the student was prepared to take time beyond the normal period required for graduation.

Do curricular adaptations of the kind I was inquiring into represent sound provision for individual differences or educational abandonment of individuals? The data we gathered on within-school curriculum variability suggest to me the latter conclusion.

Most of the secondary schools, both junior and senior high, made two major curricular adjustments to encompass or provide for student variability in academic attainment and assumed ability. The first was a separation into two broad divisions—one primarily academic and the other heavily vocational. The second was a division of courses into high, middle, and low tracks. Neither, usually, was the result of clearly articulated policy. Rather, both served as organizational, curricular, and pedagogical devices for accommodating substantial differences in the academic progress of the student body.

In most of the secondary schools we studied there was not an articulated policy or plan for assuring each student balanced exposure to the major curricular domains. Only rarely did I encounter the view (and commensurate practice) that all students should enroll in vocational education classes as part of their general education. Indeed, academically oriented students seeking such classes usually were blocked from them by schedules or because they lacked prerequisites for what often proved to be a sequence of courses in a job-training program (for example, cosmetology). Vocationally oriented students in turn frequently took their academic courses together, because of scheduling problems, track placement, or both. Various internal assumptions and arrangements conspired to segregate students according to academic accomplishments or career goals. There was, it turned out, a disproportionately large percentage of students from low-income families in job-oriented vocational programs, a disproportionately large proportion of whom were from minority groups in those schools made up of mixed racial populations.[11]

The secondary schools in our sample were predominantly tracked in the four basic subjects usually required for college admission: mathematics, English, social studies, and science. That is, students were assigned to high, middle, or low sections of the several subjects. It generally is assumed that this separation is designed to facilitate their differential rate of speed through the material. What is much less often assumed is that tracking creates other significantly differentiated provisions.

We analyzed hundreds of these tracked classes and ferreted out some of what went on in them. First, the differences in the content taught in high-track classes as compared with low-track classes in mathematics and English were such as to suggest virtually different subjects in the two tracks studied.[12] In English, high-track students read standard works of literature, engaged in expository writing, used grammar in language analyses, and prepared for the Scholastic Aptitude Test. They spent part of their learning time engaged in making judgments, drawing inferences, effecting syntheses, and using symbolism. Their teachers included in lists of what they were trying to teach such things as self-direction, creativity, and critical thinking.

Low-track classes in English were far more likely to be found practicing basic reading skills and the mechanics of language, writing simple narratives, and learning to fill out forms. They spent more time listening to their teachers than did students in the high tracks; there was a great deal more rote learning. Their teachers listed for them expectations of conforming: working quietly, being punctual, improving study habits, getting along with others, and obeying rules and regulations.

But these were not the only differences. Teaching practices upheld in the literature as most conducive to learning were observed most frequently in the upper tracks and least frequently in the lower; and practices associated negatively with student satisfaction and achievement were perceived most frequently in the lower tracks. Teachers in the upper tracks were clearer in their directions, more enthusiastic, more likely to give feedback with guidance, and perceived by students to be less punitive and more concerned about them as individuals. Students in high-track classes were more positive about their class experiences: they reported the highest levels of peer esteem and the lowest level of disruption and hostility among their classmates.

In several significant respects, then, students supposedly studying the same subjects were encountering different content, pedagogy, and class climate. The opportunities to gain access to knowledge were not at all the same or equal, the differences favoring students gaining greatest success in academic studies. And these upper-track students were disproportionately from the higher-income families and white.

It is worth noting that the heterogeneous classes (of randomly mixed student achievement and ability) in our sample more closely resembled the upper than the lower tracks in the several characteristics described. This is contrary to the conventional wisdom, which supports the belief that mixed classes tend to deteriorate in most respects to a lowest common denominator of expectations, pedagogy, and accomplishment, even though tracking has not been shown through research to be commonly beneficial. Increasingly, it appears, the burden of proof is on tracking, not mixed grouping.

I have provided in the foregoing only a sketchy account of data from "A Study of Schooling" that are relevant to this chapter. To the degree the schools studied are representative of schools generally, the data suggest several critical problem areas regarding the goal of providing a reasonably common curriculum and simultaneously accommodating individual differences among students. First, there is little consciousness among local school authorities and personnel regarding the need to provide a curriculum balanced among the goals of schooling and the domains of knowledge. Second, there is little in the guidelines and specifications of courses of study and textbooks to assure that the central elements of subject matter and ways of knowing will be commonly emphasized. Third, the commonly practiced ways of accommodating individual differences, clearly revealed in the tracking practices of secondary schools, appear more to sacrifice and penalize individuals than to cultivate their individuality. Fourth, the apparent between-school and within-school curricular and pedagogical differences create inequities, some of which are associated with low-income and minority status.

Some Directions for Improvement

Given the difficulties of considering in limited space ways of addressing all of these problem areas, I limit myself primarily to the goal of achieving for all students in elementary and secondary schools reasonably well-balanced access to the major domains of knowledge and knowing. In the process, I endeavor to suggest some degrees of freedom for accommodating differences in the three aspects of individuality discussed at the outset.

The Harvard Report, *General Education in a Free Society*, published in 1945, identified "five fingers" of human knowledge and organized experience: mathematics and science, literature and language, society and social studies, the arts, and the vocations.[13] I doubt that a similar committee appointed today would come up with a markedly different framework for a general, liberal program of studies. Inclusion of the vocations was forward-looking and gave Conant a dimension needed for the comprehensive high school he recommended in 1959.[14] There was substantial provision for vocational education in the junior high schools we studied and this field took up the largest number of teachers, on the average, among the senior highs. The rest of the curriculum at both levels was distributed among the other "fingers" plus physical education. But the gross variations among schools suggest the need for some guiding policies.

I resist the most commonly exercised guidelines—namely, college admission requirements—which constitute a meat-axe approach. The curricula of the high schools of California, for example, are being shoved about to meet the new admission requirements of the University of California, approved in 1982. Yet, only 4 percent of current secondary school enrollees, according to recent statistics, are likely to attend the University.

What is required as both a necessary confronting of first questions and some protection against the time-worn intrusions on sound curriculum planning is a definition of general education for children and youth. Some potentially useful definitions exist; there is no need to build them anew. The history of the emergence of four broad educational areas in goals for our schools—academic, social/civic, vocational, and personal—provides an initial consensus on breadth of commitment.[15] The Harvard Report and similar efforts, which differ only modestly in their outcomes, translate this commitment into substance. The rhetoric accompanying statements of state goals and most reports such as those of the Harvard Committee make clear that the domains are for all students—commonly and equally. Individual schools have no right to deny students access to some common learnings in these domains, to so emphasize one or two as to squeeze out the arts, or to train some students for jobs to the denial of vocational education for those who may not apply the learnings to a job but probably will use them as homemakers. How do we assure the implied access without the indiscriminate imposition of curricular requirements on all schools to satisfy the demands of special interest groups such as the faculty and trustees of tertiary institutions?

Let us specify, at the state level, percentages and degrees of freedom for each of the domains. I'll not quarrel over a few percentage points either way but here is my prescription for a four-year secondary curriculum (part of a reorganized continuum of early childhood, elementary, and secondary education which I describe elsewhere[16]): 18 percent of a student's program to literature and language (English and other); 18 percent to mathematics and science; 15 percent to each of the other three fingers; and 10 percent to physical education. This gives us a total of 91 percent of a student's total curricular time. The guidelines would permit a variation of up to 20 percent—which means that a student could take as much as 18 percent or as little as 12 percent in the arts, for example. Two students of quite different abilities and interests in mathematics, for instance, might take as much as 21 percent of their programs in mathematics and science, one taking an advanced course or two and the other seeking mastery in the common part of this domain. But neither student would be permitted either to opt out of the common portion or to stress one domain at the expense of any other. Simultaneously, teachers would be prevented from deciding to rule out the arts for a student for purposes of doing make-up work in English.

By adhering precisely to the recommended percentages or electing a downward variance of 20 percent in several domains, a student would leave free from 9 percent to 20 percent of his or her curriculum. This would be used for talent development in the arts, an academic subject such as mathematics, or sports. Students would be provided with vouchers for purposes of purchasing instruction in the public or private sector: college classes for advanced mathematics, a private tutor for instruction in singing, a professional trainer for swimming.

Bloom has effectively described and contrasted the unique differences between conditions promoting the development of talent and those employed to promote learning in schools.[17] The former emerges out of a fully supporting environment, modeled practice with immediate feedback, performance before an audience, and association with a like-minded peer group. Mastery and the development of personal style ultimately emerge. Surely the resulting satisfaction brings enrichment to the individual and, to a degree, carries one through the necessary demands of less preferred learnings. The potential for talent transcends socioeconomic level, ethnicity, and race. And so should provision for its development.

Beyond these curricular arrangements for both commonality and diversity, most provisions for individual differences should be in the organization of groups and in pedagogy. Our findings in "A Study of Schooling" revealed those schools that were in the top quartile for satisfaction and nearly all other characteristics to be almost invariably among the smallest in our sample; those in the bottom quartile on these same characteristics were among the largest. The studies of Barker and

Gump suggest the greater involvement of students in school affairs in small schools and their greater alienation in large ones.[18] A recent summary of research reports a falling off in curricular and economic advantages often assumed to be associated with larger schools, occurring in the 400 to 500 range in enrollment for elementary schools and the 600 to 800 range at the secondary level.[19] I often have feared that increased school size brought with it not only anonymity and alienation for teachers and students alike but also an invitation for electives to multiply with abandon. When Conant recommended a graduating class of 100 to assure the curriculum he wanted, surely he was not implying that bigger was necessarily better.

To secure for students a sense of identity, belonging, and closeness to teachers, I recommend that schools be kept small—below 400, 600, and 800 students at the three successive levels, respectively. Instead, we are closing our small schools! I recommend, further, that clusters of teachers and aides (up to four or five full-time equivalents in elementary schools and six or seven full-time equivalents in secondary schools), each including a head teacher, be associated with a group of from 100 to 150 students over the entire four-year span of a primary, elementary, or secondary phase of schooling. Each cluster would plan and provide the entire curriculum, except for the talent development sector. From twenty to thirty students would enter and a corresponding number would leave each of these largely self-contained units each year. Given the four years of association, teachers and students together would provide the support, analyses, and specific assistance required. The goal of assuring the learning of everyone else would parallel the goal of personal accomplishment in all domains except the sixth—the one reserved exclusively for developing the special interests and talents of individuals.

It is easy to envision in the environments proposed provision for attenuating the progress of gifted students and alleviating the deficiencies of those experiencing learning difficulties. Surely, administrators and teachers would not resort to the heavy-handedness of tracking. I hesitate to call for state-wide abolition of tracking, as has taken place in Sweden, simply because we resort too frequently to legislated solutions, whether or not well-advised.

I am seeking not either-or, familiar solutions to old and much argued issues but, rather, approaches that have at their heart the individual worth and welfare of persons engaged in the vital pursuit of education. Learning and doing common things commonly constitutes the essence of community, whether in school or out of it.

FOOTNOTES

1. An extreme position, reserved primarily for students disinterested in and ill-disposed to profiting from what schools have to offer—to the point of disrupting others who wish to learn—is to remove deviating individuals from school. See Robert L. Ebel, "What Are Schools For?" *Phi Delta Kappan* 54 (September 1972): 7.

2. James B. Conant, *The American High School Today* (New York: McGraw-Hill, 1959).

3. John B. Carroll, "A Model of School Learning," *Teachers College Record* 64 (May 1963): 723-33.

4. Benjamin S. Bloom, *All Our Children Learning* (New York: McGraw-Hill, 1981).

5. Jerome S. Bruner, *The Process of Education* (Cambridge, Mass.: Harvard University Press, 1960), p. 33.

6. Information from this study, providing probably the largest data bank on schools available to date, is drawn on extensively in this chapter. For a full report, see John I. Goodlad, *A Place Called School* (New York: McGraw-Hill, 1983).

7. Joseph J. Schwab, "Education and the State: Learning Community," in *The Great Ideas Today* (Chicago: Encyclopaedia Britannica, 1976), p. 235.

8. Educational Development Center, *American Schools Today and Tomorrow: A Summary of Eighteen Key Research Projects* (Newton, Mass.: The Center, 1981).

9. For a report on the findings, see Kenneth A. Sirotnik, *What You See Is What You Get: A Summary of Observations in Over 1000 Elementary and Secondary Classrooms*, Technical Report no. 29, A Study of Schooling (Los Angeles: Laboratory in School and Community Education, Graduate School of Education, University of California, 1981).

10. John I. Goodlad, M. Frances Klein, and Associates, *Looking Behind the Classroom Door* (Worthington, Ohio: Charles A. Jones Publishing Co., 1974).

11. Jeannie Oakes, *Limiting Opportunity: Student Race and Curricular Differences in Secondary Vocational Education*, Technical Report no. 28, A Study of Schooling (Los Angeles: Laboratory in School and Community Education, Graduate School of Education, University of California, 1981).

12. Jeannie Oakes, *A Question of Access: Tracking and Curriculum Differentiation in a National Sample of English and Mathematics Classes*, Technical Report no. 24, A Study of Schooling (Los Angeles: Laboratory in School and Community Education, Graduate School of Education, University of California, 1981).

13. Report of the Harvard Committee, *General Education in a Free Society* (Cambridge, Mass.: Harvard University Press, 1945), p. 102.

14. Conant, *The American High School Today*.

15. See John I. Goodlad, *What Schools Are For* (Bloomington, Ind.: Phi Delta Kappa Educational Foundation, 1979), pp. 46-52.

16. Goodlad, *A Place Called School*.

17. Benjamin S. Bloom and Lauren A. Sosniak, "Talent Development vs. Schooling," *Educational Leadership* 39 (November 1981): 86-94.

18. R. G. Barker and P. V. Gump, *Big School, Small School* (Stanford, Calif.: Stanford University Press, 1964).

19. John Ainley et al., *Resource Allocation in the Government Schools of Australia and New Zealand* (Melbourne, Australia: Australian Education Council, in press).

Name Index

Abel, David, 99
Abeson, Alan, 99
Adelson, Joseph, 270, 279
Ainley, John, 318
Amarel, Marianne, 43
Ames, Carole, 22, 23, 24, 40, 41
Ames, Russell, 24, 41
Anastasi, Ann, 159
Anderson-Levitt, Kathryn, 42
Anyon, Jean, 137, 157, 277
Apple, Michael W., 72, 73, 157, 183
Applebee, Arthur N., 190, 191, 193, 196, 216, 217, 218
Argyris, Chris, 177, 184
Aristotle, 225
Armstrong, Ellen, 298
Arnheim, Rudolph, 245
Artley, A. Sterl, 12, 39
Austin, George, 30, 42

Bach, G. L., 278
Bacon, Phillip, 278
Bain, John D., 43
Bank, Barbara J., 39
Barker, R. G., 315, 318
Barr, Robert D., 280
Basalla, George, 184
Beck, Lewis W., 72
Becker, James M., 262, 278, 279
Beery, Richard G., 39, 40
Bell, Eric T., 123, 156
Bernard, Claude, 115
Bernstein, Basil B., 51, 52, 53, 64, 66, 73
Berry, J. W., 31, 42
Bestor, Arthur, 190
Beyer, Barry K., 279
Bibby, John F., 278
Biddle, Bruce J., 39
Black, John G., 142, 158
Blackburn, Robert, 298
Blackman, Sheldon, 42
Blanpied, William A., 184
Bledstein, Burton J., 73
Block, James, 23, 40, 41
Bloom, Benjamin S., 40, 52, 73, 136, 302, 315, 317, 318

Bobrow, D. H., 157
Bolick, Nancy, 99
Borg, Walter R., 39
Bossert, Steven T., 40
Bower, Gordon H., 142, 158
Branson, Margaret Stimmann, 278
Bregand, Eleanore, 246
Brennan, Justice William J., 98
Broek, Jan O. M., 278
Broening, Angela M., 216
Brophy, Jere, 39, 42, 43
Broudy, H. S., 219, 245, 246, 283, 286, 289
Brown, Governor Jerry, 290
Brownell, John A., 156
Brownell, William, 142, 157
Bruner, Jerome S., 30, 42, 136, 190, 302, 317
Bryan, M. W., 39
Bryant, Brenda K., 40, 41
Buckholdt, David R., 42
Bullough, Edward, 245
Burnett, Joe R., 246
Burns, Robert B., 23, 40, 41
Butts, R. Freeman, 249, 263, 277

Cagan, Elizabeth, 152, 159
Calderwood, James D., 278
Califano, Joseph, 98
Cannon, Walter, 115
Carroll, John B., 40, 302, 317
Cazden, Courtney, 186
Champagne, Audrey B., 170, 184
Chapin, June R., 279
Christenbury, Leila Mayo, 196, 217
Cirrincione, Joseph M., 278
Clapp, Ouida H., 199, 200, 217
Clark, Gilbert A., 245
Cobb, Russell L., 279
Cogan, Morris L., 184
Cohen, Alan S., 24, 40, 41
Collins, A., 157
Collins, Peter, 73
Conant, James B., 301, 313, 316, 317
Conrad, Clifton, 298

Subject Index

Ability, as input variable and as outcome, 17-18

Ability grouping, criticisms of, 11-12. *See also,* Tracked programs.

Aesthetic experience, 226-28

Aesthetic judgment, 237-38

Aesthetic perception, 229-34

Aesthetic properties, of objects, 229-32

Aptitude-by-treatment interaction (ATI): limited usefulness of studies of, in curriculum planning, 13-16; need for continued research on, 17

Arts education: factors related to justification of, 221-24; problems of setting common curriculum for, 226-29; roles of teacher and arts specialist in, 222; skills in performance as goal of, 234-35; use of exemplars in, 240-242. *See also,* Common curriculum (fine arts).

"A Study of Schooling," findings of, related to individual differences and curricular practice, 305-13

Attitudes: and development of civic participatory competence, 266; toward science, 172-73

Basic skills, as goals of social studies education, 264-65

Bill of Rights, 77

Biological Science Curriculum Study, 181

Black English, litigation regarding, 88-89

Brown vs. Board of Education of Topeka, 78, 82

California State Board of Education, handbook of, for curriculum revision, 291

California State University and College System: admission requirements of, 287-88; expenditures of, for remedial education, 287

Christianity, sixteenth-century educational aims of, 55-56

Civil Rights Act (1964), 88

Classroom organization: relationship of, to optimization of learning, 19; reward structures, as features of, 19-20

Cognitive style, 29-30. *See also,* Field dependence/independence.

College Entrance Examination Board, statement of, on academic competencies and curriculum, 288

Commission on the English Curriculum, 189, 190, 198, 203

Common curriculum: contradictions in concept of, 71-72; guide for deliberations on, 292-95; increasing need for, 304; recommendations regarding, in secondary schools, 314-15

Common Curriculum (fine arts): characteristics of, 242-43; cultivation of aesthetic judgment in, 237-38; determining essential learnings in, 224-26; "enlightened cherishing" as goal of, 235-38; meeting individual differences in, 243-44; rationale for, 224-29; skills of aesthetic perception in, 229-33; skills of performance in, 234-35; use of exemplars in, 240-42. *See also,* Arts education.

Common curriculum (language and literature): goals and themes as definers of, 186; issues in planning of, 211-15; providing for individual differences in, 214-15; suggested goals for, 205-7. *See also,* English curriculum.

Common curriculum (mathematics): interest group claims regarding, 150-52; need for new approach to, 154-56; principles for development of, 138-50; provision for individual differences in, 150-56. *See also,* Mathematics.

Common curriculum (natural science): components of, 181; context as key to new view of, 180; difficulties with traditional approaches to, 162; importance of students' choice in, 181-83; need for new conceptualization of, 162-63. *See also,* Science education.

Common curriculum (social studies): developmental changes (in students) in relation to, 254, 267-73; essential learn-

325

INFORMATION ABOUT MEMBERSHIP IN THE SOCIETY

From its small beginnings in the early 1900s, the National Society for the Study of Education has grown to a major educational organization with more than 3,000 members in the United States, Canada, and overseas. Members include professors, researchers, graduate students, and administrators in colleges and universities; teachers, supervisors, curriculum specialists, and administrators in elementary and secondary schools; and a considerable number of persons who are not formally connected with an educational institution. Membership in the Society is open to all persons who desire to receive its publications.

Since its establishment the Society has sought to promote its central purpose—the stimulation of investigations and discussions of important educational issues—through regular publication of a two-volume yearbook that is sent to all members. Many of these volumes have been so well received throughout the profession that they have gone into several printings. A recently inaugurated series of substantial paperbacks on Contemporary Educational Issues supplements the series of yearbooks and allows for treatment of a wider range of educational topics than can be addressed each year through the yearbooks alone.

Through membership in the Society one can add regularly to one's professional library at a very reasonable cost. Members also help to sustain a publication program that is widely recognized for its unique contributions to the literature of education.

The categories of membership, and the current dues in each category, are as follows:

> *Regular.* The member receives a clothbound copy of each part of the two-volume yearbook (approximately 300 pages per volume). Annual dues, $20.

> *Comprehensive.* The member receives clothbound copies of the two-volume yearbook and the two volumes in the current paperback series. Annual dues, $35.

> *Retirees and Graduate Students.* Reduced dues—Regular, $16; Comprehensive, $31.
> The above reduced dues are available to (a) those who have retired or are over sixty-five years of age and who have been members of the Society for at least ten years, and (b) graduate students in their first year of membership.

Life Membership. Persons sixty years of age or over may hold a Regular Membership for life upon payment of a lump sum based upon the life expectancy for their age group. Consult the Secretary-Treasurer for further details.

New members are required to pay an entrance fee of $1, in addition to the dues, in their first year of membership.

Membership is for the calendar year and dues are payable on or before January 1. A reinstatement fee of $.50 must be added to dues payments made after January 1.

In addition to receiving the publications of the Society as described above, members participate in the nomination and election of the six-member Board of Directors, which is responsible for managing the business and affairs of the Society, including the authorization of volumes to appear in the yearbook series. Two members of the Board are elected each year for three-year terms. Members of the Society who have contributed to its publications and who indicate a willingness to serve are eligible for election to the Board.

Members are urged to attend the one or more meetings of the Society that are arranged each year in conjunction with the annual meetings of major educational organizations. The purpose of such meetings is to present, discuss, and critique volumes in the current yearbook series. Announcements of meetings for the ensuing year are sent to members in December.

Upon written request from a member, the Secretary-Treasurer will send the current directory of members, synopses of meetings of the Board of Directors, and the annual financial report.

Persons desiring further information about membership may write to

KENNETH J. REHAGE, Secretary-Treasurer
National Society for the Study of Education

5835 Kimbark Ave.
Chicago, Ill. 60637

PUBLICATIONS OF THE NATIONAL SOCIETY FOR THE STUDY OF EDUCATION

1. The Yearbooks

NOTICE: Many of the early yearbooks of this series are now out of print. In the following list, those titles to which an asterisk is prefixed are not available for purchase.

*First Yearbook, 1902, Part I—*Some Principles in the Teaching of History.* Lucy M. Salmon.

*First Yearbook, 1902, Part II—*The Progress of Geography in the Schools.* W. M. Davis and H. M. Wilson.

*Second Yearbook, 1903, Part I—*The Course of Study in History in the Common School.* Isabel Lawrence, C. A. McMurray, Frank McMurry, E. C. Page, and E. J. Rice.

*Second Yearbook, 1903, Part II—*The Relation of Theory to Practice in Education.* M. J. Holmes, J. A. Keith, and Levi Seeley.

*Third Yearbook, 1904, Part I—*The Relation of Theory to Practice in the Education of Teachers.* John Dewey, Sarah C. Brooks, F. M. McMurry, et al.

*Third Yearbook, 1904, Part II—*Nature Study.* W. S. Jackman.

*Fourth Yearbook, 1905, Part I—*The Education and Training of Secondary Teachers.* E. C. Elliott, E. G. Dexter, M. J. Holmes, et al.

*Fourth Yearbook, 1905, Part II—*The Place of Vocational Subjects in the High-School Curriculum.* J. S. Brown, G. B. Morrison, and Ellen Richards.

*Fifth Yearbook, 1906, Part I—*On the Teaching of English in Elementary and High Schools.* G. P. Brown and Emerson Davis.

*Fifth Yearbook, 1906, Part II—*The Certification of Teachers.* E. P. Cubberley.

*Sixth Yearbook, 1907, Part I—*Vocational Studies for College Entrance.* C. A. Herrick, H. W. Holmes, T. deLaguna, V. Prettyman, and W. J. S. Bryan.

*Sixth Yearbook, 1907, Part II—*The Kindergarten and Its Relation to Elementary Education.* Ada Van Stone Harris, E. A. Kirkpatrick, Marie Kraus-Boelté, Patty S. Hill, Harriette M. Mills, and Nina Vandewalker.

*Seventh Yearbook, 1908, Part I—*The Relation of Superintendents and Principals to the Training and Professional Improvement of Their Teachers.* Charles D. Lowry.

*Seventh Yearbook, 1908, Part II—*The Co-ordination of the Kindergarten and the Elementary School.* B. J. Gregory, Jennie B. Merrill, Bertha Payne, and Margaret Giddings.

*Eighth Yearbook, 1909, Part I—*Education with Reference to Sex: Pathological, Economic, and Social Aspects.* C. R. Henderson.

*Eighth Yearbook, 1909, Part II—*Education with Reference to Sex: Agencies and Methods.* C. R. Henderson and Helen C. Putnam.

*Ninth Yearbook, 1910, Part I—*Health and Education.* T. D. Wood.

*Ninth Yearbook, 1910, Part II—*The Nurses in Education.* T. D. Wood, et al.

*Tenth Yearbook, 1911, Part I—*The City School as a Community Center.* H. C. Leipziger, Sarah E. Hyre, R. D. Warden, C. Ward Crampton, E. W. Stitt, E. J. Ward, Mrs. T. C. Grice, and C. A. Perry.

*Tenth Yearbook, 1911, Part II—*The Rural School as a Community Center.* B. H. Crocheron, Jessie Field, F. W. Howe, E. C. Bishop, A. B. Graham, O. J. Kern, M. T. Scudder, and B. M. Davis.

*Eleventh Yearbook, 1912, Part I—*Industrial Education: Typical Experiments Described and Interpreted.* J. F. Barker, M. Bloomfield, B. W. Johnson, P. Johnson, L. M. Leavitt, G. A. Mirick, M. W. Murray, C. F. Perry, A. L. Stafford, and H. B. Wilson.

*Eleventh Yearbook, 1912, Part II—*Agricultural Education in Secondary Schools.* A. C. Monahan, R. W. Stimson, D. J. Crosby, W. H. French, H. F. Button, F. R. Crane, W. R. Hart, and G. F. Warren.

*Twelfth Yearbook, 1913, Part I—*The Supervision of City Schools.* Franklin Bobbitt, J. W. Hall, and J. D. Wolcott.

*Twelfth Yearbook, 1913, Part II—*The Supervision of Rural Schools.* A. C. Monahan, L. J. Hanifan, J. E. Warren, Wallace Lund, U. J. Hoffman, A. S. Cook, E. M. Rapp, Jackson Davis, J. D. Wolcott.

*Thirteenth Yearbook, 1914, Part I—*Some Aspects of High-School Instruction and Administration.* H. C. Morrison, E. R. Breslich, W. A. Jessup, and L. D. Coffman.

*Thirteenth Yearbook, 1914, Part II—*Plans for Organizing School Surveys, with a Summary of Typical School Surveys.* Charles H. Judd and Henry L. Smith.

*Fourteenth Yearbook, 1915, Part I—*Minimum Essentials in Elementary School Subjects—Standards and Current Practices.* H. B. Wilson, H. W. Holmes, F. E. Thompson, R. G. Jones, S. A. Courtis, W. S. Gray, F. N. Freeman, H. C. Pryor, J. F. Hosic, W. A. Jessup, and W. C. Bagley.

*Fourteenth Yearbook, 1915, Part II—*Methods for Measuring Teachers' Efficiency.* Arthur C Boyce.

*Fifteenth Yearbook, 1916, Part I—*Standards and Tests for the Measurement of the Efficiency of Schools and School Systems.* G. D. Strayer, Bird T. Baldwin, B. R. Buckingham, F. W. Ballou, D. C. Bliss, H. G. Childs, S. A. Courtis, E. P. Cubberley, C. H. Judd, George Melcher, E. E. Oberholtzer, J. B. Sears, Daniel Starch, M. R. Trabue, and G. M. Whipple.

*Fifteenth Yearbook, 1916, Part II—*The Relationship between Persistence in School and Home Conditions.* Charles E. Holley.
*Fifteenth Yearbook, 1916, Part III—*The Junior High School.* Aubrey A. Douglass.
*Sixteenth Yearbook, 1917, Part I—*Second Report of the Committee on Minimum Essentials in Elementary-School Subjects.* W. C. Bagley, W. W. Charters, F. N. Freeman, W. S. Gray, Ernest Horn, J. H. Hoskinson, W. S. Monroe, C. F. Munson, H. C. Pryor, L. W. Rapeer, G. M. Wilson, and H. B. Wilson.
*Sixteenth Yearbook, 1917, Part II—*The Efficiency of College Students as Conditioned by Age at Entrance and Size of High School.* B. F. Pittenger.
*Seventeenth Yearbook, 1918, Part I—*Third Report of the Committee on Economy of Time in Education.* W. C. Bagley, B. B. Bassett, M. E. Branom, Alice Camerer, J. E. Dealey, C. A. Ellwood, E. B. Greene, A. B. Hart, J. F. Hosic, E. T. Housh, W. H. Mace, L. R. Marston, H. C. McKown, H. E. Mitchell, W. V. Reavis, D. Snedden, and H. B. Wilson.
*Seventeenth Yearbook, 1918, Part II—*The Measurement of Educational Products.* E. J. Ashbaugh, W. A. Averill, L. P. Ayers, F. W. Ballou, Edna Bryner, B. R. Buckingham, S. A. Courtis, M. E. Haggerty, C. H. Judd, George Melcher, W. S. Monroe, E. A. Nifenecker, and E. L. Thorndike.
*Eighteenth Yearbook, 1919, Part I—*The Professional Preparation of High-School Teachers.* G. N. Cade, S. S. Colvin, Charles Fordyce, H. H. Foster, T. S. Gosling, W. S. Gray, L. V. Koos, A. R. Mead, H. L. Miller, F. C. Whitcomb, and Clifford Woody.
*Eighteenth Yearbook, 1919, Part II—*Fourth Report of Committee on Economy of Time in Education.* F. C. Ayer, F. N. Freeman, W. S. Gray, Ernest Horn, W. S. Monroe, and C. E. Seashore.
*Nineteenth Yearbook, 1920, Part I—*New Materials of Instruction.* Prepared by the Society's Committee on Materials of Instruction.
*Nineteenth Yearbook, 1920, Part II—*Classroom Problems in the Education of Gifted Children.* T. S. Henry.
*Twentieth Yearbook, 1921, Part I—*New Materials of Instruction.* Second Report by Society's Committee.
*Twentieth Yearbook, 1921, Part II—*Report of the Society's Committee on Silent Reading.* M. A. Burgess, S. A. Courtis, C. E. Germane, W. S. Gray, H. A. Greene, Regina R. Heller, J. H. Hoover, J. A. O'Brien, J. L. Packer, Daniel Starch, W. W. Theisen, G. A. Yoakam, and representatives of other school systems.
*Twenty-first Yearbook, 1922, Parts I and II—*Intelligence Tests and Their Use,* Part I—*The Nature, History, and General Principles of Intelligence Testing.* E. L. Thorndike, S. S. Colvin, Harold Rugg, G. M. Whipple, Part II—*The Administrative Use of Intelligence Tests.* H. W. Holmes, W. K. Layton, Helen Davis, Agnes L. Rogers, Rudolf Pintner, M. R. Trabue, W. S. Miller, Bessie L. Gambrill, and others. The two parts are bound together.
*Twenty-second Yearbook, 1923, Part I—*English Composition: Its Aims, Methods and Measurements.* Earl Hudelson.
*Twenty-second Yearbook, 1923, Part II—*The Social Studies in the Elementary and Secondary School.* A. S. Barr, J. J. Coss, Henry Harap, R. W. Hatch, H. C. Hill, Ernest Horn, C. H. Judd, L. C. Marshall, F. M. McMurry, Earle Rugg, H. O. Rugg, Emma Schweppe, Mabel Snedaker, and C. W. Washburne.
*Twenty-third Yearbook, 1924, Part I—*The Education of Gifted Children.* Report of the Society's Committee. Guy M. Whipple, Chairman.
*Twenty-third Yearbook, 1924, Part II—*Vocational Guidance and Vocational Education for Industries.* A. H. Edgerton and others.
*Twenty-fourth Yearbook, 1925, Part I—*Report of the National Committee on Reading.* W. S. Gray, Chairman, F. W. Ballou, Rose L. Hardy, Ernest Horn, Francis Jenkins, S. A. Leonard, Estaline Wilson, and Laura Zirbes.
*Twenty-fourth Yearbook, 1925, Part II—*Adapting the Schools to Individual Differences.* Report of the Society's Committee. Carleton W. Washburne, Chairman.
*Twenty-fifth Yearbook, 1926, Part I—*The Present Status of Safety Education.* Report of the Society's Committee. Guy M. Whipple, Chairman.
*Twenty-fifth Yearbook, 1926, Part II—*Extra-Curricular Activities.* Report of the Society's Committee. Leonard V. Koos, Chairman.
*Twenty-sixth Yearbook, 1927, Part I—*Curriculum-making: Past and Present.* Report of the Society's Committee. Harold O. Rugg, Chairman.
*Twenty-sixth Yearbook, 1927, Part II—*The Foundations of Curriculum-making.* Prepared by individual members of the Society's Committee. Harold O. Rugg, Chairman.
*Twenty-seventh Yearbook, 1928, Part I—*Nature and Nurture: Their Influence upon Intelligence.* Prepared by the Society's Committee. Lewis M. Terman, Chairman.
*Twenty-seventh Yearbook, 1928, Part II—*Nature and Nurture: Their Influence upon Achievement.* Prepared by the Society's Committee. Lewis M. Terman, Chairman.
*Twenty-eighth Yearbook, 1929, Parts I and II—*Preschool and Parental Education,* Part I—*Organization and Development.* Part II—*Research and Method.* Prepared by the Society's Committee. Lois H. Meek, Chairman. Bound in one volume. Cloth.
*Twenty-ninth Yearbook, 1930, Parts I and II—*Report of the Society's Committee on Arithmetic.* Part I—*Some Aspects of Modern Thought on Arithmetic.* Part II—*Research in Arithmetic.* Prepared by the Society's Committee. F. B. Knight, Chairman. Bound in one volume.
*Thirtieth Yearbook, 1931, Part I—*The Status of Rural Education.* First Report of the Society's Committee on Rural Education. Orville G. Brim, Chairman.
Thirtieth Yearbook, 1931, Part II—*The Textbook in American Education.* Report of the Society's Committee on the Textbook, J. B. Edmonson, Chairman. Cloth, Paper.

*Thirty-first Yearbook, 1932, Part I—*A Program for Teaching Science*. Prepared by the Society's Committee on the Teaching of Science. S. Ralph Powers, Chairman.
*Thirty-first Yearbook, 1932, Part II—*Changes and Experiments in Liberal-Arts Education*. Prepared by Kathryn McHale, with numerous collaborators.
*Thirty-second Yearbook, 1933—*The Teaching of Geography*. Prepared by the Society's Committee on the Teaching of Geography. A. E. Parkins, Chairman.
*Thirty-third Yearbook, 1934, Part I—*The Planning and Construction of School Buildings*. Prepared by the Society's Committee on School Buildings. N. L. Engelhardt, Chairman.
*Thirty-third Yearbook, 1934, Part II—*The Activity Movement*. Prepared by the Society's Committee on the Activity Movement. Lois Coffey Mossman, Chairman.
Thirty-fourth Yearbook, 1935—*Educational Diagnosis*. Prepared by the Society's Committee on Educational Diagnosis. L. J. Brueckner, Chairman. Paper.
*Thirty-fifth Yearbook, 1936, Part I—*The Grouping of Pupils*. Prepared by the Society's Committee. W. W. Coxe, Chairman.
*Thirty-fifth Yearbook, 1936, Part II—*Music Education*. Prepared by the Society's Committee. W. L. Uhl, Chairman.
*Thirty-sixth Yearbook, 1937, Part I—*The Teaching of Reading*. Prepared by the Society's Committee. W. S. Gray, Chairman.
*Thirty-sixth Yearbook, 1937, Part II—*International Understanding through the Public-School Curriculum*. Prepared by the Society's Committee. I. L. Kandel, Chairman.
*Thirty-seventh Yearbook, 1938, Part I—*Guidance in Educational Institutions*. Prepared by the Society's Committee. G. N. Kefauver, Chairman.
*Thirty-seventh Yearbook, 1938, Part II—*The Scientific Movement in Education*. Prepared by the Society's Committee. F. N. Freeman, Chairman.
*Thirty-eighth Yearbook, 1939, Part I—*Child Development and the Curriculum*. Prepared by the Society's Committee. Carleton Washburne, Chairman.
*Thirty-eighth Yearbook, 1939, Part II—*General Education in the American College*. Prepared by the Society's Committee. Alvin Eurich, Chairman. Cloth.
*Thirty-ninth Yearbook, 1940, Part I—*Intelligence: Its Nature and Nurture. Comparative and Critical Exposition*. Prepared by the Society's Committee. G. D. Stoddard, Chairman.
*Thirty-ninth Yearbook, 1940, Part II—*Intelligence: Its Nature and Nurture. Original Studies and Experiments*. Prepared by the Society's Committee. G. D. Stoddard, Chairman.
*Fortieth Yearbook, 1941—*Art in American Life and Education*. Prepared by the Society's Committee. Thomas Munro, Chairman.
Forty-first Yearbook, 1942, Part I—*Philosophies of Education*. Prepared by the Society's Committee. John S. Brubacher, Chairman. Paper.
Forty-first Yearbook, 1942, Part II—*The Psychology of Learning*. Prepared by the Society's Committee. T. R. McConnell, Chairman. Cloth.
*Forty-second Yearbook, 1943, Part I—*Vocational Education*. Prepared by the Society's Committee. F. J. Keller, Chairman.
*Forty-second Yearbook, 1943, Part II—*The Library in General Education*. Prepared by the Society's Committee. L. R. Wilson, Chairman.
Forty-third Yearbook, 1944, Part I—*Adolescence*. Prepared by the Society's Committee. Harold E. Jones, Chairman. Paper.
*Forty-third Yearbook, 1944, Part II—*Teaching Language in the Elementary School*. Prepared by the Society's Committee. M. R. Trabue, Chairman.
*Forty-fourth Yearbook, 1945, Part I—*American Education in the Postwar Period: Curriculum Reconstruction*. Prepared by the Society's Committee. Ralph W. Tyler, Chairman.
*Forty-fourth Yearbook, 1945, Part II—*American Education in the Postwar Period: Structural Reorganization*. Prepared by the Society's Committee. Bess Goodykoontz, Chairman. Paper.
*Forty-fifth Yearbook, 1946, Part I—*The Measurement of Understanding*. Prepared by the Society's Committee. William A. Brownell, Chairman.
*Forty-fifth Yearbook, 1946, Part II—*Changing Conceptions in Educational Administration*. Prepared by the Society's Committee. Alonzo G. Grace, Chairman.
*Forty-sixth Yearbook, 1947, Part I—*Science Education in American Schools*. Prepared by the Society's Committee. Victor H. Noll, Chairman.
*Forty-sixth Yearbook, 1947, Part II—*Early Childhood Education*. Prepared by the Society's Committee. N. Searle Light, Chairman. Paper.
Forty-seventh Yearbook, 1948, Part I—*Juvenile Delinquency and the Schools*. Prepared by the Society's Committee. Ruth Strang, Chairman. Cloth.
Forty-seventh Yearbook, 1948, Part II—*Reading in the High School and College*. Prepared by the Society's Committee. William S. Gray. Chairman. Cloth. Paper.
*Forty-eighth Yearbook, 1949, Part I—*Audio-visual Materials of Instruction*. Prepared by the Society's Committee. Stephen M. Corey, Chairman. Cloth.
*Forty-eighth Yearbook, 1949, Part II—*Reading in the Elementary School*. Prepared by the Society's Committee. Arthur I. Gates, Chairman.
*Forty-ninth Yearbook, 1950, Part I—*Learning and Instruction*. Prepared by the Society's Committee. G. Lester Anderson, Chairman.
*Forty-ninth Yearbook, 1950, Part II—*The Education of Exceptional Children*. Prepared by the Society's Committee. Samuel A. Kirk, Chairman.
Fiftieth Yearbook, 1951, Part I—*Graduate Study in Education*. Prepared by the Society's Board of Directors. Ralph W. Tyler, Chairman. Paper.
Fiftieth Yearbook, 1951, Part II—*The Teaching of Arithmetic*. Prepared by the Society's Committee. G. T. Buswell, Chairman. Cloth, Paper.
Fifty-first Yearbook, 1952, Part I—*General Education*. Prepared by the Society's Committee. T. R. McConnell, Chairman. Cloth, Paper.

Seventieth Yearbook, 1971, Part II—*Leaders in American Education*. Prepared by the Society's Committee. Robert J. Havighurst, Editor. Cloth.
Seventy-first Yearbook, 1972, Part I—*Philosophical Redirection of Educational Research*. Prepared by the Society's Committee. Lawrence G. Thomas, Editor. Cloth.
Seventy-first Yearbook, 1972, Part II—*Early Childhood Education*. Prepared by the Society's Committee. Ira J. Gordon, Editor. Paper.
Seventy-second Yearbook, 1973, Part I—*Behavior Modification in Education*. Prepared by the Society's Committee. Carl E. Thoresen, Editor. Cloth.
Seventy-second Yearbook, 1973, Part II—*The Elementary School in the United States*. Prepared by the Society's Committee. John I. Goodlad and Harold G. Shane, Editors. Cloth.
Seventy-third Yearbook, 1974, Part I—*Media and Symbols: The Forms of Expression, Communication, and Education*. Prepared by the Society's Committee. David R. Olson, Editor. Cloth.
Seventy-third Yearbook, 1974, Part II—*Uses of the Sociology of Education*. Prepared by the Society's Committee. C. Wayne Gordon, Editor. Cloth.
Seventy-fourth Yearbook, 1975, Part I—*Youth*. Prepared by the Society's Committee. Robert J. Havighurst and Philip H. Dreyer, Editors. Cloth.
Seventy-fourth Yearbook, 1975, Part II—*Teacher Education*. Prepared by the Society's Committee. Kevin Ryan, Editor. Cloth.
Seventy-fifth Yearbook, 1976, Part I—*Psychology of Teaching Methods*. Prepared by the Society's Committee. N. L. Gage, Editor. Paper.
*Seventy-fifth Yearbook, 1976, Part II—*Issues in Secondary Education*. Prepared by the Society's Committee. William Van Til, Editor. Cloth.
Seventy-sixth Yearbook, 1977, Part I—*The Teaching of English*. Prepared by the Society's Committee. James R. Squire, Editor. Cloth.
Seventy-sixth Yearbook, 1977, Part II—*The Politics of Education*. Prepared by the Society's Committee. Jay D. Scribner, Editor. Paper.
Seventy-seventh Yearbook, 1978, Part I—*The Courts and Education*, Clifford P. Hooker, Editor. Cloth.
Seventy-seventh Yearbook, 1978, Part II—*Education and the Brain*, Jeanne Chall and Allan F. Mirsky, Editors. Cloth.
Seventy-eighth Yearbook, 1979, Part I—*The Gifted and the Talented: Their Education and Development*, A. Harry Passow. Editor. Cloth.
Seventy-eighth Yearbook, 1979, Part II—*Classroom Management*, Daniel L. Duke, Editor. Paper.
Seventy-ninth Yearbook, 1980, Part I—*Toward Adolescence: The Middle School Years*, Mauritz Johnson, Editor. Cloth.
Seventy-ninth Yearbook, 1980, Part II—*Learning a Second Language*, Frank M. Grittner, Editor. Cloth.
Eightieth Yearbook, 1981, Part I—*Philosophy and Education*, Jonas F. Soltis, Editor. Cloth.
Eightieth Yearbook, 1981, Part II—*The Social Studies*, Howard D. Mehlinger and O. L. Davis, Jr., Editors. Cloth.
Eighty-first Yearbook, 1982, Part I—*Policy Making in Education*, Ann Lieberman and Milbrey W. McLaughlin, Editors. Cloth.
Eighty-first Yearbook, 1982, Part II—*Education and Work*, Harry F. Silberman, Editor. Cloth.
Eighty-second Yearbook, 1983, Part I—*Individual Differences and the Common Curriculum*, Gary D Fenstermacher and John I. Goodlad, Editors. Cloth.
Eighty-second Yearbook, 1983, Part II—*Staff Development*, Gary Griffin, Editor. Cloth.

Yearbooks of the National Society are distributed by

UNIVERSITY OF CHICAGO PRESS, 5801 ELLIS AVE.,
CHICAGO, ILLINOIS 60637

Please direct inquiries regarding prices of volumes still available to the University of Chicago Press. Orders for these volumes should be sent to the University of Chicago Press, not to the offices of the National Society.

2. The Series on Contemporary Educational Issues

In addition to its Yearbooks the Society now publishes volumes in a series on Contemporary Educational Issues. These volumes are prepared under the supervision of the Society's Commission on an Expanded Publication Program.

The 1983 Titles

The Hidden Curriculum and Moral Education (Henry A. Giroux and David Purpel, eds.)

The Dynamics of Organizational Change in Education (J. Victor Baldridge and Terrance Deal, eds.)

338   PUBLICATIONS

The 1982 Titles
    *Improving Educational Standards and Productivity: The Re-
    search Basis for Policy* (Herbert J. Walberg, ed.)
    Schools in Conflict: The Politics of Education (Frederick M.
    Wirt and Michael W. Kirst)

The 1981 Titles
    Psychology and Education: The State of the Union (Frank H. Far-
    ley and Neal J. Gordon, eds.)
    Selected Issues in Mathematics Education (Mary M. Lindquist, ed.)

The 1980 Titles
    *Minimum Competency Achievement Testing: Motives, Models, Mea-
    sures, and Consequences* (Richard M. Jaeger and Carol K. Tittle,
    eds.)
    Collective Bargaining in Public Education (Anthony M. Cresswell,
    Michael J. Murphy, with Charles T. Kerchner)

The 1979 Titles
    *Educational Environments and Effects: Evaluation, Policy, and Pro-
    ductivity* (Herbert J. Walberg, ed.)
    Research on Teaching: Concepts, Findings, and Implications (Pen-
    elope L. Peterson and Herbert J. Walberg, eds.)
    The Principal in Metropolitan Schools (Donald A. Erickson and
    Theodore L. Reller, eds.)

The 1978 Titles
    Aspects of Reading Education (Susanna Pflaum-Connor, ed.)
    *History, Education, and Public Policy: Recovering the American
    Educational Past* (Donald R. Warren, ed.)
    *From Youth to Constructive Adult Life: The Role of the Public
    School* (Ralph W. Tyler, ed.)

The 1977 Titles
    Early Childhood Education: Issues and Insights (Bernard Spodek
    and Herbert J. Walberg, eds.)
    *The Future of Big City Schools: Desegregation Policies and Magnet
    Alternatives* (Daniel U. Levine and Robert J. Havighurst, eds.)
    Educational Administration: The Developing Decades (Luvern L.
    Cunningham, Walter G. Hack, and Raphael O. Nystrand, eds.)

The 1976 Titles
    Prospects for Research and Development in Education (Ralph W.
    Tyler, ed.)
    Public Testimony on Public Schools (Commission on Educational
    Governance)
    Counseling Children and Adolescents (William M. Walsh, ed.)

The 1975 Titles

Schooling and the Rights of Children (Vernon Haubrich and Michael Apple, eds.)

Systems of Individualized Education (Harriet Talmage, ed.)

Educational Policy and International Assessment: Implications of the IEA Assessment of Achievement (Alan Purves and Daniel U. Levine, eds.)

The 1974 Titles

Crucial Issues in Testing (Ralph W. Tyler and Richard M. Wolf, eds.)

Conflicting Conceptions of Curriculum (Elliott Eisner and Elizabeth Vallance, eds.)

Cultural Pluralism (Edgar G. Epps, ed.)

Rethinking Educational Equality (Andrew T. Kopan and Herbert J. Walberg, eds.)

All of the preceding volumes may be ordered from

McCutchan Publishing Corporation
2526 Grove Street
Berkeley, California 94704

The 1972 Titles

Black Students in White Schools (Edgar G. Epps, ed.)

Flexibility in School Programs (W. J. Congreve and G. L. Rinehart, eds.)

Performance Contracting—1969-1971 (J. A. Mecklenburger)

The Potential of Educational Futures (Michael Marien and W. L. Ziegler, eds.)

Sex Differences and Discrimination in Education (Scarvia Anderson, ed.)

The 1971 Titles

Accountability in Education (Leon M. Lessinger and Ralph W. Tyler, eds.)

Farewell to Schools??? (D. U. Levine and R. J. Havighurst, eds.)

Models for Integrated Education (D. U. Levine, ed.)

PYGMALION *Reconsidered* (J. D. Elashoff and R. E. Snow)

Reactions to Silberman's CRISIS IN THE CLASSROOM (A. Harry Passow, ed.)

The 1971 and 1972 titles in this series are now out of print.